Critical Years in Immigration:
Canada and Australia Compared

McGILL-QUEEN'S STUDIES IN ETHNIC HISTORY
Donald Harman Akenson, Editor

Critical Years in Immigration: Canada and Australia Compared

FREDA HAWKINS

SECOND EDITION

McGill-Queen's University Press
Montreal & Kingston • London • Buffalo

© McGill-Queen's University Press 1991
ISBN 0-7735-0852-X

Legal deposit fourth quarter 1991
Bibliothèque nationale du Québec
First edition published in cloth 1989
Second edition published in paper 1991

Printed in Canada on acid-free paper

Publication has been supported by the Canada Council
through its block grant program.

Canadian Cataloguing in Publication Data

Hawkins, Freda, 1918-
   Critical years in immigration: Canada and Australia
   compared
   (McGill-Queen's studies in ethnic history) 2nd ed.
   Includes bibliographical references and index.
   ISBN 0-7735-0852-X
   1. Canada – Emigration and immigration – Government
   policy. 2. Australia – Emigration and immigration –
   Government policy. I. Title. II. Series.
   JV7225.H34 1991   325.71   C91-090407-3

Contents

Tables

Figures and Maps

Acknowledgments

This study is the outcome of several years of research in Canada and Australia, during which I have had a great deal of help from government, the academic community, the voluntary sector, and many individuals involved in the world of immigrants and refugees, and I am very grateful for this. I would like to thank particularly the immigration officers of the Canada Employment and Immigration Commission and the officers of Australia's Department of Immigration and Ethnic Affairs, whose assistance – based in each case on very liberal legal agreements – has been invaluable. In the course of this research, I have talked at some length with nearly all the ministers who have held the portfolio of immigration or immigration and employment in Canada and Australia in recent years, and with many of the senior officials in their departments. I have also had the great advantage of access to policy files in Ottawa and Canberra.

I am indebted to my own Department of Political Science at the University of Toronto and to the Department of Demography at the Australian National University in Canberra, where I was a Visiting Fellow for some time; both have given strong support to this study.

I would like to thank, too, all those who have provided research or secretarial assistance, including Janet Fitzpatrick, Carol Putt, and Elaine Droy of Toronto, and the staff of The Electronic Office of Leamington Spa in Britain who typed the final version of my manuscript most efficiently. I would like to express my special thanks, however, to Margaret Mansfield of Canberra, now a librarian at the National Library of Australia, who has been my research assistant from the outset, providing me with a superb research and information-gathering service and a great deal of practical help; and to my Canadian friends Paula Hitze of Toronto and Arthur and Mavis Stinson of Ottawa for their continued interest and support.

Finally, I would like to express my gratitude and thanks to Professors

Joy Esberey, Peter Russell, and Kenneth McNaught of the University of Toronto and Dr. Charles Price of the Australian National University, who kindly read the manuscript and made a number of very helpful suggestions. I am particularly grateful to Charles Price who has been a source of help and encouragement throughout this study. Warmest thanks also go to the Social Sciences and Humanities Research Council of Canada, to the Department of the Secretary of State and to the Canada Employment and Immigration Commission for their very generous financing of this project.

Preface to the
Second Edition

Nothing illustrates so well the rapid pace of development in immigration and international migration today as the changes which have taken place in Canadian and Australian immigration in the last five years. Since this book was originally completed in 1986, Canada has embarked upon a new five-year immigration plan in which annual levels of immigration will be substantially increased. Australia has overhauled and modernized almost her entire system of immigration law following the recommendations of the Fitzgerald Committee which reported to the Hawke government in 1988. There have been new developments in multiculturalism, immigration appeal systems, and refugee status determination. Dramatic events on the international scene, including the ending of the Cold War, the unification of Germany, increasing political and economic turbulence in the Soviet Union, the exodus from Hong Kong, war and its aftermath in the Middle East, and the ever-growing movement of asylum seekers towards affluent countries which began in the 1980s, are presenting the international community with new and urgent problems in international migration.

In the midst of serious constitutional deliberations and not far perhaps from a profound restructuring of her constitution, Canada is proceeding with an ambitious and courageous immigration plan involving longer-term planning and much higher annual immigration levels. As suggested in the final chapter of this book, the period of restricted immigration (following the recession of 1979–82), when levels declined to below 100,000, did not last very long. It was followed in 1985 by a decision by the Mulroney government to "restore and revitalize" the immigration program. The government then announced that "a policy of moderate growth" would be pursued, based on the recognition that immigration brought "economic, social, demographic, humanitarian, cultural and international benefits to Canada." This policy continued until October 18, 1989 when Barbara McDougall, then a very able Minister of Employment and Immigration and now Secretary of State for External Affairs, announced in the House of Commons that it had been decided to move from then on to a five-year immigration plan. This decision, she said, represented "a shift from short to long-term planning, to more comprehensive consultations on immigration issues, and to a more comprehensive view of the immigration process itself." The plan would be developed after extensive consultations were held across Canada in the next few months.

These consultations took place between November 1989 and March 1990 and included a much wider range of representatives and individuals than the earlier annual consultations had done. There were eight national meetings in the larger cities from Halifax to Vancouver and twenty regional meetings to cover regional, local, and community interests. More extensive consultations were held with all the provinces and many written submissions were received. The Minister and her senior officials played an active part throughout this national consultative exercise.

Participants in all these non-governmental meetings were asked to focus on four areas: (1) the number of immigrants Canada should accept in the future and the pace at which increases should proceed, (2) the balance among categories of immigrants, (3) the settlement and integration of immigrants, and (4) the factors affecting the distribution of immigrants across Canada.

A rather remarkable degree of consensus emerged from these consultations, at least on the principal issues involved. There was a widely held view among participants that immigration was good for Canada and that levels should be increased during the next five years. In all provinces, it was felt that increased immigration would be of great benefit economically and would contribute to Canada's future in many ways.[1] There was universal support also for the admission of increased numbers of independent immigrants selected on the basis of skills and talents and without family connections. This category, it was felt, had always been the valuable core of Canada's immigration program but had been seriously reduced by the restrictions of the early eighties. Refugees and refugee programs were also strongly supported in all regions. On the important question of the settlement and integration of immigrants, there was similar agreement on the need for considerable improvement in Canada's settlement services for immigrants and refugees, particularly in language training programs which, it was felt, should be more widely available and less specifically related to labour

---

[1] Quebec now has a new agreement with the federal government which came into force on April 1, 1991. This agreement enhances her control over the immigration policies which directly affect the province, and gives her exclusive responsibility in the selection of her own independent immigrants. Among other advantages, Quebec will be able to receive up to 30 per cent of all the immigrants coming to Canada from now on. With the lowest fertility rate in Canada, it can be seen that Quebec does indeed have a strong interest in high levels of Canadian immigration.

Figure I
THE 1991–95 IMMIGRATION PLAN

Component	Estimated 1990	Planned 1991	1992	1993	1994	1995
FAMILY CLASS	72,500	80,000	100,000	95,000	85,000	85,000
REFUGEES						
• Government-assisted Refugees and Members of Designated Classes (selected abroad)	13,000	13,000	13,000	13,000	13,000	13,000
• Privately sponsored refugees and members of Designated Classes (selected abroad)	24,000	23,500	20,000	20,000	15,000	15,000
• Refugees landed in Canada (after Jan. 1, 1989)	5,000	10,000	25,000	25,000	25,000	25,000
INDEPENDENT IMMIGRANTS						
• principal applicants	19,500	20,000	21,500	22,500	29,000	29,000
• spouses and other accompanying dependents	25,500	21,000	20,000	25,000	33,000	33,000
ASSISTED RELATIVES						
• principal applicants	7,000	7,000	7,000	8,500	11,500	11,500
• spouses and other accompanying dependents	11,000	12,500	12,500	15,000	19,000	19,000
BUSINESS IMMIGRANTS						
• principal applicants	5,000	7,000	7,000	6,500	5,000	5,000
• spouses and other accompanying dependents	13,500	21,000	21,000	19,500	14,500	14,500
RETIREES	4,000	5,000	3,000	0	0	0
TOTAL	200,000	220,000	250,000	250,000	250,000	250,000

Source: Employment and Immigration Canada, Annual Report to Parliament, Immigration Plan for 1991–95.

force participation. Many participants emphasized the importance of helping immigrants to identify with their new country and develop a sense of belonging and being part of Canadian life. Government was urged to devote additional resources to the development of better integration services.

The Minister tabled Canada's first five-year immigration plan on October 25, 1990. Under this plan, immigration will rise from 200,000 in 1990 to 220,000 in 1991 and 250,000 in 1992 where it will be stabilized for the rest of the planning period (see Figure I). Within these numbers, a reasonable balance will be maintained between the family, refugee, and independent categories. Minor changes will be made in family-related regulations to allow Canadians to sponsor – as well as other family class members – children who are in fact dependent on their parents, but not adult non-dependent children as before. Canada's international commitments relating to refugees will be maintained through both government and private sponsorship programs and the new system for refugee claiments already in Canada. The independent and assisted relatives components of the immigration program will be maintained at current levels during the early years of the plan, but the number and overall proportion of skilled workers will increase in later years. Retirees will no longer be admitted and the retiree program will be discontinued after 1990. Those who were born in Canada, however, and wish to return, having given up their citizenship while working abroad, will still be able to do so.

There will also be a new "federal integration strategy," developed in co-operation with the provinces, municipal agencies, and other groups, that will improve language training programs and provide immigrants with a wide range of co-ordinated services to help them settle in their new communities and participate fully in society. A new emphasis will be placed on "helping immigrants learn about Canadian values and on helping Canadians understand the diverse backgrounds of newcomers." An annual program review will assess the operation of the plan and allow for adjustments if necessary. There will also be a review of the policy direction and objectives underlying the plan after three years, to prepare for the next five-year planning period.

In the present Canadian climate of constitutional uncertainty, the five year plan and prospect of much higher annual levels of immigration have aroused relatively little opposition. They are seen by many as a move towards the kind of immigration planning on a much larger scale which Canada will probably be involved in in the coming years. We can say today that the plan and its higher annual immigration levels offer the following advantages: (1) They enable control to be established at a time of rising pressures in all categories. (2) They allow a better balance to be achieved among the three categories of immigrants – family, refugees, and independents. (3) They may permit, at least for the time being, control to be achieved over the rising tide of asylum seekers by establishing fixed limits to entry, as well as generous entry quotas. (4) They will offer valuable experience for the management of the larger immigration movements to Canada which lie ahead.

Australia has been no less active and innovative in the immigration field in the last few years, although Australians are more divided today on the benefits of immigration – particularly of higher levels of admission – than Canadians are and the two major parties are still divided as this issue. A vigorous debate on the economic, demographic, and environmental impact of immigration has taken place in the media and in academic circles during this period. The hard working National Population Council has now been asked by the government to undertake an inquiry into "the impact of population increase on the economy, environment, human service delivery, infrastructure, social equity and international obligations" and to report by September 1991. The Structural Adjustment Committee of the Cabinet is also examining the question of population growth. Prime Minister Bob Hawke has said on more than one occasion that he favours expansion and that the Government believes that, with proper planning, Australia could absorb a growing population. In an interesting recent interview in *The Age* (February 21, 1990), he said – in answer to the question "Given the economic downturn, do you think there will be a case for reducing the migrant intake?":

I know that it will be argued. Generally speaking I am in favour of higher migration intakes rather than lower ones, because I think this country is going to be a better country. It is going to provide better services and better environment for its citizens with a somewhat larger population. Now I understand that this is a complex issue. I understand that there are widely diverging views about it. I understand that the economics profession is seriously divided on it. You could say the economic jury is out ... (But) there will still be the family reunion element. There will still be a significant place for business migrants and there will still be the humanitarian component. Now I frankly couldn't see that, looking to the next period, there is a case for any significant lowering of the figure we've got at the present time. But we as a Cabinet will consider that matter.

Nevertheless, the Cabinet did agree on a fairly substantial reduction in the numbers of new settlers for 1990–91. The present Minister for Immigration, Local Government[2] and Ethnic Affairs, Gerry Hand, announced on June 27, 1990 that the Government had decided on a balanced reduction from the 1989–90 announced program planning level of 140,000 places. The new planning level would be 126,000, including 64,000 for family migration, 50,000 for skill migration, 11,000 (including a contingency reserve of 1,000 places) for humanitarian migration, and a small special eligibility category of 1,000 places. This decision was applauded by conservation groups and condemned by ethnic group leaders, with some politicans, academics, journalists, and others taking sides in a continuing debate. There was a further reduction to 111,000 in 1991–92, but there are plans to bring this level up to 128,000 in 1993–94.

---

[2] The Office of Local Government was incorporated in the department in July 1987.

Australia's major effort in the past few years, however, has been to reform and modernize her immigration legislation and improve her methods of immigration planning and management. Billed in official publicity as "the biggest reform of migration for 20 years" (when the Whitlam Government got rid of the White Australia policy), this period of energetic reform can be compared with the similar Canadian effort that took place a decade earlier and is recorded in Chapter 2. Disatisfaction with Australian immigration law, particularly with her basic Migration Act of 1958, had existed for a long time. Proposals for reform of the Act had been put forward by the Administrative Review Council and by the former Human Rights Commission. A major effort to examine Australian immigration law and management and identify their deficiencies took place in the late seventies when a full-time task force was appointed within the Department of Immigration and Ethnic Affairs to carry out a thorough examination and review of the Department's responsibilities and operations. The task force gave special attention to the performance of the Migration Act, the problems of illegal migration, the effectiveness or otherwise of the existing migrant selection system, and the state of staff morale within the Department. Their final report was presented in July 1978. (See pp. 122–25)

Very much the same kind of concerns occupied the Committee to Advise on Australia's Immigration Policies (CAAIP) appointed by the Hawke Government in September 1987 and chaired by Dr Stephen Fitzgerald, an academic, businessman, and former Ambassador to China, although the Committee's terms of reference were much wider. The Committee was asked to report to the Minister of Immigration, Local Government and Ethnic Affairs in March 1988 on Australian immigration policies, addressing "all pertinent matters" including, in broad terms, the following:

- the relationship between immigration and the economy, including the effects on the labour market and economic development;
- the relationship between immigration and Australia's social and cultural development as a multicultural society;
- the relationship between immigration and key population issues;
- the overall capacity of Australia to receive significant immigration; and
- the relationship between immigration policies, including compliance, and the administrative and legislative processes involved.

In carrying out its work, the Committee was also required to note that: (1) Australia's immigration policies were non-discriminatory in respect of national or ethnic origin, race, sex, and religion and that it is a sovereign right of the Australian Government to determine who should enter; (2) Australia had a continuing commitment to play its part in providing international humanitarian assistance to those in need; (3) the Government had ruled out an amnesty for illegal immigrants; (4) while bearing settlement experiences in mind insofar as they are relevant to the framing of immigration policies, the Government was separately developing a National Agenda for a Multicultural Australia; and (5) full consultation with interested parties through written and oral submissions and other appropriate means should be undertaken.

The Fitzgerald or CAAIP Report was duly submitted to the Minister on March 16, 1988 and is, in many respects, the basis of the reforms in Australian immigration law and management which have been carried out since then, although the Government did not accept all the Committee's recommendations. The Committee had some very important things to say about immigration which, they pointed out, was under pressure worldwide. In these circumstances, Australia's immigration policies were not managing the increasing demand, in their view, and the planned immigration program would probably be exceeded by tens of thousands of immigrants unless there were immediate reform. In addition, "widespread mistrust and failing consensus" threatened community support of immigration and the program was not identified in the public mind with the national interest. Many Australians were not convinced that immigrants were making a commitment to their new country and were troubled by the inevitable changes which immigration brought to their society. The status of citizenship, which should reflect a commitment to Australia and its institutions and principles was felt to be seriously undervalued. Although warned off multiculturalism by the Government, the Committee said that the philosophy of multiculturalism was not widely understood in Australia and that the "uninformed ensuing debate" was damaging the cause it seeks to serve.

The Fitzgerald Committee urged that a coherent philosophy of immigration be developed now which would emphasize – among other things – the Australian context of immigration and allow Australians to understand the effect of immigration now and in the future and the many benefits it brings. Immigration was for all Australians, not for sectional interest groups. It must not be allowed "to slide into the margins of government decision-making". It must be in the mainstream. A total of 73 separate recommendations were made by the Committee, including a model bill which could form the basis of a new Migration Act.

The Government's response to the CAAIP Report came on December 8, 1988 when the previous Minister, Senator Robert Ray, gave a ministerial statement outlining the new immigration policies which had been approved. Since the submission of the Report on March 16, an interdepartment committee representing 12 government departments had examined it. Working parties of the National Population Council had studied selection systems and the problem of overseas qualification recognition. Senator Ray himself had visited all the state and territories to discuss the Report with his counterparts, had held public meetings on the subject in all capital cities, and had received over 120 submissions from individuals and organisations. Following this public consultation, Senator Ray said, the Government had adopted many of the theories of the Fitzgerald Committee's Report and the substance of many of its recommendations. In some areas, the Government supported its underlying concepts, although the approach differed in detail. In others, the Committee's response differed significantly from the Committee's proposals. In general, however, the Government accepted the Committee's message that immigration should be for all Australians and in the national interest.

The following are the major changes in immigration policy, law, and management announced by Senator Ray on December 8, 1988. They came into effect on December 19, 1989 and amounted to a complete overhaul of the old Migration Act of 1958. Extensive amendments to the Act had received royal assent on June 19.[3] Some additional changes and modifications were announced by Senator Ray's successor, Gerry Hand, during the following year.

The Government's response to the CAAIP Report consisted of the following elements:

1 The Government's commitment to a non-discriminatory approach to migrant selection on a global basis was reaffirmed.

2 The Immigration Department was authorized to develop a research capacity to bring immigration into the mainstream of economic and social planning. A Bureau of Immigration Research would be established to undertake major, systematic research and improve public comprehension of immigration issues. There would also be "upgraded consultative mechanisms," including Immigration Outlook Conferences.

3 The immigration program of 140,000 for 1989–90 would be divided into three main streams – family, skilled, and humanitarian migration – plus a small special eligibility category. Each of these streams would be "capped" to ensure that the migration program did not overrun the levels set by the government.

4 The family migration stream would comprise (a) the immediate family (spouses, fiancé(e)s, dependent children and parents with the balance of family in Australia[4] with no limits set on numbers, and (b) the extended family (siblings, non-dependent children, nieces and nephews and parents without the balance of family in Australia). Extended family members

---

[3] Migration Legislation Amendment Act 1989.

[4] Only those with more of their children living in Australia than in any single other country, or at least as many in Australia as overseas, would qualify as close family without a points test being applied.

would be subject to a points test with a "floating" passmark to allocate the limited places in the program fairly.

5 The skilled migration stream would consist of (a) an employer/business element which would include the Business Migration Program, the Employer Nomination Scheme, negotiated industry arrangements, and a "special skills" group (numbers would be subject to demand), and (b) a "labour force enhancement element" including the Occupational Shares System and Independent Migrants. Everyone in this category would be subject to a points test with a floating passmark.

The National Population Council had developed a new points system to meet these needs. Future overseas recruitment of skilled labour and the recognition of overseas qualifications would be referred to the Structural Adjustment Committee of the Cabinet for early consideration.

6 A major change in the review of immigration decisions would be introduced through a statutory two-tiered system of review. The first tier would involve a statutory and independent review by a special unit in the Immigration Department which would be independent of the primary decision-making areas. The second tier of review would be formed by a substantial restructuring of the former Immigration Review Panels. This new body would be set up under the Migration Act and empowered to consider cases on their merits and make a final decision. It would be represented in all states and territories. Fees would be charged for each tier of review, with a lower fee for the first tier.

7 The Secretary of the Department of Immigration, Local Government and Ethnic Affairs rather than the Minister would be the principal decision-maker on most immigration cases to guarantee fairness and equity for immigration decisions, to ensure that decisions were open to scrutiny and to remove the possibility of political interference. The Minister, however, would retain the power to determine several classes of decision, notably those involving the deportation of criminals, security matters, and refugee determinations.

8 There would be changes in the laws governing the detention and deportation of people who were in Australia illegally. A major effort would be made to reduce their numbers.

Implementation of most of these policies and programs took place during the following year and, as noted, became law on December 19, 1989. On December 18, Senator Ray made another major statement saying that he was proud to have presided over the long reform process – the most exhaustive and comprehensive review of immigration in Australian history – that had culminated in the introduction of the amended Migration Act and its new regulations. "[This] package of legislation substantially tightens our management of the immigration program," Senator Ray said. "It also provides for a much fairer system of reviewing migration decisions, and improves our ability to curb abuse of the immigration program by people seeking to come to Australia illegally. [But] perhaps the most important result is the establishment of immigration rules and criteria within the legislation which will ensure accountable and consistent decision-making, open and fair to all."

Following the re-election of the Hawke Government in March 1990, Senator Ray became Minister for Defence and Gerry Hand took over the portfolio of Minister for Immigration, Local Government and Ethnic Affairs and Minister assisting the Prime Minister for Multicultural Affairs. Since then Mr. Hand has presided over the necessary process of fitting this large package of law and regulations into place and making the necessary adjustments and additions where the fit was not satisfactory. In a parliamentary statement on May 9, 1990, he said that large sections of the amended Act and new regulations were operating satisfactorily, but the Government had heard a good deal of criticism of parts of the new system and had decided to rectify a number of procedural flaws. A process of parliamentary scrutiny and public consultation would also be set up to examine any further changes which might be necessary.

The Canadian equivalent to this major Australian reform effort took place, as discussed in Chapter 2, in the 1970s when her old, illiberal Immigration Act of 1952 was finally abandoned and replaced with the far better, liberal, and workable Immigration Act of 1976 which has served the country very well so far. During that decade Australia, whose governments had been much more aware of population issues since World War II, set up a National Population Inquiry which investigated Australia's demographic situation in considerable depth and reported to the Minister for Labour and Immigration in 1975 (see pp. 111–15). The Inquiry's Report did not produce policy recommendations, but offered a discussion of Australia's demographic options on the basis of the considerable amount of demographic information which had been accumulated. Canada also made what proved to be an abortive effort in the 1970s to raise the level of public consciousness on population issues and to formulate, if not a population policy, at least a set of useful "population guidelines" for Canada. This plan was defeated by a majority of the provinces who were not ready at that point to think about Canada's demographic future (see pp. 66–70). In the 1980s, however, the Mulroney Government, increasingly disturbed, like other Western governments, by the problem of low fertility and the prospect of an ageing and ultimately declining population, tried again.

A "Review of Demography and Its Implications for Economic and Social Policy" was set up on April 29, 1986, with its headquarters in the Department of Health and Welfare. The Review was directed to study possible changes in the size, structure, and distribution of the population of Canada to 2025 and to report on how these changes might affect Canada's social and economic life. The first major report of the Demographic Review, *Charting Canada's Future*, appeared in 1989.[5] During the previous three years, a total of 167 studies had been commissioned from Canadian demographers, economists, and other social scientists at a cost of over $2 million. In 1989–90, the Review secretariat discussed their findings with 2 Cabinet committees, the senior management of 21 federal departments, all provincial and territorial governments, and a large number of private sector groups. These findings were also reported to all the immigration consultative meetings which took place between November 1989 and March 1990, prior to the announcement in October 1990 of Canada's first five-year immigration plan.

Charting Canada's Future is an interesting and informative document, presented in an attractive diagrammatic form that, as intended, makes its demographic material easy to understand. The following is a summary of its major conclusions relating particularly to immigration.

1 Canadian fertility rates are below the replacement level, but because a large proportion of the population is currently in the childbearing ages, the population will, if current rates continue, grow until 2026. At that time, the population will begin a long, slow decline, returning to the level of the 1986 census – 25 million – in 2086 and continuing to decline, eventually stabilizing at about 18 million or roughly the size of the country in the late 1950s. This is the shape of the demograhic future for all Western countries; that is, for all countries that experienced a post-World War II baby boom followed by fertility rates below the replacement level.

2 Without immigration, continuation of Canada's below-replacement fertility rates would eventually lead to Canada's disappearance. The large proportion of the population currently in the childbearing ages would again maintain growth in the short term – the population would grow to a peak of 28 million in 2011 – but the subsequent decline would never cease. The decline, however, would be relatively slow: the population would still be above 19 million 100 years hence.

3 Regional population growth in Canada will follow similar trends, growing slowly over the next 40 years before beginning a possible long-term decline. The exceptions are Ontario, which may grow slightly faster than the rest of Canada, and Quebec, which faces the possibility of relatively slower growth.

---

[5] *Charting Canada's Future*, Report of The Demographic Review (Ottawa: Health and Welfare Canada, 1989).

4 Linguistic duality has been an integral part of Canadian society since
  its beginning. From 1850 to 1950, the proportion of the two charter
  groups in Canada has been maintained at approximately 60 per cent
  anglophone and 30 per cent francophone. This long period of equilibrium
  ended at the close of World War II when all the demolinguistic factors
  (differential fertility, immigration, and linguistic mobility) started to
  exert downward pressure on the proportion of francophones. They now
  form 23 per cent of the Canadian population. Superimposed on the
  linguistic duality of Canada is a growing territorial duality. In 1986,
  nearly 90 per cent of all francophones lived in Quebec, where
  they accounted for 83 per cent of the population. On the other hand,
  95 per cent of anglophones lived in the other provinces where they
  accounted for 80 per cent of the population.

5 The consensus among those economists who have considered the question
  is that, within broad limits, population growth or sheer numbers of
  people are not a major factor in economic growth or economic well-
  being in modern economies that play an active role in world trade.
  Canada is such an economy. Recent studies indicate that it is not so
  much the numbers of people that will affect Canadians' economic well-
  being as their skills, and the effective development of those skills.

6 The Canadian population is ageing in the demographic sense that future
  populations will have a higher proportion of the population in the older
  age groups. This is a long-term trend caused by the historical decline
  in fertility. Compared with some developed countries (e.g., Germany
  and Sweden), however, Canada's population is relatively young. This
  is because those countries have comparatively lower fertility rates than
  Canada and the process of ageing has not been delayed by a marked
  baby boom, as it has in this country.

7 In a low-mortality country such as Canada, fertility is the major demographic force affecting the age structure. As long as the age structure
  of immigrants stays the same, immigration affects the overall age structure
  only in the short term. Increases in immigration to levels as high as
  600,000 per year have, in the long term, no impact. An increase in
  fertility to replacement levels also produces only a minor impact. Only
  a significant increase in the fertility rate – for example to 3.1 (from
  Canada's rate of 1.7 in 1986) – would change the long-term trend toward
  an older society.

8 Canadian immigration is far more diverse now than it was a quarter of
  a century ago in terms of the national, linguistic, religious, and racial
  backgrounds of immigrants. This is changing the face of Canada, but
  the impact is largely an urban phenomenon and, except for Montreal,
  it takes place west of Quebec. The 1986 census counted 110,000 immigrants in Ottawa-Hull and 120,000 in all of Canada east of Ontario,

excluding Montreal. To cite just one example of these differential impacts, in 1951, Halifax and Toronto had roughly the same kind of ethnic structure: three-quarters of their populations were of British origin and the other quarter was divided among a variety of ethnic origins. Despite 25 years of immigration that was shifting towards non-traditional sources, Halifax in 1986 still had the same ethnic structure, but Toronto had been transformed. In fact, immigration for the past few decades has not been a national but a highly focused phenomenon, focused on the large cities: Montreal and the large cities west of Quebec, especially Toronto and Vancouver.

9 The overall contribution that immigrants make to the economy of their new country is an important issue. Average income is a fair measure of economic contribution and the average income of immigrants in Canada is higher than the national average (although their social and economic experiences can vary widely). Part of the reason for their comparative economic success is their higher average level of education compared with the Canadian-born. This is true of immigrants from both traditional and non-traditional sources. Educational attainment in the family class and among refugees, though somewhat lower than in other immigrant groups, is still above that of the Canadian-born. Immigrants thus continue their historical role of reinforcing the trends in Canadian society, in particular the trend towards a better-educated, culturally diverse, urban, cosmopolitan society.

Charting Canada's Future has come in for a fair amount of criticism from Canadian demographers, some of whom find it too bland and simplistic and lacking in rigorous intellectual discussion. The Report certainly informs very effectively, but does not challenge or disturb, nor does it make specific proposals for action. The Research Secretariat have emphasized, however, that this Report is only the important first stage in a major information and educational effort designed to increase the public's awareness and understanding of population issues, and they claim that it has already raised a great deal of interest across Canada. Perhaps the major criticism which can be levelled against the Report, however, is that, by its own admission, it does not deal in any way with world population problems today, nor was it required by Government to do so. There is no discussion, for example, of the huge, continuing increases in the world's population and their probable effect on Canada. But it is doubtful whether the outside world can in fact be excluded in this way. This point has been well put by one academic critic:

"... in the face of a world trying to cope with more than 10 million refugees, with starvation in Africa, with the turmoil in Eastern Europe and the misery of Central

America, with the transfer of Hong Kong to the People's Republic of China in 1997, with demographic explosions in a score of Third World metropolises, is it really thinkable that our vast and wealthy land will accept no more than 100,000–400,000 immigrants in any year in the next 50? Is it not more likely that there will be years, perhaps many years, of a million or more immigrants – the equivalent of the yearly 3% of population – who came in as immigrants in some years at the turn of the 19th Century?"[6]

The pressures of rising world population and the increasing dissatisfaction with the economic disparity between the affluent countries and those of the Third World are already being felt in Canada and Australia. We have noted that the Fitzgerald Committee in Australia pointed out that immigration was now under pressure worldwide. Among the policy changes announced by Mr. Hand a year after the amended Migration Act came into force was the introduction of a new system and additional resources for determining claims for refugee status and humanitarian stay in Australia which came into force on December 10, 1990. These changes were necessary, Mr. Hand said, in order to deal with the growing number of people applying to stay in Australia on refugee and humanitarian grounds. The new system would have three stages:

1 a primary stage in which applications would be assessed and decisions made quickly on refugee status;
2 a review stage where there were negative assessments; and
3 a third stage where, although there were clear grounds for humanitarian stay, refugee status would not be recommended, but there would be Ministerial approval for temporary entry on humanitarian grounds.

A Refugee Status Review Committee would be established at the review stage which would replace the existing Determination of Refugee Status (DORS) Committee.

For the first time, a non-Government representative would be involved in the refugee decision-making process. A representative nominated by the Refugee Council of Australia would be a member of the Committee together with representatives of the Department of Foreign Affairs and Trade, the Attorney General's Department, and the Department of Immigration, Local Government and Ethnic Affairs (Chair). A representative of the United Nations High Commissioner for Refugees (UNHCR) would continue to attend meetings in an advisory capacity. The Minister said

---

[6] Federation of Canadian Demographers, *Comments on Charting Canada's Future* (London, Ont.: University of Western Ontario Population Studies Centre, 1990) p. 6.

that the Government had agreed to a significant increase in the resources available to process applications for refugee status in order to speed up decision making. It was essential that Australia should be able to decide refugee applications quickly and fairly, Mr. Hand said, and the Government was committed to a system which dealt with asylum seekers in Australia in a compassionate and humane way. Applicants who were granted permission by the Minister to remain in Australia on humanitarian grounds would receive a four-year temporary entry permit on the same conditions as a refugee.

In creating this new system, Australia would have been well aware of Canada's battle with the asylum-seeker problem. The "Canada-Australia watch" referred to in Chapter 6 (p. 243) has, if anything, speeded up and Ottawa has seen several important Australian delegations recently. The annual number of applications for refugee status in Australia is relatively low at present compared with those of Canada and some other industrialized countries, but there is no reason to think that it will remain at this level. The introduction of the new system of refugee status determination is, therefore, a timely move.

The 1980s have seen a remarkable escalation in the numbers of un-documented migrants, now more commonly described as asylum seekers or claimants for refugee status (as refugee status is now seen as a possible means of entry to many countries), now leaving developing countries and seeking a better life, generally in the more affluent countries to the north. More than 80 million people are believed to be involved in this large population movement and most industrialized countries have been inundated in the 1980s with refugee status claimants and have developed large backlogs in the process of dealing with their claims. The centuries-old international commerce of migration is prospering today as never before and becoming more sophisticated all the time. It provides – in many different ways, ranging from jet planes to rowing boats – the essential transportation for these migrants. Five hundred claims for refugee status were made in Canada in 1977. In 1983–84 the number had increased to over 6,000 and in 1986 to 18,000 with a backlog of over 20,000. This backlog grew to 60,000 in 1988 and to well over 100,000 in 1990 as the number of applications for refugee status continued to increase.

Canada's need for a more effective refugee status determination system was therefore urgent. The two bills mentioned in Chapter 4, Bill C55, which created a new refugee status determination system, and C84, known as the "Deterrents and Detention Bill" and designed to stop abuse of this system by firm deterrent measures, were passed without difficulty, despite a good deal of opposition from the Liberal and New Democratic parties, non-governmental organizations, and certain sections of the legal profession. They were then incorporated in an amended Immigration Act 1976 which received royal assent in July 1988. The new system, consisting of a new national board, the Immigration and Refugee Board (IRB), which includes two distinct divisions: the Convention Refugee Determination Division and the Immigration Appeal Division, is described briefly on pp. 192–93. It has now been in place for a little over two years. The Board is Canada's largest administrative tribunal with over 120 full-time members in the Refugee Division and about 22 in the Immigration Appeal Division. Both Divisions may take on as many part-time or additional full-time members as they require. The IRB is headed by a Chairman who is the chief executive officer of the Board with a Deputy Chairman for each Division. The IRB has its national headquarters in Ottawa and five regional offices located in Montreal, Toronto, Winnipeg, and Vancouver.

Thus far, Canada's new refugee status determination system has not been able to deal with demand or backlog any more effectively than the past system, not least because the flow of asylum seekers and number of refugee claims continues to grow. Canadian acceptance rates have been very high – around 90 per cent in the summer of 1990. This rate is far higher than those of other countries in similar circumstances and efforts are being made to bring it down. The planned levels for the three categories of refugees defined in Canada's new five-year immigration plan should help to establish some control over numbers. It is increasingly evident, however, that the continuing efforts of asylum seekers to gain entry to the more affluent countries of the Western world – their individual response to poverty and disadvantage – can only be handled internationally. Radical revision of the ideas of the international community about refugees and their protection, and the management of refugee movements of different kinds, is urgently needed.

Canada is also proceeding with the process of institutionalizing multiculturalism in her present political system that began in 1982 with the entrenchment of "the multicultural heritage of Canadians" in the Charter of Rights and Freedoms. Since then, Canada has acquired (in 1988) a Multiculturalism Act. A new full Department of Multiculturalism and Citizenship has been created, as well as a fully fledged House of Commons Standing Committee on Multiculturalism and Citizenship. With these and other developments, what has been called "the dizzying rise of multiculturalism as a national ideal in Canada"[7] has appeared to reach a plateau, with a reasonable level of public acceptance but perhaps slightly less enthusiasm than in the past. Further developments at the federal and provincial levels await the outcome of constitutional discussions.

---

[7] Canadian Human Rights Foundation, *Multiculturalism and the Charter, A Legal Perspective* (Toronto: Carswell, 1987).

In Australia, however, where public acceptance and understanding of multiculturalism has been less certain, the Prime Minister, the Office of Multicultural Affairs, and the Advisory Council on Multicultural Affairs have made a major effort to make the multicultural nature of Australian society better understood, to explain the government's multicultural policy, and "to lay to rest many of the concerns and misapprehensions that continue to be expressed about multiculturalism."[8] Following extensive consultations by the Office of Multicultural Affairs and the Advisory Council with all the state and with national and voluntary organizations, the Council prepared a discussion paper entitled "Towards a National Agenda for a Multicultural Australia" which was presented to the Prime Minister in September 1988 and then released publicly. The Council developed eight goals for a multicultural Australia that were accepted by the Commonwealth Government and are the basis of a number of new initiatives in this field. Among these new initiatives, the Office of Multicultural Affairs is examining the desirability of a Multiculturalism Act for Australia.

The last few years in Canada and Australia have indeed been critical years for both countries in immigration, population, refugee policy, and multiculturalism. If Canada is moving ahead somewhat – in a numbers sense – in coming to terms with world-wide migration pressures, Australia may move in this direction later, now that her immigration laws and regulations have been revised and modernized. In many areas, however, not least in the actual management of annual immigration and refugee movements, policies in the two countries are converging.

Whether the exclusive national management of immigration can survive for very long in the next century remains to be seen. It is certain, however, that Canadian and Australian experience in the migration field will be invaluable in helping the international community to develop the new initiatives and new kinds of international collaboration which will be badly needed in the coming years.

---

[8] Advisory Council on Multicultural Affairs, *Towards a National Agenda for a Multicultural Australia* Canberra: Australian Government Publishing Service, 1988.

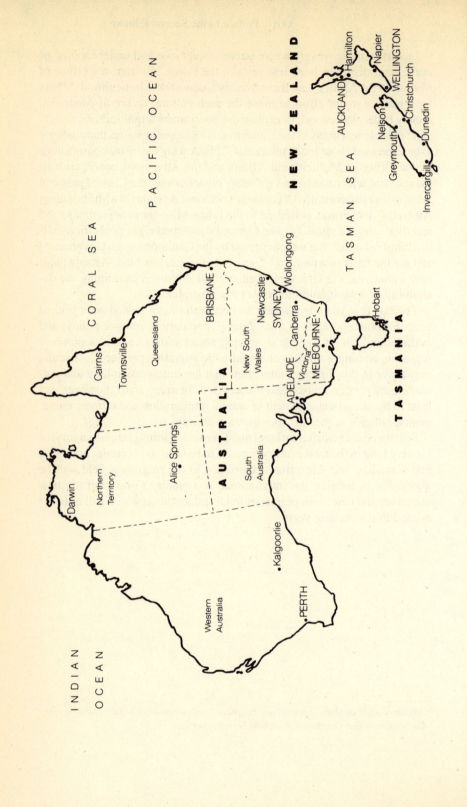

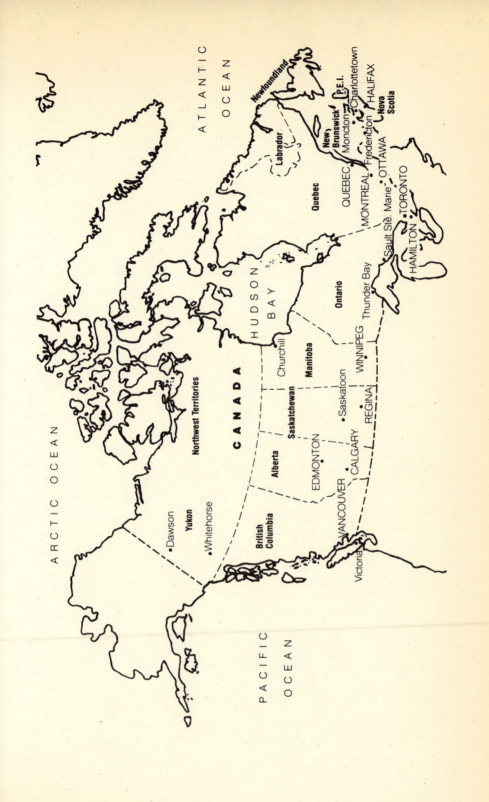

Introduction

Canada and Australia have many things in common and not the least of these is their possession of vast territories, impressive resources, and small populations. These factors in themselves account for the fact that these two countries have been among the foremost receiving countries in international migration in recent times, and for their acceptance of large numbers of displaced persons and refugees for permanent settlement since World War II. With populations today of only 26 and 17 million, the low fertility common to industrialized countries, and the prospect of population decline in the next century, it seems certain that Canada and Australia will continue to admit substantial numbers of immigrants and refugees for a long time to come. In addition to their present demographic problems, the major reviews of immigration, population, and refugee policies and programs which have taken place in both countries in recent years, clearly favoured continued population growth despite economic difficulties, and confirmed the fact that immigration will be the major instrument for achieving this.

The immense size of the Canadian and Australian territories, with areas of 9.9 and 7.6 million square kilometers respectively, is hard to visualize. A common and convenient way of expressing it is to say that Canada is about the same size as Europe without the Soviet Union, while Australia is as large as the United States without Hawaii and Alaska, or nearly as large as Brazil but with less than a sixth of Brazil's population. Within their vast domains, both Canada and Australia possess large areas of inhospitable country – Canada's frozen north and Australia's arid or semi-arid land. More than half of Australia is designated as desert or semi-desert. Canada's arctic and sub-arctic regions comprise at least two thirds of the nation. Both countries, one a continent in itself and the other the northern half of the North American land mass reaching to the Arctic, have interminable coastlines which are impossible to guard adequately and huge distances between regions and between cities. They have therefore had serious communication problems and costly and time-consuming internal travel which has had important social and political consequences.

Size and distance have imposed serious constraints on both countries from the beginning. They have also been, at all periods of Canadian and Australian history, a siren call to politicians and developers, immigrants and fortune hunters who have seen in their vast frozen or arid lands the promise of a spectacular future and great wealth. In recent years, not even the dire forebodings of a Club of Rome or a Zero Population Growth morement, nor a severe recession have restrained the imagination of those who look ahead in Canada and Australia, or dimmed the popular view that the future holds great possibilities. And perhaps the approach of the twenty-first century with its promise of fabulous technologies for resource extraction, for creative northern development, and for the flowering of deserts is making their optimism more credible at last.

Thus the opening paragraph of Australia's 1977 Green Paper, *Immigration Policies and Australia's Population*, states that "Australians, in good times and bad, have held to the belief that Australia is a land of great promise and potential. Traditionally, they have believed that such a vast area of the world's surface, which despite its dryness has many natural advantages and abundant mineral resources, must continue to prosper and its population expand." In the same vein, the Task Force on Canadian Unity which held public hearings across Canada in 1977 and 1978 noted how often they had heard statements about Canada's great natural wealth and abundant resources. In their final report they quote a comment made in the Prairie provinces that Canada has an abundance of natural resources of all types and descriptions and "what may be more important in the future, room to move, room to expand ..."

These have not been the only voices to be heard on Canadian and Australian development, however. For a long time, important elements in both countries have advocated caution, sternly realistic attitudes towards growth, and images of Canada and Australia which in their present form emphasize moderate size, high technical and social achievement, and a comfortable life preserved for the relatively few. Sobered by historical experience and aware of the serious problems that extreme climates and fragile ecology can pose, they are not seduced by visions of dramatic development and future expansion. Nevertheless, it seems evident that optimism and high expectations for the future are endemic in Canada and Australia, and are likely to remain the majority view.

The sense of space – room to move and room to expand, the chance to make a living in a free, open and earlier less developed society – has been, with flight from poverty and danger, the major factor in attracting migrants to Canada and Australia from the earliest times. What motives brought Canada's native peoples, her first known citizens, across the northern land bridge from Asia into North America long before Europeans appeared on the scene? What impelled Australia's Aborigines to move down to that vast dry land from their earlier settlements in the Southeast Asian archipelago or in Asia itself thousands of years ago? Were their motives very different from those of the 50 million Europeans who moved to North America between 1850 and 1920, or those of the large numbers of immigrants who have settled permanently in Canada and Australia since World War II? Today, on the streets and in the bars and cafes of Toronto and Sydney, cities with very large foreign-born populations, immigrants are likely to tell you that space, in the widest possible sense, is what they really value in their adopted lands, for themselves and for their children.

For many migrants from Europe, and more recently from other parts of the world, an agonizing choice has often had to be made between Canada and Australia as ultimate destinations for settlement. The choice, though less agonizing now and far from irretrievable, is still being made today. For Europeans, the appeal of Australia's warm climate has had to be balanced against the advantages of the shorter journey to Canada and a cheaper fare home if things went badly. For all migrants, the factors to be considered have included the presence of relatives or friends, and perhaps a larger ethnic community; the choice that Canada offered until recently of moving on to the United States if prospects looked brighter there; and the strong appeal of an assisted passage to Australia available to some. In addition to official information, migrants have studied the latest news, if any, about Canada and Australia and their economic prospects; have sought advice from relatives and friends already established there; and have often picked up information from what is known as the "migration grapevine" which has long proved to be a remarkable communications network. Many immigrants have changed their minds later. From the earliest years on, there have been a few, increasing to a small annual two-way movement today, of migrants of all nationalities who have tried Canada first and moved on to Australia later or vice versa.

Since World War II, Canada has admitted just over five and Australia just over four million immigrants and refugees. Through the combined effects of natural increase and immigration, both countries have doubled their populations in little more than a quarter of a century, with very little stress or strain, and with a very positive impact on national growth and development. Since their racially discriminatory immigration policies of earlier years were abandoned, by Canada in 1962 and Australia in 1973, they have admitted increasing numbers of immigrants from the developing world, and both have become important countries of permanent settlement for refugees. This study records and analyses this common experience, setting it in its historical context, examining the ways that immigration policies, law, and management have evolved in this century and looking ahead to the role of immigration in Canada and Australia in the future.

Although the term "Critical Years" does not apply to the contemporary period only, the major focus of the study is on the years after 1972 when a remarkable process of liberalization and modernization in immigration policies and programs took place in both countries. The period began in Canada with the arrival on the scene of a very concerned and energetic Liberal Minister of Manpower and Immigration, Robert Andras; and in Australia with the election of a Labor government under Prime Minister Gough Whitlam, after Labor had spent 23 years in opposition. These were critical years indeed, when both countries made major changes in this area of public policy, reviewing their immigration and population policies and laws, expanding the role of government in this field, creating new systems of immigration and refugee planning and immigrant selection, consulting the public on a regular basis, and adopting multiculturalism as a national policy. There are differences, of course, in the ways in which Canadian and Australian governments have handled these new developments, but the overall similarities are striking. It is the purpose of this study, however, not only to show how immigration has been managed in Canada and Australia, but also to add, if possible, to the mutual awareness and understanding of these two countries who have a great deal in common but, even for the informed public outside government, little access still to detailed information about each other.

Although it is hoped that the study will be widely used by scholars and students, it has not been written primarily for the academic community. It has been written for politicians and bureaucrats, policy-makers and managers at all levels, and for all those who are concerned about immigration, immigrants, and refugees and who have, or wish to have, an input into the policy-making process in this field. Reviewers should note also that it is not concerned with theories of migration or with theories of public policy-making. It is very much concerned with what governments, parliaments, political parties, and interest groups do in this field and with the actual *content* of policies, laws, and programs in immigration and related policy areas. It also seeks to show how two major countries of immigration have developed over time some useful principles and good ways of managing a difficult and sensitive area of public policy, and the extent to which they have shared their experiences and can still profitably learn from each other.

Although Canadian and Australian governments have developed a strong leadership role in the immigration field, particularly since World War II, and have been well ahead of public opinion in recent years, most

Canadian and Australian politicians have handled this area of public policy warily. They have been nervous of public reaction and of a backlash from some quarter or another, and always apprehensive about the possible loss of electoral support through unpopular immigration policies. They have been worried in times of recession about immigration and unemployment; and they have been harassed to a considerable extent by the ever-present volume of group and individual representations on issues like family reunion and on individual cases. There is some evidence to show, however, that as immigration has become better managed in recent years, these anxieties have been receding to some extent. By contrast immigration has evoked in Canada and Australia a remarkable and identical dedication and often lifetime interest among immigration officials which is particularly evident at the more senior levels. This dedication is explained by them in terms of the wide-ranging human interest of immigration and the satisfactory sense it gives, in these major receiving countries, of contributing, in the long term at least, to national growth and development.

Although Canadian and Australian immigration policies have become more alike in recent years, Australia has consistently given immigration a higher place on her national agenda. In Canada in the 1960s and 1970s, the Pearson and Trudeau governments failed to treat immigration as an area of public policy in its own right and to ensure that it had the kind of administrative structure and authority which it requires, simply making it serve their plans in manpower development and employment. These two Liberal governments, in power from 1963 to 1984 with only one short break, also allowed a fragmentation of immigration management to take place, dispersing vital parts of the operation to the departments of the Secretary of State and External Affairs where they received less direct attention and concern. Canada's great achievement during these years, however, has been to produce an excellent new Immigration Act in 1976, which is one of the best pieces of immigration legislation to be found anywhere; and, by means of this Act, to develop much closer collaboration with the provinces in immigration and new consultative procedures in immigration and refugee planning.

Although imminent, Australia has not yet replaced her elderly and illiberal Migration Act of 1958, although it has been amended quite often in minor ways and bypassed in some respects by subsequent regulations and programs. But in her Department of Immigration and Ethnic Affairs she has retained and developed an effective and unified administrative agency in immigration, which is responsible for all the major activities involved in this area of public policy, and is visible and accessible to the public. A glance at any issue of this department's highly informative, interesting, and lively Annual Review, as well as the DILGEA organization chart in Appendix 3, will show what a sensible arrangement this is.

It is often said that diffusion of responsibility fosters inaction. In Canada, diffusion of responsibility in immigration has seriously weakened authority in this area and made it impossible to manage and develop the immigration field as a whole. Just as Australia undoubtedly needs a new Migration Act, it is essential that in Canada immigration should be rescued from its present plight of being managed by a very able but small and invisible secretariat in a vast, highly regionalized employment agency (the Canada Employment and Immigration Commission). The constituent elements of immigration management should be reassembled as soon as possible and authority restored. This is particularly important in view of Canada's pressing demographic needs, discussed in the final chapter.

These and other critical issues in the contemporary management of immigration in Canada and Australia are explored in this study. It begins in the opening years of this century when the long period of free world migration was coming to an end, and when Canada and Australia were putting their immigration policies into a definite shape, deciding whom to admit, whom to exclude, and how to do it. It ends in 1986, spilling over a little into 1987 to include several major policy developments. In an area of public policy in which there is a great deal of detailed information to be absorbed, it has been planned with a view to achieving an effective joint examination and analysis of Canadian and Australian policies and programs, with as much clarity and readability as possible. Analysis is not confined by any means to the final chapter, but is an important part of the book as a whole. Comprehensive immigration and population statistics for the entire period under discussion will be found in Appendix 1 and are intended to be used for reference throughout this study. Other statistical material will be found in individual chapters. One final point should be mentioned here. Canada uses the words "immigration" and "immigrant" exclusively. Australia, on the other hand, uses "migration" and "migrant" most frequently, but "immigration" and "immigrant" sometimes. These words are used interchangeably in this study. Australia also uses the traditional word "settler" which is used here where appropriate.

Critical Years in Immigration:
Canada and Australia Compared

CHAPTER ONE

Immigration in the Twentieth Century, 1900–1972

We will first explore the major features of Canadian and Australian immigration during the period from 1900 to 1972, before a more detailed examination of contemporary policies and programs. This 70-year period falls naturally into two parts, with the Second World War providing the dividing line between them.

The century began for both countries with exceptionally large immigration movements which continued until the outbreak of World War I in 1914: to Canada from Britain, the United States and Europe and to Australia almost entirely from Britain. In Canada the early years of the century were notable for vigorous immigration management and development under a very remarkable Liberal minister, Clifford Sifton. In both countries, these were the years when the White Canada and White Australia immigration policies were enshrined in the law, and when politicians and the public strongly supported them.

After the end of World War II in Europe and the Far East, governments began to assume much wider responsibilities in immigration. Refugees in large numbers gradually became an accepted fact of life, and refugee policy with its international obligations became an established element in immigration planning and management. Most important, the deliberately discriminatory immigration policies involved in the image of a White Canada and a White Australia, implemented in one way or another by both countries from the late nineteenth century onwards, were abandoned – first by Canada in 1962, then by Australia in 1973.

1900–1945

Canada: The Sifton Era[1]

Some two and a half million immigrants came to Canada between 1896 and 1914. Of these, it is estimated that close to a million came from Britain; more than three quarters of a million came from the United States, many of them returning Canadians; and more than half a million came from continental Europe.[2] Not all of these immigrants settled in Western Canada as is widely believed. Many were attracted to the growing cities and towns in the east. Nevertheless, more than a million settlers from all three groups arrived on the Prairies and in British Columbia during the peak period of immigration between 1901 and 1911. While the majority were English-speaking, there were considerable numbers from Germany, Scandinavia, the Netherlands, Russia (including many from the Ukraine), Austria, Hungary, Italy, and what is now Poland, as well as a large Jewish group.[3] It was the beginning of the diversification of Canada's population and the point of origin of some of her largest, present-day ethnic communities.

The chief planner and promoter of this large immigration movement was Clifford Sifton, Minister of the Interior in the Laurier government from 1896 to 1905 who was knighted in World War I. There is no figure like him in the history of Canadian immigration to the present day and his actual works, in addition to his often-quoted opinions, deserve to be much better known. The only comparable figure in the immigration field can be found not in Canada, but in Australia half a century later, in Arthur Calwell, Minister of Information and Immigration in the Chifley government of 1946–1949, creator, as we shall see later, of Australia's "Populate or Perish" post-war immigration program, and a developer of similar talents and determination. Both Sifton and Calwell were men of strong views and strong prejudices and both were convinced all their lives that their approach to immigration was the right and the only one. But both showed in dramatic ways what can be done in immigration planning, development, and management, if the political will is there.

Clifford Sifton was born in London Township in Middlesex County, Ontario in 1861. His father John Wright Sifton, a keen Methodist and energetic Liberal supporter, moved the family to Manitoba in 1875 where he entered the provincial legislature; he was made Speaker of the House in 1878. His sons, Arthur and Clifford, became students at the Methodist Victoria College in Toronto, returning to Manitoba to practice law. Both had distinguished careers, Arthur eventually becoming Premier of Alberta and later a Dominion cabinet minister. Clifford was first elected to the Manitoba Legislature in 1888. In 1891 he became provincial Attorney-General and was also responsible for education and provincial crown lands. Five years later, he was invited by Wilfrid Laurier to join the new Liberal cabinet in Ottawa. As Minister of the Interior and responsible both for Dominion lands and immigration he is said to have insisted that he must have complete freedom to organize the settlement and development of the West, and this he proceeded to do with tremendous energy and dedication.

Shortly after his arrival in Ottawa, Sifton began to develop a well-organized Immigration Branch within the Ministry of the Interior, where it had been transferred in 1891 from its earlier home in Agriculture. He appointed a Superintendent of Immigration based in Ottawa with a corps of civil servants to assist him. Most of them were "Sifton men," often westerners, chosen by the Minister himself. The Ottawa group was to be responsible for recruiting immigrants in the United States, Britain, and Europe, as well as supervising the government agents who would promote immigration to Canada and do the actual recruiting. A subdivision of the Immigration Branch was established in Winnipeg to look after the placement and settlement of these new immigrants in the West.[4] At the same time, Sifton made a determined and successful effort to free railway lands and Dominion lands for immediate settlement and to make sure that the new settlers whom he planned to recruit would be able to acquire land and settle on it with reasonable speed. This together with improvements in transportation were essential elements in his program. Sifton planned to settle the West with farmers, experienced farmers from the American Middle West and Britain (if available), peasant farmers from Europe, or simply people who had been born on the land, preferably in northern regions, and who were accustomed to a pioneering life. As he said himself, he did not want artisans, mechanics, labourers, small shopkeepers, and the like who were town-dwellers who knew nothing about farming. In an article written for Macleans Magazine 25 years later, he described his objectives:

In those days, settlers were sought from three sources: one was the United States. The American settlers did not need sifting; they were of the finest quality and the most desirable settlers. In Great Britain we confined our efforts very largely to the North of England and Scotland, and for the purpose of sifting the settlers we doubled the bonuses to the agents in the North of England and cut them down as much as possible in the South. The result was that we got a fairly steady stream of people from the North of England and from Scotland and they were the very best settlers in the world ...

Our work was largely done in the North ... Then came the continent where the great emigrating centre was Hamburg. Steamships go there to load up with people who are desirous of leaving Europe ... We made an arrangement with the booking agencies in Hamburg, under which they winnowed out this flood of people, picked out the agriculturists and peasants and sent them to Canada, sending nobody else. We paid, I think, $5,000 per head for the farmer and $2,000 per head for the other members of the family.[5]

Sifton's most famous remark appeared in the same article, although he must have expressed this thought on many occasions. This was his idea of a farmer. "I think a stalwart peasant in a sheepskin coat," he wrote, "born on the soil, whose forefathers have been farmers for ten generations, with a stout wife and a half dozen children, is good quality." It was men like these, in his view, along with other experienced farmers, who were needed in Canada "to fight the battle of the pioneer" and settle the West.

Sifton's major effort to attract and recruit settlers for Canada, however, was undoubtedly made in the United States and, according to his biographer John Dafoe, he had his eye on American farmers from the beginning.[6] In 1897, the Department of the Interior established nine Canadian agencies south of the border, increasing the number gradually to 18 in 1904 and to 21 in 1914. Full-time Canadian agents were in charge of these offices, using numerous sub-agents who worked on commission. An extensive newspaper advertising campaign was started immediately, and within a year or two advertisements describing land purchase and settlement opportunities in Canada were appearing regularly in American agricultural papers. The Department of the Interior appointed its own press agent in the US, to establish good relations with the national press and to keep Canada's advertising campaign up to date. In all this, the Department worked with the Canadian Pacific Railway which had its own settler recruitment campaign in the American Middle West and elsewhere. In the summer of 1897, Sifton and the president of the Canadian Pacific, Sir William Van Horne, issued a joint invitation to newspaper editors in Minnesota to take a trip through the Canadian West as their guests. The invitation was repeated later that summer for Wisconsin editors and in 1899 for the 600 members of the National Editorial Association of the United States.

The Department also produced a mass of supporting literature on the Canadian West – pamphlets, booklets, maps, and circulars – which could be given to editors, journalists, and interested individuals, or distributed by its agents and sub-agents through the American farming communities. One of the most popular pamphlets which was reprinted year after year and distributed widely had the now well-known title "The Last Best West," but there were many others. "The Wondrous West," "Canada, Land of Opportunity," "Prosperity Follows Settlement," "The Story of a Manitoba Farmer," "Canada, the Land of the Prairies," "Peace River Trail" were among the titles; and there were information booklets also with such titles as "One Thousand Facts about Canada," "Canada in a Nutshell," "Canadian West" and "Canadian Winter." It was a lively and innovative promotion campaign and remarkably successful.[7]

American farmers and others who responded to these blandishments were warmly welcomed in Canada and with the exception of one group given every assistance. American negroes were not welcome and were not encouraged to come; and, although no law was passed to exclude them, careful administrative procedures ensured that their applications would be rejected. There was in fact no mass demand to come to Canada on the part of American negroes who were often too poor and disadvantaged to contemplate migration. But their situation was worsening in the United States around the turn of the century, with discrimination, segregation, and outright hostility against them increasing; and some negro groups and individuals, who became aware of Canada's need for settlers, expressed a real interest in moving there. A few did manage to acquire land and settle on the Canadian Prairies, but their relatives and friends, the necessary "reinforcements" for these small settlements, were hardly ever allowed to join them. In this, the Immigration Branch was undoubtedly in tune with public opinion in the West and elsewhere in Canada – as expressed in the press, through local councils, boards of trade, voluntary organizations, and in other ways – which was totally opposed to the admission of negroes. White settlers were insisting that the Prairies be kept white. As only one example, in 1911 the Edmonton Board of Trade organized a petition to the federal government demanding the exclusion of negroes and in the same year the Edmonton Municipal Council passed a resolution calling on the federal government "to take all action necessary to prevent the expected influx of negroes."[8]

Clifford Sifton resigned from the Laurier cabinet in 1905 after a disagreement with the Prime Minister over the separate school rights question. He stayed on in Parliament as a backbencher until 1911, but remained a powerful and influential figure in the Liberal Party and in public affairs generally until shortly before his death in 1929. He also became a wealthy businessman and was the principal proprietor of the Manitoba Free Press for many years. Later on, increasing deafness limited direct participation in the public issues of the day, but he continued to exercise a major influence through speeches, articles, and personal contacts. He always believed that his kind of immigration planning and development, "the great Sifton plan of western settlement" as Dafoe puts it,[9] was good for Canada. After World War I, he proposed a similar plan for the development of Canada's empty northern lands from the St. Lawrence to the Rockies, involving another major scheme to recruit farmers to settle and develop them. But the prevailing mood in Canada in the early twenties favoured exclusion not expansion and there was no Sifton to carry such a plan through.

As Minister of the Interior from 1896 to 1905 and later, Sifton had encountered plenty of opposition to his western settlement plan and made many enemies, but his status, talents, and the sheer force of his personality enabled him to push the plan through. The major accusations levelled against him were that his immigration policies were non-selective and

indiscriminate, and that he was admitting "illiterate Slavs in overwhelming numbers." His successor as Minister of the Interior, Frank Oliver,
another westerner who was by no means a whole-hearted supporter of the
Sifton plan, put it this way: "... there is nothing [the westerners] more
earnestly resent than the idea of settling up the country with people who
will be a drag on our civilisation and progress. We did not go out to that
country simply to produce wheat. We went to build up a nation, a civilisation, a social system that we could enjoy, be proud of and transmit to our
children; and we resent the idea of having the millstone of this Slav
population hung around our necks in our efforts to build up, beautify and
improve the country, and so improve the whole of Canada."[10] Oliver
produced two new immigration acts in 1906 and 1910 which greatly
increased the powers of immigration officers to reject "undesirable elements." But, before World War I, the tide of new immigrants to Canada
from Britain, the United States, and Europe created by Sifton was not to
be turned back, and the excitement of expansion and prosperity held
prejudice (against some white newcomers) at bay. World War I, however,
ushered in a new era in which Canadian immigration would be severely
restricted and prejudice would be the order of the day.

Origins of the White Australia and White Canada Policies[11]

The White Australia and White Canada immigration policies, abandoned
only in 1973 and 1962, have their roots in the mid-nineteenth century.
Their gradual formulation coincided with the critical period of nation-
building and constitution-making in both countries from the mid-century
onwards. In Canada, in a national sense, these early origins and indeed the
whole lengthy episode of White Canada is often downplayed, or clothed in
discreet silence, or simply not extrapolated from its historical context. In
Australia, however, this is not the case. There, White Australia has been a
public policy in the plainest sense of the term.

Hostility against non-white immigrants plus a determination to keep
them out or reduce their numbers began in both Canada and Australia
during the early gold rushes. It was generated first by the migration of
considerable numbers of Chinese to California after the discovery of gold
there in 1848, then by similar movements to Britain's growing Pacific
colonies, as gold was discovered in Australia in 1851, in British Columbia
in 1858, and in New Zealand in 1861. Nearly all the Chinese who emigrated during this period came from the Cantonese region of Kwantung
Province. The large majority were rural and urban workers, artisans and
small traders accustomed to a life of peasant toil, thrift, and often extreme
poverty. All were organized in a very ancient and complex family lineage

system which commanded life-long loyalty and which had a profound effect on their manner of emigrating.

With the opening of Hong Kong as a British port in 1842, and the declaration the same year of Amoy, Canton, Foochow, Ningpo, and Shanghai as treaty ports for European trade, plus the advent of faster sailing ships to be followed later by steamships, a thriving maritime and overseas trade was developing along this southern China shore. There were numerous merchant houses and commercial enterprises to sustain it and emigration became one of these enterprises which would remain viable, in one way or another, for over 100 years.[12] The following is a description of the way it was organized during this period: "This method of emigrating became known as the "credit-ticket" system: merchants or brokers advanced passage costs in exchange for an agreement requiring the emigrant to work for a low fixed wage or to make regular agreed repayments of both loan and interest; all this on the security of the emigrant's title to village land or of the persons of his wife and children. Only when the loan and interest were repaid could the emigrant start sending his entire savings back to the family."[13]

Like other gold seekers, the primary motive for expeditions to the Pacific goldfields was profit – for the Chinese mainly profit for their families in China and for the firms who had financed these ventures. Although some stayed overseas, a great many returned to China after a few years. If they stayed, it was to create their own communities in foreign lands and often to continue to contribute to family finances in China, or in some cases, to represent Chinese commercial interests. Little or no thought was given by these migrants or their organizers to the history and probable development of the societies to which they emigrated, or of adjusting to foreign ways beyond respecting local laws which were not very numerous in those days. We can speculate now that had they had a friendlier reception on the gold fields, the Chinese might have developed the desire to assimilate to some degree in the new communities around them. As it was, in these early years of emigration they lived, worked, dressed, and used what leisure they had much as they had in China. An Australian newspaper, the Bathurst Free Press, published this report in 1858 of Chinese diggers prospecting and moving from one gold field to another:

They travelled in gangs of 20–200, carrying their gear on bamboo poles slung over the shoulder, neither walking nor running but moving with a short trot timed to the swing of the load, their loose shoes slapping against the soles of their feet or dragging along the ground with a harsh grating noise that provided a continuous accompaniment to their high sing-song voices. For clothing they wore full coloured trousers, loose jackets, pig-tails and large umbrella-like rattan hats sometimes six feet wide ... When on a gold field, they pitched tents, stacked with strange-looking cooking utensils on the outside and coloured prints on the inside, in orderly "villages" well apart from the Europeans ... On the whole, their mining was cooperative on a larger scale than European mining – the large groups as distinct from small groups of diggers and "mates."[14]

The Chinese were slow to respond to the California gold rush, but by the end of 1850 about 1,000 had arrived on the U.S. west coast. About 6,000 more came in 1851 and another 20,000 in 1852. Most began digging for gold, but a small number, some 2,000, found work in San Francisco laundries and restaurants or started small businesses of their own. As numbers increased, open hostility to the Chinese appeared in the mining areas and anti-Chinese feeling spread to San Francisco, and began to appear elsewhere in the United States. It was the beginning of a long series of events in California and at the federal level in the United States which led eventually to the Chinese Exclusion Act of 1882, and other restrictive measures against the Chinese community in the States and to prevent further immigration from China.

Attitudes towards the Chinese in the United States, and particularly in California from the 1850s onwards, had a direct effect on public opinion and on lawmakers in Australia and British Columbia. Gold created an international mining community as diggers moved from one gold field or one country to another. The large majority were white and most were English-speaking or quickly acquired some knowledge of the language. They were not prepared to accept a totally alien race, as they saw it, with a different language, clothing, customs and way of life, cutting in on their territory, taking a share of their findings (and sending the profits home) and, in their view, generally depreciating working and living standards on the gold fields.

To the white diggers and to a growing section of public opinion in these pioneering communities in North America and Australasia, the Chinese were not only alien, they were often seen as evil and dangerous as well. Profoundly ignorant of life in the ancient civilization of China which had been closed to foreigners for so long (although it was then on the verge of revolutionary change), but aware of its poverty and teeming population, they easily absorbed tales of the "yellow peril" which would soon engulf the white countries of the Pacific if allowed to do so. The Chinese were seen as having dark and hideous vices; of running, at least in cities, horrible dens and infamous houses where opium-smoking, gambling, rape, prostitution, and other evil practices were rife; of being ignorant of the most elementary principles of sanitation and of being the bearers of "loathsome diseases" – smallpox, cholera, leprosy, and venereal diseases – which would soon infect entire populations. Few voices were raised any-where to point to the hard-working, thrifty, and orderly nature of most

Chinese immigrants and communities, whose crime rate was noticeably less than that of Europeans and Americans, and whose vices, contemporary ignorance of sanitation, and proneness to deadly diseases were no worse than those of many peoples in many cities in the nineteenth century.[15] These attitudes were firmly entrenched, however, and were to harden and intensify each time the numbers of Chinese immigrants increased, becoming a major factor in the development of discriminatory immigration policies in Canada and Australia in the late nineteenth and early twentieth centuries.

White Australia

Australian historians see four distinct stages in the development of the White Australia policy in the latter half of the nineteenth century:

- minor and often temporary restrictive action by individual colonies against Chinese immigrants in the 1850s and 1860s;
- an attempt at concerted restrictive action involving all the colonies in the early 1880s;
- the adoption of fairly uniform restrictive measures against the Chinese in 1888;
- the official adoption of a White Australia policy by the Commonwealth of Australia in 1901.[16]

During the 1880s, the desire among colonists to keep Chinese immigration in check gradually turned into a belief that exclusion was the only feasible policy. In the *History of the White Australia Policy to 1920*, Myra Willard suggests that several factors account for this hardening of opinion. First, experience of a resident and what was regarded as a "permanently alien" Chinese population confirmed the colonists' view that the numbers of these immigrants should not be allowed to increase. Secondly, Australia was beginning to take an interest in the wider world as the Pacific itself was becoming a centre of European and Asiatic activity. Thus "the Australian people instinctively began to draw together, not only to consolidate what they already held, but also to obtain what they felt was essential to their future safe development." Thirdly, in 1888, there was a sudden influx of Chinese into the hitherto "unprotected" Northern Territory, partly to work on the railway being built between Palmeston and Pine Creek, and partly, it was believed, in response to the discovery of rubies in the Mac-Donnell Ranges. Fourthly, there was evidence that would-be Chinese immigrants were evading immigration restrictions wherever they could, in the belief that these were totally unjustified. Finally, the idea began to circulate – and was even supported by the then premier of New South

Wales, Sir Henry Parkes – that Chinese immigration, particularly to the Northern Territory, was part of a deliberate plan by the Chinese government to establish a colony in Northern Australia. There was also a strong public demand at this time in public meetings, petitions and deputations to governments, for further restrictive measures against the Chinese.[17]

Should Britain negotiate a treaty with China restricting immigration to the Australian colonies, or should the colonies themselves introduce comprehensive restrictive legislation? After informal discussions among the colonies in 1887 and 1888 as to the best line of action, South Australia proposed that a conference of all the colonies be held to establish a uniform policy on the Chinese question. The delegates to the conference, held in Sydney, June 12–14, 1888, agreed unanimously that restriction of Chinese immigration was essential to the welfare of the Australian colonies, and that it could best be effected by the dual means of diplomatic action by the Imperial Government and uniform legislation introduced by all the colonies. Although both proved difficult to achieve, it has been said that from 1888 onwards "Australia had virtually uniform and almost prohibitive laws against Chinese immigration in Queensland, Victoria, South Australia and the Northern Territory, an almost prohibitive law of another kind in New South Wales, and a milder law in Tasmania."[18] The majority of delegates at the 1888 conference also agreed to prohibit or reject all further Chinese applications for citizenship of their respective colonies. These measures were carefully implemented and the number of Chinese in Australia declined considerably after 1888.

During the 1890s, the major issue of the day was the achievement of federal union. In the minds of many Australian politicians, the vital question was what kind of country Australia was going to be. Whatever form the constitution itself might take, no one doubted that Australian society – apart from the Aborigines – should remain white and homogeneous, and should be shaped according to what was best in their British inheritance. The idea became widely accepted that in a part of the world inhabited by many millions of people with alien religions and social customs, endemic poverty and disease, and very low wages, it would be wise to exclude immigration from all non-white countries from the outset. In the Legislative Assembly in 1896, the Premier of New South Wales, George Reid, expressed the thought that this would be "an infinitely more humane policy than that of allowing tens of thousands of people from these coloured races to drift into this country, innocently and according to law, in order that from the contact between the white and the coloured races here all sorts of evils, all manner of dissensions and perhaps a great deal of bloodshed might ultimately follow, embroiling this, and perhaps the mother country, with these great populous nations of the East."[19]

A few immigrants from India and Japan had also begun to arrive in the

Australian colonies at this time. In 1891, for example, there were 2,503 "Asiatics," of whom 1,800 were East Indians, in New South Wales, in addition to the Chinese. In the whole of Australia by 1901 there were 4,383 immigrants from India and Ceylon, as well as a few Japanese, Syrians, and Afghans. No one doubted that in future these nationalities must be excluded, even though many of those from India and Ceylon were British subjects. (Within a decade, we should note, the inhabitants of British Columbia were protesting vigorously against and clamouring for the exclusion of immigrants from precisely the same countries.) Meeting in Sydney in March 1896, the premiers and representatives of the six colonies resolved to extend without delay the provisions of the 1888 legislation to include "all coloured races" and to alter the clause which precluded its application to British subjects. Queensland agreed provided her right to recruit Pacific island labor (Kanakas) for her sugar and cotton-growing plantations, embodied in her Pacific Island Laborers Act, renewed in 1892, should continue.

The Kanaka issue had caused bitter controversy in Queensland and elsewhere in the colonies for more than 20 years, and had become an important aspect of the White Australia question. Since the earliest days, Australia had suffered from a serious shortage of labour mainly to work on the land and on her northern plantations. Queensland, where it was discovered that sugar and cotton could be produced in large quantities in the coastal regions, had a particularly urgent need for labour which was easy to recruit and did not require high wages. Later South Australia was to make repeated and unsuccessful efforts to secure "coolie labour" for the production of sugar, rice, and coffee in the Northern Territory for which she had become responsible. Much thought and a number of private initiatives went into the possible recruitment of Indian indentured labour, as employed on plantations in Mauritius and the West Indies, but nothing of a substantial kind had come of it. Thought was also given to recruiting labour in the Pacific islands and this did produce the following results: "Between 1847 and 1904 nearly 60,000 Islanders generally known as *Kanakas* (from a Melanesian word for man) were imported into Queensland. The recruiting agents, commonly known as *blackbirders*, often employed deceit, violence or murder to obtain their complement of Kanakas. Once landed in Queensland, conditions were better than on the recruiting ships, thanks to the colonial government's protective legislation; but even so their death rate was several times higher than that of the white population."[20]

It was a brutal system, particularly in the early years, part of a wide range of cruel and unscrupulous behaviour the Pacific islanders experienced at the hands of white men from their first contact with Europeans onwards. Not only was it objectionable on humanitarian grounds, it clearly did not fit in with the concept of an Australia, desired by many

Australians, in which there would be social justice, a fair deal for labour, equal opportunities, and a reasonable standard of living for all. After a long struggle on the part of those who wanted to get rid of the system, with strong opposition from the Queensland sugar planters (who were eventually compensated by a combination of bounties and tariff protection), the system was finally abolished in 1901 as part of a body of law passed by the first Commonwealth parliament to establish a comprehensive White Australia policy.

The basis for this policy lay in the Commonwealth of Australia Constitution Act of 1900 which was passed by the Parliament of the United Kingdom on July 5, 1900 and came into force on January 1, 1901. Under this Act, the powers of the Commonwealth parliament included the power to make laws for the peace, order, and good government of the Commonwealth with respect to naturalization and aliens; the people of any race, other than the aboriginal race in any state, for whom it was deemed necessary to make special laws; emigration; and the relations of the Commonwealth with the islands of the Pacific.

The new Commonwealth parliament proceeded to enact laws which ensured that, with very few exceptions, non-whites would not be permitted to settle, work, or live temporarily or permanently in Australia. The first of these laws was the Commonwealth Posts and Telegraph Act of 1901. Under a section of this Act, no contract or arrangement for the carriage of mails, by sea or by land, was to be entered into on behalf of the Commonwealth unless it contained a condition that only white labour would be employed in such carriage. Secondly, the Commonwealth parliament passed the Immigration Restriction Act of 1901, followed in the same year by the Pacific Island Laborers Act. In 1902 a Commonwealth Franchise Act was passed which among other provisions established that no aboriginal native of Australia, Asia, Africa, or the islands of the Pacific except New Zealand, was entitled to have his name placed on the electoral roll, unless so entitled by Section 41 of the constitution which conferred the Commonwealth franchise on all those entitled to be enrolled in their own state. In 1908, a section of the Invalid and Old Age Pensioners Act provided that Asiatics (except those born in Australia) and aboriginal natives of Australia, Africa, and the islands of the Pacific would not be entitled to a pension.

Edmund Barton, a Sydney barrister, politician and leader of the New South Wales federation movement, who was soon knighted, was Australia's first Commonwealth Prime Minister. The Barton government decided on the "Natal Method" of a dictation test as the means of exclusion in the Immigration Restriction Act 1901. This method, which is easy to manipulate to achieve any result desired by the authorities, had been adopted by the Government of Natal in 1897 to exclude immigrants from the Indian sub-continent. Urged by the British Colonial Secretary, Joseph Chamberlain, to give the least possible offense to India and other parts of the Empire, or to Japan with whom Britain was negotiating an alliance, the Australian government hoped (in vain) that a dictation test would give less offense than actually naming the nationalities it intended to exclude. Section 3 of the Immigration Restriction Act therefore provided that, among other prohibited classes, any person who failed to pass a dictation test of 50 words in a European language could be declared a prohibited immigrant. Immigrants resident in Australia for less than five years could also be required to take the test; if they failed they could be deported.

In this manner, the White Australia policy was enshrined in the law as one of the first acts of the new Commonwealth government. The Immigration Restriction Act was amended on a number of occasions during the next half century (in 1905, 1910, 1912, 1920, 1935, 1940, and 1949), mainly to incorporate the concessions already mentioned and to strengthen its provisions in relation to illegal entry.

In 1905, the words "European language" were changed to "prescribed language," mainly to appease the Japanese who were greatly offended by the Act. In the same year, students, tourists, and businessmen from India and Japan were permitted to enter and stay in Australia for a maximum of five years; this concession was extended to the Chinese in 1912. In 1918, following a Dominions conference in London, Indians resident in Australia were permitted to bring in their wives and minor children for residence.[21]

The Pacific Island Laborers Act of 1901, which brought an end to the Kanaka recruitment system, gave the Commonwealth government the power to deport any Kanaka found in Australia after December 1906. After March 1904, no more Kanakas were to be recruited and only a limited number of licences to recruit them were to be issued for 1902 and 1903. In 1906, another, more considerate, act was passed which exempted from deportation on compassionate grounds all Kanakas who were in Queensland before October 1879, those who had lived there continuously for 20 years, those whose return because of their marriage involved risk to themselves or their families, the very old and infirm, and the owners of freehold land.[22]

The White Australia policy remained in force for 72 years. The Immigration Restriction Act was eventually replaced by the Migration Act 1958 which left the policy unchanged but substituted ministerial discretion for the "dictation test" method of exclusion. The White Australia policy itself was abolished by the Labor government under Gough Whitlam in 1973 (see Chapter 3). Later in this chapter, we will look at the modifications in the policy introduced after World War II. White Australia received a considerable boost with the arrival of 393,048 British immigrants between

1906 and 1914. Of these, some 184,605 had received some kind of federal or state assistance in the form of free or partly paid passage or an offer of cheap land. Combined with natural increase, this very large migration led to a substantial increase in Australia's population which reached 4,940,000 in 1914.[23]

Australians, politicians and public alike, believed in the White Australia policy. They believed in it almost to a man and for a very long time they were proud of it. Serious criticism of the policy within Australia only began to appear in the early 1960s,[24] and until the latter years of that decade it enjoyed the unqualified support of both major political parties. Serious criticism outside Australia, however, began when the Immigration Restriction Act was passed in 1901. It continued throughout the century and was particularly damaging to Australia's reputation in the international community after World War II.

We will now examine the parallel evolution of the less well-known White Canada immigration policy which also began with the restriction and exclusion of the Chinese in the 1880s and continued into the twentieth century until 1962. Then we will discuss the similar motivation which inspired both countries to develop these restrictive immigration policies and maintain them for so long.

White Canada

There have been six important immigration acts since Canadian Confederation in 1867, as well as a number of minor and amending acts, orders-in-council relating to immigration, immigration regulations and laws to discourage the entry of or exclude the Chinese. The six important immigration acts are those of 1869, 1906, 1910, 1919 (an amending act), 1952, and 1976. While Canada did not have an act specifically called an immigration restriction act, elements of restriction, directed first against the Chinese and later against all potential non-white immigrants, were present in her immigration legislation from the 1880s onwards. The power to exclude would-be immigrants in certain categories and of certain origins, on which the White Canada policy was based, was laid down in the Immigration Act of 1910, amended by the Act of 1919. More detailed information on precisely who would be excluded was provided in subsequent orders-in-council for those who cared to read them. Laws to discourage the entry of the Chinese or to exclude them altogether were passed by the federal parliament in 1885, 1900, 1903, and 1923.

Section 38 of the Immigration Act of 1910 provided that the governor-in-council might, by proclamation or order:

a. Prohibit the landing in Canada or at any specified port of entry in Canada of any immigrant who has come to Canada otherwise than by continuous journey from the country of which he is a native or naturalised citizen, and upon a through ticket purchased in that country, or prepaid in Canada.

b. Prohibit the landing in Canada of passengers brought to Canada by a transportation company which refuses or neglects to comply with the provisions of this Act.

c. Prohibit for a stated period, or permanently, the landing in Canada, or the landing at any specified port of entry in Canada, of immigrants belonging to any race deemed unsuited to the climate or requirements of Canada, or of immigrants of any specified class, occupation or character.

Clause c was the critical clause. It was expanded in the amending Act of 1919 to read:

c. Prohibit or limit in number for a stated period or permanently the landing in Canada or the landing at any specified port or ports of entry in Canada, of immigrants belonging to any nationality or race or of immigrants of any specified class or occupation, by reason of any economic, industrial or other condition temporarily existing in Canada or because such immigrants are deemed unsuitable having regard to the climatic, industrial, social, educational, labour or other conditions or requirements of Canada or because such immigrants are deemed undesirable owing to their peculiar customs, habits, modes of life and methods of holding property, and because of their probable inability to become readily assimilated or to assume the duties and responsibilities of Canadian citizenship within a reasonable time after their entry.

Similar wording with only minor changes ("ethnic group" is substituted for "race," for example) may be found in the next major immigration act, the post-World War II Immigration Act of 1952. This clause was the principal instrument through which the White Canada policy in immigration was implemented; it was in active use for 50 years.

The "continuous journey" rule, expressed in Clause a. and first issued as an order-in-council in 1908, was aimed at the East Indians and Japanese who were beginning to arrive in British Columbia in increasing numbers. In those days steamships made a stop in Hawaii in their passage from ports in Asia across the Pacific to BC. The requirement of a continuous journey could be used as a way to close the Pacific migration route. Later, when direct journeys by sea from Calcutta, Hong Kong, and other Asian ports to Vancouver became commonplace, this method of exclusion was abandoned. The 1908 order-in-council requiring a continuous journey had been introduced as an emergency measure as a result of the following events. In 1906 and 1907, approximately 4,700 East Indians, mainly Sikhs from Punjab, arrived in Vancouver. Some went on to the United States, a few returned to India, but the large majority stayed on in British Columbia, settling in the area of Vancouver and New Westminster. At the same time, despite a heavy head tax imposed on Chinese immigrants in 1903, there was a sharp increase in arrivals from China and from Japan as well. In 1907 alone, more than 2,300 Japanese newcomers arrived in British Columbia.[25]

These arrivals, all within a period of two years, caused great alarm among the white population of British Columbia which feared an imminent Asian takeover of their province, a degree of alarm described by the Minister of the Interior, Frank Oliver, who was visiting BC at the time, as "almost hysterical."[26] On September 7, 1907, an "Anti-Asiatic Parade," organized by a local group known as the Asian Exclusion League, erupted into a riot in which thousands of dollars of property damage was done in Vancouver's Chinatown and in the small Japanese quarter. Soon afterwards, W.L. Mackenzie King, later Prime Minister of Canada for nearly 22 years and then deputy minister of the federal Department of Labour, was sent to investigate the origins of the riot and to compensate the victims.[27] It was King who urged the prohibition of immigration by way of Hawaii, among other proposals. He had come to the firm conclusion that all Asian immigrants should be excluded for their own good and safety. In his report written in 1908, after a subsequent visit to London to confer with the British authorities on the subject of immigration to Canada from the Orient, and from India in particular, he expressed his views on East Indian immigrants. They would be reflected many years later in his famous 1947 prime ministerial statement on Canada's post-war immigration policy. "It was clearly recognised with regard to emigration from India to Canada, that the native of India is not a person suited to this country, that, accustomed as many of them are to the conditions of a tropical climate, and possessing manners and customs so unlike those of our own people, their inability to readily adapt themselves to surroundings entirely different could not do other than entail an amount of privation and suffering which render a discontinuance of such immigration most desirable in the interests of the Indians themselves."[28]

A dramatic incident relating specifically to East Indian immigration to British Columbia took place a few years later. On May 23, 1914 a ship named the *Komagata Maru* from Hong Kong, under charter to a wealthy Sikh merchant and contractor, docked in Vancouver harbour close to the shore, with 376 East Indian migrants aboard, despite a recent federal order-in-council that temporarily prohibited laborers and artisans from entering the province. This provoked furious public protests in Vancouver, firm federal intervention and an appeal to the B.C. Supreme Court which caused some delay. Eventually, however, after two months in Vancouver harbour, the *Komagata Maru* set sail again for Hong Kong without discharging her passengers. This symbolic incident was a *cause célèbre* in Vancouver for some time, but there was no rioting or violence because, it is said, the government and people of British Columbia at last believed that the federal government (now a Conservative administration under Robert Borden) was solidly behind them in their desire to prevent all immigration from Asia. This was indeed the case, but it did not solve the problems, as the white inhabitants saw them, of Asians already established in the province, or of what they suspected were persistent evasions of immigration restrictions, particularly by the Chinese. Soon after World War I a strong wave of anti-orientalism reappeared in British Columbia and to a lesser extent elsewhere in Canada, compounded by the serious economic difficulties of the immediate post-war period. With it came demands for tougher and more explicit immigration laws to achieve the total exclusion of the Chinese, East Indians, and Japanese.[29]

We will now examine the special case of the Chinese who because of China's weak international position in the late nineteenth century and the first half of the twentieth century were even more vulnerable than their counterparts from India and Japan. British Columbia made urgent pleas in the latter part of the nineteenth century for federal assistance in discouraging the Chinese and other Asian immigrants already in Canada from contemplating permanent settlement, and in excluding any others who wished to come. Federal governments, unwilling at first to impose a total ban (for various reasons, including the need for Chinese labour in railway construction), responded cautiously, appointing no fewer than three royal commissions (in 1884, 1902, and 1907) to investigate first Chinese immigration, secondly Chinese and Japanese immigration, and finally Asian immigration in general. Nevertheless, in 1885 "an Act to restrict and regulate Chinese immigration into Canada" was passed, providing that no vessel carrying Chinese immigrants to any port in Canada should carry more than one such immigrant for every 50 tons of cargo; and that every person of Chinese origin entering Canada at a port or other place of entry should pay a head or entry tax of $50. The head tax was increased to $100 in 1900 and to $500 in 1903.

In addition to the restrictive powers acquired by the federal government under the 1910 and 1919 acts, and under strong pressure again from British Columbia, the Chinese Immigration Act of 1923 was passed to ensure the complete termination of Chinese immigration. A Liberal government had been in power since 1921 with Mackenzie King as Prime Minister. Under this Act, the final act of exclusion, a head tax was no longer required, but the entry to or landing in Canada of persons of Chinese origin or descent, irrespective of allegiance or citizenship, was confined to (a) diplomatic and consular personnel; (b) children born in Canada of Chinese race or descent who had left Canada for educational or other purposes; (c) merchants, a merchant being defined as "a person who devoted his undivided attention to mercantile pursuits, who had not less than $2,500 invested in an enterprise importing to Canada or exporting to China goods of Chinese or Canadian origin or manufacture, and who had conducted such a business for at least three years"; and (d) students coming to Canada for study at or in attendance at recognized Canadian educational institutions. No mention was made in the Act of relatives of Canadians of Chinese descent or of persons of Chinese origin living in Canada, and no relatives were admitted. The Act was effective, and it had profound effects on the size and composition of the Chinese community in Canada for a quarter of a century. There were many desperate protests from the Chinese community itself when the Act was passed, but no one spoke up for the Chinese in Parliament and very few voices were raised in their defence outside.[30]

Following the Immigration Act of 1919 there were, as mentioned earlier, a number of orders-in-council relating to immigration. The most important were P.C. 182 and P.C. 183 of January 1923, and P.C. 695 of March 1931, the latter remaining valid until after World War II. P.C. 182 excluded "any immigrant of any Asiatic race" except bona fide agriculturalists and farm labourers, female domestic servants, and "the wife and child under 18 years of age of any person legally admitted to and resident in Canada, who is in a position to receive and care for his dependents." (After June 1923, this order-in-council did not apply to the Chinese.) In 1930–1931, with the onset of the world-wide depression, these exceptions were removed, barring the admission of the wives and children of Asiatics.

P.C. 183 (1923) and P.C. 695 (1931) laid down exactly who might be admitted to Canada. Although they are very similar, P.C. 695 was slightly more restrictive in excluding (white) farm labourers and female domestic servants who could be admitted under the 1923 order-in-council. P.C. 695 is summarized below. Under this order-in-council, immigrants of all classes and occupations were prohibited, but the immigration officer-in-charge might permit the landing in Canada of the following persons:

1 A British subject entering Canada directly or indirectly from Great Britain or Northern Ireland, the Irish Free State, Newfoundland, the United States of America, New Zealand, Australia, or the Union of South Africa, who has sufficient means to maintain himself until employment is secured; provided that the only persons admissible under the authority of this clause are British subjects by reason of birth or naturalization in Great Britain or Northern Ireland, the Irish Free State, Newfoundland, New Zealand, Australia, or the Union of South Africa.

2 A United States citizen entering Canada from the United States who

has sufficient means to maintain himself until employment is secured.
3 The wife or unmarried child under 18 years of age of any person legally admitted to be resident in Canada who is in a position to receive and care for his dependents.
4 An agriculturalist having sufficient means to farm in Canada.

Like P.C. 183, P.C. 695 explicitly stated that its provisions did not apply to immigrants of any Asiatic race.

It is most important to bear in mind what the words "Asia" and "Asiatics" meant to Canadian politicians and officials of that day. Although "Asiatic" was mainly applied to the Chinese, East Indians, and Japanese, the term "Asia" embraced a large part of the globe. The following comment from the author's earlier study of Canadian immigration relating to the immediate post-World War II period is just as relevant for the inter-war years:

In this connection, it is important to remember where Asia was in 1947. In the public mind, western Asia has now receded to the shores of the Arabian Sea and the borders of Afghanistan. A new political and geographic entity, the Middle East, occupies the territory between Istanbul and Karachi. But in the minds of the Canadian Liberal government in 1947, Asia meant almost everything in the Eastern Hemisphere outside Europe. Its northwest frontier ran along the southern border of the Soviet Union and the Black Sea and round the eastern and southern coasts of the Mediterranean. All Turkey and lands to the south, were in Asia.[31]

Thus by excluding Asians or "Asiatics," and by association and extension Africans also (who lived then almost entirely under colonial rule), Canada was prepared to accept only one kind of immigrant from the Eastern Hemisphere – the immigrant of European origin. During the inter-war years as we have seen this was confined by order-in-council to immigrants from Britain, Ireland, the dominions, and the United States.

One other important aspect of discrimination against Asian immigrants in Canada, and one which helped to exclude them from Canadian society and politics for a long time, should be mentioned. This was denial of the franchise. An amendment to the Franchise Act was introduced by the Prime Minister, Sir John A. Macdonald, in 1885 and passed after an angry debate in the Commons, to prevent "any persons of Mongolian or Chinese race from voting in federal elections." In 1895, the British Columbia Provincial Elections Act denied the vote to all persons of Asian ancestry. Eventually all Asian immigrants were disenfranchised both federally and provincially. Canadians of Chinese and East Indian origin finally regained the vote in 1947 following World War II. The Japanese obtained it two years later.

White Immigration Policies: Motives and Reasons

What induced Canadians and Australians to move with such determination to exclude Asians, and by extension all non-white immigrants, from their countries from the 1880s to the second half of the twentieth century? It may be useful to consider this question at this point in our discussion, i.e., during the inter-war years when discrimination was at its height.

As we have seen, Canada began moving towards the total exclusion of non-whites some 9 years later than Australia and abandoned her racially discriminatory immigration policy 11 years earlier, but these time differences are not significant. What is significant is their common strength of feeling on this subject, the unanimity with which their politicians and officials pursued the goal of a White Canada and a White Australia, and the obvious approval of their respective publics. In Canada, every prime minister from Sir John A. Macdonald at Confederation to Louis St. Laurent in the 1950s clearly approved of it. In Australia, every prime minister from Sir Edmund Barton in the early 1900s to Sir William McMahon in the early 1970s either strongly approved of White Australia or stood by it. No political party came out against it in Canada, and the decision to abandon the White Canada policy in 1962 was inspired by officials and not by politicians. In Australia, both the major parties supported White Australia until the late sixties. Before the policy was changed in Canada in 1962, there was no public protest of any kind on the subject. In Australia, small groups of reformers, often centred in the universities, appeared in the sixties but not before.

We look back disparagingly and even apologetically today, from the vantage point of our established pluralistic and multicultural societies, at the illiberality and insensitivity of these policies and their practitioners. But we do less than justice to our political forbears if we do not examine carefully their primary motivation and reasoning in developing and maintaining these white immigration policies so wholeheartedly, and for such a comparatively long period of time. It is essential also to see these policies in the context of a century of nation-building by very small populations in immense, undeveloped territories.

The primary and identical motivation of Canadian and Australian politicians in trying to exclude first the Chinese, then other Asian migrants, and finally all potential non-white immigrants, was the desire to build and preserve societies and political systems in their hard-won, distant lands very like those of the United Kingdom. They also wished to establish without challenge the primary role there of her founding peoples of European origin, the British and French in Canada and the British in Australia. Undisputed ownership of these territories of continental size was felt to be confirmed forever, not only by the fact of possession, but by the hardships and dangers endured by the early explorers and settlers; the years of back-breaking work to build the foundations of urban and rural life; the efforts involved in discovering and harnessing natural resources and learning to use the land successfully in unfamiliar climates; and the difficulties and struggles of early political development and the establishment of law and order. The idea that other peoples, who had taken no part in these pioneering efforts, might simply arrive in large numbers to exploit important local resources, or to take advantage of these earlier settlement efforts, was anathema.

It is also important to remember that Canada and Australia were founded during the long period of Pax Britannica. They owed their safety and their opportunities for peaceful, uninterrupted development to the powerful world role of Britain in the nineteenth century, and to her almost total domination of navigation on the high seas. It is plain to see how closely tied they were to the mother country during the early stages of their development, and how much they relied on Britain as a major source of political ideas, development capital, technical expertise, and useful experience in creating the necessary structures and systems, large and small, of a modern state.

It is difficult to exaggerate the enormous prestige and high standing of Britain in the latter half of the nineteenth century, or the respect and admiration, if not envy, which her liberal political system, advanced technologies, and role as the world's leading manufacturer, financier, trader, carrier, insurer, and commercial agent, as well as empire-builder, engendered in many quarters.[32] Trying though their dealings with Britain may often have been, Canadian and Australian politicians constantly reflect this attitude of admiration. In addition, their own populations were substantially of British origin (in Australia almost entirely so) since some ten million emigrants had left Britain between 1850 and 1900 for the United States, Canada, and Australia. It seemed natural therefore to develop these new societies in all the ways that were feasible, and particularly in politics, law and administration on the successful and, to most people, congenial and familiar British model, and to conceive it as a duty to exclude "alien" elements which might change their basic character. It was widely believed that the homogeneous and unified character of the British people contributed in no small measure to Britain's success in peace and war, and that this quality of homogeneity (British in Australia and British-French in Canada) should be fostered as a guarantee of future harmony. Sir Henry Parkes, Premier of New South Wales, expressed this thought in a circular from his government to other Australian state governments in 1887: "[It is] a question of policy of the first magnitude to cement society together by the same principles of faith and jurisprudence, the same influence of language and the same national habits of life."[33] A year later in the Legislative Assembly, he affirmed that "It is our duty to preserve the type of the British nation and we ought not, for any consideration whatever, to admit any element that would detract from or in any appreciable degree lower that admirable type of nationality."[34]

Behind these attitudes in Australia and in Canada lay a profound ignorance of Asian and other non-European societies, and a fear of difference which no liberal thoughts or aspirations could quell. It was a fear expressed very clearly in the famous Section 38 of Canada's Immigration Act of 1910, as amended in 1919, which gave the governor-in-council the power to prohibit the landing of "[immigrants] deemed undesirable owing to their peculiar customs, habits, modes of life and methods of holding property, and because of their probable inability to become readily assimilated or to assume the duties and responsibilities of Canadian citizenship within a reasonable time after their entry." It is important to try to visualize the world as the Victorians and their immediate successors saw it, with large tracts of Africa and Asia still relatively unknown to the peoples of the western world, and subject to the same romantic and often alarming speculation with which we treat the nearer universe today. It is necessary also to understand their automatic assumption of the superiority of the white nations over all others, arising not only from Britain's vast "dominion over palm and pine," but from what has been described as "Europe's assault on the world" which began after 1500. By the end of the eighteenth century, the major European nations including Russia had "already laid claim to more than half the world's land surface and, in varying degree, actually controlled more than a third of it." They had met with little more than local resistance.[35]

Other factors which help to explain the Canadian and Australian white immigration policies include Australia's proximity to Asia and her real fear of invasion or invasion through infiltration. This fear continued through the twentieth century and was shared to a considerable extent by British Columbia, the only Canadian province which faces the Pacific and which is partly cut off from the rest of Canada, physically and psychologically, by the barrier of the Rocky Mountains. They include also the attitudes of the Canadian and Australian labour movements, both strongly opposed to the recruitment of what they saw as "cheap coolie labour." For a long time they were opposed to any form of Asian immigration, which they felt would inevitably undermine their hard-won wage and living standards. To some extent these attitudes have been adapted to contemporary economic conditions and to changing world relationships in recent years, but elements of them are still firmly entrenched in both countries.

Geography has had an important influence in Canada too, giving Canadians a sense of security in being part of an Anglo-Saxon majority which reached right across North America, but creating also a strong desire to steer clear of the racial conflicts and minority problems observed for so long in the United States. The latter was a factor which had an influence in Australia also. Some Canadians of both British and French origin also developed a belief, held with different degrees of conviction, in the virtues of northernness – "the true north strong and free" – the north being synonymous with strength, self-reliance, energy, stamina, morality, and liberty. This quality, it was believed, should not be contaminated by contact with the weaker races from warmer southern climes, where moral laxness, indolence, corruption, and decay were believed to prevail.[36] Canada, it was felt, had a lasting affinity with the peoples of northern Europe, and her doors should remain closed to immigrants from other lands.

The principal driving force behind the White Canada and White Australia policies, however, was the collective national desire to remain British in political principles and institutions, and to remain white like their forbears from Europe. Thus, Robert Borden, Leader of the Opposition and later Laurier's successor as Prime Minister of Canada, when touring British Columbia in September 1907 at the time of the Vancouver riot, proclaimed that "The Conservative Party ... will ever maintain one supreme consideration to which all material considerations must give way and it is this: British Columbia must remain a British and Canadian Province, inhabited and dominated by men in whose veins runs the blood of those great pioneering races which built up and developed not only Western but Eastern Canada."[37] A few years earlier the first attorney-general of Australia, Alfred Deakin, who followed Sir Edmund Barton as prime minister in 1903, and was one of the finest speakers of his day and a very talented politician, said in the House of Representatives: "No motive power operated more universally on this Continent, or in the beautiful island of Tasmania, certainly no motive power operated more powerfully in dissolving the technical and arbitrary political divisions which previously separated us than the desire that we should be one people, and remain one people, without the admixture of other races."[38]

The Inter-War Years, 1919–1939

The inter-war years – a decade of uncertain and uneven prosperity followed by a decade of dire depression – were a troubled and inglorious period in Canadian and Australian history, as they were in other democratic states. It was not a time when immigration was likely to flourish or, as Canada and Australia rapidly but almost unknowingly evolved into urban and industrial societies, be turned to very good account. Nor, given the growing class and sectional differences, intolerance, and narrow nationalisms developing in the international community, was it a time when immigrants would be welcomed or immigration policies become more liberal.

Both Canadian and Australian immigration was now tightly controlled. The major immigration objective of the 1920s in both countries, implemented through assisted passages and settlement schemes of various kinds, was to attract and recruit British immigrants. In Canada, American immigrants and to a limited extent immigrants from what were called "the preferred countries" of central and northern Europe were also welcomed. A few immigrants from Italy, Greece, Malta, Yugoslavia, and a few other European countries, mainly family-sponsored, were admitted to Australia during this period, but even these small numbers caused hostility and alarm in some quarters.

As we have seen, "Asiatics" in the contemporary sense of that word were not admitted to either country except for a small number of necessary diplomatic personnel, well-established merchants and their families, and students.[39] In Australia, the Commonwealth government accepted responsibility for migrant selection in 1920, and in 1921 took over from the states control of all Australian migration operations in the United Kingdom.

Empire settlement schemes which involved direct collaboration with Britain, introduced shortly after the end of the war, were a special feature of this period. Immigration to Canada and Australia had inevitably declined during World War I, although not to the rock-bottom levels it was to reach in the 1930s and during World War II (see Appendix 1). Despite the priorities and problems of demobilization, both countries made an effort to get immigration going again and to benefit from a possible British post-war urge to emigrate. This effort is reflected in the increasing number of immigrants admitted in 1919 and 1920. Early in 1919, Britain launched an emigration scheme in which ex-servicemen could apply to emigrate to the Dominions and, if accepted, have their fares paid by the British government. After the whole question of emigration to the Dominions had been discussed at the 1921 Imperial Conference in London, the British Parliament passed the Empire Settlement Act on May 31, 1922. The Act established that the British government might collaborate with Dominion governments, public authorities, or private organizations in the development of emigration and settlement schemes.

The idea of land settlement for immigrants still prevailed. Under the Empire Settlement Act, assisted passages and sometimes training opportunities were provided for married couples, single agricultural labourers, domestics, and juveniles between the ages of 14 and 17 who were given free passages; most of them were expected to settle on the land. There were other public and private schemes. In Canada, the "3,000 Families

Scheme," for example, gave assistance to British families who wished to settle on the land. The Dominion-Provincial Land Settlement Scheme and the Dominion-Provincial Training Farms Plan provided young British boys with Canadian farming experience. Australia also offered various dominion-state land settlement schemes, and there were efforts by private organizations like the Dreadnought Trust, Dr. Barnado's and the Big Brother movement to bring British boys to Australia and train them to become agricultural workers. Of the 282,000 British immigrants who arrived in Australia between 1922 and 1931, 212,000 received assistance under the Empire Settlement Act. Canada fared less well. Only 130,000 Canadian immigrants were assisted under the Act, but it probably encouraged many more to come on their own. There are no reliable statistics to tell us how many of these immigrants actually settled on the land in Australia and Canada, or remained in agricultural pursuits for any length of time. It is very likely that many of them actually preferred and eventually settled in the growing towns and cities where, along with large numbers of Canadians and Australians, many had a very tough time during the depression.

After the Empire Settlement Act had been passed and when prosperity seemed to be returning, the Canadian government (the Liberals under Mackenzie King were in power) decided in 1928 cautiously but deliberately to encourage immigration once again, from Britain and from a number of preferred countries designated as Norway, Sweden, Denmark, Finland, Germany, Switzerland, Holland, Belgium, and France. Canadian government offices were opened or reopened in these countries, and railways and private agencies were also encouraged to start recruiting immigrants. Only agricultural workers, domestics, and family-sponsored applicants were to be admitted from non-preferred countries, listed as Austria, Hungary, Poland, Romania, Lithuania, Estonia, Latvia, Bulgaria, Yugoslavia, and Czechoslovakia. Southern Europe was not mentioned. Two years later, on September 1, 1925, the government entered into the "Railways Agreement" with the Canadian Pacific and Canadian National Railways (which still had some land to dispose of) whereby the railways were authorized to invite citizens or residents of the non-preferred countries to emigrate to Canada and settle there as "agriculturalists, agricultural workers and domestic servants." The railways agreed to invite only persons of these specified classes, and to return to their countries of origin all those who refused to engage in agriculture or domestic service, or became public charges within one year of their admission to Canada. The agreement was to last for two years but was later extended for another three.[40] The "preferred" and "non-preferred" countries plan lasted only a short time, however, and was never revived. It was overwhelmed by the crash of the New York stock market in the fall of 1929 and the subsequent collapse of the Canadian economy. By 1931 no further immigrant recruitment was possible.

We need not record in detail the dismal facts of the world-wide depression of the 1930s, which caused such havoc in the trading system of the western world. Canada and Australia were particularly vulnerable and particularly hard-hit, with their only partly developed industrial systems and heavy reliance on foreign trade and the export of grain, wool in Australia, and raw materials. In Canada, the Prairies and the Maritimes suffered a catastrophic economic decline, compounded on the Prairies by severe drought, which caused widespread destitution. By 1933 about 26 per cent of the labour force in Canada was unemployed, compared with 3 per cent in 1929. In Australia, unemployment reached a peak of nearly 30 per cent in the winter of 1932. Neither country had any effective machinery to deal with mass unemployment and destitution; their politicians were baffled by these events and uncertain how to deal with them. The 1930s were years of great hardship and, although the Canadian and Australian economies began to revive from the mid-thirties onwards, it was not until World War II that the major effects of this far-reaching depression could be said to be overcome.

The inter-war years were not tolerant years in Canada and Australia. No one felt secure enough or concerned enough to propose or even to contemplate anything like a non-discriminatory immigration policy, let alone a program of multiculturalism. Groups hostile to non-British immigrants and often to all immigrants were active in both countries during this period. The exhaustion which followed World War I, with its appalling losses in human life, had produced strong anti-democratic and nationalist sentiments in many countries together with a yearning for firm, authoritarian control. These tendencies were as evident in Canada and Australia as they were in other democratic states. Both Canadian and Australian societies were narrow and inward-looking in the inter-war years, with little interest in the outside world, until events in Germany forced them to acknowledge its existence. Charles Price has described Australia during this period:

At the outbreak of World War II, the Australian people were basically "British-Australian," a curious mixture of British peoples and traditions, slowly developing a distinctive Australian character. Moreover, most Australians looked askance at anything else. The bulk of the population were descended from migrants of lower middle class and laboring background: classes which had little experience of other peoples and cultures and tended to be suspicious of anything strange or different. Geographical isolation merely aggravated this. As a consequence, non-British immigrants were looked at suspiciously, being expected to learn English immediately, to refrain from forming immigrant groups and societies, and to intermix and intermarry with British-Australians. Complete assimilation in one generation was the philosophy behind Australian attitudes to newcomers. Even immigrants from the United Kingdom were expected to conform, those who kept their English accent or opinions too long receiving the name "Pommy," sometimes as a term of affection, but more often as a term of abuse.[41]

One of the strongest voices in Australia between the wars, speaking out against immigration and against foreigners and foreign influence, was the RSL, the Returned Soldiers and Sailors Imperial League of Australia. Now called the Returned Services League of Australia, it has become a powerful, conservative pressure group watching over the interests of present and former members of the armed forces and their families, but also intervening directly in politics in support of right-wing causes and objectives. It was the RSL which played the major role in the 1920s in establishing the anniversary of the Gallipoli landing in World War I as an Australian National Day (Anzac Day), now an important annual occasion. The general influence of the RSL between the wars has been described by an Australian historian:

More generally throughout the period between the wars, the RSL did a great deal to make the values associated with Anzac Day and the "old digger" dominant in the Australian community. Along with the virtues ascribed to the idealised digger – courage, loyalty, mateship and democratic levelling – went other less admirable characteristics. The stereotyped figure exhibited also tough, sardonic contempt for coloured people and foreigners generally, for minority views, for art, literature, culture and learning ... The tone of most of the writing in the *Bulletin* or *Smiths' Weekly* at this period exactly mirrors the prevailing ethos – levelling values, rough manners and philistine tastes as the outer form; conformity, conservatism and unquestioning Anglo-Australian patriotism as the inner content.[42]

Canada had no real counterpart to the RSL in strength and influence, but conservatism, conformity, and fear and dislike of minority views and what were felt to be foreign influences were certainly the order of the day. In politics, the inter-war years were dominated by the unappealing and complex character of Mackenzie King, Prime Minister of Canada and Leader of the Liberal Party from 1921 to 1926, 1926 to 1936 and 1935 to 1948, the depths of whose neurotic personality are only now being plumbed.[43] King, who has been over-praised by some Canadian historians for his manipulative and long-lasting political skills, had only two political objectives: to keep Canada united and to stay in power. He was successful in both. Unity, as he and his indispensable Quebec colleague Ernest Lapointe saw it, required "near paralysis on the social reform front,

extreme sensitivity to provincial rights, fiscal orthodoxy and non-commit-
ment either to the Empire-Commonwealth or to the League of Nations."[44]
He had no interest whatsoever in collective security and, it has been said,
"really disliked the world beyond the North Atlantic Triangle."[45] It was a
deeply uninspiring philosophy, which shaded off into anti-semitism and a
total indifference to the plight of Jewish refugees in Europe in the 1930s.
In political terms it was implemented by what one Canadian historian has
called "unremitting insistence on the need for caution – caution in foreign
policy, caution in dominion-provincial relations, caution in governmental
intervention in the social economy. His formulation of what might be
called the politics of fear left a lasting impression upon Canadian attitudes
and no doubt also expressed a deep conservatism in Canadian society – at
least the Canadian society of the 1930s and 1940s."[46] There were other
ways in which Canadian unity, not to mention some other laudable
national objectives, might have been achieved, but neither King nor the
Liberal Party of that day ever explored them.

The short interval between the two world wars came to an end when
Hitler invaded Poland on September 1, 1939. Britain and France declared
war on Germany two days later. Australia automatically followed suit, the
Australian government taking the view that as Britain was at war with
Germany from September 3 onwards, so was Australia. No separate declaration of war was made. The Canadian parliament, however, made its
own declaration of war on September 10.

THE POST-WAR PERIOD: PROSPERITY, DEVELOPMENT, AND EXPANSION

Wars are well-known as powerful agents of change. For Canada and
Australia the Second World War, one of the few major wars fought in a
just cause, achieved much more than change. It set in motion a remarkable
transformation in both countries, accelerating their political, economic,
technological, social, and cultural development to an astonishing degree.
The small, insecure, inward-looking, and narrow-minded societies we saw
in the inter-war years steadily retreated after the war, to be replaced over
the next 30 years by two far more responsible, humane, better governed,
socially conscious, and internationally concerned nations.

Industrialization and diversification proceeded rapidly in both countries. Living standards rose to a remarkable degree and there were major
improvements in public administration and education at all levels. Comprehensive social security systems were put in place. The protection of
human rights and the promotion of equal rights and opportunities for
women began to get attention; and at last, after centuries of neglect and
abuse, native and aboriginal peoples began to get a fair deal. None of this,

of course, produced a perfect world; progress was uneven and a great deal remains to be done. In Canada, development began a little earlier and moved faster in some areas, particularly in the sixties. Nevertheless, the achievements in both Canada and Australia in such a short period of time have been considerable. In all this, the greatly increased immigration of the post-war period has played a very important part, enabling both countries, by adding substantially to their own natural increase, to double their populations in little more than 30 years; and providing them with a range of skills and talents and a degree of creative energy and cultural diversity they could not have acquired in any other way.

Immigration policy and management in both countries from the end of World War II to the early seventies are considered in the final section of this chapter. In Chapters 2 and 3 we will examine the important changes and new directions in immigration policy introduced in Canada and Australia from the early seventies onwards.

Australia 1945–1972

World War II, which was much more of a global war than World War I had been, threatened Australia's security far more directly than it did Canada's, and was a more traumatic experience for the Australian people. In 1938, following her occupation of Manchuria in 1931 and invasion of China in 1937, Japan had proclaimed her plan for a "Greater East Asia Co-prosperity Sphere." In 1940, she signed a three-power pact, followed in 1942 by a military alliance with Germany and Italy designed "to reorder Europe and the Far East," and in 1941 a non-aggression pact with the USSR. In December 1941 came the Japanese air attack on Pearl Harbor, followed by the invasion of Malaya and the capture of Hong Kong and Singapore (which took place on February 15, 1942 with the surrender of 60,000 British, Indian, and Dominion troops including large contingents of Australians and Canadians). Then came the occupation of Burma and the seizure of the Phillipines and the Dutch East Indies, as well as a number of other Pacific islands, giving Japan dominion over territories with a combined population of 450 million. The Japanese occupation of the island of Timor in February-March 1942, and a landing on the north coast of New Guinea - repulsed as they advanced inland by Australian troops - brought Japan's military might very close to the Australian continent, and for a while there was a real possibility of invasion. It was not only this threat of invasion, however, which made Australia's situation seem so vulnerable, but also the collapse, from the fall of Singapore onwards, of the British security system in the Pacific on which she had so long relied for protection.

The wartime Labor government under Ben Chifley responded decisively to this situation as the war in Europe came to an end. A member of the cabinet, Arthur A. Calwell, was appointed Australia's first Minister for Immigration. On August 2, 1945, he announced in the House of Representatives a large scale post-war immigration program, designed to strengthen national security and economic development by increased population growth; meet post-war labour shortages; and fill the serious gaps in the age structure of the existing population. "If Australians have learned one lesson from the Pacific war now moving to a successful conclusion," he said, "it is that we cannot continue to hold our island continent for ourselves and our descendants unless we greatly increase our numbers ... Our first requirement is additional population. We need it for reasons of defence and for the fullest expansion of our economy."[47]

An old slogan of "populate or perish" became associated with the Calwell program. It was to involve diversifying Australia's migrant sources while keeping a British majority; resuming and extending the pre-war assisted passage schemes for migrants (to offset the cost of a long journey and competition from other receiving countries); providing short-term accommodation for assisted migrants who needed it; and, in a remarkable piece of political innovation at that time, formally consulting with and involving the Australian community in this nation-building exercise. A small planning staff was set up within the new federal department and a blueprint worked out for a substantial degree of community participation in the form of Immigration Advisory and Planning Councils (and later of a Publicity Council); Good Neighbour Councils as a means to coordinate and stimulate voluntary efforts for immigrants; annual citizenship conventions; and other developments. The Immigration Advisory Council was set up in 1947, and the Immigration Planning Council, conceived as a senior group with direct access to the Cabinet, in 1949. The Good Neighbour Councils were created shortly afterwards and the other parts of the plan implemented in due course. Although the Chifley government was defeated in December 1949, the Liberal government under Robert Menzies simply continued these policies and programs, as did their successors. Menzies, who was a personal friend of Calwell, had in fact strongly supported him from the start. This consensus lasted until the critical moment in 1972 when the Australian electorate returned a Labor government (the Whitlam government) to power once again. Labor had then been in opposition for 23 years.

The original target proposed by Arthur Calwell in 1945 was to increase Australia's population through immigration by one per cent per annum and this remained the official goal until the early 1970s. Initially it was proposed to admit British and European migrants in a ratio of 10 to 1, but the urgent needs of Europe's displaced and homeless peoples, and the shortage of shipping from Britain immediately after the war, led to a major change in immigration policy which permitted the entry of some 170,000 displaced persons from Europe between 1947 and 1952. This paved the way for a much broader recruitment in the 1950s, which included all European nationalities and even some limited recruitment in parts of the Middle East. This major change in Australia's immigration policy was already reflected in the 1961 census which showed that, of a total population of 10.5 million, 8 per cent of Australians were now European-born. The largest groups were Italians (228,000), Germans (109,000), Greeks (77,000), Poles (60,000), Yugoslavs (50,000) and Hungarians (30,000), with smaller groups of Austrians, Latvians, Russians, and Ukrainians.

While the main features of the White Australia policy stood firm (Arthur Calwell himself had strong prejudices against Asian immigration which he kept all his life – he died in 1973) a series of minor relaxations in the policy were made as time went on. They included more lenient provisions for the temporary residence of non-Europeans admitted for business reasons; the eligibility of non-Europeans for naturalization; and the admission of "distinguished and highly qualified non-Europeans" and persons of mixed descent. In 1966, a definite step was taken to make the admission and permanent settlement of non-Europeans somewhat easier. It was announced on March 9 in the House of Representatives by the Minister for Immigration, Hubert Opperman who said that from then on: "applications for entry for people wishing to settle in Australia with their wives and children will be considered on the basis of their suitability as settlers, their ability to integrate readily and the possession of qualifications which are in fact positively useful to Australia. Those approved will initially be admitted on five year permits and will then be able to apply for resident status and citizenship." Mr. Opperman added that the number of people entering Australia under the new arrangement would be controlled by careful assessment of individual qualifications, and that the aim of preserving a homogeneous population would be maintained.[48] This rather cautious measure resulted in the admission of only a few thousand non-Europeans and persons of mixed descent a year, increasing to approximately 10,000 by 1971–1972. It did open the door to a limited extent, however, and also established the principle of skill as an important criterion for admission and as a means of entry.

There were other important elements in this post-war exercise in immigration planning. A new Migration Act was passed in 1958, which, as we have seen, abolished the old dictation test introduced in 1901. It also sorted out a tangle of minor amendments introduced over the preceding half century. The new Act limited the powers of the Minister to deport anyone within five years after entry, and provided some safeguards for persons arrested as prohibited immigrants or as deportees, providing that they be given facilities to obtain legal advice and to institute legal proceedings. But essentially the Act vests enormous discretionary powers relating to admission and deportation in the Minister, as did Canada's Immigration Act of 1952 (discussed in the final part of this chapter). Both acts produced the same results – a mass of time-consuming representations which had to be dealt with by the Minister and his officials. The Migration Act of 1958 is still Australia's principal immigration statute, but it has been very substantially amended and these discretionary powers no longer apply.

The Calwell plan called, as we have seen, for new assisted passage schemes. Immediately after the war, two migration agreements were negotiated between the Australian and British governments which came into operation in March 1947. The first one provided for the grant of free passage to British ex-servicemen and their dependents; it was terminated in February 1955. Under the second, which continued until the early seventies, each British migrant 19 years of age or over contributed £10 towards his or her passage costs (the famous £10 passage). Migrants under 19 made no contribution. The Australian government met all but a small fraction of the remaining costs. Between January 1947 and June 1971, 991,431 British migrants arrived in Australia under these assisted passage schemes. Some years later, in 1966, a Special Passage Assisted Program (SPAP) was introduced to provide financial assistance for European migrants and some others who were ineligible under other schemes. Up to A$335 was provided for those 19 and over and A$360 for those under 19. A similar program was later established for North and South America. In addition both federal and state governments provided initial accommodation for migrants if needed.

In 1952, Commonwealth Hostels Ltd., a non-profit, government-sponsored company reporting to the Minister of Housing, was created with the specific task of providing initial accommodation, mainly for assisted migrants nominated by the Commonwealth government, in government hostels and other types of accommodation. By the mid-seventies these hostels (later managed by a similar company called the Commonwealth Accommodation and Catering Services Ltd.) could accommodate about 17,000 migrants at any one time and a further 1,850 in self-contained flats. Hostel accommodation was available for up to 12 months and flats for up to 6 months. The hostels have been an invaluable resource for Australia, and have been particularly useful from the late 1970s onwards for refugees (see Chapter 4). In 1982–1983 the Department of Immigration and Ethnic Affairs assumed responsibility for managing this network of temporary accommodation.

Another interesting feature of Australia's post-war immigration program was a firm belief in the value of direct bilateral agreements with some of the countries of emigration, permitting a reasonably secure and agreed flow of migrants. From the late 1950s onwards, migration agreements were negotiated with Malta, The Netherlands, and Italy, followed by others with West Germany, Austria, Belgium, Greece, Spain, Turkey, and Yugoslavia. In the late seventies, when economic circumstances caused a reduction in intake and when large numbers of refugees began to arrive, these agreements found less favour and some were discontinued.

This post-war national effort produced the greatest sustained migration in Australia's history and a remarkable degree of population growth managed without undue stress or strain. Before 1973, concern about the White Australia policy in the international community tended to divert attention from this considerable achievement. In June 1947, Australia's population stood at 7.5 million. By June 1982, it had reached 15.2 million of which about 20.6 per cent were overseas born. Although Calwell's goal of a one per cent population increase a year through net immigration was only achieved from time to time, it was felt to have been valuable as a target.

In November 1966, the Immigration Planning Council established a Committee on Long-Term Planning in response to a request from the Minister of Immigration, B.M. (Billy) Snedden. The committee submitted its report in June 1968. Stating that its inquiry and recommendations should be seen in the context of some 20 years of planned immigration which had started in 1947, the committee concluded: "In this period the evidence showed clearly that immigration had received the unqualified backing of successive Australian governments, both as a national policy and in the direction of full financial support for its implementation. There had been a high degree of co-operation between all government departments and instrumentalities involved, and the Commonwealth Department of Immigration had been most flexible in initiating new policies and developments to meet changing conditions and circumstances."[49]

Canada 1945–1972

Immigration worked well for Canada also and, although not the most important factor overall in population growth, also permitted a doubling of population between World War II and the 1970s.[50] Demand to emigrate to Canada has been high in the post-war period and Canada's power to retain immigrants once they arrived – assisted by restrictive immigration legislation in the United States – has increased.[51] Nevertheless, there is a striking difference between the way immigration was managed and developed during this period in Canada and Australia, a much greater difference than is found before World War II or today, when their policies and programs have become very similar. The difference can be accounted for in the main by the security factor.

As we have seen, Australia felt an urgent need for a high level of immigration after World War II to achieve fast population growth. Her security seemed to depend on it and she gave this area of public policy very high priority. Canada felt no such need. Comfortably protected by her common border with the United States, she was not unduly threatened in a security sense by the decline in British imperial power. While Canada was ready to help solve the problem of Europe's nine million displaced persons, and prepared to believe that immigration might be an important factor in national economic development and population growth, immigration was certainly not given high priority, nor was it ever given ample funds. It was simply put in order after the war. Its purposes were outlined in a short statement by the Prime Minister in 1947, and for a few years it was provided with a federal department of its own (the Department of Citizenship and Immigration), a new immigration act, and a modestly enlarged staff at home and overseas.

Among Canadian politicians, the Citizenship and Immigration portfolio was never seen as a prestigious or politically rewarding one. Within the public service, and particularly within Canada's growing foreign service, immigration officers were regarded as rather lowly beings and given low classifications. As an area of public policy deemed of low priority, immigration received far less than its share of political and administrative creativity, and no share at all of any development funds which might have been available. Apart from rather limited and inexpensive joint arrangements with the provinces for evening language classes for immigrants, next to no money was provided for immigrant services either directly or through the funding of voluntary agencies. Proper funding for voluntary agencies in this field only became available from the mid-seventies onwards.

In 1965, the Liberal government under Lester Pearson, disturbed by accumulating evidence of the unskilled character of the Canadian labour force and impressed by the then fashionable possibilities of manpower development programs, abolished the uninfluential Department of Citizenship and Immigration. Immigration then became a very junior partner within a large, well-financed new Department of Manpower and Immigration, with "Immigration" added to the title only at the last moment. While there were some gains in this new setting for immigration, including improved funding, higher status and better use of employment services for immigrants, there were serious losses as well. The most serious of these were the loss of a separate and clearly recognizable identity for immigration within the public service, and the loss of important responsibilities in the service area to the Department of the Secretary of State. The result was a serious fragmentation of immigration management in Canada which has continued to this day.

To add to these problems of priority, status, and lack of a well-established place for immigration in the public service, post-war Canadian governments and Canadian politicians generally have been nervous about immigration. They have been worried, as already mentioned, that immigration might become a political battleground or cause some kind of backlash; worried that new measures might upset ethnic groups and thereby lose votes; and worried that immigration might get out of control in one way or another. Happy when it is well-managed but inconspicuous, governments and politicians have probably been more comfortable when immigration operates anonymously, as it does now within a large manpower agency (the Canada Employment and Immigration Commission which replaced the Department of Manpower and Immigration in 1978). Until recently the same syndrome has affected the provinces, although they have also had reasons of their own for a "hands off" policy. Although immigration is a concurrent jurisdiction under the British North America Act, none of the provinces with the exception of Quebec have wanted to accept any responsibility for immigration policy or to be involved in the policy-making process. This began to change, however, with the conclusion of federal-provincial agreements with some of the provinces in the 1970s and with the passage of a new immigration act in 1976.

The critical dates in the evolution of Canada's post-war immigration policy are 1947, 1962, 1966–1967, and 1976. (Developments after 1972 will be considered in the next chapter.) On May 1, 1947, not long before his retirement the following year, Prime Minister Mackenzie King made a statement in the House of Commons on post-war immigration policy. His government had already made important decisions relating to the admission of displaced persons from Europe, a movement which began on April 1, 1947 (186,154 were admitted between 1947 and 1952); the repeal of the 1923 Chinese Immigration Act; the admission of relatives, an urgent post-war problem; and arrangements for special movements of immigrants such as Polish ex-servicemen. Canadian citizenship had also been defined for the first time in the Canadian Citizenship Act of 1946.

The Prime Minister's statement on immigration policy was a cautious and unenthusiastic one which effectively preserved the White Canada immigration policy for the next 15 years. It established that the general objectives of Canada's post-war immigration policy must be to enlarge the population of the country, because it would be dangerous for a small population to try to hold "so great a heritage as ours"; to improve the Canadian standard of living; and to help to develop Canadian resources, enlarge her domestic market and reduce her dependence on the export of primary products. Immigration would be selective, the Prime Minister said, and related to absorptive capacity. It was a matter of domestic policy, subject to the control of Parliament, and Canada was perfectly within her rights in selecting the immigrants she wanted. The people of Canada, he asserted, did not wish to make a fundamental alteration in the character of their population through mass immigration. The government was therefore opposed to "large-scale immigration from the Orient," and the existing restrictions on Asiatic immigration must remain. The Prime Minister also said it was the government's intention to expand and strengthen that part of the public service which related to immigration.

Mackenzie King retired as Prime Minister in November 1948 and died on July 22, 1950. He was succeeded by his own nominee Louis St. Laurent, an able and well-to-do corporation lawyer from Quebec. On November 6, 1949, St. Laurent introduced bills in the House to create three new government departments, including a Department of Citizenship and Immigration which opened its doors on January 18, 1950. A new Immigration Act, passed in 1952, became effective on June 1, 1953. Although it had serious defects, and a number of efforts were made to change it beginning in the 1950s, the Act was to stay on the statute book until 1976. To some extent it was by-passed by subsequent immigration regulations, but it remained valid in the area of control and enforcement. As we have seen, the Act gave the Minister and his officials substantial powers over the selection, admission, and deportation of immigrants; and it gave the governor-in-council the all-embracing power to refuse admission on grounds of nationality, geographical area of origin, peculiar customs, habits and modes of life, unsuitability with regard to the climate, probable inability to become readily assimilated, and other similar reasons.[52]

In the federal election of June 1957, a Conservative government was elected for the first time since the early 1930s. John Diefenbaker became Prime Minister and in his election campaign promised that a Conservative government would develop a vigorous immigration policy in co-operation with the provinces and would overhaul the Immigration Act. Canada must "populate or perish" he proclaimed. In 1959 a cabinet committee was established to consider the issues, and in the fall of 1960 it was announced in the Speech from the Throne that the Government would produce a new immigration act. Nothing happened, however, and finally, owing to what was seen as the difficulty of getting such an act through Parliament, the Minister of Citizenship and Immigration, Ellen Fairclough, and her Deputy Minister, Dr. George Davidson (who later became a senior administrator at the United Nations), decided to introduce new immigration regulations to "eliminate all discrimination based on colour, race or creed" and to think about a new act later on. This was one of a number of similar postponements.

The new Immigration Regulations tabled in the House by Mrs. Fairclough on January 19, 1962, represented a radical new departure. They removed racial discrimination as the major feature of Canada's immigration policy, retaining only one privilege for European immigrants over most non-Europeans – the sponsoring of a wider range of relatives. This clause (Section 31d) was inserted at the last minute, it is said, because of Dr. Davidson's fear of an influx of relatives from India – large numbers of immigrants from India were then arriving in the United Kingdom. The clause was removed in the Immigration Regulations of 1967. With the introduction of the 1962 Regulations, however, the White Canada policy was virtually dead. This very important policy change was made not as a result of parliamentary or popular demand, but because some senior officials in Canada, including Dr. Davidson, rightly saw that Canada could not operate effectively within the United Nations, or in the multiracial Commonwealth, with the millstone of a racially discriminatory immigration policy round her neck. Apart from all other considerations, this decision undoubtedly proved beneficial for Canada's international image and effectiveness during the 1960s, when empires were ending and so many new independent states were being created.

The third critical date in policy evolution was the period between 1966 and 1967 when a completely new immigrant selection system – the Canadian points system – was invented and incorporated in the Immigration Regulations of October 1, 1967. If the selection of immigrants was no longer to be based on nationality or race, some other system had to be devised which could be used on a universal basis and would be reasonably fair and objective. Today the United States has a system of six preferences, Canada has her points system, and Australia her own migrant selection system, partly based on the Canadian points system (see Chapter 3). This system was invented by an official in the Canadian overseas immigration service and came to the attention of the Deputy Minister of the recently established Department of Manpower and Immigration, Tom Kent. In 1966, Kent appointed a task force of four senior immigration officials and told them to use this idea as the basis for a new selection system but to refine and improve it. The result was the points system incorporated in the 1967 Regulations. There is no doubt that it has been a very good selection system and has been popular with both immigration officials and immigrants. It is simple, easy to understand, and can be used anywhere. It does, however, require regular monitoring and adapting from time to time to changing circumstances. This did not happen for the first few years (except in a minor way in 1974), but with the new Immigration Act of 1976 described in the next chapter, and the Immigration Regulations which followed it, this principle was adopted and some very useful changes were made. The selection criteria for Independent immigrants were revised again in 1985.

Two other government initiatives in the late 1960s should be mentioned.

The first was the Immigration Appeal Board Act passed on November 13, 1967 which created a new and wholly independent Immigration Appeal Board. The Board has had a rather tumultuous history and has had to deal with some difficult problems, particularly relating to illegal immigration and refugee status determination. It has survived, however, and has proved to be a valuable and independent-minded institution. The second initiative was the Canada Manpower and Immigration Council Act passed on December 21, 1967. This was Canada's first attempt to establish a formal process of consultation and advice to the Minister in the manpower and immigration field, on the lines of Australia's advisory councils in immigration created immediately after World War II. The Act provided for the creation of a Canada Manpower and Immigration Council, consisting mainly of generalists, and four advisory boards of specialists on adult occupational training, the adjustment of immigrants, the co-ordination of rehabilitation services for disabled persons, and manpower and immigration research.

Only two of these advisory boards survived – the boards on adult occupational training and on the adjustment of immigrants. The author was a member of the latter for nine years and had the opportunity to observe the operation of the council and boards very closely. They were a failure, although not a disastrous one, and made only a small contribution to policy development in manpower or immigration. This was partly due to the fact that the structure itself was defective and the idea of a council of non-specialists which reviewed specialist advice before it went to the Minister was very inadequate. But the main reason for failure was that the Trudeau government, which took over in 1968, did not want advice or not of this kind, and while the council and boards were there, policy was being made all the time without them. Although always well looked-after, they operated at a middle management level and rarely saw the Minister and Deputy Minister; and this lack of status and lack of a sense of being entrusted with important tasks caused them quite literally to wither away.

We now turn to the period from 1972 to 1984, when the scene changes altogether. This period begins in Australia with the election of the Whitlam government, involving a major change in political mood and objectives and finally, a very serious constitutional crisis; and in Canada with the appointment in the fall of 1972 of an energetic and purposeful immigration minister, the first for many years. Refugees appeared now in much greater numbers and illegal immigration increased. Multiculturalism was invented as a national policy and public consultation in immigration became an established tool of both governments. At the same time, immi-

gration planning and immigration management became more sophisticated and, on the whole, more humane. Overall, a remarkable degree of
liberalization and innovation took place in both countries in immigration
policy, law and programs.

CHAPTER TWO

Canadian Immigration Policy and Management, 1972–1986

The alternately inactive and turbulent years of the Trudeau administration in the 1970s would not seem the best time to introduce major changes in immigration policy. Public support for the Prime Minister swung dramatically back and forth; the Canadian economy was plagued with unrelenting inflation and unemployment, moving into a severe recession towards the end of the decade; and the clear priorities, forward planning, and policy co-ordination expected from this government never really materialized. That these changes were made is probably due to three principal factors: first, they were long overdue; secondly, they had the support of all political parties at the federal level and, except in one area, encountered no significant provincial opposition; and thirdly, they had the drive of a very able minister with a strong voice in Cabinet behind them.[1]

The cornerstone of these policy developments was a new Immigration Act passed in 1976. An admirable piece of legislation, it put Canadian immigration law on a sound basis and helped to create a very positive climate in immigration management. It also contained a number of innovative provisions which paved the way for further constructive developments in immigration, after the Act came into force in 1978. This chapter records and analyses the considerable effort made in Ottawa after 1972 to get a new Act and the positive consequences which followed.

Between 1968, when Pierre Elliott Trudeau became Leader of the Liberal Party and Prime Minister of Canada, and 1972, three ministers of Manpower and Immigration followed each other in rapid succession. They were Alan MacEachen (July 1968 to September 1970), Otto Lang (September 1970 to January 1972), and Bryce Mackasey (January 1972 to November 1972, when he resigned). None of them made any significant impact on public policy in this area except perhaps Bryce Mackasey, who gave strong personal support to a sizeable movement of Ugandan Asian refugees accepted for permanent settlement in Canada in the fall of 1972. The terms of office of these three ministers coincided with the first period of Pierre Trudeau's leadership when there was much talk of planning and priorities and very little action on any front.

There were urgent matters to be dealt with in the immigration field, however, in particular the pressing need for a new immigration act to replace Canada's old, outdated, and illiberal Immigration Act of 1952 which had already been bypassed in important ways by subsequent regulations. A cautious minister, Alan MacEachen believed that nothing radical should be attempted, at least before the next election in 1972. When urged by his officials he authorized some preparatory work on a new act, but would go no further. Otto Lang, on the other hand, wanted some quick action but without radical change. On his instructions a new immigration bill, incorporating limited improvements, was drafted and sent to Cabinet, where it was rejected as inadequate. Bryce Mackasey, who had previously been Minister of Labour and was the author of some recent and controversial reforms in unemployment insurance, showed no interest in a new act during his brief period as Minister.[2] It was the next Minister of Manpower and Immigration, Robert Andras, who took the task of producing a new, modern immigration act seriously.

Formerly president of a group of automotive sales and rental firms and a prominent businessman in the Thunder Bay district of Ontario, Mr. Andras was persuaded to run in the 1965 federal election. He won the Thunder Bay–Nipigon seat for the Liberal Party. In 1968 he joined the first Trudeau government as Minister without Portfolio, acting first in a supporting role to Jean Chrétien, Minister of Indian Affairs and Northern Development, and then as Minister responsible for Housing in 1969 and Minister of State for Urban Affairs in June 1971. From there he moved to Consumer and Corporate Affairs, and to Manpower and Immigration in November 1972. He retired from politics for health reasons in December 1979 at 58 after a short but remarkably successful political career. He had been a Liberal Member of Parliament for 14 years and a Cabinet minister for 11.

Bob Andras came to the Department of Manpower and Immigration determined to get a new Immigration Act.[3] Privately, and later publicly, the Prime Minister had authorized him to be the minister responsible for population policy. Population had been included on the list of major policy areas the Trudeau government hoped to explore in a careful and methodical way on assuming office in 1968. Unlike foreign policy, defence, taxation, prices and incomes, housing, communications, and other important policy areas, however, which were given to special task forces for study and review, population issues were the subject of minor research activity and occasional papers emanating from the new departments of

Regional Economic Expansion and Urban Affairs and from the Privy Council office. These papers were then submitted to Cabinet. Mr. Andras' own interest in the subject was aroused, he said, by his own previous experience in the Cabinet, particularly as Minister of State for Urban Affairs.

Population problems were becoming the subject of increasing international concern at this time, however, and this gave a definite boost to Canada's hitherto lukewarm interest in the field. In December 1970, the General Assembly of the United Nations designated 1974 World Population Year. During the final months of 1972 and the first six months of 1973, at the request of the U.N., an Inter-Departmental Committee on Population convened by the Department of External Affairs prepared a "country statement" on Canadian population growth and its impact on economic and social development, for a World Population Conference in Bucharest in August 1974. For a while, therefore, and coinciding with Mr. Andras' term of office in Manpower and Immigration, population policy stood somewhat higher than usual on the national agenda.

When Bob Andras took up his new assignment in November 1972, he found not only that there were urgent policy matters to be resolved, but also that the department itself was in very poor shape. The major developments which had followed the creation of this large department in 1966 – including building a truly national employment service and Canada-wide manpower training, mobility and other programs, introduction of the points system in immigration, and creation of the Immigration Appeal Board and Canada Manpower and Immigration Advisory Council and advisory boards – had not been followed by a period of effective consolidation. There had been a high turnover of deputy ministers as well as ministers. A disastrous organization structure had been inflicted on the Department whereby all effective decision-making was concentrated in a central Operations Division, reducing the other major divisions, including immigration, to near impotence. At this point, the Immigration Division had in effect no operational responsibility in Canada whatsoever. Already feeling swamped in its new manpower environment and "downgraded to a manpower policy," as it was then described, this situation was hardly conducive to high morale.[4] There were serious problems on the manpower side, too, where unforeseen difficulties in meeting ambitious national objectives had already emerged.

The new Minister described all this in an interview with the author as "a terrible mess." The existing organization was stultifying, he said, and hardly anyone could communicate with the field. Morale in the Department was very low. Marchand,[5] MacEachen, Lang and Mackasey had succeeded each other in swift succession and the deputy ministers had done the same. Hardly anyone had got a real grip on this territory and it was clear that substantial management changes had to be made. In addition, the Unemployment Insurance Commission, for which he was also responsible, was at its lowest ebb. The immigration points system, the Minister said, had never been properly reviewed and provided no control over numbers. Because of a loophole in the 1967 Regulations, illegal immigration was becoming critical and the backlog of cases before the Immigration Appeal Board was increasing all the time.[6]

By all accounts, Mr. Andras moved quickly. The existing senior management was dispersed, and within a few months the new Minister had brought in Alan Gotlieb, a very able senior official from the Department of External Affairs, as Deputy Minister. Gotlieb was later to become Under Secretary of State in that department and afterwards Canadian Ambassador in Washington. For the next four years the two men formed a very influential political partnership. While not all their efforts were successful nor always in the best interests of immigration, they were the principal architects of Canada's new Immigration Act of 1976, providing the major thrust behind the creation of this important piece of legislation. They began thinking about possible amalgamation of the Unemployment Insurance Commission and the Department of Manpower and Immigration about 1974, if not earlier. (It eventually took place in 1978.) Mr. Andras was convinced from the beginning that this was a logical and desirable step; Mr. Gotlieb was less certain but was finally persuaded. They made a deliberate and ultimately successful effort to involve the provinces in the policy-making process in immigration and they attempted – unsuccessfully as it turned out – to provide Canada with at least the basic elements of a population policy. Before these developments took place, however, Mr. Andras and his Department had to deal with a major immigration crisis on the home front.

IMMIGRATION OUT OF CONTROL

The 1967 Immigration Regulations contained an important provision, Section 34, permitting visitors to apply for landed immigrant status from within Canada.[7] In the same year, as we have seen, the Immigration Appeal Board Act was passed, creating an independent appeals tribunal in immigration with authority to make final and binding decisions on deportation. The Act gave anyone who had been ordered deported the right to appeal to the Board, no matter what his or her status under the Immigration Act. The special opportunities provided by these combined provisions began to be appreciated within a remarkably short time, particularly by the many practitioners of the ancient commerce of migration in every part of the world. Floods of visitors began to arrive in Canada with the obvious intention of staying, applying for landed immigrant status and, if refused, submitting an appeal to the Immigration Appeal Board, which had the power to permit them to stay in Canada on compassionate or humanitarian grounds. The longer they stayed and the more successfully they settled in, the more compelling, obviously, those grounds would be.

The events that took place between 1970 and 1973 in Canada are worth describing in some detail, as they illustrate a dilemma which faces all immigrant receiving countries – namely the unforeseen consequences of new or untried immigration laws and regulations, and the extreme care that must be taken in areas like internal change of status. At the same time, they show how easily would-be immigrants can be persuaded to take considerable risks, often selling all their possessions in the process, for the chance of a better life in a safe, stable, and affluent country. It was Canada's most dramatic experience in recent years of the problems of illegal or undocumented migration.

Initially nothing of any consequence happened as a result of Section 34 of the new Immigration Regulations, but within the space of two years at most it became evident that a special and growing movement of visitors to Canada was under way from the United States, Europe, Latin America, Asia, the Caribbean, and elsewhere. These visitors had learned, or had been told, that the fastest way to get into Canada and settle there was simply to come, apply for landed immigrant status and, if refused, submit an appeal to the Immigration Appeal Board. As the number of visitors arriving at Canada's international airports began to increase alarmingly so did the number of cases before the Immigration Appeal Board, until a sizeable backlog developed. Approximately 45,000 visitors in Canada applied for landed immigrant status in 1970, one sixth of all the applications made in Canada and overseas.

In 1972, the situation became critical. Between January and August, the average monthly rate of applications from visitors for landed immigrant status was about 4,600 and each month the backlog of cases before the Immigration Appeal Board grew larger. In June, the Department instituted a review of appeal cases with a view to reducing the backlog. But word of the review rapidly spread around the world and what were sensed as impending changes in the regulations spurred travel agents and other commercial operators, as well as would-be immigrants, to desperate efforts. By September, the rate of applications from visitors for landed immigrant status had increased to 6,900; in October it went up to 8,700. At the same time, the number of suspected "non–bona fide visitors" arriving at the international airports of Toronto, Montreal, and Vancouver was escalating in the same way. As many as 4,500 arrived at Toronto International Airport during one weekend in October.

At this point, the Liberal government decided that action must be taken to bring the situation under control. On November 3, 1972, Section 34 of the 1967 Immigration Regulations was revoked. On January 1, 1973, a further step was taken. Regulations were introduced requiring all visitors staying in Canada for more than three months to register, and for all those seeking jobs to obtain employment visas. Because of the number of visitors who had already arrived in Canada and applied for landing, however, there were 12,700 people awaiting a hearing before the Immigration Appeal Board on January 1 and 17,472 by the end of May, an increase of almost 1,000 a month. Ninety per cent of these cases involved either visitors or illegal entrants. The Board was able to handle only about 100 cases a month.

Two problems now faced the government as they saw it — the plight of the Immigration Appeal Board, which could not handle the huge backlog of cases without assistance; and the large number of visitors already in Canada by the beginning of November 1972 who had not yet applied for landed immigrant status and were caught by the November third announcement. The government decided to tackle the first problem by amending the Immigration Appeal Board Act as soon as possible, and the second by offering the opportunity of adjustment of status to visitors who had lived in Canada continuously since November 1972.

The Bill to amend the Immigration Appeal Board Act was introduced in the House of Commons on July 18, 1973; the critical Second Reading began two days later. The Bill consisted of a number of permanent amendments to the Act to prevent a recurrence of the crisis, and a group of temporary amendments to deal with the backlog. At the same time, the Minister announced a 60-day Adjustment of Status Program to allow those who had been in Canada continuously since November 30, 1972 to regularize their status.[8] The main permanent amendments to the Act provided for the appointment whenever desirable of seven additional temporary members of the Board; and for the modification of existing appeal rights, confining them in future to permanent residents, those who had a valid immigrant or non-immigrant visa when applying for admission to Canada, and those who had a substantial claim to refugee status or Canadian citizenship.

The Minister explained the reasons for this two-pronged approach in his opening speech in the House of Commons. If the appeal process was put on a fair and workable footing, which had to be done first, it would then be possible to offer the large numbers of people then in Canada illegally "the opportunity to get their life in Canada off to a new and legal start." He did not condone violation of the law, the Minister said, but many of these people were perhaps "the unfortunate victims of unscrupulous, self-styled immigration counsellors, whom we know exist, who for a fee may have convinced them that they were doing no wrong in short-circuiting Canadian immigration law. Others who knowingly violated the law in the way they entered Canada and remained here have nevertheless put down their roots, established families and settled into productive work."[9]

The Adjustment of Status Program, Mr. Andras said, was intended to accommodate most of the people caught by the November third announcement revoking Section 34 of the 1967 Immigration Regulations, as well as many people who had lived in Canada for years without legal status. "The right to apply in Canada for immigrant status," he said, "was a noble experiment that proved unworkable and has had to be laid to rest, but I think decency demands that it be done fairly."[10] These people would be allowed to regularize their status within a 60-day period only. "The clock starts ticking," Mr. Andras said, "on the day this Bill is proclaimed, and the opportunity runs out permanently 60 days later."[11] Applications for immigrant status would be judged in the light of such criteria as length of residence in Canada, family relationships, financial stability, and employment records, as well as compelling grounds for compassionate consideration. It was expected that the great majority of those who came forward would be successful in their applications for landed immigrant status.

It is important to note here that, although it had many similar features, the Adjustment of Status Program of 1973 was never seen by the Liberal government as an amnesty.[12] It was seen as a decent gesture, an act of fairness towards those who, whatever their motives in coming to Canada, had suddenly been deprived of rights they thought they had and on which they intended to rely. At the same time, equal opportunity to acquire legal status in Canada had to be offered to the unknown number of residents who had been living in the country illegally for varying periods of time.

The Adjustment of Status Program went into effect on August 15 and ended on October 15, 1973. It was carried out with verve and imagination and is a fine example of what can be done with a government program when it has the right resources, the right management, and the right degree of support at the top. It also had the active support of all political parties at the federal level, and all the media. A major effort was made to reach as many illegal immigrants as possible and to offer the widest possible facilities for them to apply for landed immigrant status. When the program ended and all were counted, some 39,000 people from more than 150 countries had obtained landed immigrant status. Of these, 60 per cent were in Canada illegally and 40 per cent had legal status of some kind. A few had lived in Canada illegally for decades. A further 13,000 people obtained landed immigrant status as a result of the first administrative measures taken in 1972 to attempt to reduce the backlog in the inquiry system (the first stage of the examination and appeal process), and the larger number of cases heard by the Immigration Appeal Board after the

Table 1
Canada: Adjustment of Status Program, 1973

Last Permanent Residence of Successful Applicants (15 Principal Countries)	Number	Percent
United States	7,259	28.4
Hong Kong	5,619	22.0
Jamaica	1,420	5.5
Trinidad	1,055	4.1
India	852	3.3
Great Britain	833	3.3
Guyana	799	3.1
Greece	695	2.7
Portugal	690	2.7
South Vietnam	363	1.4
Haiti	351	1.4
France	349	1.4
Ecuador	339	1.3
Japan	312	1.2
Malaysia	303	1.2
Others	4,354	17.0
TOTAL	25,593	100.0

Source: Department of Manpower and Immigration, Immigrant Landings – Adjustment of Status Program to July 31, 1974.

amendment of the Act. This makes a final score for the whole effort of some 52,000 people.

There are other interesting statistics. The program cost an extra $2 million above the normal operating costs of the Department, mainly in overtime and travel expenses. The distribution of cases across Canada reflected the normal pattern of immigrant settlement, with more than half coming from Ontario and a substantial proportion of that half from Toronto. Table 1 shows the 15 principal countries from which the majority of those accepted for landing during the 60-day program had come.

The table shows an interesting world-wide spread, confirming the well-known fact that illegal immigrants come from everywhere. Proximity is always important, however (the United States and the Caribbean in this case), since it provides greater opportunity. Many of the immigrants from the United States were former draft evaders and deserters from the Vietnam war period who had entered Canada mainly in the late sixties. The high proportion of successful applicants from Hong Kong indicates that familiarity with the English language and British institutions may have been an advantage, and also that the well-known illegal migration industry in Hong Kong was still alive and well in 1972.

The Adjustment of Status Program was widely felt in Canada to have been a great success. An American observer who came to study it and to learn its possible lessons for the United States was impressed with the political harmony which prevailed throughout. "[The] Government was able to build substantial political support for its program," he wrote in his report. "It then proceeded to manage the politics of the situation skilfully, moved its program through from inception to fruition quickly and then opened and closed the operation with dispatch ... By American standards, it was a political honeymoon from start to finish." He noted also how swiftly the necessary legislation was passed by Parliament, how supportive the press had been throughout, and how impressive he had found the calibre, skills, and dedication of the Canadian immigration officials involved.[13]

As the Program closed on October 15, a more controversial note was struck in Parliament. The Opposition – supported outside by elements of the press and voluntary sector – urged that the program be extended for a few days, a month, or even another 60 days, to take full advantage of the climate of trust which had been created so successfully. After reflection the government decided against any extension of the program, and suc-ceeding administrations have been opposed to any repetition of it. The main reason – still felt to be valid – was given by Mr. Andras in the House of Commons later that year. Repetition of the program in any form, he said, would indicate "a lack of will to hold firm to our immigration laws," and might in fact, if only from time to time, legitimize illegal immigration instead of reducing it.[14]

IMMIGRATION AND POPULATION REVIEW

The success of the Adjustment of Status Program and the widespread interest and support it aroused revived the flagging spirits of the Immigra-tion Division of the Department of Manpower and Immigration. The whole Department was also beginning to see that Bob Andras was one of the best ministers they had ever worked with. Always in close touch with his officials, he absorbed complex information quickly and soon had a very good grasp of existing immigration law and regulations, and a clear idea of what he wanted to achieve. At the same time, everyone found him very approachable and a good, sympathetic listener. There are many peo-ple in immigration today who still speak of Robert Andras with affection and remember what a good minister he was.

After the Adjustment of Status Program was well under way, the next step, as the Minister and his senior officials saw it, was to initiate a thorough review of existing immigration policies and practice, leading to a Green Paper or some kind of discussion document. This document could then be the basis of a public debate on critical issues of immigration and population policy, prior to the creation of a new immigration act.

The review was officially announced by the Minister in the House of Commons on September 15, 1973. He described it as "action to create a new long-term basis for Canada's immigration and population policy." A special task force, later called the Canadian Immigration and Population Study, was being created within the Department of Manpower and Immigration to study policy options and organize the whole review process. A senior official on loan from the Department of External Affairs had been named chairman, and the task force would be supported by a group of non-government experts and consultants. He was writing that day to the provinces and to more than 100 organizations, inviting their help Mr. Andras said and he had asked the task force to proceed with special studies focusing on a range of problems in this area. He intended to publish a Green Paper outlining the many available options in immigration in the spring of 1974. The following summer would be devoted to intensive public discussion of the Green Paper in the form of submissions and briefs, and an immigration and population conference would be held under the auspices of the Department of Manpower and Immigration. The aim was to establish a forward-looking immigration policy, backed by new legislation to be presented to Parliament as soon as possible. The task was "enormous and difficult," Mr. Andras said, and would need the help of all Canadians. He looked forward to an open and fruitful discussion.[15]

The task was indeed difficult and the proposed timetable too ambitious. It took nearly 15 months to produce a Green Paper on immigration and population policy, instead of the six months envisaged. Public discussion could not begin until this had been done. Little thought had been given to the role of Parliament other than as final judge of the proposed legislation. It was highly unrealistic to think that one national conference, in addition to briefs and submissions, would be an adequate instrument of public participation.

The main obstacle to the brisk policy-making process Mr. Andras and his officials hoped to launch was the sheer lack of basic research and published work in the immigration and population fields in Canada. The author's 1972 study had been the only major work on immigration published in Canada since the Corbett study in 1957.[16] There was only a handful of Canadian "experts and consultants" in either area. Canada had very few senior academic demographers, for example, and they had been working mainly in other fields. In addition, as the task force discovered, the Immigration Division of the Department of Manpower and Immigration was unaccustomed to "displaying its wares" in a public discussion document.[17] The last occasion of this kind was in 1966 when the division produced a very cautious and carefully written White Paper on Canadian Immigration Policy, which was then discussed by a Special Joint Committee of the Senate and the House of Commons which failed to produce a report.[18] In 1973 there were very few internal studies the task force could use.

A further obstacle to the production of an effective Green Paper was the strong desire of Mr. Andras and his colleagues to press on and get the job done quickly. This stemmed in part from the persistent belief among Canadian politicians and officials that immigration is controversial, hard to manage, and subject to awkward political pressures; and that policy issues in this field should not float freely in the public arena for too long. Speaking later to the Special Joint Committee of the Senate and the House of Commons appointed to examine the Green Paper and hold hearings on it across Canada, Mr. Andras said that immigration was so sensitive an issue it might not be advisable to prolong public debate on future policy and he added, "One has to ask how long a debate on this issue can go on in this country and remain constructive."[19]

There was more to it, however, than just the sensitive nature of the issue. Mr. Andras' paramount concern was to get a new immigration act. Throughout the period from the appointment of the Green Paper task force in 1973 to the tabling of the Immigration Bill by his successor, Bud Cullen, on November 22, 1976, he was fearful that something might go wrong or that the national debate might get bogged down and that, as had happened so often in the past, no new act would emerge. Even when he had, somewhat reluctantly, accepted the Prime Minister's proposal made in 1976 that he take the senior cabinet post of President of the Treasury Board, his concern continued. In conversation with the author during the second reading of the Bill in the spring of 1977, he confessed that he wished that he could be there to steer the Bill through the Commons. He was worried that his colleague Bud Cullen was not pushing hard enough. Time and political will were getting short. The Bill might easily die on the order paper, he said, and we might never get another piece of immigration legislation as good as this one. As it turned out, however, these fears were unfounded. The new Immigration Bill was passed without major difficulties and received royal assent on August 5, 1977.

As we have seen, Mr. Andras and his deputy minister were driving hard for a new immigration act from 1973 onwards. But they also wanted to involve the hitherto reluctant provinces in the policy-making process in immigration, and, if possible, to establish some "population guidelines" for Canada on which the federal government and the provinces could agree. These policy objectives were very clear. The Green Paper and the national debate which was planned to follow it were seen much less as a way of seeking information and guidance from the Canadian public on immigration policy, than as a means of *educating* the provinces and public on the critical decisions in immigration and population which would have to be made in Canada in the very near future. The brisk timetable, limited resources devoted to the production of the Green Paper, the restricted concept of what a national debate on the subject should involve, all reflect this approach. And it is interesting to note that the other major policy development under active consideration from 1974 onwards, the possible amalgamation of the Department of Manpower and Immigration and the Unemployment Insurance Commission, was never put to the public at all, although it was discussed with the provinces later. This amalgamation would create a large, quasi-independent agency with extensive resources (later called the Canada Employment and Immigration Commission) which could deal effectively with Canada's serious unemployment and labour force development problems. This possibility was not even mentioned in the Green Paper, in which the central issue of immigration management was ignored, nor was it seriously considered by the Special Joint Committee of Parliament which examined the Green Paper.

GREEN PAPER ON IMMIGRATION POLICY

The Green Paper was finally completed and submitted to Cabinet in the fall of 1974, and tabled in the House of Commons by the Minister on February 3, 1975.[20] It consisted of four separate volumes and eight supplementary studies (several of which appeared a little later), written either by academic consultants or officials.[21] The first volume, "Immigration Policy Perspectives," was the most important. It contained a short essay on contemporary immigration policy in which the important issues the government and its principal policy makers wished to put before the public were discussed or mentioned briefly. Volume 2, "The Immigration Program," was more substantial and factual, providing a brief account of the evolution of Canadian immigration policy and law since Confederation, and a description of current immigration policies and practice. Volume 3 offered a comprehensive set of immigration and population statistics, as well as some population projections to the year 2001 recently published by Statistics Canada. The first report of the Department of Manpower and Immigration's longitudinal survey of the economic and social adaptation of immigrants, which was started in 1969 was published in Volume 4.[22]

The Green Paper was accompanied by an explanatory statement from the Minister which was a clear and forthright piece of work and the best part of the materials laid before Parliament on that day.[23] It stressed, first of all, the importance of the occasion and the need to see immigration policy in a very wide framework. It was not, the Minister said, merely a question of regulations or procedures, nor of Canada's economic or humanitarian concerns: "... what finally is at stake is no less than the future of Canada's population – its size, rate of growth, distribution and composition – and the basic principles that should govern our decisions to augment the nation's human resources through the admission of migrants from abroad." There were key elements in Canada's present policy which, it was believed, Canadians would wish to preserve. These were non-discrimination, the importance of family reunion, compassionate considerations relating to refugees and others, and an immigration policy in close harmony with other major areas of economic and social policy. Nevertheless immigration policy must be related to contemporary Canadian needs and international pressures, and must be designed to support the attainment of long-range national goals. It was hoped, therefore, that the Green Paper would help to stimulate a country-wide debate on immigration policy that would embrace not only the important practical questions of immigration management, but also the development of a population policy for Canada which future immigration to this country could be fashioned to support.

"We need a set of flexible guidelines," the Minister said, "to which policies which affect our population future may be related. The formulation of such guidelines – which would need to be kept under constant review in the light of changing conditions and national priorities – is a subject to which the government attaches great weight." It would require close collaboration between Ottawa, the provinces, and the municipalities. The federal government was taking a series of steps, he said, to foster "the widest possible measure of agreement about Canada's population future." The Prime Minister had written to the provincial premiers to ask them to designate "lead ministers" to participate in this enterprise. In Ottawa, the government had appointed a Demographic Policy Steering Group of deputy ministers, under the chairmanship of the Deputy Minister of Manpower and Immigration, "to develop the federal view in the demographic policy area and to coordinate the federal input into the consultative process." A National Demographic Policy Secretariat, headed by a senior officer in the Department of Manpower and Immigration, had been created to support the work of the Policy Steering Group and to undertake consultations with the provinces and the public.

The Minister then turned to the plans made for the national debate and consultation which would take place now that the Green Paper had been published. While the review of immigration policy leading to this discussion paper was under way, he had invited contributions from the provinces and from interested organizations across Canada and views had been submitted from many quarters. He looked forward to receiving further proposals and representations from organizations and individuals after they had studied the Green Paper, which would also be referred to a committee of Parliament in the near future. In addition, Mr. Andras said, he would himself be visiting the provincial capitals for "initial exchanges with the provincial ministers designated to participate with us in the discussion of demographic goals." Finally, he referred to the urgent and widely acknowledged need for a new immigration act and announced that the government proposed to place an immigration bill before Parliament at an early date.

After this positive beginning, the Green Paper itself, and particularly Volume 1, "Immigration Policy Perspectives," proved to be disappointing. It simply did not live up to the occasion and inevitably got a cool reception in the media. It compares very unfavourably with the Australian Green Paper "Immigration Policies and Australia's Population," produced two years later, written by a sub-committee of the former Australian Population and Immigration Council. In addition, public relations for the Canadian Green Paper were handled much less skilfully by the Department than they had been for the Adjustment of Status Program. Although the inadequacies of the Green Paper were not significant in the long run, they undoubtedly did some damage to the quality of the debate that followed, and provided ammunition for the small but vocal group of Canadians who were hostile to this process.

The critical Volume 1, "Immigration Policy Perspectives," discussed in greater detail the issues raised in the Minister's explanatory statement. It examined Canada's population problems, labour market needs, national interest and international responsibilities in this field, federal-provincial relations in immigration, existing immigration law and the possible content of a new immigration act. Lacking both clarity and depth, as well as an intimate understanding of and feel for the immigration field in Canada, Volume 1 probably offended most by its ambiguous language, pessimistic tone, and failure to speak plainly. These were most evident in the discussion of Canada's multiracial immigration movement, and the problems of urban congestion and incipient social tensions in our largest cities. Here it simply invited accusations of racism, although these were unwarranted. In addition, a thinly-veiled bias against an "expansionist" immigration program, as well as a tendency to emphasize economic factors and ignore political ones, was evident throughout the paper. Although it attempted to take a rather elevated, impartial position and to reflect all sides of the immigration question, the Green Paper in fact presented a rather narrow and depressing view of the immigration scene in Canada. It is not at all surprising that the media as well as many individual Canadians reacted against it.

Why did this inadequate document pass muster in the middle of a determined, responsible, and creative effort to improve Canadian immigration policy and law? The major reasons could be summarized as inexperience at a senior level, excessive caution, and lack of consultation with anyone on the part of those who were ultimately responsible for it. In its final form, the Green Paper was in fact a very private document, produced by a small group in the Department of Manpower and Immigration, and written and edited by its senior management. There had been major changes in senior management since Bob Andras took charge in November 1972 and highly talented as the new entrants were, their experience of immigration was very limited. They had had no field experience of any kind and at that point no direct exposure to immigration's special sensitivities. At the same time they were over-cautious, almost to the point of inflexibility, about the problems this area of public policy could produce. Finally, the Immigration Division had lost some very good people since the late sixties, partly due to the Department of Manpower and Immigration's frustrating management structure already referred to, and partly because they had been attracted to what seemed to be better prospects on the more influential manpower side. When the Canadian Population and Immigration Study started work on the Green Paper, much of the talent in the Immigration Division was concentrated in the Foreign Branch. Only a few senior immigration officers in Ottawa had extensive experience that could be drawn on, and they were very much occupied with day-to-day management.

There were, however, other sources of experience and advice very close at hand. Among the academic consultants who were asked to write supplementary studies to the Green Paper, at least three had had wide-ranging experience of immigration. They produced the required papers. They had informal talks with the Chairman of the Canadian Immigration and Population Study and his staff, but they were never consulted about the document itself. If they had been, the Green Paper might have been a more stimulating piece of work or, at the very least, some of its ambiguities could have been removed. Similarly, the Department and the Canadian Immigration and Population Study made only minimal use of the Canada Manpower and Immigration Advisory Council and its Advisory Boards, while proclaiming the need for the widest possible consultation with the public.

In Australia by contrast, the actual task of writing a Green Paper on immigration was given, as we have seen, to the Australian Population and Immigration Council, with the necessary support from the Department of Immigration and Ethnic Affairs.[24] The members of this council were a highly qualified group and a number of them had had extensive experience of the immigration field. Drafted by a small sub-committee and then submitted to the council as a whole, the Green Paper had the benefit of a critical review by a group of very knowledgeable people. The result was an excellent discussion paper which in little more than 100 pages, deals with the issues involved in Australian immigration today in a very competent and straightforward way.

All that can be said now for the Canadian Green Paper is that at least it got the debate going. Within nine months its significance faded with the publication of the Report of Parliament of the Special Joint Committee of the Senate and the House of Commons on Immigration Policy.

THE SPECIAL JOINT COMMITTEE

Cabinet was divided on the best way to handle a national debate on the Green Paper, and on the desirability of appointing a parliamentary committee to examine the issues involved and to hold public hearings on them. Although the Minister himself was in favour of a parliamentary committee, provided it got down to work quickly, an initial decision was made by Cabinet in favour of the earlier plan to have a national conference and other meetings, organized by a few well-known national organizations and voluntary agencies involved in immigration. When this decision became known in the House, the Liberal caucus reacted strongly against it. They wanted a committee and so did the opposition parties, both believing that Parliament must be directly involved in any major examination of the public's views in this important policy area. Eventually the strength of feeling in the caucus won the day and the Cabinet decision was reversed. A Special Joint Committee of the Senate and the House of Commons on Immigration Policy was appointed in March 1975 to examine the Green Paper and to hold public hearings on it across Canada.

Under the joint chairmanship of Martin O'Connell, a former Liberal cabinet minister, and Senator Maurice Riel, the Special Joint Committee proved to be able, dedicated, and hard-working. Fifty public hearings on the Green Paper and the major policy issues involved were held in 21 cities across Canada, and the Committee heard some 400 witnesses and received more than 1400 briefs. In November the Committee produced an excellent *Report to Parliament* which made a major contribution to the immigration and population debate.[25] Although there were a few topics, such as immigrant services and refugees, on which they might have been more helpful and occasionally more liberal, the Committee spoke out firmly and positively on nearly all the essential matters. It is sad to have to record that, whereas the Green Paper received a good deal of attention in the media, the Committee's final report – a much better and more important piece of work – received almost none.

In addition to the Minutes of Proceedings and Evidence,[26] we have a good account of the work of the Parliamentary Committee written by their special adviser, Peter Dobell, Director of the Parliamentary Centre for Foreign Affairs and Foreign Trade, and Susan d'Aquino, a staff member of the Centre, for the Canadian Institute of International Affairs' *Behind the Headlines* series.[27] Both were part of the small support staff of the Committee. It was in no small part due to the very professional efforts of this small group that the Committee functioned so effectively, and produced such a good report within a relatively short time.

Dobell and d'Aquino were impressed with the mutual understanding and trust that developed among the members of this all-party parliamentary committee. Perhaps 15 out of 23 members, they said, formed a hard core who participated regularly during all stages of the Committee's proceedings, and became well-informed on the issues and the wider implications of various courses of action. They were impressed with the chairmanship of the Committee in which Martin O'Connell, who did much of the travelling, played a major part. They noted that, although the public hearings were not as representative of Canadian public opinion as the Committee would have wished, members were satisfied that they had heard from "every relevant sort of group and individual" with views on the subject, through briefs, personal appearances, and expert presentations. They noted that "immigration proved to be one area of public policy where the opinions which Canadians expressed did not differ significantly along regional lines."

The Committee's patience was sorely tried at the public hearings, however, by the frequent disruption of small, mainly young, far-left groups. As these authors put it, "The Marxist-Leninist Committee Against Racism (formed by the Communist Party of Canada (Marxist-Leninist), popularly called "Maoists") and several other allied or sympathetic groups, set out to dominate or abort a number of meetings through disruptive tactics, such as shouting, chanting, heckling witnesses they did not agree with, and in one case completely drowning out another group's presentation." They did this despite being offered the opportunity to come forward and express their views from the witness table. Perhaps the most damaging aspect of these interventions was the claim made by the groups, without any authority, that they were the true spokesmen for Third World immigrants and the newer ethnic groups from Asia and the Caribbean. In fact, as Dobell and d'Aquino point out, "... with very few exceptions, the Marxist-Leninist groups were composed of young, middle-class white Canadians." A major focus of their attacks was that the Green Paper was a racist document and promoted racism.[28]

The members of the Special Joint Committee, facing fierce attacks of this kind and other critical but less hostile witnesses, were ambivalent about the Green Paper, as Dobell and d'Aquino record, and clearly did not wish to be held responsible for it. Quite a few members, in conversation with the author, expressed reservations about its style and content. At public hearings, the Committee frequently emphasized that it was conducting its own independent inquiry into the contemporary problems of immigration and population in Canada.

According to the original timetable, the Committee was required to complete its inquiry and submit a report by July 31, which gave them only four months to do a difficult job which involved considerable travelling. This timetable caused concern to members of the Committee and to a number of organizations who felt they would have difficulty consulting their memberships and studying the matter thoroughly in such a short time. With some reluctance, the Government eventually agreed to extend the deadline to October 31.[29]

While the Committee's public hearings were in progress, the criticism was made that they were not reaching the general public and that "ordinary Canadians" were not being involved. When the author discussed the national debate later with Martin O'Connell, Co-Chairman of the Special Joint Committee, he said it was true that the Committee had not reached the general public. They had reached national organizations, ethnic groups, voluntary agencies, and individuals who were already concerned with immigration and had views and proposals which they wished to present. With only a few exceptions, he said, the Committee did not reach the schools or young people generally. They did not reach labour, and reached business to only a limited extent. Furthermore, the Prime Minister and other cabinet ministers did not participate in what was meant to be a national debate, or only very occasionally. Mr. Andras in fact carried the whole load. Concerning radio and television coverage, Mr. O'Connell said the Canadian Broadcasting Corporation was a total failure as far as the Committee's endeavours and national issues were concerned. They simply did nothing. The press was just as inadequate, totally ignoring the Committee's final report. O'Connell noted also that the Committee lost a lot of time through the irresponsible activities of the Marxist-Leninist "stage army" which attended almost every meeting and antagonized everyone.

For the Committee itself, however, Mr. O'Connell had warm words. They were hard-working and effective, and did a very good job in the time available to them. Although Committee members did not divide on party lines, they did divide to some extent philosophically. They turned their backs very firmly on racist mail and presentations, of which they were some, and on irrational anti-immigration briefs. They were good at compromise and had a strong feeling and concern for Canada's future needs and development.[30]

THE COMMITTEE'S RECOMMENDATIONS

The Report to Parliament of the Special Joint Committee had a warm reception in Parliament, in the Department, and in immigration circles generally. Sad to say, since the press failed to comment on the report and the electronic media had remained uninvolved, the Canadian public heard little of it. The Minister himself responded very positively to the report. A few months later when he presented the main estimates of his department to the Standing Committee on Labour, Manpower, and Immigration, he congratulated the Committee on a masterful performance.[31] Sixty of the 65 recommendations of the Special Joint Committee were accepted by the Government. They formed the main basis of the new Immigration Act.

The Committee's major recommendations are listed below. It is most important that they should both be more widely known in Canada and not forgotten by those involved in immigration policy-making today.

1 Canada should continue to be a country of immigration for demographic, economic, family, and humanitarian reasons.

2 A new Immigration Act should contain a clear statement of principles and objectives including those pertaining to admission, non-discrimination, sponsorship of relatives, refugees, and the prohibition of certain classes of immigrants. Operational details and procedures should be specified in regulations.

3 The principle of non-discrimination in immigration on the basis of race, creed, nationality, ethnic origin, and sex should be continued and should be formally set out in the new Immigration Act.

4 A clear statement of Canada's refugee policy should now be made.

5 Immigration should be treated in future as a central variable in a national population policy. A country as large and thinly populated as Canada cannot afford the declining population which is indicated by current trends in fertility, and must continue to welcome a minimum of 100,000 immigrants a year as long as present fertility rates prevail. Major efforts should also be made to forestall a further decline in Canada's French-speaking population.

6 Annual admission figures should be calculated on the basis of this 100,000 minimum, plus an annual target figure to be adjusted from time to time to achieve an even rate of population growth, and to take account of changing economic conditions.

7 The Minister of Manpower and Immigration should propose an annual target figure after consultation with the provinces. This target should then be subject to parliamentary scrutiny.

8 Immigration is a long-term investment in human resources. Our present rapid rate of labour force expansion is likely to decline abruptly around 1980. From then on, future economic development might actually be held back by labour shortages unless immigration is continued.

9 The settlement of post-war immigrants alongside our founding cultures had been one of the most positive chapters in Canada's post-war history, and the Committee looked to immigration to continue to contribute to the economic, cultural, and social well-being of the coun-

try. Nevertheless our present immigration system needs modifying and modernizing with the objective of regulating our immigration flow to achieve desired population growth.

10 A permanent joint federal-provincial committee should co-ordinate the development and implementation of immigration policy.

11 The points system should be retained but modified in certain respects; the category of area demand in the points system should be used experimentally to encourage immigrants to settle in areas requiring development and population growth.

12 More thorough follow-up, control, and enforcement procedures relating to illegal immigration within Canada should be introduced, and more immigration staff and better support services provided at Canadian–U.S. border crossing points.

13 Because deportation carries a stigma with it, the introduction of a simple "required to depart" procedure is recommended to be used in cases of minor breaches of the Immigration Act or regulations.

14 Increased attention should now be given by the Department of Manpower and Immigration to the planning, development, and co-ordination of immigrant services in Canada, in consultation with other levels of government.[32]

There were many other recommendations on a wide range of practical matters: selection criteria; prohibited classes and control and enforcement; refugees; temporary workers and foreign students; immigrant services and department organization. On the latter point – the question of whether immigration should remain in the same department with manpower, or be separated from it, the Committee members were divided, as were the submissions they received. According to the report, however, "of the several proposals put to the Committee, the one which attracted most support was that Immigration be detached from Manpower and the Unemployment Insurance Commission, and instead be linked with citizenship, multiculturalism and population to form a new portfolio. It was felt this represented a rational grouping of federal responsibilities, and a Minister with such a portfolio could expect to carry considerable weight in the Cabinet."[33]

The Committee members were not unanimous on every element in their recommendations. The day their report was tabled, three members of the Committee – Monique Bégin, Andrew Brewin and David Macdonald, together with two other members of Parliament who had been closely involved, Peter Stollery and David Orlikow – issued a short statement saying that while they accepted many of the proposals and recommendations of the report, there were certain items with which they did not agree. These included the jurisdiction of the Immigration Appeal Board (which they believed should be widened); the recommendation to eliminate the concept of domicile from the Immigration Act (which they thought should be retained); the view that foreign students should not be permitted to work during their vacations (with which they disagreed); and the recommendation that the right to sponsor relatives be confined to Canadian citizens (which they thought should apply to all lawful residents of Canada). They were also concerned to see that under the new Immigration Act, admission should not be denied because an applicant might become a public charge, and that landed immigrants who became a public charge should not be deported – a distinctive feature of the 1952 Act.[34]

David Macdonald, then Member of Parliament for the Egmont riding of Prince Edward Island and a well-known "Red Tory,"[35] went further. He issued his own statement entitled "Some Critical Observations on the Report of the Special Parliamentary Committee on Immigration." Mr. Macdonald had a number of specific objections to the stand taken by the Special Joint Committee on immigration and population issues. Fundamentally, however, he disagreed with Canada's whole approach to immigration. His views are important because he represents a small but ever-present minority in the immigration debate in Canada and Australia. The members of this minority cannot accept the idea of immigration as a national policy designed primarily to serve Canadian or Australian interests, even though this policy may be managed in a reasonably open and liberal way, may be tolerant on the question of family reunion, and may permit the admission of large numbers of refugees. In their view, this is not enough. Immigration to these affluent countries should be used almost entirely for compassionate purposes.

After their Report to Parliament had been tabled in the House of Commons, the Special Joint Committee on Immigration Policy ceased to exist. Some of its members were already or became members of the Standing Committee on Labour, Manpower and Immigration. One of the beneficial results of this exercise, however, was to create a larger group of members in the House who were really interested in and knowledgeable about this area of public policy. As we have seen, the recommendations of the Committee were easy for the government to live with. They coincided to a remarkable degree with the views of the Minister, the Deputy Minister, and the Minister's other sources of advice. The important matter now was to move ahead with the task of writing an immigration bill incorporating the Committee's recommendations. To write a wholly new piece of immigration legislation including new regulations, to meet the requirements of Canadian law and public policy, and to avoid the pitfalls which beset the legislator in this field is no light task. The Interdepartmental Committee created in April 1975, with representatives of the Departments of Justice, Manpower and Immigration, External Affairs, and Secretary of State, managed it in another 12 months after the tabling of the Committee's report. The Immigration Bill had its first reading on November 22, 1976.

Looking back on this national debate on immigration and population which lasted for six months at most, it can be said now that it was a very effective one-time consultation with the immigration world, and with those Canadian institutions and organizations to whom immigration is an important matter. It did not reach "the average Canadian" for one simple reason: because the Minister and Cabinet did not trust the average Canadian to respond in a positive way on this issue, and thought this would create more trouble than it was worth. As a result of this view, they did not want to commit the funds to organize extensive public participation, and made only a minimal effort to mobilize the media on behalf of a truly national debate. The principal benefit of this approach was that the badly needed new Immigration Act was on the statute book only a little later than Mr. Andras and his colleagues originally envisaged. The principal loss was what some would regard as a golden opportunity to bring a great many individual Canadians together, to discuss the future of their vast under-populated land.

Throughout this effective but limited debate, immigration issues were discussed with much more care and in greater depth than demographic ones. As we shall see, the effort to establish a population policy or acceptable population guidelines for Canada, as well as creating a new Immigration Act, was ultimately frustrated by the provinces, by a lack of sustained concern and determination in Ottawa, and by the sheer difficulty and size of the task, which daunted many federal and provincial policy makers.

THE POPULATION QUESTION

There were two separate strands of development in the population field in Canada in the 1970s. The first was concerned with world population issues and focused on the UN World Population Conference at Bucharest in August 1974. The second related to the Department of Manpower and Immigration's mandate in the area of Canadian demographic objectives, and the Andras-Gotlieb effort in 1975 to establish a framework at least for the development of a population policy for Canada. Although the Canadian Immigration and Population Study was represented on the Interdepartmental Committee which prepared Canada's "country statement" for Bucharest, and although the preparation of the Green Paper and the statement were taking place at the same time, the two activities were carefully kept apart by the Liberal government. Canada's country state-

Table 2
Statistics Canada: Population Projections to 2001

	Assumed Total Fertility Rate for Canada by 1985	Annual Net International Migration	Population 2001
Projection A	2.6	100,000	34,611,000
Projection B	2.2	60,000	30,656,000
Projection C	1.8	60,000	28,370,000
Projection D	1.8	60,000	28,360,000

ment made no mention of the immigration and population review and forthcoming Green Paper, and the Green Paper made only one minor reference to the World Population Conference.

The Canadian Immigration and Population Study (CIPS) did make some special efforts in the population field, however. In the fall of 1973, a wholly new set of population projections was commissioned to show the effect of different annual levels of immigration on Canada's population. But in 1974, Statistics Canada produced its own comprehensive set of population projections, the first to be released in an official publication, and they became an important factor in the immigration and population debate in 1975. They were mentioned in Volume 1 of the Green Paper as part of the discussion on population growth, where they were described as yielding "a fan of possibilities for the total population of between 28.4 million and 34.6 million by 2001."[36] Four of these projections were published in Volume 3 of the Green Paper, "*Immigration and Population Statistics*," with a short preamble pointing out that they were not predictions, but were intended to show what the growth and distribution of Canada's population would be under stated assumptions.[37] Looking simply at the immigration and emigration assumptions used in the projections, it is interesting to note that they were based on the experience of the 1960s. During that decade, according to the preamble, "three-year averages for gross immigration ranged from 80,000 a year to 200,000 a year during the period of highest immigration. Estimated emigration fluctuated within a narrow range around 60,000 a year. From this analysis four immigration assumptions (ranging from 80,000 to 200,000) and one emigration assumption (60,000) were used for the projections, giving a net immigration ranging from 20,000 to 140,000."[38] The four projections are shown in Table 2. (See note 38 for an explanation of the other assumptions.)

CIPS commissioned supplementary studies to the Green Paper from two of Canada's best known demographers, Warren Kalbach of the University of Toronto and Jacques Henripin of the University of Montreal, which resulted in two interesting papers, "The Effect of Immigration on Population" and "Immigration and Language Imbalance."[39] The latter was a study of the linguistic composition of the Canadian population and the impact immigration has had or may have on the relative size of Canada's language groups. In this study, Professor Henripin concluded that the English language had been gaining ground in Canada since 1941, due mainly to the marked preference for English shown by immigrants. French, on the other hand, had been losing ground since 1950, particularly outside Quebec. Professor Henripin predicted that the absolute number of francophones in Canada would diminish in almost all provinces – Ontario was one exception – and that their comparative numbers would decline throughout the country. In the year 2000, he wrote, from 92 to 95 per cent of francophones will be concentrated in the province of Quebec. He expected that languages other than English and French would lose significance, and that around the year 2000 only 8 to 12 per cent of the Canadian population would have a language other than English or French as its mother tongue.

In his study, "The Effect of Immigration on Population" Professor Kalbach assessed the relative impact of immigration on the Canadian population as a whole, among other areas of enquiry. Various characteristics of immigrants and the foreign-born population in Canada were examined, with special emphasis on the inter-censal decade 1961–1971, because of the major changes in Canadian immigration policy during that period: the introduction of a universal non-discriminatory immigration policy in 1962 and the Canadian points system in 1967. Immigration was then examined as a component of the growth and distribution of Canada's population from 1941 to 1971 when the population nearly doubled. For the entire 30-year period, more than one fifth of the population growth in Canada was due to net immigration, which contributed most during the 1966–1971 period and least from 1951 to 1961 which were years of high fertility.

Professor Kalbach concluded, however, that immigration seemed likely to become increasingly important as a determinant of population growth in the face of Canada's declining birth rates and continuing losses through emigration.[40] In relation to the ratio of emigration to immigration he stressed the simple but often ignored fact that for every migrant stream in one direction, there is a counter-stream in the opposite direction, and pointed out that Canada has probably never done better in the sense of "holding power" than she has during the post-war period. During this period, her capacity to attract immigrants has been enhanced by increasing industrial and resource development, rapid urbanization and urban growth, and increased international recognition as an important and peaceable middle power.[41]

Among Canada's small constituency of government officials, academics and members of national organizations, churches and voluntary agencies who were beginning to develop some concern about her population problems, these problems were taking a more definite shape by the mid-seventies. No doubt the immigration and population review, the preparations for Bucharest, the briefs that were written for both and the limited public consultations on this question all contributed towards crystalizing a general concern into something more specific. The problems perceived then, not all of them seen by everyone, might be listed as follows:

1 Finding a workable answer to the question "How big should Canada's population eventually be?"
2 Ameliorating the demographic and linguistic problems of Quebec.
3 Finding an acceptable means of achieving a more balanced distribution of population in Canada, between regions and between urban and rural areas.
4 Mitigating the continuing trend towards rapid urbanization in Canada: the prospect of between 80 and 90 per cent of all Canadians living in cities by the year 2000, and the possible development of huge megalopolises such as a densely populated Quebec-Windsor corridor.
5 Protecting the Canadian environment and preserving Canada's limited supply of good agricultural land against human depredation, as well as industrial and commercial development and resource extraction.
6 Recognizing and doing something about the fact that Canada had no institution (apart from rather small sectors in one or two universities) devoted to the study and dissemination of information about Canadian population issues, no federal or provincial government departments equipped to manage this area of public policy, and no policies to manage.

It is interesting to note that concern about Canada's steadily declining fertility rate and the prospect of future population decline, which would become a major issue in the next decade, had not yet emerged.

To this list, however, can be added a major problem for the federal government alone: how to interest and involve the provinces in Canadian demographic concerns. Since hardly any of Canada's principal population difficulties could be resolved or even reduced without the provinces, they had to be brought into the act. To this end, the Minister, Bob Andras, set off on a planned tour of the provinces immediately after the Green Paper on Immigration Policy was tabled in the House of Commons on February 3, 1975.

VANISHING POPULATION GUIDELINES

The purpose of the Minister's tour was to discuss population issues, and the possible formulation of population guidelines for Canada, with the "lead ministers" the provinces had been asked to appoint. According to a working paper produced at the time by the new Demographic Policy Secretariat, "The Federal Government has proposed that a jointly elaborated consensus be developed with the provinces, setting out a framework for national demographic objectives which would include population size and rate of growth, geographic distribution, age and linguistic structure."[42] The idea was that the federal government would seek to discover provincial preferences in these areas and would then attempt to aggregate them. Thus it could be said that a rough national consensus had been established.

Most of the provinces were in no mood for this, however, and Mr. Andras had an unexpectedly cool reception. There were two exceptions: Quebec, where the demographic objectives of the federal government and the province coincided, and any effort to examine Canada's population problems was welcomed; and the then prosperous province of Alberta, where a planning and development exercise involving population, resources and land use had already begun. The other provinces were simply not prepared to get involved at this stage in trying to plan Canada's demographic future. They had too many problems of their own, and had neither the time nor the staff to work out preferences in matters of population size, rate of growth, linguistic structure, and the like.

Interviewed later on this provincial response, Mr. Andras said that he was very disappointed that the provinces did not react more positively. He had hoped for a mutual attack on the problem. Although he felt that this might change with time, most of the provinces had refused to get involved, would not take a longer view, and simply wished to concentrate on their own regional and local problems which they felt had to be solved first. Quebec and Alberta were the only provinces where the response had been positive. Nevertheless, Andras was determined that some consultation with the provinces on immigration and population objectives would take place. Therefore consultation with the provinces by the Minister of Manpower and Immigration on annual levels for immigration, as recommended by the Special Joint Committee, would be mandatory in the new immigration act. He and the Prime Minister had agreed on this and this provision was there in the Immigration Bill.[43]

The author explored the attitudes of five provinces towards this post-Green Paper effort by the federal government in a series of interviews with provincial politicians and officials in the spring of 1977. Four of these provinces – British Columbia, Alberta, Saskatchewan, and Manitoba – welcomed the federal government's initiative in trying to establish closer consultation with the provinces in immigration planning, as laid down in the new immigration bill (which received royal assent in August of that year), provided immigration was seen as an element in the total context of economic development. Only Alberta showed some interest in demographic questions, however. New Brunswick, on the other hand, was quite hostile to any involvement in immigration or population issues. The province's minister of Labour and Manpower, as well as his deputy minister, insisted that immigration was simply not on their agenda. They had too many other pressing problems, and immigration was too far off and too threatening, in the sense that it might involve them in commitments they not did want to undertake. Nor had they any desire to be involved in formulating population guidelines for Canada. Immigration must *follow* economic development, they said. Unemployment in New Brunswick was then about 14 per cent with a disturbing recent increase in the 16 to 24 age group. On this account, and because the large French-speaking community in the province would not welcome a larger influx of mainly English-speaking immigrants, New Brunswick was not interested in increasing its immigrant intake.[44]

Officials in Saskatchewan made the important point that, in their view, the Minister had appeared too soon for discussions on population questions. The Department of Manpower and Immigration, which they considered to be a very aggressive federal department, was rushing it. The Government of Saskatchewan, they said, was not hostile to the idea of population guidelines, but no one had given any real thought to the subject. A lot more work and research would be needed before they could make a useful contribution.

When discussing his unsuccessful provincial tour, Mr. Andras also mentioned that Ontario had been particularly cool to the idea of population guidelines, although he felt they might come round to this in a few year's time. But in conversation with the author somewhat later, a senior Ontario official who took part in the discussions said that he doubted this. Ontario, he said, "had had a hand in killing the idea of a population policy for Canada." All the provinces disliked the idea. It was totally unmanageable and would only have led to a huge and ineffective bureaucracy.[45]

Faced with this provincial rebuff, the federal government tried a new approach. Bilateral and multilateral meetings with provincial officials continued after the Minister's tour, but little progress was made. At one of these meetings, in December 1975, it is reported that provincial officials asked why, if this matter was so important to the federal government, had they adopted such a low profile on it? Why had the Prime Minister not addressed Parliament and the nation on Canada's population problems and the need for a population policy, and why were other ministers besides Mr. Andras not involved? It was a good question, and no clear answer seemed to be available.

The federal government then considered producing a policy statement of its own.[46] But the statement never materialized, and the government appeared to content itself, at least for the time being, with a modest "population input" in the new immigration bill, which was introduced in the House on November 22, 1976 and became law on August 5, 1977. This input consists first of an important statement of principle, the first in the list of policy objectives which forms the opening section of Part 1 of the Act and reads as follows: "... Canadian immigration policy ... shall be designed and administered in such a manner as to promote the domestic and international interests of Canada recognizing the need (a) to support the attainment of such demographic goals as may be established by the Government of Canada from time to time in respect of the size, rate of growth, structure and geographic distribution of the Canadian population."

Under the Act, the Minister is also required to lay before Parliament an annual statement specifying the number of immigrants who will be admitted "during any specific time," as well as the manner in which demographic considerations have been taken into account in determining that number. This is to be done "after consultation with the provinces concerning regional demographic needs and labour market considerations" (Part 1, Section 7), and has in fact taken place each year since the Act came into force on April 10, 1978. Further on, in Part VII of the Act, the Minister is required to "consult with the provinces respecting the measures to be undertaken to facilitate the adaptation of permanent residents to Canadian society and the pattern of immigrant settlement in Canada in relation to regional demographic requirements" (Part VII, Section 109(1)).

And that was the end of a rather remarkable effort to induce Canada's 11 governments to work together towards some medium- and long-term demographic planning and policy making. By then, the driving force behind it – the Andras-Gotlieb partnership, reinforced by Mr. Andras' strong belief that Canada badly needed a population policy – was being diverted into other channels. In September 1976, Mr. Andras became President of the Treasury Board at the Prime Minister's urgent request.[47] In May 1977, Mr. Gotlieb became Under-Secretary of State for External Affairs. During the previous year, the latter had been deeply preoccupied with the amalgamation of the Department of Manpower and Immigration and the Unemployment Insurance Commission, to form the Canada Employment and Immigration Commission (created under the Employment and Immigration Reorganization Act, 1978). From November 1976 onwards, the attention of Parliament was directly focused on a new immigration act.

The Demographic Policy Steering Group of 14 federal deputy ministers, created at the time of the publication of the Green Paper on Immigration Policy, did not survive very long, nor did the Demographic Policy Secretariat established within the Department of Manpower and Immigration. The secretariat was never adequately funded or staffed, although it might have been if a population policy or population guidelines for Canada had become a reality. During its brief existence of less than two years, the secretariat was managed by a senior official in the Department with the aid of a very small support staff which included no qualified full-time demographers.

We will now examine the new Immigration Act and Regulations, which emerged from the Department's two-year immigration and population review, the Green Paper on Immigration Policy, and the Report to Parliament of the Special Joint Committee of the Senate and the House of Commons on Immigration Policy. Canada's present concerns in the field of population and population policy are discussed in the final chapter. It would not be long before population problems once again became a serious concern of the Canadian government.

THE IMMIGRATION ACT 1976

In contrast to the failure of Canada's first effort to formulate a population policy, the outcome of this three year period of review and discussion on the immigration side was very satisfactory. The 1976 Immigration Act is an innovative, liberal, and effective piece of legislation and a vast improvement on its 1952 predecessor. In the main, it does what the Special Joint Committee and the many other Canadians who contributed to the 1975 national debate on immigration hoped it would do. As the new Minister, Bud Cullen, said when tabling the Bill in the House of Commons on November 22, 1976, "The Act explicitly affirms, for the first time, the fundamental objectives of Canadian immigration law: family reunion, non-discrimination, concern for refugees and the promotion of Canada's demographic, economic, social and cultural goals. It removes inequalities in the present law; it provides a modern flexible framework for the future development of immigration policy, and it makes future immigration levels a matter for open decision and public announcement in advance by government." One of its two prime movers, Alan Gotlieb, described it to the author as "a beautiful piece of work -logical, well-constructed, liberal, and workable." No piece of legislation is perfect and this one has several provisions which have needed or may need improvement, but on the whole it has come in for very little criticism since it became law in 1978.

The major provisions of the Act fall into certain well-defined areas: immigration policy, immigration planning and management, admission to Canada, refugees, inadmissible classes, control and enforcement, and other provisions. Brief comments in each of these areas follow. Then we

will examine the new Immigration Regulations that accompanied the Act
and which contain among other things, a revised and improved version of
the Canadian Points System.

Immigration Policy

As recommended by the Special Joint Committee, the principles of Canadian immigration policy are set out clearly in Part 1 of the Act. This
statement of principles is a completely new provision in Canadian immigration law and, according to Bob Andras, it required a considerable
effort to get it through Cabinet. Apparently some Cabinet members were
afraid the principles represented too much of a commitment, and would
be too difficult to change. Their inclusion in the Act was approved nonetheless.

The 10 principles of immigration policy relate to Canada's demographic
goals; enriching the cultural and social fabric of Canada, taking into
account its federal and bilingual character; family reunion; federal-provin-
cial-municipal and voluntary sector collaboration in immigrant settlement; the fostering of trade, commerce, tourism, cultural and scientific
activities, and international understanding; non-discrimination in immigration policy; refugee policy; economic prosperity in all Canadian
regions; the health, safety, and good order of Canadian society; and the
exclusion of persons likely to engage in criminal activity. (The principles
are listed in full in Appendix 2.) This part of the Act also makes it clear
that the admission of immigrants and the admission and stay of visitors to
Canada are matters of privilege and not of right.

Immigration Planning and Management

The Act contains several very important and completely new provisions
relating to the planning and management of Canadian immigration. They
include an ingenious and effective way to involve the provinces more
closely in planning and decision-making, and to make this process more
open to public discussion and scrutiny. Section 109 of the Act makes
consultation with the provinces mandatory for the Minister, and enables
him to enter into agreements relating to immigration with a province or a
group of provinces. Section 7 requires the Minister, after consulting the
provinces and "such other persons, organizations and institutions as he
deems appropriate," to announce annually in Parliament the number of
immigrants which the government proposes to admit during any specified
period of time, together, as mentioned earlier, with an account of "the
manner in which demographic considerations have been taken into
account in determining that number." An "Annual Report to Parliament

on Immigration Levels" has been tabled by the Minister for each year since the Act came into effect in 1978.

Admission to Canada

The Act and Regulations establish three classes of immigrants who will be admitted to Canada: first, a family class which includes the immediate family and dependent children, and parents and grandparents over 60 (or under 60 if widowed or incapable of gainful employment, or parents of any age if sponsored by a Canadian citizen); second, refugees, including Convention refugees or members of a specially designated class of refugees; and third, other applicants consisting of immigrants selected on the basis of the points system, including independent applicants and what are now called assisted relatives (i.e., more distant relatives sponsored by a family member in Canada). In addition, the Act requires all visitors and students who wish to work temporarily, or study in Canada, to obtain prior authorization abroad. Once admitted, neither visitors nor students may normally change their status. Temporary workers who change jobs and students who change their course of study without proper authorization, plus all visitors who remain in Canada beyond the period for which they were admitted, are subject to removal. (Since April 1978, all parents under 60 and their dependents have been included in the Family Class provided they are sponsored by a Canadian citizen.)

Refugees

This is one of the shorter but more complex parts of the Act. In Part 1, Canada's commitment to fulfil its international legal obligations in relation to refugees, and "to uphold its humanitarian tradition with respect to the displaced and the persecuted," is established as a fundamental principle of immigration policy for the first time in Canadian immigration law. The Act also codifies and improves existing procedures for determining refugee status. It provides for the establishment by regulation of special selection standards for refugees and for special classes of refugees. The purpose of the latter provision was to meet the needs of groups of displaced persons who are de facto refugees but do not qualify as refugees under the definition laid down in the Geneva Convention and Protocol of the Office of the UN High Commissioner for Refugees. The Act also formally establishes a Refugee Status Advisory Committee, to advise the Minister on the determination of refugee status in individual cases (replacing an unofficial committee which had existed for some years), and includes important new provisions for refugee sponsorship. (See Chapter 4 for recent developments in relation to this section of the Act and to refugee status determination generally.)

Inadmissible Classes

Part III of the Act, which deals with "Exclusion and Removal," begins with a completely revised section on inadmissible classes, known in the 1952 Act as "prohibited classes." Substantive changes here reflect far more liberal and sensible attitudes to the question of exclusion. The 1952 Act established an absolute veto on the entry of a now familiar and depressing list of those regarded as undesirable, including idiots, imbeciles or morons, the insane, epileptics, persons with tuberculosis, the dumb, blind, or otherwise physically defective, those guilty of "moral turpitude" and many others, as well as those believed to be involved in or found guilty of subversive activities, espionage, sabotage, or high treason. While some of these grounds for exclusion had been officially abandoned for some time, or had fallen into disuse, or had been used very rarely, this section remained a viable part of Canada's immigration law until 1976.

Fortunately this list has now been abolished and in its place the 1976 Act identifies certain broad classes of persons whose entry to Canada might endanger public health, welfare, order, security, or the integrity of the immigration program. Grounds for exclusion now include a degree of health impairment, judged on an individual's total health profile, that would constitute a threat to public health or safety, or cause excessive demands to be made on health or social services; the lack of means of support or evident capacity to acquire them; criminal offences of a severe character without evidence of rehabilitation; and involvement in criminal activity (such as organized crime) or in espionage, subversion, or acts of violence (such as terrorism and hijacking). The concept of moral turpitude has been eliminated at last, and all offences committed outside Canada are directly related to comparable offences under Canadian law, and are judged in relation to admissibility by the sentence that would have been imposed in this country.

Control and Enforcement

The Act introduced major changes in control and enforcement which, among other provisions, seek: (a) to improve the conduct of inquiries relating to persons subject to removal from Canada; (b) to provide new ways to protect the fundamental rights of persons subject to an inquiry; and (c) to offer – instead of deportation in all cases requiring removal, as laid down in the 1952 Act – three different instruments for removal depending on the gravity of the case. They are a deportation order, an exclusion order, and a departure notice (the latter being a recommendation of the Special Joint Committee).

The Act extended to all those who are believed to be subject to removal, whether seeking admission or already in Canada, the right to a full and impartial immigration inquiry. Inquiries are open to the public unless there are valid reasons in individual cases for not doing so. Special provisions are included to protect people who are not competent to look after their own interests, especially minor children. Every person with respect to whom an inquiry is to be held has a right to counsel and must be informed of this right. All persons against whom a removal order is made, following an inquiry, must receive an explanation of the reasons for this decision, and must be informed of their rights of appeal.

The Special Inquiry Officers responsible for the conduct of immigration inquiries under the 1952 Act, often regular immigration officers who had been given these additional responsibilities, have been replaced by a new class of specially trained officials known as "adjudicators." Unlike the sios, the adjudicators are totally removed from the process of producing evidence. Their only task is to weigh the evidence presented to them before deciding on a person's admissibility in accordance with the law.

Among the three instruments established under the Act for effecting removal from Canada, a deportation order is mandatory in the case of a permanent resident, and of any person seeking admission to or in Canada, who is found liable to removal for serious reasons. It compels a person's departure and has serious consequences for any future return to Canada. A deportation order can, however, be appealed to the Division of the Immigration and Refugee Appeal Board. An exclusion order is mandatory in the case of a person seeking to come into Canada who is found inadmissible for relatively minor reasons, i.e., temporary illness or inadequate documentation. It compels departure for a 12 month period only and the fact of having been excluded has no effect on a renewed application for admission. It is appealable in the same way as a deportation order, but in fact this occurs rarely in either case. A departure notice is not appealable, but a subsequent deportation order might be in certain circumstances.

The Act also provides for moderate penalties against employers who knowingly employ persons who are neither Canadian citizens nor permanent residents. On conviction on indictment for such an offence, employers are liable to a fine not exceeding $5,000 or imprisonment for a term not exceeding two years or both; on summary conviction, they are liable to a fine not exceeding $1,000 or imprisonment for a term not exceeding six months or both. As a way of identifying illegal immigrants, the Act also permits the Minister to direct that social insurance number cards be issued to persons other than Canadian citizens or permanent residents, indicating that such persons may be required to have the proper authorization to work in Canada (see Chapter 4).

Other Provisions

The Act contains other important provisions. Part IV, for example, concerns the Immigration Appeal Board and incorporates most of the provisions of the Immigration Appeal Board Act of 1967 which established, for the first time in Canada, a fully independent body to hear immigration appeals. In 1988, however, the Act was amended and the Board replaced by the Immigration Appeal Division of the Immigration and Refugee Board. (See Appendix 6)

The Immigration Act 1976 also contained what were then completely new provisions relating to the security aspects of immigration. These have since been superseded by the provisions of the Canadian Security Intelligence Service Act which became law on June 28, 1984. This Act established a Canadian Security Intelligence Service, and a Security Intelligence Review Committee which reviews the performance of the Service on a continuing basis. Among its other functions, the Committee conducts investigations into immigration cases, involving persons other than Canadian citizens, which may represent a threat to the security of Canada. The Act repeals the sections of the Immigration Act 1976 that deal with security matters.

Immigration legislation should always provide for the unusual case, or the case where extra compassion or special consideration is required. This has normally been done by ministerial discretion but under the new Act, which attempts to reduce this kind of discretion to a minimum, this is provided for by the well-tried system of Minister's permits. The Minister may admit anyone he sees fit to admit, or delay the departure of anyone against whom removal proceedings are contemplated, but for a period of 12 months only. He must provide Parliament with an annual report on the total number of permits issued during the preceding calendar year. The number of Minister's permits issued each year from 1975 to 1989 are shown in Table 3.

IMMIGRATION REGULATIONS 1978

The 1952 Immigration Act placed considerable reliance on the power established under the Act to make regulations in certain important areas, defined in very broad terms. One of the best known of these related, as we have seen, to "the prohibiting or limiting of admission of persons by reasons of (i) nationality, citizenship, ethnic group, occupation, class or geographical area of origin; (ii) peculiar customs, habits, modes of life or methods of holding property ..." and other grounds for unsuitability.

Table 3
Canada: Minister's Permits, 1975–1989

Year	Permits	Year	Permits
1975	21,202	1983	11,829
1976	11,281	1984	14,118
1977	10,281	1985	14,811
1978	17,121	1986	20,186
1979	9,104	1987	17,641
1980	8,231	1988	16,216
1981	12,601	1989	17,457
1982	12,585		

Almost any member of the human race could have been excluded for one or another of these reasons. Fortunately, there is nothing like this in the new Act. The 1976 Act establishes the power of the governor-in-council to make regulations, but it specifies each separate matter on which regulations are or may be required.[48] If a particular matter is not so identified, no regulations can be made without an amendment to the regulation-making powers. Section 115 of the Act specifies the precise areas in which regulations can be made. The list is a long one, but it is both useful in itself and protection against the excessive use of regulations as a tool of management.

The Immigration Regulations 1978 complement the Immigration Act and specify the conditions of admission relating to the points system, employment authorizations, visitors visas, and student authorizations, as well as the admissible classes. The revised points system is contained in Schedule 1 of the Regulations and there is also an important section on priority processing. The Regulations also expand the refugee provisions of the Act, and set out a new refugee sponsorship program. This proved very successful for the Indochinese refugee movement, and set a pattern for the management of future refugee movements. In addition to the more routine matters such as passports and travel documents, medical examinations, deposits and bonds, transportation and assistance loans, and the obligations of transportation companies, the Regulations also spell out the requirements for the conduct of inquiries by adjudicators in great detail. They also affirm the rights of appeal to the Immigration Appeal Division of those whose claim to be a Convention refugee has been denied under subsection 45(5) of the Act, and of Canadian citizens who have sponsored an application which has been refused.

Two other interesting items in the new Regulations might be mentioned, before we look in more detail at the revised points system. The first is what might be called a "Canadians first" provision whereby immigration officers may not issue an employment authorization unless they have first considered whether the prospective employer has made reasonable efforts to hire or train Canadian citizens or permanent residents for this job. The second quietly lays to rest a small but long-standing controversy in Canada as to whether immigration officers should be authorized to take fingerprints for identification, or for crime detection in special cases. This was not permitted under earlier immigration regulations. The 1966 White Paper on Immigration Policy even affirmed that there was a "national repugnance" to finger printing. Times have changed, however, crime has increased, and under the 1978 Immigration Regulations this power has finally been accorded to immigration officers.[49]

We will simply note here the significant differences between the 1978 revised version of the Canadian points system and the earlier version introduced in the Immigration Regulations of 1967. The need for an explicit selection system, as well as the interesting differences between Canada's points system and Australia's present selection system will be discussed in the next chapter. Charts describing the Canadian points system for the assessment and selection of immigrants as well as Australia's new selection system may be found in Appendix 5.

The Revised Points System

The points system, as revised in the 1978 Immigration Regulations, had the same basic structure as the 1967 version. Numerical weights are attached to a set of 10 factors (9 in the earlier version) which attempt to assess the qualifications of an applicant for landed immigrant status in the broad areas of education, training and experience, occupation and intended destination, age, knowledge of English and/or French, personal suitability, and the presence or otherwise of relatives in Canada. As a general rule, the pass mark was 60 points out of 100. Members of the family class and retired persons are not selected according to these criteria. Three of the 10 factors do not apply to assisted relatives. Convention refugees are assessed by means of the points system, to enable immigration officers to learn about their background, qualifications, and experience, but are not given a point rating.

In contrast to the earlier version, the 1978 version of the points system placed more emphasis on practical training and experience than on formal education. The maximum number of points awarded for educational attainment dropped from 20 to 12 points, while vocational training and job experience together account for a maximum of 23 points. This change had been widely recommended. The 1978 version also introduced the concepts of "designated occupation" and "designated area," to meet skill shortages and to provide a means, if only a limited one, of steering immigrants away from the major metropolitan areas.

In another interesting modification in the points system, a maximum of only 10 points was allowed for personal suitability, whereas the maximum awarded for "personal assessment" under the former system was 15. This quality is described as "the personal suitability of the person and his dependants to become successfully established in Canada based on the person's adaptability, motivation, initiative, resourcefulness and other similar qualities." The immigration officer can still recommend to the director of his Immigration Office, however, that a candidate who has failed to secure the required number of points should nevertheless be accepted, and vice versa. This change reflects a continuing trend in Canada, particularly among parliamentarians, to reduce the amount of individual discretion allowed to immigration officers, and to try to establish even more objective criteria for admission. Some would argue that this is not necessarily a wise course. In their view, nothing replaces the judgment of an experienced immigration officer who has interviewed and talked to the candidate and family. The Australians certainly believe this and, as we shall see, accord far more weight to the personal characteristics of the applicant, which they feel may be decisive in settlement and adjustment.

The points system has become a barometer for measuring the intentions of government in immigration policy and planning. New selection criteria for independent immigrants were announced in 1985. The changes will make it easier for the government to raise levels and achieve announced targets.

Refugee Sponsorship

Finally, we should mention briefly the Refugee Sponsorship Plan outlined in the new Immigration Regulations (discussed in more detail in Chapter 4). It was a major innovation, and it is important to note that it was in place in the new Act and Regulations before the Indochinese refugee movement began to accelerate alarmingly in the early summer of 1979. This occurred just after the Progressive Conservative government under Joe Clark, which took some important decisions relating to this refugee movement, had been elected to power for what proved to be a very brief nine month period. The plan represents a deliberate effort to involve the voluntary sector and the public generally in the settlement and adjustment of refugees. It provides for the sponsorship of a refugee family by any group of not less than five individual Canadian citizens, or permanent residents, who are over the age of 18 and live in the "expected community of settlement"; or by a corporation which is properly incorporated under the laws of Canada, or of any province, and has representatives in the expected community of settlement. The group or corporation must give a written undertaking to the Minister "to make provision for lodging, care, maintenance, and resettlement assistance for the Convention refugee and his accompanying dependents for a period of one year." The group or corporation must make adequate arrangements in the community of expected settlement for the reception of this refugee family and must have sufficient financial resources and expertise to carry out this undertaking. It was a very timely plan.

PROBLEMS OF MANAGEMENT

The new Immigration Act received royal assent on August 5, 1977 and came into effect on April 10, 1978. The new Immigration Regulations were approved by the governor-in-council on February 23, 1978. After the major effort of producing the new Act, a lull seemed to ensue in immigration in Canada. At the political level, it was felt that a great many matters had been settled, a very good piece of legislation had been produced, and it was time to think of other things. For immigration management, however, it was a period of intense activity. The Act had to be put to work. An extensive staff training program was launched; new manuals were provided for immigration officers; all the forms used in immigration operations in Canada and overseas had to be reviewed and revised; data systems supporting the immigration program had to be rewritten and new publicity materials written. A major public information campaign was undertaken to tell the Canadian public in general and ethnic communities in particular about the new Act, and the new cadre of adjudicators had to be recruited and placed in all the major Immigration Centres, ports of entry including international airports, and other locations.

This was only part of the general upheaval and reorganization which began in the fall of 1977. On August 14, 1977, the Employment and Immigration Reorganization Act became law, providing for the integration of the Department of Manpower and Immigration and the Unemployment Insurance Commission, in order to create a Canada Employment and Immigration Commission and a small Department of Employment and Immigration. The Commission would be a very large quasi-independent agency, which would eventually have some 26,000 employees and an elaborate regional structure. The major purpose of this move was to create a more effective, innovative, and reasonably independent institution to deal with Canada's serious problems of employment and unemployment, and to put the substantial funds of the Unemployment Insurance Commission to work in the service of this cause. A small Department of Employment and Immigration, which would in fact be part of the Commission, was brought into being to give this important new institution a voice in Cabinet. Immigration and all its works were also to serve what was seen by those who planned this development in the mid-seventies – with the Andras-Gotlieb team in a leading role – as an over-riding Canadian need.

Immigration then became part of or embedded in a vast cross-Canada organization, a good deal larger than the former Department of Manpower and Immigration, whose scope can be seen from the organization chart in Appendix 3. It has no direct voice in the top management of the Commission, which consists of a chairman, vice-chairman, and two commissioners who represent workers and employers respectively. The Immigration Group is one of *seven* similar groups within the Commission, each of which is headed by an executive director or director general. It has no authority outside Ottawa and very little in it, and no direct lines of communication with immigration officers in the regions. At the regional level, the senior immigration officer reports to the Regional Director General who reports in turn to the Chairman of the Commission. It is a wholly inadequate organization structure for the management of such an important area of public policy.

The Employment and Immigration Reorganization Act 1977 also created a Canada Employment and Immigration Advisory Council (CEIAC), which was also designed with no regard for immigration. The Council was to have a chairman and no fewer than 15 or more than 21 members to be appointed by the governor-in-council. Its members were not appointed until December 1979, due, it was said, to the lengthy consultations involved. The Act stipulates that one third of the Council's members are to be appointed after consultation with "organizations representative of workers" and one third after consultation with "organizations representative of employers." This left one third of the places on the Council (a maximum of seven) for immigration, if in fact they were used in that way, with no requirements for prior consultations. The outgoing Council – the Canada Manpower and Immigration Advisory Council and its Advisory Board on the Adjustment of Immigrants – protested strongly to the Minister and Deputy Minister (Bob Andras and Alan Gotlieb) that the proposed structure of the Council did not meet the needs of immigration in any way, let alone leave room for the varied representation immigration requires. Their protests went unheard.

The outcome on the immigration side of this poorly structured council, together with the former Liberal government's appalling patronage practices in relation to councils of this kind, have been exactly as foreseen. At the time of writing, there is no single member of the Council who can be said to be really knowledgeable in the immigration field; there are no academic specialists on the Council either in employment or in immigration; and the work of the Council in immigration so far has been undistinguished to say the least. As part of this completely inadequate scenario, it might be mentioned that the Immigration Group within the Commission has no links to the Council and no regular connection with it of any kind. The contrast between these arrangements and the way advisory councils have been run in Australia is striking. (This matter will be discussed again in the final chapter.)

The Liberal governments of Lester Pearson and Pierre Trudeau, governing for close to 21 years with only one brief interruption in 1979 (until the Trudeau government was defeated by the Progressive Conservatives under Brian Mulroney in September 1984), showed much greater concern for the liberality and effectiveness of immigration policy and law than they did for the needs of immigration management. The concerns and attitudes of the able Andras-Gotlieb team are unfortunately typical of the Liberal position in this area of public policy. Since the mid-sixties, immigration has served other causes. Three different departments or agencies have been responsible for it during the post-war period: the Department of Citizenship and Immigration from 1950 to 1965, the Department of Manpower and Immigration from 1966 to 1977 and the Canada Employment and Immigration Commission from 1977 onwards.

Today, the responsibilities involved in immigration management in Canada are split in four ways. First, they are divided between the federal government and the provinces under Section 95 of the British North America Act 1867 (although this shared jurisdiction is only now becoming a reality with the passage of the new Immigration Act in 1976). Secondly, the responsibilities of the federal government relating to the short and longer term settlement and adjustment of immigrants are divided between the Commission and the Department of the Secretary of State, under an agreement arrived at between that department and the Department of Manpower and Immigration in 1966-1967. Under this short-sighted and mistaken arrangement, it was agreed that the Department of Manpower and Immigration would be primarily responsible for the individual immigrant worker and his family, providing reception services and employment and family counselling to assist in their early settlement in the community. Manpower and Immigration would also pay for the cost of language training for adult immigrants in the labour force, where it was established that the immigrant must have some knowledge of English or French; and would work with voluntary agencies where they supplemented these primary services. The Department of the Secretary of State, on the other hand, would be responsible for the longer-term social, political, and cultural integration of immigrants. The Citizenship Branch, which had been transferred to the Department of the Secretary of State in 1966 from the old Department of Citizenship and Immigration, would continue to work with the provinces and voluntary organizations to provide combined language training and citizenship classes for immigrants. In fact there would be two language training programs for immigrants, one oriented to employability and the other to the integration process generally.

Outside the field of language training, however, the Department of the Secretary of State has never been provided with the funds to carry out these responsibilities effectively and has never really shouldered the task. In 1971, the Department became responsible for the management of the new $5 million dollar multicultural policies and programs announced by the Prime Minister in October of that year. For some years, this seems to have entirely absorbed its immigration concerns, although today, a fairly substantial part of the now larger multiculturalism budget is devoted to supporting various programs and services for immigrants. The informal agreement arrived at in 1966–1967 with the Department of Manpower and Immigration, however, never led to effective joint consultation or to joint action in the immigration field. For many years, it led in fact to a federal twilight zone in the planning and development of immigrant services, since neither department felt totally responsible for immigrants in Canada, and neither initiated a process of coordination and joint development in immigrant programs. The fact that settlement services have been for so long the weakest part of immigration management in Canada is due in no small part to this agreement and its consequences.

There have been further developments in immigrant services, however. Briefly, as an outcome of the Report of a Task Force on Programs and Services for Immigrants, Migrants and Refugees, established by the Citizenship Branch of the Department of the Secretary of State in 1971–1972 and directed by the author, followed up by an interdepartmental committee working through the following year, a small Settlement Branch was created in 1973 within the Department of Manpower and Immigration. Still constrained by the division of responsibilities with the Department of the Secretary of State and very weakly funded at the outset (Canada was now in a period of increasing inflation and unemployment) the Settlement Branch has managed slowly to increase its budget, to improve reception services at points of entry, and to develop and manage several quite substantial funding programs. These include the Immigrant Settlement and Adaptation Program (ISAP), created in 1974, through which voluntary agencies providing essential services to immigrants across Canada are funded on a fee-for-service basis; and the Adjustment Assistance Program (AAP) which provides grants to immigrants and refugees needing food, clothing, shelter and other necessities, and loans for what is called "labour market access." A Settlement Grants Program and a Refugee Settlement Liaison Program were added later.

Since the creation of the Canada Employment and Immigration Commission in 1977–1978, there has been more consultation with the Department of the Secretary of State and more joint effort in the service field. But services for immigrants and refugees, particularly in the longer term, are not yet adequate in Canada mainly because they still lack overall planning, direction, and co-ordination, as well as proper funding.[50] The provision of reasonably equal services in all parts of Canada with substantial immigrant and refugee settlement has also not yet been achieved. Initial orientation programs for immigrants are still very limited in number and availability, and further improvements are needed in the provision of language training for adults and children.

The third way in which national immigration responsibilities are divided in Canada, between the federal government and the provinces and between departments and agencies, relates to the former Foreign Branch or Foreign Region of the Immigration Service. This has now been separated bodily from the Immigration Group in the Canada Employment and Immigration Commission and transferred to the Department of External Affairs. The purpose of this move was not to improve the management of immigration overseas, but to serve the cause of the integration of the foreign operations of Canadian government, mainly involving the departments of External Affairs and Industry, Trade and Commerce, as well as the former Department of Manpower and Immigration and now the new Canada Employment and Immigration Commission.

The concept of an impressive Canadian foreign service, well-managed, program-oriented, and integrated – that is, embracing all the important activities of the Canadian government overseas – was a goal of the first Trudeau administration, and a cause dear to the heart of Prime Minister Trudeau who gave it a firm, personal thrust forward. A special study of foreign service integration was commissioned by the new Trudeau government in 1968, followed in 1970 by the appointment of an Interdepartmental Committee on External Relations (ICER) at the deputy minister level to guide the integration process. Integration proceeded slowly through the seventies with functional integration — office staff, premises, and equipment for example – proving much easier to integrate than professional staffing and career development. Determined resistance to total integration was put up by the departments of Industry, Trade and Commerce and Manpower and Immigration. They argued that they had developed highly professional overseas services in their respective fields, and that this professionalism and the dedication that went with it would be lost if a total merger took place. The resistance of Industry, Trade and Commerce, however, was somewhat more successful than that of the Immigration Service, whose position within the powerful new Canada Employment and Immigration Commission certainly did not give them a strong voice in interdepartmental discussions. In any event, the Foreign Branch of the Immigration Service has now been merged with External Affairs. No-one could say today, however, that the merger as a whole has been an unqualified success.

The merger was announced in a joint press release issued on April 1, 1981, by the Secretary of State for External Affairs, Mark MacGuigan, the Minister of Employment and Immigration, Lloyd Axworthy, and the Minister of Industry, Trade and Commerce, Herb Gray, stating that some 350 foreign service personnel from the Canada Employment and Immigration Commission would shortly be transferred to the Department of External Affairs. According to the press release, this would not mean any change in the way immigration services were provided to individuals. The Department of External Affairs would simply be assuming responsibility for the delivery of immigration programs abroad. Policy development, program design, and legislative interpretation would remain with Employment and Immigration, which would continue to administer the provisions of the Immigration Act and its application at home and abroad. This would improve the career prospects of these foreign service officers and lead to "more efficient and effective foreign operations" through integration at foreign posts. The Trade Commissioner Service of the Department of Industry, Trade and Commerce (which that department had striven hard to preserve) would remain where it was, but would assume responsibility for the foreign operations of the Canadian Government Office of Tourism. The Department of External Affairs would assume management responsibility for the executive level of the foreign service and would provide program services abroad to the Canadian International Development Agency (CIDA).[51]

The loss of the Foreign Branch, and the further subdivision of immigration responsibilities which it entailed, was a bitter blow to immigration officials in Ottawa and elsewhere, although this development clearly offered some career advantages to the overseas staff. The former Foreign Branch is now the Immigration and Social Affairs Bureau of the Department of External Affairs. It is part of the Social Affairs and Programs Branch which includes two other bureaus: the Cultural and Public Information Bureau and the Federal-Provincial Relations and Francophone Affairs Bureau. In the Department's annual report for 1982–1983, immigration – simply called "Immigrants and Refugees" – rated only half a page; in 1983–1984, about two pages.

None of the five ministers (three Liberals and one Conservative) who succeeded Bob Andras before the Mulroney victory in September 1984 did anything about this fragmentation of immigration management. The ministers were Bud Cullen (September 14, 1976 to June 4, 1979) who steered the Immigration Bill through its final stages in Parliament; Ron Atkey (June 4, 1979 to March 3, 1980), Minister of Employment and Immigration in the short-lived Clark government; Lloyd Axworthy

(March 3, 1980 to August 12, 1983); and John Roberts (August 12, 1983 to September 17, 1984). The Clark government made some good decisions relating to the Indochinese refugee movement, then escalating rapidly, but the Minister, Ron Atkey, had little time to do anything else. Of the three other ministers only Lloyd Axworthy made a real contribution to the immigration field.

Mr. Axworthy was a determined and liberal minister responsible for immigration. Not particularly tactful, and not very popular with his officials since he always seemed to distrust the bureaucracy and prefer private sources of advice, he nevertheless flung himself energetically into this part of his portfolio, beavering away or inducing others to do so at some of its dilemmas and inequities. He first tackled the problem of family reunion which seemed to occupy an ever-increasing proportion of Canada's annual immigration movement.

FAMILY REUNION

In all countries of immigration, not least in Canada and Australia, family reunion has become a sacred subject which can only be handled with extreme care.[52] Hardly any Canadian politician fails to do homage to it at the appropriate moment, and every Canadian bureaucrat puts some soothing reference to it in any ministerial speech concerned with immigration. Although it is an official objective of Canadian immigration policy, family reunion is and always has been a problematical area of immigration management. This should be faced more frankly and openly than it usually has been by politicians and by ethnic groups.

In the past in Canada, the problem never lay with the immediate family of an immigrant, although the definition of the immediate family, that is precisely which members should be included in it, was always an important matter. The difficulty has been the size of the family element in the annual immigration movement and its potential for rapid escalation. In the past, the unstable element in family immigration has been the more distant relatives – the uncles and aunts, nephews, nieces, and cousins – as well as brothers and sisters and their spouses and families whom immigrants wished to sponsor. This element in family reunion could easily escalate into a flood. It should be noted here that, in the past, Australia kept a tighter rein on the large potential influx of relatives than Canada, although this has changed markedly under the Hawke government which is giving family reunion high priority.

Another difficult aspect of family reunion is that the demand for it is so uneven among national groups. Some nationalities wish to sponsor large numbers of relatives; others only a few, if any. In an immigration movement like Canada's, which has achieved a good but always precarious balance among world regions, a large movement of relatives from a few countries can make that balance unattainable. In addition, a large family element in an annual immigration movement limits the space available for independent applicants, who may have no family connections overseas to assist them. It also limits the choice of skills and talents available to the country of immigration. Relatives of all kinds are in general less qualified than independent applicants, and may also have skills which are not in current demand. Furthermore, it is difficult to influence their choice of destination in Canada, that is, to steer them away from the major metropolitan centres, since they naturally tend to settle where their sponsors are. None of this says that there should not be a regular policy of admission of both close and more distant relatives, but it does say that the policy must be managed with care. In earlier days, a rough rule of "not more than 50 per cent" was regarded by immigration officers as a useful guideline for the total family element in an annual immigration movement.

Surprisingly, however, in the kind of unexpected development which makes immigration and its consequences so hard to predict, it is not the assisted relatives whose numbers have escalated in the last few years, but the family class itself. Since the mid-seventies, both the independent and assisted relative classes have declined sharply while the family class has steadily increased. This situation is described in the Annual Report to Parliament on Immigration Levels 1981, the third "Levels" report to Parliament as required under the new Immigration Act: "The family class is now the predominant part of the immigration movement and has been so since 1976. Between 1970 and 1975, immigrants in the family class increased from 32,000 to 64,000 or from 22 to 34 percent of the total. Family class arrivals were just under 47,000 in 1979, which was 42 percent of the total intake for that year." The decline in the number of assisted relatives was attributed partly to the fact that the family class had been enlarged under the 1978 Immigration Regulations, and partly because more of those who formerly entered as assisted relatives were now qualifying as independent immigrants. One important consequence of these developments has been that, because of the admission of substantial numbers of both relatives and refugees, the space available for independent applicants has been relatively small, at a time when skilled immigrants of certain kinds are in increasingly high demand in Canada once again.

The Immigration Regulations 1978 made generous provision for the family class. From the beginning of the debate on the immigration bill, a small group of Liberal MPs had worked hard, mainly through the Liberal caucus, to get as generous an interpretation of family reunion as possible. These efforts are reflected in the Act and Regulations. Their motives? Perhaps a combination of genuine conviction that only this approach would really satisfy human rights requirements and foster good community relations in Canada, along with a desire to please ethnic groups and respond positively to continuing pressures from them on this subject. No doubt they also believed this approach would fit in well with the Liberal government's multiculturalism policy and would, as usual, benefit the Liberal Party at the polls. In any event, those who framed the new Immigration Regulations were aware that the current climate in Cabinet and caucus in relation to family reunion was a positive one.

One of Mr. Axworthy's first acts as Minister of Employment and Immigration was to refer the question of the large numbers of family class immigrants then being admitted to the new Canada Employment and Immigration Advisory Council, which met for the first time in January 1980. The Council, which responded with reasonable speed, favoured a cutback in the size of the family reunion element, but showed no awareness whatever of the political complexities of the issue. Their principal recommendations were that the concept of family reunion should be sacred, but should apply only to the close, dependent relatives of the sponsor; and that the obligations of the sponsors towards their relatives should be more clearly defined and more effectively enforced. They also found what they called "an inordinate number of exceptional situations" leading to admission by Minister's permit, a device which they felt was superfluous. No sympathy was expressed in their report for the human dilemmas which might be caused by a reduction in the number of relatives admitted. No understanding was shown of the value of a system of Minister's permits even if used in a more restricted way.[53]

The Council's report was later set aside and for the time being the matter of family reunion was left to be monitored in the annual reports to Parliament on immigration levels. Between 1980 and 1984, landings in the family class have averaged about 50,000 a year. In 1983, family class landings totalled 48,698 which represented about 55 per cent of the total movement of 89,157.[54] The 1986 Annual Report to Parliament on Immigration Levels reported that when family class landings are added to the landings of spouses and other dependants of immigrants in other categories, almost 75 per cent of the total is attributable to immediate family migration. An important new element may have to be taken into account in relation to the family class, however: Canada's future population needs. If immigration levels need to be increased substantially from now on, in order to mitigate the certain prospect of a declining Canadian population after the turn of the century, the family class may prove to be an unexpected asset. A sure and stable source of immigrant supply which requires no promotion, it may form the backbone of the larger immigration movements of the future. This question is discussed further in the final chapter.

While handing this difficult assignment to the Canada Employment and

Immigration Advisory Council, Mr. Axworthy evidently decided to set up a task force of his own to investigate current problems in immigration. Accordingly, a Task Force on Immigration Practices and Procedures was appointed in September 1980, consisting entirely of lawyers who were mainly well-known to the Minister. Their mandate was to advise him on "the apparent objectives of the Immigration Act 1976 and on the extent to which these objectives are being met under existing regulations, procedures and practices ..." The members of the task force were W.G. Robinson (chairman), barrister, Vancouver; Carter Hoppe, barrister, Toronto; David Mantas, barrister, Winnipeg; Ed Ratushny, law professor, Ottawa; and Manon Vennat, barrister, Montreal. It was a Liberal and Axworthy task force and did not last beyond his ministry, although its chairman, W.G. Robinson, prepared a special report for the Minister on *Illegal Immigrants in Canada*, submitted in June 1983, and subsequently became chairman of the Long-Term Illegal Migrant Review Committee. He resigned after the defeat of the Liberal government in September 1984. The report is discussed in Chapter 4.

During its short life, the Task Force on Immigration Practices and Procedures produced three useful reports: *Domestic Workers on Employment Authorizations* (April 1981), a study of the working conditions of foreign domestic workers and the opportunities or lack of them, available to these workers to achieve landed immigrant status; *The Exploitation of Potential Immigrants by Unscrupulous Consultants* (April 1981), a discussion paper with a listing of the options available for better control in this area; and *The Refugee Status Determination Process* (November 1981).[55] The latter, which is the most substantial of the three reports, is also discussed in Chapter 4.

IMMIGRATION PLANNING

One of the most important innovations introduced in the Immigration Act 1976 was a new process of immigration planning, which involved annual consultations by the Minister with the provinces and with "such other persons, organizations and institutions as he deems appropriate," and which lead to the annual announcement of the number of immigrants to be admitted during a specified period. This specified period was first interpreted as the following year, but after 1981, the Australian idea of "three-year rolling programs" was adopted and three-year projections began. At the time of writing, an Annual Report to Parliament on Immigration Levels (now described as "Future Immigration Levels") for the eight years from 1978 to 1986, have been tabled in the House of Commons. They are very useful reports, improving in quality and density of information in each succeeding year, and they are now accompanied by an equally useful background paper.

The Immigration Group within the Canada Employment and Immigration Commission has worked out a detailed annual immigration levels cycle, a work schedule for the months leading up to the Minister's statement in Parliament. First a spring Cabinet submission is prepared in January and February, when work is also started on a basic document for the forthcoming consultations (entitled "Immigration Levels: Basic Federal Considerations") and other supporting documents. In March and April, the spring Cabinet submission is considered by the deputy ministers of the Ministry of State for Social Development and then by the Social Development and Priorities and Planning committees of the Cabinet where, if all goes well, it is approved. At this time, letters and consultative documents go out from the Minister to his provincial counterparts, and to a larger number of non-governmental organizations (NGO)s and groups. In May, June, and July, consultations take place with the provinces and replies begin to come in from the NGOs. In July, work begins on the preparation of a fall Cabinet submission and in August a draft annual report is prepared. In September, the draft goes to the departments of External Affairs, Secretary of State and National Health and Welfare, and to the Royal Canadian Mounted Police, for comment. The fall Cabinet submission is also considered by the senior officials of the Ministry of State for Social Development. In October, the fall Cabinet submission is submitted to the Social Development and Priorities and Planning committees of Cabinet for their approval. On November 1, or earlier, the Annual Report to Parliament on Immigration Levels is tabled in the House of Commons.[56]

This planning and consultative process is fairly complicated and time-consuming. Is it worth it? What purposes do the tabling of the Annual Report and the consultations which precede it really serve? Do the consultations have any significant influence on the announced levels and how do the levels themselves relate to the actual numbers of immigrants admitted?

It should be said first that the annual reports so far do have weaknesses. They tell us very little, for example, about the demand side of immigration and nothing at all about our overseas immigration service. (From reading these reports, one might not know that it even exists.) Thus we learn nothing about the current volume of applications for landed immigrant status in different parts of the world; or about the present availability or otherwise of professional and skilled workers; or about the present opportunities and difficulties of our overseas service in attempting to meet or diffuse the demand to come to Canada. These weaknesses could easily be remedied.

Table 4
Canadian Immigration: Projected Levels and Immigration by Calendar Year, 1979–1984

Projected Levels		Immigration by Calendar Year	
1979	100,000	1979	112,096
1980	120,000	1980	143,117
1981	130 – 140,000	1981	128,618
1982	130 – 135,000	1982	121,147
1983	134 – 144,000		
1984	130 – 145,000		
1983	105 – 110,000	1983	89,157
1984	115 – 125,000		
1985	120 – 135,000		
1984	85 – 90,000	1984	88,000

Source: Canada Employment and Immigration Commission.
Note: In November 1981, it was decided to move to a three-year planning cycle with annual reviews and adjustments. In November 1984, in the light of an imminent review of immigration policies and programs, the Mulroney government announced that it would make only a one-year projection.

Another major weakness lies in the treatment of the demographic material in the reports which has been very bland so far and in the words of the authors, "passive" – a good description. The reason for this is that, despite appearances, until very recently demographic considerations have *not* been taken into account by Cabinet or anyone else in the annual computing of these immigration levels. But it seems certain that from now on they will have to be, and that the demographic section of the Annual Report will have to be more than background material.

How do the projected annual immigration levels compare with the number of immigrants actually admitted? Eight years is too short a time to come to any firm conclusion on this question, but it looks at present as if the performance is distinctly mixed, as Table 4 shows.

Members of the Immigration Group in Ottawa believe that the immigration levels projections will work, i.e., will be a useful planning tool and will correspond reasonably well to actual admissions, in conditions of economic stability. But they are likely to be very vulnerable in conditions of economic instability, and may not hold up in the face of economic downturn. The reason for the sharp decline in admissions in 1982–1983, for example, and the disparity between these figures and the announced immigration levels for those and the following years, was a decision announced by the Minister of Employment and Immigration on May 1, 1982. Due to Canada's increasingly high levels of unemployment, it was decided to impose a freeze on the recruiting of any future independent immigrants, unless they had a validated job offer from a Canadian employer. Following this decision, the number of independent immigrants declined sharply. By a further decision of Cabinet, no reduction was made in the family class or in refugee admissions.

What value, then, do the annual statements on immigration levels have, if the levels themselves can be pushed aside so easily? There is no doubt that they have a valuable public relations effect, in good times and bad. They give the impression that this difficult and often unpredictable area of public policy is well under control. They add greatly, therefore, to the necessary political element of good management in this field. In addition, the immigration planners may get better with more experience, and their forecasting may become more accurate. If their forecasts are reasonably accurate, there is no doubt that the announced immigration levels are very useful for certain federal departments and agencies, for the provinces and for overseas staff planning in immigration. The information and background material provided also have educational value in an area where public information has been very limited. Above all, they have considerable value as a shared program in which many people and institutions are involved, and as an easily understood statement of government objectives in immigration.

One further question might be considered. Apart from discussions with the provinces, how useful are the annual national and regional consultations on the forthcoming immigration levels statement, other than as a way of legitimizing government policies and educating the informed public on immigration and related areas of public policy? Do they really contribute to policy development? Until recently, the national consultations have taken place in an exchange of letters, together with the submission of briefs in some cases. In the regions, on the other hand, annual meetings have taken place with non-governmental organizations which can discuss all aspects of the forthcoming immigration levels, but tend to focus on refugee and settlement matters, because that is what these organizations are primarily interested in. In addition, there have been annual meetings with the Standing Conference of Canadian Organizations Concerned for Refugees.

It is interesting to note that in 1984, approximately 115 national groups and organizations were contacted, but only 25 replied and, according to CEIC, their replies were of mixed quality. Apparently the most useful contributions still come from the provinces, government departments and agencies, and the larger interest groups such as business and labour. This is no doubt due to the fact that immigration and immigration planning are very technical questions. Probably only government institutions and large interest groups have been able to afford the staff or staff time to do a good paper or prepare a set of recommendations in this area. However, the consultative process involved in determining immigration levels is now changing, becoming more elaborate and better organized, and involving meetings and seminars at the national level. In 1986, some 650 NGOs were consulted at the national, regional, and local levels, and about 40 Canadian

academics with expertise in aspects of immigration were invited to participate in consultations. In addition, changes in the points system (discussed
in the final chapter) which came into effect on January 1, 1986 introduced
a new factor called *levels control* for which up to 10 extra points may be
awarded. This factor is intended to help ensure that actual landings are
numerically consistent with announced immigration levels. As of October
30, 1986, the full 10 units of assessment are being awarded under the levels
control factor. This is consistent with the government's announced intention to achieve the higher end of the 1987 immigration levels planning
range which is 115,000 to 125,000.

It will be seen that the period from 1972 to 1984 was one of very
significant growth and development in Canadian immigration. There were
important developments too in refugee policy, illegal or undocumented
immigration, and multiculturalism which will be discussed in later chapters. It was a very necessary process of modernization and liberalization in
which the cornerstone was the new Immigration Act. As we shall see in the
next chapter, a very similar process was taking place in Australia during
these years. Today, immigration in Canada is entering a new phase and
another serious review of immigration and population is under way. This
time, the major focus is on Canada's present and future demographic
needs and their implications for immigration which could be momentous.

CHAPTER THREE

Australian Immigration Policy and Management, 1972–1986

In Australia, the McMahon Liberal–National Country Party government was defeated on December 2, 1972, and a Labor government was elected after 23 years in opposition. The new government, under Gough Whitlam, had a majority of nine in the House of Representatives, but there was no Senate election in December 1972 and the party standings in the Senate at that point were: Australian Labor Party (ALP) 26, Liberal–National Country Party (LNCP) 26, Democratic Labor Party (DLP) 5, and Independents 3. The new government was totally dependent, therefore, on the DLP and the Independents to get its legislative program through Parliament. On May 18, 1974, in the face of early efforts by the Opposition in the Senate to delay supply, the Prime Minister called a double dissolution. The Labor government was returned to power in the 1974 election, but its majority in the House of Representatives was reduced to five, and it still did not get a majority in the Senate where the situation, if anything, worsened (ALP 29, LNCP 29, Independents (both former Liberals) 2.) Nevertheless, the Whitlam government went ahead with a major reform program on a wide front, arousing great enthusiasm and high expectations among its supporters and considerable hostility and anxiety elsewhere.[1]

It is against this background of parliamentary instability and, what soon proved to be a period of intense and turbulent politics leading to the decline and dismissal of the Whitlam government by the Governor General in 1975, that the remarkable changes in immigration during this administration must be seen. The changes were largely the work of the Prime Minister and his close advisers, aided initially by his first Minister for Immigration, A.J. Grassby.

Gough Whitlam was a highly articulate, able, and forceful prime minister with a charismatic personality and great eloquence, but a tragic lack of diplomatic skills. His interest in immigration derived directly from his passionate concern for foreign affairs. He was not interested in population policy, nor in the present or potential contribution of migrants to the Australian economy. He was not particularly concerned about questions of settlement, except as they related to equal rights and non-discrimination, and he was not well informed about nor really interested in the technical problems of immigration management. Foreign affairs and Australia's image abroad, particularly in the Pacific region, were a profound concern, however, and he gave this area of public policy top priority and direct personal attention, taking on the portfolio of Foreign Minister as well as that of Prime Minister in 1972.[2]

THE DEMISE OF THE WHITE AUSTRALIA POLICY

When sworn in on December 5, Mr. Whitlam said the change of government provided a new opportunity to reassess the whole range of Australian foreign policies and attitudes, with a view to developing more constructive, flexible, and progressive approaches to a number of issues. "Our thinking," he said, "is towards a more independent Australian stance in international affairs and towards an Australia which will be less militarily oriented and not open to suggestions of racism, an Australia which will enjoy a growing standing as a distinctive, tolerant, co-operative and well-regarded nation not only in the Asian and Pacific region but in the world at large."[3] Five months later, when this reassessment had taken place, the Prime Minister made a foreign policy statement in the House of Representatives from which it was clear that racial discrimination, which had been a major feature of Australia's immigration policy throughout this century, was no longer acceptable and would be removed:

One of the crucial ways in which we must improve our global reputation is to apply an aspiration for equality at home to our relations with the peoples of the world as a whole. Just as we have embarked on a determined campaign to restore the Australian aborigines to their rightful place in Australian society, so we have an obligation to remove methodically from Australia's laws and practices all racially discriminatory provisions, and from international activities any hint or suggestion that we favour policies, decrees or resolutions that seek to differentiate between peoples on the basis of their skin. As an island nation of predominantly European inhabitants situated on the edge of Asia, we cannot afford the stigma of racialism.[4]

Thus the White Australia policy came to an end — eleven years after Mrs. Ellen Fairclough, then Canada's Minister of Citizenship and Immigration, tabled new Immigration Regulations making Canada's immigration policy universal and nondiscriminatory; and eight years after Lyndon

B. Johnson, President of the United States after the assassination of John F. Kennedy, signed the 1965 Kennedy Amendments to the Immigration Act into law, achieving the same objective when the amendments came into force in 1968. It is sometimes suggested that this Whitlam move had no particular significance, since it was simply the final blow in a slow process of demolition which began in the 1950s. But this is to diminish an act of leadership in a climate of very considerable uncertainty within the major political parties in the early seventies, on the subject of the White Australia policy and on the objectives of immigration in general. In the uneasy months leading up to the December 1972 election, when it became increasingly likely that the Australian Labor Party would win, immigration policy became front page news on more than one occasion. In a speech delivered in Perth in January 1972, Dr. A.J. Forbes, Minister for Immigration in the McMahon government, had delivered a major attack on the ALP's immigration policies, no doubt in anticipation that immigration would become an election issue. If the ALP's policies were introduced, Dr. Forbes said, there would be a progressive escalation of non-European migration to Australia. If assisted passages were made available to non-European migrants as they proposed, he predicted that assisted migration from Britain would be cut by more than 60 per cent and migration from countries such as Germany, the Netherlands, Finland, Sweden, Denmark, Norway, France, Switzerland, the United States, and Latin America would be virtually eliminated.[5]

Liberal and Country Party politicians appeared at this point to be holding on to the White Australia policy defiantly, but with an evident sense of standing on shifting ground. In March 1971, Phillip Lynch, Dr. Forbes's predecessor, produced what was intended to be a definitive statement on the Government's immigration policy (essentially on White Australia), emphasizing its evolutionary approach to and progressive relaxation of a total ban on non-European migration. The statement had been carefully drafted in the Department of Immigration. Entitled "The Evolution of a Policy," it was an unconvincing and defensive piece of work. It failed to discuss the central issue of racial discrimination, avoided the critical question of Australia's image in the international community, and assumed a tone of benevolent liberality almost totally belied, at that point, by the facts of the case.[6]

Dr. Forbes continued to take the same approach in a speech to the North Sydney Federal Electorate Conference on July 31, 1972, when he warned of the danger of "self-perpetuating enclaves and undigested minorities," and stressed that what Australians wanted was a homogeneous society, that is, "a cohesive integrated society, one that is essentially undivided, without permanent minorities and free of avoidable tensions." The Government was therefore correct in following its present course of prudent realism and would not depart from it. "We have not abandoned our essential policies," he said, "nor do we intend to do so."

On this occasion, the Minister listed the numbers of non-Europeans and persons of mixed descent actually admitted to Australia under existing immigration regulations in 1971. The ban on non-European migration was certainly not total at that point, but the numbers admitted were still very small. Of the 155,525 settlers from all sources who arrived in Australia in 1971, 2,696 were non-Europeans and 6,054 were persons of mixed descent. Among the former group, 707 persons with a total of 1,125 dependents had been admitted on the basis of their qualifications. Of these, 177 were medical practitioners and 153 were teachers. The main nationalities were Indians (639), Malaysians (450), Chinese (185), and Filipinos (158). In addition, 916 non-Europeans already in Australia were granted resident status. More than 80 per cent of the 6,054 persons of mixed descent admitted in 1971 were admitted on the basis of family relationships with residents of Australia. They came from India (2,088), Ceylon (813), Mauritius (737), Burma (716), and South Africa (410).[7]

It is interesting to look at comparable figures for Canada where, as we know, a universal, nondiscriminatory immigration policy had been in operation since 1962. 1971 was a year of low intake in immigration; only 121,900 immigrants were admitted. Nevertheless the numbers of what Australia would then have regarded as non-Europeans were substantial. Table 5 shows the largest groups admitted to Canada in 1971 from countries outside Europe, the Middle East, and North and South America. (The figures are taken from the "Country of Former Residence" category in Canada's annual immigration statistics. Since Canada does not seek to define "ethnic origin," a few immigrants of European or partly European origin may have been included in some of these totals.)[8]

After the 1969 Commonwealth election, and while John Gorton was Prime Minister, a lesser aspect of the White Australia policy had arisen to embarrass the Government. This concerned the question of racial discrimination in the allocation of assisted passages to British citizens wishing to migrate to Australia – part of the wider question of the denial by Australia up to that point of assisted passages to non-Europeans. Britain now had sizeable numbers of citizens of West Indian and Asian origin. Could Australia discriminate between them and other British citizens in the allocation of assisted passages (the famous £10 passages which made a considerable difference to would-be migrants)? In November 1970, the British Race Relations Board made an official request to the Australian government to reconsider its approach to the question, and specifically asked for an assisted passage for a Mr. Jan Augustine Allen, a computer engineer, aged 36, his French-born wife and their three young children. Mr. Allen was born in Jamaica, but was now a British citizen. The British

Table 5
Canada: Leading Countries of Origin of Immigrants, 1971*

Country of Origin	No. Immigrating to Canada	Country of Origin	No. Immigrating to Canada
West Indies	10,843	Africa (n.e.s.)**	1,220
India	5,313	Pakistan	968
Hong Kong	5,009	Japan	883
Philippines	4,180	Taiwan	761
Asia (n.e.s.)*	2,912	South Africa	729

Source: Department of Manpower and Immigration
 *Outside the Middle East and North and South America.
**Countries not elsewhere specified.

case was thought to be made somewhat stronger by the fact that Britain, through an agreement due to expire in 1972, paid £150,000 a year towards the assisted passage scheme. The British Prime Minister, Edward Heath, was due to meet John Gorton at a Commonwealth conference in Singapore in January 1971, and it was confidently expected that they would discuss the matter there.

The Australian government, however, chose to take a firm stand on the issue and to take umbrage at this intervention by the Race Relations Board. On January 7, 1971, it made an official reply to the Board through the British Foreign and Commonwealth Office. The reply, it was reported, had been prepared after long discussions between Mr. Gorton, the then Foreign Minister Mr. McMahon, the Attorney General Mr. Hughes, and Mr. Lynch. The basic question, the Australians said, was whether any British instrumentality could interfere with the sovereign rights of Australia to determine those migrants to whom the Australian government was prepared to grant assisted passage. Their answer was: "The Australian government cannot consider itself bound in this or other aspects by statutory bodies set up under the laws of other countries." And there the matter had to rest for the time being.

Unfortunately for Canberra, anxious at that point to play down the harsher aspects of the White Australia policy and to convey an impression of totally reasonable immigration management, a State Minister for Immigration, Mr. Vance Dickie of Victoria, was in London at the time as head of a "Migrate to Victoria" campaign, and he had no inhibitions about calling a spade a spade. Interviewed by *The Guardian* on the subject of assisted passages, Mr. Dickie said that Australia deliberately rejected "99 per cent of all people with dark blood, even if only one member of their family has dark blood," adding that only in a few very special cases would non-Europeans be allowed into Australia on the assisted passage scheme. Asked on a BBC public affairs program at the time if this was a racialist policy, Mr. Dickie said, "I suppose if you want to call it that, I suppose that is exactly what the attitude of the Australian people is." Sir Alex Downer, a former Minister for Immigration and the incumbent Australian High Commissioner to Britain then entered the fray, obviously trying to put things in a more acceptable light. On the eve of leaving London to join the Australian team at a Commonwealth conference in Singapore, he spoke with the press and stressed that since 1956 it had been possible for non-Europeans within certain classes, including the close relatives of persons already resident in Australia, to be admitted to Australia for residence. Following a major policy review in 1966, he said, more than 12,000 non-Europeans had been admitted or granted resident status, as well as some 20,000 persons of mixed descent. However, at no time had these people been eligible for assisted passages.[9]

Discrimination between persons of European and non-European descent in the award of assisted passages to Australia did not last much longer, since the Liberal-National Country Party Coalition lost the Commonwealth election in December 1972 and the Whitlam government took over. Before this, the McMahon government did not yield on this question, although there was pressure from the churches and other groups in Australia to do so. Since the refusal of an assisted passage to Mr. Allen and the intervention of the British Race Relations Board, no ministerial discretion was exercised in the matter, either by Mr. Lynch or Dr. Forbes, except in cases where the non-European family member was an adopted child. In August 1971, however, following a submission from the Department of Immigration in which a number of sample cases were analysed, Cabinet agreed to a return to "a prudent and limited exercise of administrative discretion in cases of requests for assisted passages where the breadwinner is fully European and the wife is non-European or of mixed descent" (but not, be it noted, vice versa). This discretion would be reserved to the Minister personally and to very senior officers in Canberra, and only families of "positive value to Australia" would be approved. It was envisaged that no more than 50 families might be approved in the ensuing 12 months. The number might grow gradually in later years, but would be kept under close scrutiny.[10]

THE AUSTRALIAN LABOR PARTY AND WHITE AUSTRALIA

We have seen Liberal and Country Party politicians trying to stand firm on the White Australia policy in a world that was increasingly hostile to it. Where did the ALP stand on this question in the early seventies? They were by no means wholehearted abolitionists. Some leading members, notably Don Dunstan, ALP Premier of South Australia, had worked hard to change the party's attitude and platform, but others still had strong reservations. The ALP had been a vocal supporter of White Australia for a long time, perhaps its most vocal supporter.[11] Racial exclusiveness in immigration – white only and British if possible – had been a central feature of Labor policies of protectionism and nationalism; and to many no doubt it still seemed dangerous to abandon it. However, with Gough Whitlam at the helm from 1967 onwards, and in a mood of optimistic reformism as the prospect of electoral victory drew nearer, the views of the liberal element were prevailing.

Explicit reference to the White Australia policy had been removed from the party's platform in 1965, but a further critical step was taken at the party's conference at Launceston in Tasmania in June 1971. Prior to the Launceston conference, the ALP's position on immigration policy read as follows:

Convinced that increased population is vital to the future development of Australia, the Australian Labor Party will support and uphold a vigorous and expanding immigration program administered with sympathy, understanding and tolerance. The basis of such policy will be:
(a) Australia's national and economic security;
(b) the welfare and integration of all its citizens;
(c) the preservation of our democratic system and balanced development of our nation;
(d) the avoidance of the difficult social and economic problems which may follow from an influx of peoples having different standards of living, traditions and cultures.

At Launceston, this statement was redrafted and two important new clauses were added, so that the statement now read:

The Australian Labor Party supports an immigration policy administered with sympathy, understanding and tolerance. The basis of such a policy shall include:

(a) Australia's national and economic security;
(b) the capacity to provide employment, housing, education and social services;
(c) the welfare and integration of all her citizens;
(d) the preservation of our democratic system and the balanced development of our nation;
(e) the avoidance of the difficult social and economic problems which may follow from an influx of peoples having different standards of living, traditions and cultures;
(f) the avoidance of discrimination on any grounds of race or colour of skin or nationality.

Thus non-discrimination and the capacity to meet migrant employment, welfare, and other needs were added, and there was no longer any reference to supporting and upholding a vigorous and expanding immigration program. It was the Launceston conference, therefore, followed by the policies and programs of the Whitlam government, which brought to an end the bipartisan approach to immigration policy of the major political parties in Australia, which had been such a notable feature of the post-war period up to that point.

The ALP's critical 1971 decision to go for non-discrimination, meaning not only a universal immigration policy applied even-handedly to all nationalities, but also the removal of all traces of British preference in immigration and citizenship policies and practices, had other aspects as well. They related first to numbers and then to immigration management. From this time onwards, it seems to have been generally accepted within the ALP that these major policy changes would be accompanied by a substantial reduction in the number of migrants admitted to Australia for permanent settlement. There would also be changes in selection procedures, putting more emphasis on family reunion and much less on the deliberate government recruitment of qualified migrants.

Reduced intake was seen as vital. Dr. Forbes was quite wrong in believing, if he had believed it, that under a Labor government there would be "a progressive escalation of non-European migration to Australia." During its three years in office and with three different ministers for immigration, the Labor government progressively reduced migrant intake from 140,000 in 1972–1973 to 50,000 in 1975. If total numbers were reduced, the groups of migrants coming in from non-European countries would inevitably be small, despite a universal immigration policy. Since the numbers of non-Europeans already in Australia were also small, the movement of non-European relatives would be modest also.

This approach was used in a very explicit way to sell the ending of the White Australia policy to the party's hard-liners, and to reassure them that, if the ALP was elected in the forthcoming federal election, there would be no inrush of Asian or other migrants to take jobs away from Australians. But it also reflected a new conviction that a steadily increasing population – the basic premise of Australia's post-war immigration policy thus far – was definitely not what Australia needed at this stage. Gough Whitlam himself was far more concerned with building what he saw as a really responsible, caring society, both domestically and internationally, and with creating an effective and equitable economic system which would produce a high standard of living for all Australians, than he was with population growth and the large-scale development it might ultimately bring. He was questioned on this subject by the press on a number of occasions before and after taking office in December 1972.

On October 14, 1971, in a television program called "This Day Tonight," Mr. Whitlam was asked: "If you win the election next year, in your administration would there be more or less non-European migrants coming to Australia?" He replied, "There would be fewer. But there would probably be a decrease in the number of migrants coming to Australia anyhow." On October 7, 1972 in an editorial on immigration, the Sydney *Morning Herald* wrote:

The reasons behind the Labor Party's policy of phasing out Government recruitment of migrants are plain enough. Mr. Whitlam faced problems within his own party and in the electorate generally on the issue of coloured immigration. He has been represented by his opponents as an advocate of a large rise in coloured immigration, particularly from Asia. As he has obviously come to recognize, this is a politically dangerous label to wear. Mr. Whitlam did not need to be terribly perceptive to realize that he could not afford to run foul of the kind of sentiment involved so close to an election. Hence Labor's policy of cutting down immigration from all sources. Mr. Whitlam was commendably frank about it. Asked whether the policy got him "off the hook" on coloured migration, he replied, "Yes, for those to whom this is a great preoccupation – yes, it does, it does ..."

In addition to a firm intention, before the 1972 election, to reduce migrant intake, other ideas were simmering in Mr. Whitlam's mind on the subject of immigration management. He had always distrusted the Department of Immigration and had associated it directly with Arthur Calwell's racist ideas and policies. In an interview with the author, he described this department as "racist, sexist, narrow, and hidebound."[12] It was a weak department, he said, without good people, and was simply not doing a good job. It pre-empted all the responsibility for migrants, but did very little for them. It had no real expertise in settlement and nothing to offer migrants in the field of community services, health or education. In his view, the Department was totally wedded to the White Australia policy in all its ramifications.

It is interesting to note here that one of Mr. Whitlam's closest advisers and his Principal Private Secretary from 1972 to 1974 was Dr. Peter Wilenski, formerly of the Department of Foreign Affairs, who had spent some time in Canada, both as a graduate student at Carleton University in the mid-sixties, and working at the Australian High Commission in Ottawa in 1968–1969. While in Canada, Dr. Wilenski studied Canadian public policy and the Canadian public service with great interest and was impressed with the calibre of the latter, with some of the new institutions in Ottawa, and with some recent developments in the public policy field. He was particularly interested in the Canadian Department of Manpower and Immigration and the major investment being made in Canada, at that

time, in manpower training, mobility, and other programs.[13] He thought
this might be a useful model for Australia, and no doubt communicated
these thoughts to Mr. Whitlam as a possible way of giving much higher
priority to the manpower field – felt by the ALP to be badly needed – and of
reorganizing immigration at the same time. The fate of the Department of
Immigration hung in the balance, therefore, in December 1972 when the
ALP won the federal election. Drastic action was postponed, however,
partly because there were other more urgent priorities, and partly because
Mr. Whitlam had among those designated by the ALP caucus for Cabinet
office, A.J. Grassby, Member for the New South Wales constituency of
Riverina, whom he thought was just the right person for the immigration
portfolio because of his concern for and empathy with migrants.[14]

Six months before the election which brought the ALP to power, an
incident occurred which might be described as a last cry of anguish and
fury from one of the most determined supporters of the White Australia
policy. On May 1, television's "Monday Conference" interviewed Don
Chipp, then a Liberal and Minister for Customs and Excise in the McMahon government, and later (in 1977) to form his own party, the Australian
Democrats. Mr. Chipp was asked "What do you think are Australia's
national goals – say for the rest of this decade – what sort of things do you
have in mind?" In a short reply, Mr. Chipp ended with the following
words: "I would like to see a more tolerant nation so that we can receive
ideas and cultures and, even people, from overseas. I would like to see a
stage in the 1980s where Australia is becoming the only true multiracial
country in the world," adding that this would have to be done gradually
and sensibly. Next day, this statement was front page news and in his
autobiography, Mr. Chipp has described the reaction which followed:
"Predictably this really flushed out every racist in the country. Arthur
Calwell came out of 'retirement' to give me a vicious rebuke. As a 'red-
blooded Australian' (his words, not mine), he said he was deeply concerned about the future of this country, that he did not want a black
tragedy brought on to the scene here and despised the thought of a choco-
late-coloured Australia populated by non-whites, breeding like flies and
living on the smell of an oily rag." Mr. Chipp added that, in addition to
these remarks, he received many abusive letters, anonymous phone calls
and demands for his resignation. He also records that the Australian
Gallup Poll carried out a nationwide survey on his "Monday Conference"
statement. 37 per cent of those interviewed supported this statement while
49 per cent disapproved. However, 51 per cent of those between 16 and 20
approved, as did 40 per cent of those between 21 and 50.[15]

It was an ugly and intemperate outburst on the part of Arthur Calwell,
then on the point of resigning from his Melbourne seat in the House of
Representatives, and it was roundly condemned in the Australian media.[16]

His implacably racist views had remained unchanged since the 1940s. In addition, by all reports, he had retained a very proprietorial attitude towards immigration, implying always that only he understood Australia's real needs in this area of public policy.[17]

This then was the climate of uncertainty on all sides in which the Whitlam government decision was made in 1973 to implement the party platform and throw out the White Australia policy once and for all. It was a courageous and badly-needed decision. Once made, it would have been almost impossible to change it, and when they returned to office in December 1975, the Liberal-National Country Party Coalition did not try. It may not be too much to say that, despite the fact that White Australia sentiment was by no means dead in any of the major political parties or among the public generally, there was a general if unstated sense of relief that the matter had been settled. Soon a convenient respectability descended on the new immigration policy, liberating creative effort for other important matters. The Department of Immigration adjusted to it quickly and the states appeared to do so even if, at heart, they continued to prefer migrants from traditional sources.

The Whitlam statement which gave effect to this decision came, in fact, not a moment too soon. Although the span of years separating these policy developments in Canada, the United States, and Australia (1962, 1965, and 1973) was not significant, the period when Australia appeared to the outside world to be holding on tenaciously to its White Australia policy was. The sixties were the critical years of the ending of empires, the birth of many new nations, and the rise of the Third World in international affairs. Great damage was done to Australia and to her image in the international community, particularly among Third World countries, by this continued adherence to what was seen as a concept of racial superiority. Mr. Whitlam was right to move swiftly to correct the situation.

IMMIGRATION MANAGEMENT: THE WHITLAM YEARS

The Whitlam years (1972–1975) were as turbulent in immigration as they were in other areas of public policy, and the turbulence began almost immediately with the arrival on the scene of Al Grassby as the administration's first Minister for Immigration.[18] A.J. Grassby, a well-known public figure, has played an important role in the world of migrants and ethnic communities in Australia as a publicist, promoter, teacher, and entertainer, the like of which cannot be found in Canada. Evoking great affection among his friends and an almost obsessive dislike among his enemies, he tirelessly promoted the causes of multiculturalism and racial equality in Australia.

Born in Australia of mainly English-Irish descent, with a talent for languages and considerable experience of travel as a child in a family which uprooted itself frequently, Al Grassby was first elected to the federal Parliament for the New South Wales constituency of Riverina in 1969, having worked as a journalist and agricultural extension officer, and served in the NSW Legislative Assembly for three years. He won the seat for the ALP again in 1972, was appointed Minister for Immigration, but then unfortunately lost it in the May 1974 election, after only 15 months in the Cabinet. It was the only seat lost by the Labor government in that election, the result partly of unpopular agricultural policies in a rural constituency, but also of what Mr. Whitlam has described as "the most intensive and virulent racist campaign yet recorded in Australia."[19]

Mr. Grassby was then appointed Special Consultant to the Government on Community Relations and, with the proclamation of the Labor government's Racial Discrimination Act on October 31, 1975, became Australia's first Commissioner for Community Relations. He continued to act as Commissioner, according to the terms of reference laid down in the Act, despite a distinctly cool attitude towards his activities by the Fraser government after 1975 (including a continuing refusal to increase his budget or staff). Recently, however, a Human Rights Commission has been established in Australia under the Human Rights Commission Act proclaimed on December 10, 1981; it will now be responsible for the administration of the Whitlam government's Racial Discrimination Act which has been amended accordingly. Mr. Grassby remained Commissioner for Community Relations for his full seven year term, but was not reappointed when the term expired on October 30, 1982.

Al Grassby was an active and energetic Minister for Immigration in the short time he had, implementing some programs which had been started by the previous administration and initiating others. Within 10 months, he had presented the House of Representatives with an impressive research and action program entitled "Australia's Decade of Decision: A Report on Migration, Citizenship, Settlement and Population" which brought together every possible item on the current immigration agenda.[20] The Minister described it as "a national stocktaking of immigration" in which the Department of Immigration; the Immigration Planning, Advisory and Publicity Councils; special state task forces and all the Good Neighbour Councils were to be actively engaged. A number of new developments and programs listed in the report had been announced during the previous 10 months.

After a preamble emphasizing the "rich diversity" of Australia's population since the arrival of the first settlers in 1788, and recording the six major premises of the ALP's immigration policy (the Launceston platform), the Minister's report began with an announcement of a new admissions policy providing for three categories of migrants: (1) immediate family members sponsored by people already resident in Australia; (2) other sponsored migrants including non-dependent relatives and friends; and (3) unsponsored migrants, with or without relatives or friends in Australia, with the qualifications and experience required to meet Australia's national needs. The highest priority would be given to the reunion of immediate family members. If their accommodation and maintenance were assured, only health and character would be taken into consideration. Mr. Grassby went on to announce that the Government had approved an immigration program of 110,000 migrants for 1973–1974; that the Department of Immigration was being reorganized to give effect to the new immigration policies which involved totally new concepts; and that a new "Structured Selection Assessment System" was being introduced to improve the migrant selection process.

The Structured Selection Assessment System

The Structured Selection Assessment System (SSAS), introduced by the Whitlam government in 1973, was the first stage in an interesting process that has taken place in Australia in the 1970s and early 1980s. This has involved first a generally accepted need to improve the migrant selection system, and secondly the problem of deciding whether to introduce a "points system" like the one adopted in Canada in 1967 or some other way of giving numerical weight to migrant selection criteria in the interest of objectivity and uniformity. Up to this point, Australia's migrant selection was wholly unstructured. It was carried out by Australian immigration officers at overseas posts or in Australia. These officers had had training in interviewing techniques and in migrant assessment, but the final assessment of the migrant's suitability as well as the questions asked in the interview were left entirely to the officer's discretion.

Beginning in the late 1960s, there was a growing concern about the incidence of migrant settlement problems, and about the high rate of settler departure from Australia, raising questions about the suitability of the migrants selected for permanent settlement. In 1970, Mr. K. Kern, Chief Psychologist to the Department of Immigration, was asked by the Department to visit a number of posts in the United Kingdom, Greece, Germany, Italy, and Yugoslavia "to investigate and report on procedures for the selection of migrants." He submitted his report to the Secretary on November 13, 1970. It showed a wide variation in the factors used by interviewing officers in their assessment of migrants, in the weight given to these factors, and in the manner in which interviews were conducted. It also showed that, in many cases, future settlement difficulties should have been apparent at the time of interview, but were not being identified. As a result, the Secretary decided to set up a senior staff committee to study selection procedures. It was this committee, the Committee on the Selection of Migrants, which eventually produced the Structured Selection Assessment System, originally intended for the McMahon government but finally introduced by Mr. Grassby, on January 31, 1973. The Whitlam government, still enamoured of the Canadian experience, originally favoured a points system, but settled in 1973 for the SSAS.

This new selection system was a half-way house. It provided the immigration officer with a detailed two-part "interview report," which had to be completed. Part A related to employment or "economic factors" and provided a list of factors very similar to those in the Canadian points system as it was then. Part B, however, required the officer to make an "Assessment of Personal and Social Factors" including attitude to migration, expectations, responsiveness, initiative, self-reliance and independence, presentation (appearance, personal hygiene, speech, and behaviour), family unity, community, sport and cultural interests, and "comment on any convictions" – all elements which the Canadian system leaves to the discretion of the immigrant officers but has never spelled out. In making a final assessment in Parts A and B, the immigration officer had to use a simple scale ranging from "very good," through "good," "adequate" and "barely adequate" to "not favourable."

The Structured Selection Assessment System, while regarded as a distinct improvement on the previous wholly discretionary approach, was found to be not sufficiently precise and not capable of producing a sufficient degree of uniformity, and it did not last very long. Work began in the Department of Immigration on its possible conversion to a numerically weighted system in 1976. Later on in this chapter, we will discuss the creation of NUMAS (Numerically-weighted Multi-factor Assessment System) introduced on January 1, 1979, the hostility which it aroused in some quarters, and its subsequent modification and adaptation in stages to Australia's present Migrant Selection System.[21]

New Policies and Programs

Returning now to Al Grassby's package of new and not quite so new policies and programs, Mr. Grassby turned next to the question of Australia's future population policies and the National Population Inquiry (discussed later in this chapter) which had been set in motion in 1970 when Phillip Lynch was Minister for Immigration. He emphasized the importance of this National Inquiry and said that he expected to receive a report from the Chairman, Professor Borrie, in June 1974. Public hearings in all states had been authorized, three had already been held, and nearly 200 submissions to the Inquiry were expected. Mr. Grassby said that, as soon as the report on evidence submitted at public hearings was published, he intended to make a submission to Cabinet on the strategic objectives of Australian population policy. The Minister referred to other developments, too, on the research side. The Immigration Advisory Council's three standing committees on Social Patterns,[22] Migrant Education, and Citizenship were engaged on "a wide range of important migration studies," and a fourth Committee on Community Relations had been established "to enquire into all aspects of discrimination against migrants, to investigate exploitation of migrants and to examine the extent to which migrants use community services."

The Minister also said that a new and more vital role would have to be found for the Good Neighbour Movement throughout Australia and he proposed to explore this with its members and with other community leaders. As well, task forces had been set up in all the states, each chaired by a Labor Member of Parliament who was also a member of the Government Immigration Committee, to look into "the grass roots problems facing migrants." There would be major improvements in post-arrival services for migrants which would include more grants-in-aid to voluntary agencies working with migrants, more financial support for Good Neighbour Councils and an expansion to all state capitals of the very successful Telephone Interpreter Service (created in 1972 by the previous government), then operating in Melbourne and Sydney only (see Appendix 7).

Finally, Mr. Grassby dealt with the question of citizenship, referring to the new Australian Citizenship Act which he had introduced in the House on April 11, 1973, which established Australian citizenship for the first time on the basis of "one criteria, one national allegiance, one citizenship and one ceremony." The essential tasks for 1973-1974, he said, would be to identify and overcome the problems that inhibit the successful settlement and integration of migrants already in Australia, and to move closer to a new sense of national identity and unity. Practical expression would have to be given to the Government's global, non-discriminatory immigration policies, thereby contributing to closer relations with other nations in the Indo-Pacific area. It was important also to contribute to "the vital labor needs of a buoyant economy and to the policies of regional development and urban improvement," and to facilitate the work of the National Population Inquiry and prepare for major policy decisions following completion of its report.

It was a fine package and some of it went forward as planned. Senior immigration officers then in Canberra remember this as a very exciting time, and some of them felt, and still feel, a warm sympathy for Al Grassby in his concern for migrants and his liking for an active and innovative program. Others, however, were disturbed by his desire to liberalize everything immediately, and lack, as they saw it, of a real grasp of normal management procedures and of the precautions which must be taken in immigration in the light of possible abuse and illegality. Thus an "Easy Visa Scheme" for visitors, introduced while Mr. Grassby was Minister, had to be withdrawn later because of mounting practical difficulties and considerable abuse. In addition, by the end of 1973, the new government's lenient approach to family reunion was becoming widely known and applications in this category were escalating in a disturbing way.

The Department of Immigration Dismantled

Mr. Grassby's package of new programs and services, and the co-ordinated approach it represented, was effectively destroyed, for the time being at least, by the Whitlam government itself. When Al Grassby lost his Riverina seat in the May 1974 election and could no longer stand up for the Department of Immigration (as many think he would have done), the Prime Minister indulged his view that this department could be dispensed with in its present form.[23] In June 1974, the Department of Immigration was merged with the Department of Labor, whose offices were in Melbourne, and Clyde Cameron, a veteran labour leader and influential member of the ALP's leadership group became Minister for Labor and Immigration. Dr. Peter Wilenski was appointed permanent head of the combined department, whose immigration operations were considerably reduced in size and effectiveness by the transfer of migrant welfare and community services to the Department of Social Security; English language training to the Department of Education; migrant accommodation to the Department of Housing and Construction; publicity and information to the Department of the Media; and passports to the Department of Foreign Affairs. There was no prior consultation with senior officials in the Department of Immigration and none with the Department's advisory bodies.[24] When this development was announced, the Opposition promptly replied that when they were re-elected, they would put all these elements back together again, separate the two departments (of Labor and Immigration) and restore to the Department of Immigration its rightful place and responsibilities. They did this, in fact, within a very short time.

Six weeks later, there was a debate in the House of Representatives on a motion proposed by Michael MacKellar, the Opposition's spokesman on immigration and future Minister for Immigration, that the House debate "the confusion and uncertainty created by the Prime Minister's actions in dismembering the Department of Immigration." Opening the debate, Mr. MacKellar attacked the Prime Minister for what he called "an entirely unilateral decision" to split up the Department, and demanded a clear and detailed explanation of the reasons which lay behind it. He pointed out that the report of the National Population Inquiry which might have a

major impact on immigration policy and administration was nearly fin-
ished. Why had such sweeping changes been made before public examination and discussion of this important document? He drew attention to the
confusion which this move created in critical aspects of immigration management and gave high praise to the officers of the former department:
"No one would claim that the former Department of Immigration and its
officers were perfect, but also no one would deny that the officers of the
Department exhibited experience, expertise and dedication of an
extremely high order." For 25 years, Mr. MacKellar continued, migrants
had had a single department to turn to and knowledgeable people to help
them. The Department had had the ability and experience to respond
quickly to crisis situations and its officers had shared a comradeship and
sense of purpose. The Whitlam government's recent decision, he said, had
been a sad and sorry exercise.

Replying for the Government, the Minister, Clyde Cameron, defended
the Government's decision, emphasizing the critical importance of
employment and training for migrants and stressing the advantages for
them which the amalgamation of the two departments would bring. He
also referred to Canada's Department of Manpower and Immigration,
adding, "It works extremely well there. It works so well that Canada
obtains many more migrants than we do ... Canada had no difficulty in
welding manpower and migration to form a single department."[25]

From the 1974 election onwards, the Whitlam government ran into
serious difficulties and became increasingly crisis-prone. Its major reform
programs and deliberate expansion of the public sector, which involved a
substantial increase in public expenditures, had unfortunately coincided
with the onset of a serious world recession which would have a critical
impact on both the Australian and Canadian economies. The ALP had no
agreed strategies to deal with a high rate of inflation and mounting unemployment, and both Cabinet and caucus were reluctant to introduce the
stringent and unpopular measures now urged on them by the Treasury as
the economy deteriorated. The party still believed that it must carry out its
reform mandate come what may, and the caucus was opposed to even
mild measures of restraint. As the months passed, relations with the public
service worsened and public confidence in the competence and ability of
the Whitlam government began to ebb away.

It was during this period that Clyde Cameron was Minister for Labor
and Immigration and Dr. Wilenski commuted energetically between Melbourne and Canberra implementing the merger of the two departments,
while senior immigration officers tried to save what they could from the
wreck. Mr. Cameron's major concerns as the minister responsible for
immigration were almost wholly related to the labour market with which
he had been involved all his life. They consisted first of a decision to reduce

intake even further in the light of increasing unemployment, and secondly to recruit skilled workers, as needed, mainly from traditional sources. Much less was heard now about family reunion and "natural migration" (Mr. Whitlam's phrase). As we have seen, the immigration target for 1974–1975 was brought down to 80,000 and to 50,000 for 1975–1976. Overseas immigration officers were instructed to suspend the acceptance and processing of all applications, except those involving sponsored dependants; persons in employment categories for which there was a strong and unsatisfied demand; and refugees. It was also announced that, as from January 1, 1975, all non-immigrants, with the exception of New Zealand citizens, would require non-immigrant visas in order to enter Australia for any length of time. In a press statement issued on October 2, 1974, Mr. Cameron explained that these measures simply followed the long-established policy of adjusting the immigration program to economic realities.[26]

Clyde Cameron never concealed his views about what he felt to be the proper composition of Australia's immigration movement. These views were very different from those of his predecessor. As Minister, he made it clear on several occasions that he favoured "the best skilled workers" as he put it, and determined recruitment in Northern Europe. The best possible workers, in his view, were now to be found in Denmark and West Germany (and possibly also in Britain) and they had the advantage of not bringing many relatives with them. In an interview in August, published in the Australian public affairs journal *New Accent*, he said that the great thing about Danish and West German tradesmen was that "they come here under their own steam – well, that is with assisted passages – but they don't then bring out a whole string of brothers and sisters and close relatives who are without skills. They usually come on their own and that's the end of it."[27]

In June 1975, in response to the Government's financial problems and considerable public criticism, Mr. Whitlam announced a major Cabinet reshuffle in which Clyde Cameron was moved to Science and Consumer Affairs. There had been differences between them on wage restraint and other matters and Mr. Whitlam was apparently convinced that Cameron had "exhausted his creativity in a portfolio which meant so much to him."[28] At first, Mr. Cameron refused to go, but he was obliged to give way. In an interview with the author in Canberra three years later, he expressed very bitter feelings about this demotion, as he saw it, and about Mr. Whitlam himself. He also made the point that, in his view, although the two departments of Labor and Immigration had been merged, neither Mr. Whitlam nor Dr. Wilenski – nor, for that matter, most of the Cabinet – had any real interest in manpower questions or in manpower programs along Canadian lines which he felt were so badly needed in Australia. Mr.

Whitlam, he said, "simply wouldn't listen and wouldn't put manpower proposals on the Cabinet agenda."[29] For the few remaining months in the life of the Whitlam government, Mr. Cameron was replaced as Minister for Labor and Immigration by Senator James McClelland.

The Whitlam government made one or two further moves in the immigration and multiculturalism field during what proved to be its final year of office. The First Report of the National Population Inquiry (the Borrie Report) was tabled in February 1975 and the Government immediately announced the creation of an Australian Population and Immigration Council (APIC) replacing the Immigration Planning Council created in 1949. One of the major purposes of the new council was to monitor and evaluate demographic trends and to advise the Government on the economic and social consequences of changing population patterns. A few months later, the Labor government made the first tentative moves towards the creation of an ethnic broadcasting service. A committee was established to run two experimental radio stations in Sydney and Melbourne, initially for a trial period of 13 weeks, but eventually on a more permanent basis. The Sydney station 2EA began broadcasting in seven languages on June 8, 1975 and the Melbourne station 3EA opened on June 23 with programs in eight languages.

The National Population Inquiry

The National Population Inquiry proved to be a substantial piece of research; it investigated Australia's demographic situation in considerable depth. Its director, Professor W.D. Borrie, a New Zealander by birth and a world-renowned demographer, was Reader and then Professor of Demography at the Australian National University in Canberra from 1949 to the late 1970s.[30] As Director of a recently established Department of Demography, he brought together a small but highly talented group of demographers who have played a major role in establishing an impressive tradition of scholarly demographic research in Australia, combined with a public policy input, neither of which can be matched in Canada so far. As we have seen, the Canadian government opted in the 1970s for a policy-oriented approach to population questions, involving minimal research and an institutional structure which proved to be only a fleeting phenomenon. The Australians, on the other hand, chose to investigate their demographic situation much more thoroughly. Canada was to follow suit, however, more than a decade later.

The Inquiry was a joint government-university enterprise and was funded through and carried out at the Australian National University. Professor Borrie was assisted by an advisory committee of senior academics and immigration officials, as well as a small research staff. During the course of the Inquiry, public hearings were held across Australia and a large number of submissions received. According to the initial terms of reference, the Inquiry was required to look into all aspects of Australian population growth, including natural increase and immigration and, in the context of the academic freedom necessary for objective research, "to focus attention on matters of particular concern to the Government in order to produce results that would contribute usefully to the formulation and application of national policies." In addition, the desirable future population levels towards which immigration should contribute were to be examined. It is emphasized in the Report of the Inquiry, however, that the Inquiry was not asked to establish an "optimum" population for Australia or to determine "ultimate carrying capacity on the basis of assumed or current technologies." The Inquiry itself imposed its own limitation on forecasting – mainly to the end of the century only – because of the significant element of change evident in Australia's current demographic situation and the well-known hazards of long-term demographic forecasting.[31] The First Report of the Inquiry was submitted to the Minister for Labor and Immigration, Clyde Cameron, in January 1975. A Supplementary Report and a series of shorter research reports were submitted three years later to the Minister for Immigration and Ethnic Affairs in the Fraser government, Michael MacKellar.

The Borrie Report did not produce policy recommendations and in this it disappointed some politicians and officials, who had hoped for clearer guidelines on future population policy. Rather, it offered a discussion of Australia's demographic options, on the basis of the mass of evidence which had been assembled and analysed during the course of the three and half year inquiry. In the words of the Report itself, the intention was not to suggest the choices government should make, but rather "to indicate some of the parameters that appear to be relevant to the formulation of policy in the light of the demographic analysis presented in this Report."[32] Following is a brief listing of some of the Inquiry's principal findings, as well as the policy considerations which emerge from them and are discussed in the First and Supplementary Reports.

1   The Report dismissed as "shibboleths that grossly oversimplify the real position" the two extreme positions in the population debate in Australia, namely the traditional "populate or perish" view which inspired the post-war immigration program, and the much more recent zero population growth approach. It suggested that while majority opinion favours "a continuation of moderate growth but does not favour excessive zeal simply for the sake of reaching defined targets," there was clearly no national consensus on this question.[33] At public hearings, it was evident that while support for slowing growth was strongest in New South Wales and Victoria, the two largest states, and in South Australia, the emphasis in Queens-

land and Western Australia, which both had impressive resources and small populations, was on the need for more people. This suggested that "there was no good reason why the whole of the vast continent of Australia should either grow at the same time, or stop growing at the same time.[34]

2   The Report then examined the question of possible physical constraints on population growth, noting Australia's very large size and extremely low population density; the concentration of people in one corner of the continent between the coast and a line drawn from Brisbane to Adelaide, where the climate is temperate and rainfall and other systems favourable; and her dry and fragile physical environment with one of the most erratic rainfalls in the world. But it noted also the adequacy of food supplies for a larger population in Australia; her rich mineral resources and abundant energy reserves; and the fact that water, often seen in the past as Australia's Achilles heel, seems today much less of a constraint. Authorities were quoted to show that present supplies could definitely sustain a much larger population if this were thought desirable. The Report concluded that resources generally were not likely to impose constraints on population growth at existing standards of living. "A minimum level," it suggested, "might be three times the present population; the maximum might well be several times greater depending upon technological developments, expanding markets, and increased availability of resources compared with the present state of knowledge."[35]

3   The Report then offered some realistic population projections. It concluded that the levels of population growth implied in the fertility and immigration trends up to 1971 were no longer appropriate. A marked downswing in fertility, together with a decline in the free flow of immigration and a deliberate reduction of immigration intake to 80,000 new settlers a year by the Whitlam government, had set "the population growth pattern along a totally different course." Fertility was now expected to decline to replacement level by 1975–1976, remaining constant after that. Natural growth was expected to be very modest in the ensuing years, slowing down by the year 2001. Given these circumstances, according to the Report, the effect on population growth shown in Table 6 could be expected by the end of the century from three possible levels of net immigration: 50,000, 75,000, and 100,000 per annum.[36]

The Report's "preferred solution" in relation to net immigration levels – stated unequivocally in the Supplementary Report – was 50,000 per annum, influenced perhaps by what was called "the weight of evidence of submissions to the Inquiry" in favour of lower levels. This did not prove to be the view of the Fraser government, however, when it came to power in 1975.

4   Nevertheless, the Report suggested a "short-range flexibility in determining immigration targets and a dovetailing of immigrant flows to

Table 6
Australia: The Effect of Three Possible Levels of Net Immigration on Population
Growth, 1973–2001

| | Population (in Thousands) | | | |
| | Actual | | Projected | |
	1973	1981	1991	2001
No Immigration	13,132	13,976	15,019	15,878
Net Immigration = 50,000 p/a		14,406	16,063	17,612
Net Immigration = 75,000 p/a		14,621	16,585	18,479
Net Immigration = 100,000 p/a		14,837	17,106	19,346

Source: National Population Inquiry.

assessed manpower needs." These needs were seen as becoming more acute again in the nineties when the peak period of "baby boom" influence on the labour force would have passed.

The work of the National Population Inquiry was extended for two years after the First Report was tabled in January 1975. The principal stated purpose of this extension was to take the analysis of recent demographic trends in Australia a little further, to update the First Report, and to prepare a Supplementary Report, incorporating any new findings which might be made and relating them to the conclusions which had emerged from the Inquiry. It was, in fact, a final look at Australia's recent demographic experience and future prospects, and an attempt to see whether the observations and conclusions offered in the First Report were valid; and this was found to be the case. Although the Supplementary Report offered some interesting additional thoughts on the social implications of Australia's present demographic situation, on population distribution and immigration and population targets, the conclusions found in the First Report were generally felt to provide "a sound basis for policy determination." The final advice of the Borrie Report on population goals for Australia appeared to be that, although no national consensus had emerged on this question thus far, *both* conservative objectives in population growth and more ambitious ones (i.e., a range from 17 to 50 or 60 million) were reasonable. Although this was not stated precisely, it could be inferred that decision-making in this area still lay with the politicians.

On one point, however, the Borrie Report was very precise: the urgent need for a careful and continuous monitoring of demographic changes in Australia and of all the factors which contribute to them including immigration. The point is made several times in the First and Supplementary Reports. The final chapter of the First Report entitled "Towards an Australian Policy" concludes with the following comment: "... it is to be hoped that the new demographic patterns emerging will continue to be monitored and evaluated as they proceed, for they are already casting their shadows, or their lights, a long way ahead."[37] This was a practical recommendation to which the Whitlam government could respond immediately. As we have seen, in February 1975, a month after the Borrie Report was tabled in the House of Representatives, the Minister for Labor and Immigration, Clyde Cameron, announced the formation of the Australian Population and Immigration Council which would monitor and evaluate demographic trends and would also make a total reappraisal of immigration policies. The chairman of the new 12-member council, he said, would be the federal (ALP) Member for Perth, Mr. J.M. Berinson MP. Thus far 10 prominent Australians, including four university professors and a federal judge had accepted invitations to sit on the Council. Council members were being appointed, Mr. Cameron said, for the contribution they could make as individual experts rather than as representatives of organizations.[38]

Following Mr. Cameron's reluctant move to the Department of Science and Consumer Affairs in June, the new Minister, Senator James McClelland, made a further announcement on the subject of advisory councils in immigration. The Labor government, he said, had decided to re-establish the Immigration Advisory Council with the same chairman, Senator J.A. Mulvihill, but with much wider community involvement. Whereas the former Immigration Advisory Council, created by Arthur Calwell in 1947, had been based on nominations for membership from organizations established on a federal basis, this one would be composed of "suitably qualified Australians and new settlers" who were asked to make application for positions on the Council. The Minister hoped that this new approach would ensure "larger migrant representation."[39]

Neither of the new councils was to survive very long in the form envisaged by these two ministers, however. In the autumn of 1975, there began the now famous and dramatic sequence of events in Australian politics which led to the dismissal on November 11 of the Whitlam government by the Governor General, Sir John Kerr. On that day also, Malcolm Fraser, the opposition Liberal—National Country Party Coalition leader was installed as caretaker Prime Minister until a double dissolution election could be held. This election took place on December 13, 1975, resulting in an overwhelming electoral victory for the Coalition which was to stay in power for the next seven years.[40] On July 14, 1977, Sir John Kerr resigned as Governor General in the face of considerable public hostility and doubt as to the wisdom and propriety of his actions on November 11, 1975. On December 10, 1977, Bill Hayden, a senior member of the Whitlam Cabinet and a politician of a more moderate and conciliatory disposition, replaced Gough Whitlam as federal Labor leader, following Whitlam's resignation.

THE FRASER GOVERNMENT

Behind Malcolm Fraser, it has been said, "lie three generations of wealth and conservatism." His grandfather, Simon Fraser, who founded the family fortune, represents a distant connection with Canada. He was born in Pictou, Nova Scotia in 1832, the son of Scottish immigrants from Inverness, but set sail for Australia at the age of 21 to make his fortune in the Australian gold rush of the 1850s. After a remarkable entrepreneurial career in the State of Victoria, which covered gold digging, retail trading, railway and land development, finance, and politics, he was knighted at 86. He left to his five children and their offspring considerable wealth and a very secure existence in Victoria's well-to-do and conservative upper class.[41]

Malcolm Fraser has been one of the most interesting and complex of Australia's leading Liberal politicians in the post-war period. Hard-driving and determined, austere and authoritarian, he seemed at times the most rigid of right-wing conservatives and at others surprisingly flexible and liberal, particularly in matters of international relations. His seven years as Prime Minister of Australia were very significant for immigration and ethnic affairs in a broad context, including management, the selection and admission of migrants, the provision of migrant services and the whole area of multiculturalism. Behind these developments lay a firm belief on the part of the L-NCP Coalition in the value of a well-managed, reasonably large annual immigration movement, both for demographic reasons and as an important factor in Australian development. The record of the Fraser government in the field of refugees, which includes the very large Indochinese refugee movement taking place almost on Australia's doorstep, was impressive.

The first Minister for Immigration and Ethnic Affairs in the Fraser government was Michael MacKellar, one of the younger members of the Fraser team. A vigourous and articulate Liberal politician, he was first elected to the House of Representatives as the Member for Warringah, a "blue chip" (i.e., very safe) seat in New South Wales in the general election of October 1969. While in opposition, he served for a while as parliamentary secretary to the Leader of the Opposition and was opposition spokesman on immigration from June 1974 onwards. As Minister for Immigration and Ethnic Affairs, not a senior portfolio, he was not included in the Fraser inner Cabinet and was not influential in a larger sense. He proved to be an active and creative minister in this sensitive area of public policy, however, ready to tackle its many problems.

The new government's priorities in immigration were worked out during the final months of the Whitlam administration. In August 1975, the Liberal and National Country parties issued a policy statement on immigration and ethnic affairs, drafted by Michael MacKellar.[42] This statement deliberately linked immigration to population policy and national development, promised an active immigration program and referred to the needs of migrant peoples already in Australia in a way that suggested a considerable future commitment to multicultural policies and programs.

In practical terms, Liberal–NCP priorities in immigration in 1975–1976 were, first, to restore the Department of Immigration to its former strength and full range of responsibilities, as promised while in opposition; secondly, in a careful and gradual way to raise immigration levels again from the low point of 50,000 per annum to which they had fallen in 1975; and thirdly, to catch up with the ALP in its fairly recently established and politically valuable connections with ethnic communities.

On arrival in Australia for the first time in August 1977, the author had the first of several very interesting interviews with Mr. MacKellar, who described the situation he faced when he became Minister in December 1975. First he had to deal with a seriously fragmented department and very low morale among the remaining immigration officers in Canberra. While writing the Liberal–NCP policy statement a few months earlier, he realized that the Coalition simply had no immigration policy and was just coasting along on past achievements, so that clear policy directions had to be established. In addition, in his view, the ALP had made all the running with ethnic groups in recent years. The Liberal and National Country parties had hardly any contact with them, never talked to them, and did not know who their leaders were. He was determined to put that right. When questioned on the subject of the ending of the White Australia policy by the Whitlam government in 1973, he said he thought it would take time for this to be fully accepted in Australia; there was still a lot of racism around in his view. There was some racism in the Cabinet, and some in all the political parties. He thought the ALP would be, if anything, the more racist of the two major political groups because of the unions, which still had some strong views on this subject. Thus there would still be a good deal of anxiety in Australia about the sources of Australian migrants, and he thought that this would have to be managed carefully.

In general, Mr. MacKellar did not find that his Cabinet colleagues had a burning interest in immigration, or in ethnic groups – a conclusion which might well be echoed by any Canadian minister responsible for immigration. Both the Prime Minister and Cabinet simply wanted the whole policy area to be well managed and well controlled. If that were done, then they did not want to hear about it.

Mr. MacKellar is credited, however, by several senior immigration officers who were there at the time but have now retired, not only with rehabilitating the Department and re-establishing a fairly firm control over immigration, but also with "selling multiculturalism to the Prime

Minister and Cabinet." Although only a junior minister, and in no sense a powerful or influential one, he succeeded in persuading Mr. Fraser and his Cabinet first that multiculturalism was in the interests of the Liberal–NCP Coalition and of Australia itself, if kept well under control; and secondly, that by this means he could probably deliver a good part of the ethnic vote.

Michael MacKellar was Minister for Immigration and Ethnic Affairs for four years. In December 1979, he became Minister for Health and was succeeded in the immigration portfolio by Ian Macphee who was formerly Minister for Productivity and had considerable experience in the employment and labour relations field. In May 1982, Mr. Macphee was replaced by John Hodges, a pharmacist by profession and a former Chairman of the House of Representatives Standing Committee on Environment and Conservation. Mr. Hodges was Minister for Immigration and Ethnic Affairs for only 10 months, until the Fraser government, after seven years in office, was defeated by the ALP in the general election of March 5, 1983.

The Fraser years were years of considerable achievement in immigration, comparable in vitality and innovation to the Andras-Gotlieb period (1972–1976) and its aftermath in Canada. In immigration policy, they followed a remarkably similar pattern with a Green Paper tabled in the House of Representatives on March 17, 1977, followed by public hearings and discussion. This led to major changes in immigration policy announced by the Minister on June 7, 1978 and, in the following year, to a completely revised migrant selection system (NUMAS) which was revised again in 1982. These years also saw other significant developments:

1 The rehabilitation and strengthening of the Department of Immigration, now given the added function of Ethnic Affairs.

2 The gradual raising of immigration levels from the low points of 52,748 settler arrivals in 1975–1976 to 118,700 in 1981–1982; and the introduction in 1978–1979 of "triennial rolling programs" in a three-year immigration planning process.

3 The reshaping of the Australian Population and Immigration Council (APIC) and the creation of two more advisory councils, the Australian Ethnic Affairs Council (AEAC) and the Australian Refugee Advisory Council (ARAC) (later, for reasons of economy, they were replaced by a single council known as the Australian Council on Population and Ethnic Affairs (ACPEA)).

4 The creation in September 1977 of a valuable institution, the National Accreditation Authority for Translators and Interpreters (NAATI) which has put this profession on a much firmer basis in Australia (no comparable institution exists in Canada).

5 A continuing battle with illegal or undocumented migration, coming

from all directions including the trans-Tasman route from New Zealand; this would involve two official amnesties and several amendments to the Migration Act 1958.

6 Further progress in the development of ethnic broadcasting.

7 Significant changes in refugee policy and management, stemming in part from Australia's large Indochinese refugee movement.

8 The implementation of the recommendations of the Galbally Review of Post-arrival Programs and Services for Migrants which took place in 1978; this has created for Australia a planned and unified system of migrant services which Canada still does not have.

9 Important amendments, outlined in Parliament on May 6, 1982 by the then Minister, Mr. Macphee, to the Australian Citizenship Act 1948.

We will now examine the most important of these developments, namely the rehabilitation of the Department; the Green Paper and its consequences; immigration intake during the Fraser years; the battle with illegal immigration; the Galbally Review and its implementation and the search for a new migrant selection system. The new advisory councils in immigration, as well as the changes in refugee policy and management, will be dealt with in chapters 4 and 6.

The Department Restored

In December 1975, what was left of the former Department of Immigration occupied a depressing cluster of temporary, single-storey buildings in an obscure part of Canberra's large public service cantonment. It had been thoroughly dismembered during the final years of the Whitlam government and, as we have seen, vital parts had been handed over to the departments of Labor, Social Security, Education, Business and Consumer Affairs, and other agencies. It was reassembled first by declaration, being simply declared the Department of Immigration and Ethnic Affairs (DIEA) by the Minister on December 22. Then gradually, piece by piece, it was put together again. This took some time to accomplish and involved lengthy negotiations with the Public Service Board,[43] as well as extensive review and reorganization procedures.

The process of rehabilitation continued until the Department had, once again, almost complete responsibility at the federal level for all matters pertaining to immigration including ethnic affairs, now looked after by a new Ethnic Affairs Branch. At the end of May 1978, with the Government's acceptance of the recommendations of the Galbally Review of Post-arrival Programs and Services for Migrants (discussed below), the Department's role in implementing these recommendations, and in monitoring and evaluating all federal programs and services for migrants, was firmly established. Following the publication in the same year of an important report, *The Commonwealth Government and the Urban Environment*,[44] which emphasized Australia's need for population policies and planning, a Population Branch was created within the Department in 1980-1981 and its major responsibility in this field was also confirmed.[45] Finally, it should be recorded that at the end of 1978, a critical year in the life of the Department, preparations were being made to move into impressive new offices in a large complex of government buildings in the north Canberra area of Belconnen, out of what is described in the Department's annual review as "the hotchpotch of fibro-cement buildings on the shore of Lake Burley Griffin used by the Department since 1951."[46]

Despite these gratifying developments, the Department was in fact in need, in December 1975, of much more than a straightforward restoration and strengthening of its former functions. The old Department of Immigration in Australia bore a striking resemblance to Canada's former Department of Citizenship and Immigration which managed Canadian immigration operations from 1950 to 1965. Both were small, non-prestigious departments with limited resources and low classifications for their staff, standing always in the shadow of other more powerful departments.[47] The Australian Department of Immigration had, at the outset, a more significant mandate and more political clout than the Canadian department, and in its first two Secretaries, Tasman Hayes (1948-1961) and Peter Heydon (1961-1971), both later knighted, it had two public servants of great distinction. Nevertheless, as years went by and the initial drama of establishing a vigorous, post-war immigration program settled into a more routine operation, the strength, innovative capacities, and resources of the Department did not improve significantly. No doubt this was mainly due to the lack of development and innovation in the Australian public service itself during this period, "the years of benign complacency" as they have been called.[48] Nevertheless, even a senior public servant with the status and experience of Sir Peter Heydon was unable to get a very much better deal for the Department of Immigration from the Public Service Board. An unfinished letter to the Board, found after his sudden death in 1971, revealed that he had made no fewer than 17 applications to the Board for additional positions for the Department and higher classifications for its staff in recent years and that every one of them had been turned down.[49]

The Department's first Secretary after the change of government in December 1975 was L.F. Bott, who supervised the initial restoration of the Department. He was very close to retirement, however, and on August 10, 1977 he was replaced by L.W.B. Engeldow, previously Secretary of the Department of the Capital Territory and known as a very capable administrator. Mr. Engeldow was given the specific task of welding the Department together into an effective organization and "revitalizing it." In an interview with the author in January 1978, he explained the administrative problems he found on arrival and how he proposed to deal with them.

Several of the most difficult problems were related, fundamentally, the Secretary believed, to the nature of immigration itself. The policy area of immigration was always intriguing and absorbing to officers who liked working with people, and who were continuously fascinated by human problems and predicaments. They became completely absorbed in the field and stayed. There were too many people in the Department, he believed, who had stayed in immigration too long.[50] There were some very good younger people, but not enough. In addition, there were too many officers in Canberra bogged down in casework, chiefly due to the powers of discretion given to the Minister under the 1958 Migration Act. As a result, not enough attention was being given to policy-making. Promotion was another fundamental problem in immigration, according to Mr. Engeldow. It tended to be very slow and discouraging for able junior officers; the promotion picture was the familiar one of the flat pyramid. In immigration, there was always a lot of routine work at the bottom, but not many jobs available at the top. Thus promotion opportunities had been very limited. (It is worth noting that all the above comments could have been made with equal truth about Canadian immigration management in the fifties and early sixties.)

Mr. Engeldow's recipe for revitalizing his reconstituted department, in collaboration with a now much more co-operative Public Service Board (which had, of course, been responsible for his appointment) was not to apply shock treatment and attempt a rapid reorganization and re-staffing. Rather it was steadily to build a younger, better qualified staff with wider experience, recruiting them from other departments. He also believed that the Overseas Service needed streamlining and upgrading, and wanted to establish regional directors for the major world regions, having the same classification as that of an Assistant Secretary. Regional directors in Australia should have the same classification, so that there could be some real career mobility at this level. He also wanted to recruit more university graduates, particularly for the Overseas Service where they had been far too few in the past. And he wanted to push all casework out to the regional offices to relieve Head Office of this burden, so that it could give more attention to policy-making. These were some of his major prescriptions for revitalization.[51]

Major developments in management along these lines did take place from the latter part of 1977 onwards and we will mention just a few of the most significant ones. It is certainly true to say that by 1982 the Department was not only better housed, but in a much stronger position, with a younger and better qualified staff than it had been 10 years earlier. Mr.

Engeldow was in charge of these developments for three years, but then took an early retirement for health reasons. He was replaced in August 1980 by John Menadue who had been Secretary of the Department of the Prime Minister and Cabinet in 1975–1976 and Australia's Ambassador to Japan from 1977 onwards. He was in turn replaced in 1983 by W.A. McKinnon, formerly Chairman of the Industries Assistance Commission.[52]

One of the first moves initiated by Mr. Engeldow and his advisers was to set up a Joint Management Review of what was described as "selected aspects of the Department's functions and management." A full-time task force, appointed on November 21, 1977, worked for 15 weeks and examined the operations of a number of regional branch offices and overseas posts. The task force consisted of an external consultant engaged by the Public Service Board to head the review, a senior official from the Department, a staff member from the Public Service Board itself, and – of particular interest to this study – a Canadian immigration official, Reg Casselman, formerly Director of Immigration for the Atlantic Region of the Department of Manpower and Immigration, then on a two-year exchange visit to the Australian department. Mr. Casselman was also a member of the implementation team set up in November 1978 after the review had been completed.

The Joint Management Review was given broad terms of reference and it examined, in a careful and expeditious way, virtually every area of the Department's operations, except Australia's basic immigration and refugee policies. Special attention was given to the present performance of the Migration Act 1958, to the problems of illegal immigration (mainly related to temporary entry), to the effectiveness of the existing migrant selection system (the Structured Selection Assessment System introduced under the Labor government in 1973), and to the state of staff morale within the Department.

The review team's final report was presented in July 1978.[53] Concise, direct, and well-documented, it amounted to a major critique of Australia's Migration Act 1958 and of her system of immigration management in recent years. The report noted the serious weaknesses in the Act, including its lack of mandatory requirements in either immigration policy or practice, and its "excessive discretionary features." The latter led directly, in the team's view, to the very large number of representations (i.e., requests for ministerial intervention in cases where an unfavourable decision has been made) with which the Minister and his officials were always burdened.[54] During the 12-month period from March 1977 to March 1978, 15,500 ministerial representations had been made, 60 per cent of which required the Minister's signature. The policy problem was described as "the absence of a formal base for policy, lack of policy on all but the most basic issues and non-adherence to policy."

The report emphasized that in 1958 when the Migration Act was passed, almost all immigration to Australia came from the United Kingdom and Western Europe. The majority of all those arriving in Australia were migrants coming to settle in Australia permanently, and more than 60 per cent of all passenger traffic was by sea.[55] But 1958 was the year when commercial airlines began using inter-continental jet aircraft. The jet, which made it possible to reach virtually any part of the world in a day or less, revolutionized travel to and from Australia. This resulted in large and rapidly increasing numbers of people visiting Australia each year for business, study, or pleasure, and even greater numbers of Australian citizens and residents travelling abroad. Today, the report noted, almost all passenger traffic to Australia came by air and temporary entrants exceed migrants by almost eight to one. This made regulation and control very much more difficult and revealed in even sharper focus the weaknesses of the Migration Act.

The deficiencies of the Act were then described in detail. The following are some examples:

1 The very informal approach to policy definition, with no statutory requirement that there even be an Australian immigration policy, is a deterrent to the implementation and enforcement of the provisions of the Act and Regulations.
2 The lack of mandatory provisions in the Act means that immigration requirements and provisions can be changed arbitrarily, but also that representations cannot be rejected definitively.
3 The Act provides insufficient statutory powers for immigration officers.
4 There are no provisions in the Act for migrant selection criteria of any kind.
5 There are no sanctions against prohibited immigrants or visitors who work in contravention of their entry conditions. Similarly there are no sanctions against employers of prohibited immigrants or of visitors who work in contravention of their entry conditions.

On the vital question of immigration policy, the report stated in its conclusions that there had been a lack of policy on all but the most basic issues, leading to "confusion in the community and considerable uncertainty within the Department concerning objectives, roles, priorities and the extent to which the provisions of the legislation are to be enforced." Non-adherence to policy had been widespread, according to the report, as shown by the high percentage of approvals for change in status and variability in decisions on migrant entry and deportation cases. "The lack of firmness in enforcing policy is well known overseas and Australia is regarded as an easy country to enter and obtain residence."

The Joint Management Review team were no less categorical in their analysis of the weaknesses hitherto of departmental management. These were described as "over-centralization, poor communications, inadequate training and the absence of proper management and control systems." The review team also paid considerable attention to the problems of illegal immigration – mainly the overstayers – which was an important part of its mandate. Its conclusions and recommendations on this subject will be examined in Chapter 4, along with Canada's similar experience during this period. In all, the review team produced 96 detailed recommendations. They included such firm prescriptions to the Minister and Department as:

- Amend the Migration Act as soon as possible.
- Begin planning for a new Migration Act.
- Define migrant selection criteria more specifically, incorporating a "points system."
- Make policy statements on eligibility for visa and entry, and the Department's stance on enforcement of control provisions.
- Divert representations to departmental and external enquiry, review, and appeals machinery, and publicize this procedure.
- Publicize Australia's intent to adhere to policy.
- Lay down firm and unambiguous guidelines for the application of policies.

Of the team's 96 recommendations, 45 had been implemented by June 30, 1979. Forty-one were still in the process of being implemented. Only 10 were rejected as impracticable or had been overtaken by changes in policy and procedure. It was a remarkable achievement.

As a result of a combination of forces, therefore, including ministerial drive, a revitalized senior management and a much more development-minded Public Service Board, together with the firm recommendations of the Joint Management Review, a vigorous process of modernization and development of the Department of Immigration took place during the remaining years of the Fraser government.

Among the important events during this period, we might mention Public Service Board approval in 1979 of a new top management structure for the Department; implementation of the first stages of a long-term plan to transfer the bulk of casework from Canberra to the regional offices in Australia and overseas; and improvements in the Overseas Service including the creation of two new regional structures based in Rome and Hong

Kong under the direction of senior immigration officers, as well as a major review of the training needs of overseas staff, followed by a reorganization of the Overseas Training Course. In fiscal year 1978–1979, a new Refugee Branch was created, as well as an Australian Refugee Advisory Council (which unfortunately did not survive for very long). A Legal and Parliamentary Branch was also added; it later became the Legislation and Review Division under the new management structure. (A management organization chart for the Department in 1991 may be found in Appendix 3.)

In October 1979, two Migration Amendment Acts (Acts to amend the Migration Act 1958, one major and one minor) received royal assent. They embodied the principal recommendations of the Joint Management Review relating to legislative control and enforcement. The review team had recommended four possible strategies for changing Australia's migration legislation. Its preferred strategy, which has evidently been adopted, was to get these important amendments through quickly and then to proceed at a comfortable pace with the major task of preparing a new Migration Act. According to the advice which the team received, this would take several years at least. At the time of writing, a new Migration Act is still under consideration. On May 26, 1986, a Migration and Review Task Force was established in the Department to help analyse the Migration Act, migration policy, and decision-making and review arrangements.

The Green Paper and Public Debate

While these changes were taking place in immigration management, there were equally important policy developments. On March 30, 1976, three months after the Liberal–NCP Coalition took office, the Minister, Michael MacKellar, delivered a statement on population policy in the House of Representatives, signifying that the new government now proposed to take some action in this field. Australia, he said, was in a period of significant fertility decline. The birthrate had slumped to a long-term "no growth" level. At the same time, immigration had declined dramatically. Figures available for 1975 indicated a net migration loss of about 5,000 people – an unprecedented situation. The only major instrument available to the Government to influence the level and composition of Australia's population was immigration and this government was committed to using it. Immigration strategy must not be a "numbers game," however, but must have a sound basis which took account of the medium- and long-term implications of various growth options.[56]

The Minister then announced two important initiatives. First, he said, he was reconstituting the Australian Population and Immigration Council created by the Whitlam government a year earlier. He was appointing to the Council what he described as "A distinguished group of people with wide experience and exceptional personal qualifications." It was indeed a distinguished and able group. The present Prime Minister of Australia, Bob Hawke, was a member, in his capacity as President of the Australian Council of Trade Unions, and so was George Polites, Executive Director of the Australian Council of Employers' Federations. There were six eminent academics on the Council, including Professor W.D. Borrie of the National Population Inquiry, representing the disciplines of demography, economics, international relations, urban studies, psychology, and medicine. And there were other well-known members from business, the law, and the voluntary sector.[57] The terms of reference of the reconstituted Council were spelled out more precisely. They included:

- regularly monitoring and conducting research into population change;
- major development and research in Australia and overseas concerning population and immigration;
- recommending ways in which future immigration intakes can be planned to complement other policies;
- advising the Minister on the manpower, regional distribution, educational, economic, environmental, strategic, humanitarian, and other implications of population change.

One of APIC's first tasks, according to the Minister, would be the preparation of a Green Paper, i.e., a discussion paper on immigration and population matters. "The purposes of the Green Paper," Mr. MacKellar said, "are to stimulate interest in and debate on vital population issues and objectives; to create a better informed public opinion; and to lead to the development of policies in accord with present day values and foreseeable national needs."[58] In another very important move, not announced in Parliament, the Minister decided, for the first time in Australia's long history of advisory councils in immigration, to take the chair of APIC himself. This factor, together with the sheer talent and capacity for hard work of the new APIC membership, turned the Council into a first class policy-making instrument, which the author had the good fortune to observe at first hand during her visits to Australia.[59] The considerable advantages of this kind of advisory council and the contrast with Canada's way of appointing and managing similar councils are discussed in the final chapter.

The Australian Green Paper *Immigration Policies and Australia's Population*, tabled on March 17, 1977, came so hard on the heels of the Canadian Green Paper and the public debate that followed it, that it is difficult to avoid the view that the idea itself came from Canada. But there all likeness ends. As we have seen, the Canadian Green Paper was an inadequate and pessimistic document, although it was followed by a good and positive report from the Special Joint Committee of the Senate and the House of Commons appointed to examine it. By contrast, the Australian Green Paper was an excellent discussion paper. Informative, readable, straightforward, well-documented, and well-written, it was above all what a good Green Paper should be – an exploration of, and an invitation to explore, the complex issues and national options in a critical area of public policy. It was the work of APIC's Migration Committee.

The Green Paper examined the implications of recent trends in and prospects for population growth in Australia, drawing on the findings of the National Population Inquiry. It provided a brief survey of the history of immigration to Australia, plus a description of present immigration policies. It then explored the place of family reunion in Australia's annual immigration movement, and discussed the difficult problem of balancing this with Australia's need for skilled migrants and her commitment to helping refugees. A chapter on refugees followed, in which Australia's record was discussed, together with difficult issues relating to the determination of refugee status; the selection of refugees (how important should skill and education be?); Australia's response to the large and increasing numbers of refugees requiring resettlement; and the need for a "clear-cut refugee policy." Another chapter considered current and future options for Australia in relation to sources of migrants, and examined the "migrant potential" of various countries and regions. Finally, there were chapters dealing with the social implications of immigration and its effects on the Australian economy, on urban development and the environment, and on the relationship between population and defence and foreign policy – a long-standing national concern. Within the short space of 101 pages, the Green Paper was a mine of useful information.

The opening and closing chapters of the Green Paper dealt with policies and options. The opening chapter identified the questions which had to be asked. The final chapter took stock of the current situation and suggested possible answers in the light of existing knowledge. It also made some important statements on immigration and population issues as a basis for discussion, including the following:

1 Australia has experienced very little social tension between ethnic groups or between ethnic groups and the Australian community. Although Australians are apprehensive about this, on the basis of the experience of the last few decades there is little reason to expect racial conflict as a result of the admission of large numbers of migrants with linguistic and cultural backgrounds different from those of the host society.

2 In terms of human resources, there is little doubt that the past contribu-

tion of immigration to Australia has been positive and the immigration program has done much to put specific skills where they are needed. Whether this will continue to be of such importance depends upon the future balance between the demand for various skills, the supply of suitably trained labour by Australian education and vocational institutions and by the degree of mobility that can be generated within the Australian labour force.

3 Virtually all countries, except totalitarian regimes with closed borders, experience significant immigration and emigration. Recent experience suggests that quite apart from former immigrants leaving to settle elsewhere, Australia can expect to lose an average 30,000 to 40,000 people per year, representing a significant loss to the labour force.

4 In the short term, Australia should have the capacity to absorb at least an annual net migration gain of 50,000 each year (or about 0.4 per cent of its total population). This would represent an annual intake of about 100,000 annually (with scope for fluctuations according to prevailing circumstances).

5 In the longer term, assuming improvement in economic and employment conditions, there appears to be no major reason why Australia, with appropriate planning, should not be able to absorb an annual net migration gain of 100,000 which would require a gross intake of 170,000 to 200,000, which would bring Australia's population to 19.3 million in 2001. The major constraint on the acceptance of such a population increase would be community attitudes rather than the availability of resources.[60]

6 To facilitate better and more flexible advance planning in immigration, there is a strong case for the introduction of a "rolling program approach" covering a three year period. Adjustment of Australia's selection procedures may also be necessary. (Information is given in the Green Paper on Canada's points system of migrant selection, and the United States' system of preferences and world regional ceilings.)

Finally, the authors of the Green Paper stress that their purpose has been to identify the major issues which need to be grasped in the field of immigration and population, and to draw attention to a broad range of relevant factors. They hope that this will lead to "informed public debate which can help Government to review its policies in a way that will recognize the contemporary values and wishes of the community."[61]

The contemporary values and wishes of the community in Australia proved to be somewhat difficult to ascertain, however. The Fraser government made a more determined effort than the Trudeau government had done two years earlier to elicit public response to the Green Paper. Nearly 6,000 copies, most of them accompanied by a personal request from the

Minister for views and comments, were distributed to individuals, organizations, and groups. Advertisements inviting written submissions were placed in the national and ethnic press on April 30,1977. The Department of Immigration and Ethnic Affairs (DIEA) helped to arrange, and took part in, seven seminars on Green Paper issues and options in different parts of Australia. The views of state governments were discussed at meetings of federal and state ministers responsible for immigration and ethnic affairs. Senior DIEA officers held discussions on the Green Paper with selected Commonwealth and state departments, major trade unions, employer organizations, industries, and local government authorities. Nevertheless, even with this degree of encouragement, the volume and quality of written submissions on the Green Paper, as well as public response generally, were disappointing.

To add another dimension to this sampling of public opinion, therefore, a small Department task force was created. Its members visited 29 different localities in the states and in the Northern Territory, to hold interviews and enable people to express their views on the Green Paper directly and in confidence. Once again only a limited number of citizens came forward. The total number of submissions and recorded interviews on the Green Paper was 768 (including 456 submissions from individuals and groups and 312 interviews). It will be recalled that in Canada, with a larger population and a more formal apparatus for taking evidence (the Special Joint Committee of the Senate and the House of Commons on Immigration Policy), 1,800 individuals and groups submitted their views either in the form of written submissions or at Committee hearings. It was a larger number, but still not very impressive.

Looking back on the public debate that followed publication of the Canadian and Australian green papers on immigration and population policy, it can be said that while both produced interesting and positive results, neither was nation-wide. The Canadian effort involved Parliament to a somewhat greater extent through the creation of the Special Joint Committee, although few other members of Parliament became directly involved. The Australians attempted to reach out to the general public in an informal and low-key way, through the Department's program of public interviews, held in municipal council offices, shopping plazas, and on Good Neighbour Council premises. Neither government attempted to involve the young in this critical debate on future population size, through special programs for schools or for universities and colleges; nor was any serious attempt made to reach a wider public through the media. It is fair to say that, despite the importance of the issues under discussion, the whole debate in Canada and Australia was notable for the caution and desire not to go too far which characterizes government's relations with the public in this field. The result was limited public involvement.

The fact is that one very important element was missing in these critical public debates, without which the public was unlikely to feel that vital national questions were being discussed. Although both ministers responsible for immigration, Bob Andras in Canada and Michael MacKellar in Australia, worked exceedingly hard in the cause, their Cabinet colleagues were, with few exceptions, conspicuously absent from this public debate, while Mr. Trudeau and Mr. Fraser were positively invisible. Their absence diminished these events, and their collective behaviour clearly reflected the attitude of judicious non-involvement, provided everything was under control, sensed by Mr. MacKellar when he first took over this portfolio.

Policy Developments

Although the public debate on the Green Paper in Australia did produce some useful results, the chief value of the exercise lay in the internal review of immigration and population policies by APIC and by the Department itself,[62] which it involved, and in the fact that it paved the way for further policy developments. These developments were announced by Mr. Mac-Kellar in an important policy speech in the House of Representatives on June 7, 1978.[63]

The speech contained some very interesting announcements. The first was a statement of nine principles on which future Australian immigration policy would be based. So far – even with the amended Migration Act – no similar statement of principles has been made. (By this time in Canada, the new Immigration Act, 1976, with its statement of 10 objectives or principles on which Canadian immigration policy is based, had been the law of the land for 10 months.) Although the final report of the Joint Management Review would not be submitted for another month, its general views would have been known to senior management by then, including its strongly held belief that one of the chief weaknesses in Australia's Migration Act, 1958 was "the absence of a formal basis for policy, lack of policy on all but the most basic issues and non-adherence to policy." The statement of principles of June 1978 was no doubt designed as part of a general effort to correct this situation.

The Canadian and Australian statements of principle in immigration policy may be read in full in Appendix 2. While they have some features in common, the Australian statement places more emphasis on Australia's rights in selecting and admitting migrants; on the need to protect "social cohesiveness and harmony within the Australian community"; on the requirement that "eligibility and suitability standards for migrants will reflect Australian social mores and Australian law"; that "enclave settlement" will not be encouraged and that, although migrants will have every opportunity to preserve and disseminate their ethnic heritage, a basic premise of immigration policy will be that immigrants should integrate into Australian society. While both statements include a commitment to non-discrimination in the administration of immigration law and regulations, the Australian statement adds a rider to the effect that there are external restraints on the extent to which Australia can apply a non-discriminatory policy, in that some countries restrict emigration in various ways and there are also varying degrees of interest in migration to Australia. In addition, while refugees are mentioned in the Australian statement, there is no specific commitment, as there is in the Canadian Immigration Act, to the fulfilment of Australia's international legal obligations in relation to refugees or to continued assistance to the displaced and the persecuted.

It can be said, therefore, from a straightforward comparison, that the Canadian statement is the more liberal of the two and the less apprehensive. This is probably a direct reflection first, of the greater length of time which had elapsed since Canada adopted a universal, non-discriminatory immigration policy; and secondly, of Mr. MacKellar's own anxieties, shared by his senior officials, about the continued preference for a White Australia immigration policy in many quarters in Australia, and his belief in the need for maximum reassurance to the public in the ongoing implementation of a universal policy.

The second major announcement in Mr. MacKellar's speech related to new criteria for admission to Australia, with somewhat more emphasis on family reunion, while warning of the dangers of admitting large numbers of unskilled workers. At the same time, the Minister gave notice of the introduction of a new selection system with numerical weightings, as in the Canadian points system which had been described in the Green Paper. The details of this system were still being tested in Australia and overseas.

The new eligibility categories, described only briefly here, were as follows: (1) *Family Reunion*, consisting of the immediate family and parents of retiring age; (2) *General Eligibility*, consisting of independent applicants who possessed skills, qualifications, or other attributes which would be an economic, social, or cultural gain to Australia, as well as employment nominees; (3) *Refugees and Displaced Persons*; and (4) *Special Eligibility*, consisting of (a) applicants to be admitted under the Trans-Tasman Travel Arrangement whereby citizens of New Zealand, and Commonwealth and Irish citizens residing in New Zealand, did not normally require immigration documents when travelling to Australia directly from New Zealand[64]; (b) patrials, i.e., UK citizens with an Australian-born parent or grandparent (a reciprocal arrangement for the category of patrials in the British Immigration Act 1971)[65]; (5) entrepreneurs, and (6) self-supporting retirees. These eligibility categories were to remain in place for five years, until a Labor government took over again after the federal election of 1983. Within a few months, the new government under Bob Hawke had made significant changes reflecting very different immigration priorities.

Mr. MacKellar made three other important policy announcements in his June 1978 speech. The first concerned triennial programming (recommended in the Green Paper); the second, change of status in Australia; and the third, creation of immigration review panels within the Department as a formal appeals system.

Triennial programming was an Australian invention, adopted by Canada in 1981 as a "three year planning cycle with annual reviews and adjustments."[66] (It is interesting that neither country ever openly acknowledges the real source of these good ideas.) Instead of planning immigration on an annual basis as in the past, it would from now on be planned for a three year period with flexible annual intakes which could be adjusted within the overall target, according to circumstances. Mr. MacKellar described the new system as "triennial rolling immigration programs" which would begin with the period from 1978–1979 to 1980–1981. The main purpose of the new approach was to achieve more stability and predictability in immigration levels, and to provide a better basis for manpower and other kinds of planning in the public and private sectors in Australia, both of which were being urged on the Government by the states and by major employers. The Government had decided, the Minister went on to say, that the net annual gains in the first triennial program should be 70,000 which, given current levels of emigration, could be achieved with a gross intake of 90,000. He added: "Critical to the success of future immigration programs will be the co-ordination of manpower, population and development policies at the local, state and Commonwealth levels. In particular, the immigration program will be planned with special regard to government policies on retraining and assistance to industry. The effects of technology transfer, the needs of growth centres and specific regional needs will be reflected in each program."

Change of status, that is the possibility of changing from temporary to permanent status when already in a receiving country, is a critical issue in immigration as we have seen. It was this provision in the Canadian Immigration Regulations of 1967, together with the opportunity to appeal one's case to the newly created Immigration Appeal Board, which set off, in the early 1970s, the largest post-war illegal immigration movement Canada has seen. As a result, change of status is not now permitted in Canada, although special dispensation can be obtained in compassionate cases.

Australia has been reluctant to close off all possibilities for change of status, mainly because of the hardship created by distance for applicants who may have to re-apply from their home country (an issue which has concerned Canada also). However, the new provisions relating to change of status announced by Mr. MacKellar came close to a total embargo — tightened,in his words "as from today to reduce the incidence of circumvention." As from June 7, 1978, he said, persons who had entered Australia as visitors, temporary residents, or illegally would not be eligible to apply in Australia for change of status to permanent residence. The only exceptions would be spouses and dependent children of residents of Australia, refugees with valid entry permits, aged parents who would have qualified for admission if they had applied overseas, and private overseas students able to meet the criteria and requirements for migrant entry to Australia.

The final major policy announcement in the Minister's speech concerned the lack of an effective appeals system in Australia. The Joint Management Review team was very concerned about this, and would stress in their July report the need for review and appeals machinery. "The representation case-load will be appreciably reduced," they wrote, "only if a viable alternative – an effective system of internal and/or external review and appeals – becomes available and is used. This means that the Minister himself must be prepared to direct representations to the proper channels, and avoid protracted representations as either an alternative or an addition to the new procedures."[67] Mr. MacKellar drew attention to the fact that hundreds of thousands of prospective migrants were rejected each year. From this number, more than 40,000 requests for review of decisions affecting more than 150,000 people came in every year. To meet this need, he said, it had been decided in principle to establish review panels within the Department to deal with these requests. The advice of the Administrative Review Council would be sought on the best way to set up this system.[68]

This was an important step in creating an effective appeals system which also involved the recently created Administrative Appeals Tribunal and the Commonwealth Ombudsman.[69] Review panels, staffed by senior officers who were not involved in the original decisions, were created within DIEA. This could not be described as a fully independent appeals system, however. The present review and appeals systems of Canada and Australia are outlined in Appendix 6.

Finally, the Minister pledged that the Fraser government would continue to take a positive approach to accepting refugees for resettlement; would consult state governments on the level and content of each triennial program; would ensure that the Australian Population and Immigration Council continued to be "the prime consultative body" on immigration policies and programs and population issues; and would continue to monitor population trends carefully. Mr. MacKellar ended his speech with a peroration in which the words Australia and Canada could well be interchangeable: "Australia and its people are extremely fortunate. We have a vast land area with a low overall population density, a large share of the world's mineral resources, stable and efficient administrative systems, a high level of personal prosperity and material security, an extensive system of social services and a spirit of egalitarianism which promotes an exceptional level of social and economic mobility. We must continue to have confidence in ourselves and the future – to meet the challenge of our destiny – to build together a nation rich in diversity, yet united in purpose.[70]

The Galbally Review and Implementation Program

These developments in immigration and population policy and management were accompanied by determined action on another front: migrant services and programs. In August 1977, the Fraser government announced a review of the post-arrival programs and services provided to migrants by the Commonwealth and non-government organizations supported by Commonwealth funding. The chairman of a review group of four would be Frank E. Galbally, CBE, a prominent criminal lawyer from Melbourne. Galbally was well-acquainted with migrant groups in that city, and was also a good friend of the Prime Minister. The other three members were well-known members of the Italian, Greek, and Yugoslav communities from Sydney, Melbourne, and Perth, respectively.

The Galbally review group was asked to examine and report on "the effectiveness of the Commonwealth's programs and services for those who have migrated to Australia, including programs and services provided by non-government organizations which receive Commonwealth assistance identifying any areas of need or duplication of programs and services." It was also asked to consider "the roles and functions of government and non-government organizations respectively, and the appropriate relationship between them which would ensure the most effective planning and provision of programs and services to migrants," "which programs and services available to the general community could be better designed to ensure that migrants (especially non-English speaking migrants) are as well served as others," and a number of other requirements.

The Galbally Review of Post-Arrival Programs and Services for Migrants was completed in less than a year. Its recommendations were firm and unequivocal and the Fraser government accepted them with similar speed and firmness. On May 30, when tabling the report which he had received only a few weeks earlier, the Prime Minister announced not only that the review recommendations had been accepted, but that there would be additional expenditures of $49.7 million by the federal government on migrant services over the next three years. This would include an extra $13,290,000 for English language teaching for children and adult migrants; $12,000,000 for initial settlement services (including new settlement centres to provide 6 to 12 week orientation courses); $10,770,000 for ethnic media, including a pilot ethnic television station; and $6,800,000 for multicultural projects, including teaching community languages and setting up an Institute of Multicultural Affairs. In addition, $3,540,000 would be spent on communications, $3,460,000 for voluntary and self-help services, $770,000 for special groups (young children, migrant women, the handicapped, and the aged), and $730,000 for employment and health services for migrants.

It is widely believed in Australia that the main thrust of the Galbally Report and the amount of money to be spent on its implementation were probably agreed in advance. It can therefore be seen as a major statement of intent by the Fraser government, or as a set of rather deliberate policy initiatives relating to the settlement and integration of immigrants in Australian society; the involvement of ethnic groups in this process; and the acceptance of Australia as a multicultural society in which the right of migrants to maintain their own cultural and racial identity, if they wish to do so, must be recognized. The money to be spent on the implementation of the Galbally recommendations – roughly $15 million annually for three years – was fairly modest, given that it included initial orientation and settlement, language training, creation of settlement centres and migrant resource centres, extension of the Telephone Interpreter Service, and other items. (In fact, the ceiling of nearly $50 million over three years has now been exceeded by quite a substantial amount.) What was impressive, however, was the decisive way in which the review was set up, carried out, its recommendations accepted and given a high degree of priority, and an implementation program set up right away.[71]

Without going into the Galbally recommendations in detail, we should note the major emphases of this influential report. The report stressed:

1 The importance of an initial language training and orientation program for all migrants, described as "a comprehensive initial settlement program," to be provided at existing migrant hostels and at new settlement centres.
2 The importance of the concept of multiculturalism and the use of ethnic organizations and agencies in the delivery of services to migrants.
3 The principle of self-help which should be encouraged to help migrants become self-reliant quickly.
4 The need for language training programs catering for all age groups and for those who had not been reached by existing programs.

5 The vital importance of good information programs for all migrants, and the need therefore to strengthen the Information Branch of the Department of Immigration and Ethnic Affairs.
6 The need to extend existing translation and interpreter services, particularly the successful Telephone Interpreter Service.
7 The need for multicultural education programs in the schools to encourage "a multicultural attitude in Australian society."
8 The need for further developments in the field of ethnic broadcasting, as well as the establishment of a permanent ethnic television service within the next three years.

The extent to which the Galbally Review and recommendations were a deliberate response to the needs of Australia's increasingly multicultural society, and the need to update and improve her services and programs for migrants, may be gauged from the report's opening remarks:

We believe that Australia is at a critical stage in the development of a cohesive, united, multicultural nation. This has come about because of a number of significant changes in recent years – changes in the pattern of migration and in the structure of our population, changes in attitudes to migration and to our responsibilities for international refugees, changes in the needs of the large and growing numbers of ethnic groups in our community, and changes in the roles of governments and the community generally in responding to those needs ...

We have concluded that it is now necessary for the Commonwealth Government to change the direction of its involvement in the provision of programs and services for migrants and to take further steps to encourage multiculturalism. In taking these new directions, we stress at the outset that the closer involvement of ethnic communities themselves, and of other levels of government, is essential.[72]

The implementation of the Galbally Report's package of 57 recommendations, plus related proposals, to be introduced between 1978 and 1981, proceeded at the same cracking pace as the review itself. The Minister for Immigration and Ethnic Affairs was made responsible for implementing the Galbally Report, reporting to the Social Welfare Policy Committee of Cabinet. During the latter part of 1978, a Galbally Implementation Task Force was created under the chairmanship of Derek Volker, then the Deputy Secretary of the Department. The task force consisted of senior officials from the Commonwealth departments chiefly concerned with implementation, namely the departments of Prime Minister and Cabinet, Finance, Employment and Youth Affairs, Education, Home Affairs, the Public Service Board, and DIEA itself, which also provided the task force secretariat. Other departments, including Social Security, Health, Post and Telecommunications, and Administrative Services, participated from time to time.

The task force went at it in a very determined and energetic manner. Visits were paid to all states and mainland territories (19 of the 57 major recommendations in the Galbally Report involved state responsibilities), for talks with state and Commonwealth officials and with leaders of ethnic and other community groups, to initiate new services and programs or expand and develop old ones. Consultations were held in all the capital cities as well as in Mt. Isa, Alice Springs, Geelong, Wollongong, Albury-Wodonga, and Shepparton. Conferences, seminars, and meetings about the Galbally Report with academic, professional, business, and community groups were supported or promoted by the Department. To assist in the consultative process, and to keep the community informed, the Department distributed a useful information kit, which it updated regularly, showing the progress made in implementing the Report. In the Department's Annual Review for 1980-1981, the final year of the implementation program, it was reported that of the 57 Galbally recommendations, 51 could now be said to be "implemented, near implemented or overtaken by other initiatives."[73]

These post-arrival services are kept under review, however. In December 1985, the Minister, Chris Hurford, announced a major Review of Migrant and Multicultural Programs and Services designed to give further direction to the activities of the Post-Arrival Services and Community Affairs Program.

The Australian Institute of Multicultural Affairs

One of the major recommendations of the Galbally Report was to propose the creation of an Australian Institute of Multicultural Affairs "to engage in and commission research and advise government bodies on multicultural issues." This too was implemented quickly. The Galbally Report was tabled in the House of Representatives on May 30, 1978. A bill to establish an Australian Institute of Multicultural Affairs had its first reading on September 13, 1979 and received royal assent on November 28. Within the next few months, the Institute was set up with offices on Bourke Street in downtown Melbourne. Its chairman was Frank Galbally, its director Petro Georgiou, previously senior adviser on ethnic affairs and speech writer to the Prime Minister. The Institute consisted of a small governing council and a membership of not more than 100 persons, all of whom were to be appointed by the Minister. The council consisted of the Chairman, the Director, the Secretary (Deputy Minister) of the Commonwealth

Department of Immigration and Ethnic Affairs and not less than three or more than six other members.

The objectives of the newly-created Institute, as defined in the Act, were: (a) to develop among the members of the Australian community an awareness of the diverse cultures within that community that have arisen as a result of the migration of people to Australia; and an appreciation of the contribution of those cultures to the enrichment of that community; (b) to promote tolerance, understanding, harmonious relations, and mutual esteem among the different cultural groups and ethnic communities in Australia; (c) to promote a cohesive Australian society by assisting members of the Australian community to share with one another their diverse cultures within the legal and political structures of that society; and (d) to assist in promoting an environment that affords the members of the different cultural groups and ethnic communities in Australia the opportunity to participate fully in Australian society and achieve their own potential. As well as providing advice to the Commonwealth governments on all matters relating to the achievement of these objectives, the Institute was required to promote them by commissioning and conducting research and public education in this field.

The Institute was soon put to work by the Fraser government and one of its early tasks, requested on September 15, 1981 by the Minister for Immigration and Ethnic Affairs (Ian Macphee had replaced Michael MacKellar in December 1978), was to prepare an evaluation of the objectives and implementation of the Galbally Report. While the Institute, whose nine man governing council then included Frank Galbally himself, who was of course responsible for the Galbally Report, and John Menadue, Secretary of DIEA, who was chiefly responsible for its implementation, could therefore hardly be said to constitute an impartial evaluating body, it nevertheless carried out a thorough assessment which was submitted to the Minister on May 15, 1982.[74] The council did not subject the basic objectives and concepts of the Galbally Report to any rigorous analysis, or none that was published. It did not ask the question, for example, whether the multicultural approach to the delivery of migrant services taken by the Galbally Report was the best one, nor did it examine the political implications of multiculturalism. It might also be argued that it was rather soon to evaluate the impact and effectiveness of such a wide-ranging set of recommendations, since the implementation process had scarcely been completed. The Institute's evaluation, therefore, was really a useful progress report which identified program weaknesses, additional financial requirements, and tasks requiring further effort. By its firm approval, however, it did legitimize the Galbally Report, and helped this large package of policies and programs on its way. In relation to a longer term evaluation, the Institute did recommend that a further evaluation of migrant and multicultural programs and services should begin in 1986.

The major conclusions of the Institute's evaluation of the implementation, achievement of objectives, and financing of the Galbally Report, may be summarized as follows:

1 On implementation. The evaluation found what it called "an impressive record of implementation" whose major achievements included: (a) establishing a new intensive program to provide English instruction and essential information to new arrivals; (b) doubling the number of grants to ethnic and voluntary organizations to undertake migrant welfare services; (c) extending the Telephone Interpreter Service to Canberra, Hobart, Darwin, and several regional centres; and (d) introducing a multicultural television service in Sydney and Melbourne – foreshadowed earlier but given considerable impetus by the Galbally Report.

Set against these achievements the evaluation found instances where expectations had not been realized. Overall, however, the evaluation concluded that "implementation of the Report's proposals has been of substantial benefit to migrants both newly arrived and longer resident; to Australia's ethnic groups; and to the community as a whole. The years since the Report have seen the establishment and extension of programs and services which together make up what is perhaps the most comprehensive system of migrant and multicultural services in the world. In several key areas, Australian provisions are unique.[75]

2 On objectives. Here the evaluation states that "it is by no means a simple process to assess whether the Report's overall objectives have been achieved." Considerable unevenness was found in the degree to which the pursuit of recommendations had actually served the intended objectives. Most movement seemed to have occurred in programs and services that were relatively specific, rather than in areas where the Galbally Report had made broad proposals calling on government departments and other bodies to make changes in their general programs and policies. Nevertheless, "across the range of recommendations and associated proposals," the evaluation found "evidence of tangible and significant gains in the direction of the central objectives."

The council concluded that the Report's essential relevance was undiminished and that its guiding principles continued to be relevant as well, constituting a clear and necessary basis for effective programs and services in a multicultural society. It warned, however, that over the longer term "the achievement of overall objectives are not exclusively a matter of changes in particular policies, programs and recommendations. They depend upon the development of a recognition that the Australian community is a multicultural one, and a commitment to the principle that general programs must serve the community as a whole."[76]

3   On financing. The evaluation notes that the Galbally Report "proposed additional expenditures, over three years, of nearly $50 million above the 1977/78 base of $45 million. Spending on post-arrival programs and services for migrants increased to more than $220 million over the three years, an average of more than $70 million per year. In real terms, total expenditure in this area has matched that envisaged by the Report."[77]

The major part of the Institute's evaluation is taken up, however, with a wide range of recommendations for the improvement, adjustment, or development of some of the basic programs recommended in the Galbally Report, including the initial settlement program, the adult migrant education program, the child migrant education program, the multicultural education program and others. There were a total of 89 recommendations, some of them involving significant expenditures, others some savings or a reallocation of resources. The net additional cost to the Commonwealth budget was estimated at approximately $6 million, at current prices over the next three years.

As with the Galbally Review itself, the Fraser government moved swiftly to accept the Institute's evaluation and recommendations. On July 26, 1982, under the title "Aid for Migrants Upgraded," the *Canberra Times* reported: "The Government has decided to accept almost completely the recommendations of an evaluation study of the Galbally Report on migrant services. The Prime Minister, Mr. Fraser, announced yesterday that an extra $21 million would be spent implementing the recommendations over the next three years." It was as if nothing could go wrong in this remarkable episode in Australia's post-war immigration history, which had behind it the invincible combination of Malcolm Fraser and Frank Galbally. What went wrong with this particular scenario, of course, was that Mr. Fraser and the Liberal-National party were defeated in the election of March 5, 1983, and the Hawke government had rather different ideas on some aspects of the Galbally system of post-arrival services for migrants and, particularly, on the objectives and management of the Institute of Multicultural Affairs. Nevertheless, a large proportion of the Galbally recommendations were carried out, bringing major improvements to migrant services and programs in Australia and providing a more unified framework for delivery.

NUMAS AND THE SEARCH FOR A
MIGRANT SELECTION SYSTEM

The search for an effective and acceptable migrant selection system for Australia, which began in the early seventies, did not proceed so smoothly.

From the late sixties onwards, there was a growing feeling within the Department of Immigration that something would have to be done to replace its wholly unstructured procedures for migrant selection. As mentioned earlier, there was at that time a particularly high rate of departure from Australia of former settlers, as well as a disturbing incidence of migrant settlement problems. Concern about these problems is reflected in two studies commissioned by the Department during this period: the *Inquiry into the Departure of Settlers from Australia* by the Committee on Social Patterns of the then Immigration Advisory Council, published in July 1973; and a large-scale immigration survey of migrant experiences in Australia carried out in 1973 by the Commonwealth Bureau of Census and Statistics (now the Australian Bureau of Statistics).[78] A report on the survey and its findings was written by the Australian Population and Immigration Council and published in 1976 under the title *A Decade of Migrant Settlement*. Both reports lent weight to the view that better selection procedures, better information for migrants, and better post-arrival services for migrants were needed.[79]

Canada had produced her points system for the selection and admission of immigrants in 1967, and Australian immigration officers had been observing its performance. Some approved and would have liked to see a similar system installed in Australia. Others felt that the system was too mechanistic and left too little room for the personal evaluation of applicants by experienced immigration officers, which they felt was the most valuable element in a selection system. Nevertheless in 1970, as we have seen, the Department of Immigration set up an internal task force to study possible new selection procedures. One key factor was numerical weighting, a principal characteristic of the Canadian points system. It was relatively easy to list the factors required for successful settlement, but much more difficult and more critical for the migrant to weight the factors so they would add up to a pass or fail mark. Only this or something like it could indicate the relative importance of selection factors, bring greater uniformity to assessment of migrants, and generally free the system from the burden of personal discretion.

In 1972, the Department's task force produced a tentative Australian points system with numerical weighting which was submitted to the then Minister for Immigration, Dr. A.J. Forbes. But Dr. Forbes opted for a non-numerically-weighted system, partly because it was rumoured that Mr. Whitlam and the ALP (whose electoral prospects were looking ever brighter) were likely to favour the Canadian system, including Canada's amalgamation of employment and immigration. The Department then created the Structured Selection Assessment System (SSAS), without numerical weighting.[80] Ironically, when the ALP came to power in December of that year, with Al Grassby as Minister for Immigration, they too favoured the new Structured Selection Assessment System. It was announced by Mr. Grassby, as we have seen, on January 31, 1973.

The Structured Selection Assessment System was in fact a half-way house and of value only as a trial effort. It received careful evaluation, however. In July 1973, Mr. Grassby asked the Chairman of the Social Patterns Committee of the Immigration Advisory Council, Professor Jerzy (George) Zubrzycki, who was about to visit Canada as Visiting Research Professor of Sociology at Carleton University in Ottawa, to extend his visit to include several overseas immigration offices in Britain and Europe to see how the SSAS was working.[81] The Department of Immigration set up a working party to study its use and effectiveness, and in early 1977, the new Minister, Mr. MacKellar, asked the Social Studies Committee of the Australian Population and Immigration Council to carry out a thorough appraisal of it. The committee's preliminary findings were sufficient to show that the new system had serious shortcomings. Acting on this and its own internal evidence, the Department's working party produced an improved system which was given the name NUMAS, short for "Numerically-Weighted Multi-Factor Assessment System." After careful field testing and extensive public consultation, the new system was introduced on January 1, 1979.

The fate of NUMAS deserves a study in itself. It aroused unexpected suspicion and hostility, immediate and continuing wrath on the part of the Opposition, deep anxieties among ethnic groups and voluntary agencies, and a critical reception in the press. Like its predecessor, it did not survive for long in its original form.

NUMAS was an amalgamation of the Canadian points system and the Structured Selection Assessment System. It preserved the two-part assessment form of the SSAS (Part A: economic factors and Part B: personal and settlement – formerly social – factors), making only minor deletions and changes in terminology, but adding numerical weightings to a total of 100 as in the Canadian system. Originally all applicants for migrant entry except refugees were to be assessed under NUMAS and only spouses, dependent children, and aged parents of people already resident in Australia were not required to reach the necessary minimum number of points in either Part A or Part B. Other relatives of Australian residents, who were eligible for entry under family reunion policy, were also not required to attain a minimum number of points on economic factors, but they were required to gain a minimum of 25 points on personal and settlement factors, and were also required to show that they would not become a charge on public funds if admitted to Australia.

"Independent breadwinner applicants," however, including those nominated by Australian employers, were required to attain a minimum of 30 points on both sets of factors, although these could be averaged out if more points were obtained on one set of factors than on the other. Applicants eligible as "patrials, entrepreneurs and self-supporting retirees" were only required to obtain the minimum 30 points on personal and settlement factors alone. This applied also to fiancé(e)s of Australian residents, except that the required number of points in Part B was reduced slightly to 28.[82]

The significant differences between NUMAS and the Canadian points system were first that the Canadian system concentrates almost entirely on economic factors, leaving a maximum of 10 points only for "personal suitability," described in Canada's Immigration Regulations 1978 as "the personal suitability of the person and his dependants to become successfully established in Canada based on the person's adaptability, motivation, initiative, resourcefulness and other similar qualities." Secondly, in Canada the immediate family (the family class) have always been admitted automatically and are not assessed under the points system.

The basic objections and fears about NUMAS on the part of the informed public, which surfaced almost immediately, were first, that it laid major emphasis on skills, and therefore on the countries and regions from which skilled migrants still came in the largest numbers, namely Britain and, to a lesser extent, Northern Europe and North America. It was felt that this implied a return, to some extent, to the White Australia policy. Secondly, it was seen as giving too much weight to competence in English, discriminating against migrants from non-English-speaking countries. Thirdly, its provisions for family migration were regarded as very inadequate. There was also a general unease and discomfort with the *explicitness* of the new selection system. It seemed to be attempting to analyse and quantify too much, particularly in the personal and settlement factors in Part B.

The Australian Labor Party took a firm stand against NUMAS, finding at last some politically appealing grounds for opposing the Fraser government's immigration policies. Outlining the party's platform for the 1980 election (won by the Liberal–NCP Coalition but with a reduced majority), the Leader Bill Hayden said that if the ALP won the election, they would abolish NUMAS altogether because it was heavily biased against family reunion and against non-English-speaking immigrants. On a number of occasions, but most notably in a speech in the House of Representatives the following year, he elaborated on this position:

The populations of the countries in our region have two things in common: they are all brown-skinned and none have English as their first and basic language. The implication of NUMAS is that it discriminates in favour of Anglo-Saxons. It discriminates even more in favour of people who are higher on the socio-economic ladder. In a very important respect there is an explicit clash of principle between the application of NUMAS and the enunciated purposes of the Government's immigration policy. The Government declares that its immigration policy is based on multicultural principles, yet here we have a selection system which discriminates in a significant way – although not completely – against the development of such a principle.[83]

In the face of a distinctly adverse public reaction, even the Minister began to have misgivings. In an interview with the author in 1980, Mr. Macphee remarked "We borrowed it from you and then made it more complicated!" He thought NUMAS had to be simplified and made more comprehensible to the public.[84] After a year or more, therefore, of trial, testing, and continuing public criticism, the Fraser government began to make changes in NUMAS. In May 1980, Cabinet decided "to expand NUMAS to facilitate family reunion for Australian citizens and residents" and on May 23, the Minister announced concessions under Part A for people with relatives or friends in Australia. From July 1 onwards, the pass mark of 30 points in Part A was reduced to 24 for those nominated by a very close relative, to 26 for those nominated by a brother or sister and to 28 for those nominated by some other relative or friend. In October, just prior to the election, when the ALP was saying that it would abolish NUMAS, the Prime Minister announced that there would be a major review of the new selection system directed particularly "towards assessing whether it adequately took account of assistance provided by relatives in Australia."

This review, which had been promised by the Minister when NUMAS was introduced in January 1979, was launched by Mr. Macphee on March 6, 1981. It was to be a community-wide review with public consultations and – as with the Green Paper – submissions invited from organizations and individuals. In addition, the Minister said, "an independent committee of prominent members of the community with expertise in immigration matters" was being asked "to review the submissions, the results of the public consultations and the findings of a number of research projects being undertaken as part of the review."[85] A three-man independent review committee was appointed immediately, illustrating Australia's remarkable capacity – which will be discussed in more detail later – for using a high level of talent and experience in the service of immigration policy development. Its members were Dr. Charles Price of the Department of Demography of the Australian National University, an eminent social historian and authority on immigration, member of the Australian Refugee Advisory Council and Chairman of the recently-formed Migrant Settlement Council of the ACT (Australian Capital Territory); Mr. James Samios, MBE, Chairman of the New South Wales Ethnic Communities Council and of the N.S.W. Migrant Settlement Council; and Mr. Justice James Gobbo of the Victoria Supreme Court, Chairman of the Migration Committee of the Australian Population and Immigration Council and Chairman of the Refugee Advisory Council.

Within little more than a year, NUMAS had undergone a major transformation and the name itself, which had always sounded like a dangerous weapon, had been abandoned. On October 29, 1981, the Minister outlined in Parliament the details of a new migrant selection system for Australia which was modified further by the Hawke government after March 1983. The present system is closer to the Canadian points system than NUMAS was and shares its major emphasis on family migration and labour market needs. (The two systems may be compared in Appendix 4 where they are described in detail.)

The Minister said the Government had revised the selection system to meet two objectives: to reunite close family members and to help satisfy Australia's demand for skilled workers. At the same time, the principles of a universal non-discriminatory immigration policy were being retained. The new selection system was based on a broad range of advice which the Government had received from the Australian Council on Population and Ethnic Affairs (ACPEA which had now replaced APIC, the Australian Population and Immigration Council), the Australian Council of Trade Unions and the Confederation of Australian Industry, as well as from the Review Committee which had examined the written submissions and the views expressed at the series of public forums which had been held around Australia.

The Review Committee had found "a strong demand for an acceptable family reunion system," Mr. Macphee said, and in its report had emphasized "the importance of family and friends to settlement success." But it also found concern that "migrant entry criteria should be sensitive to current and foreseeable demands for labor," underlining evidence that the ability to get a job was vital to settlement success. The committee had discovered "widespread support for numerical weighting to yield an overall point score," but also "widespread criticism of attempts to numerically assess settlement factors, in particular such subjective factors as initiative and adaptability." On the difficult question of English-language requirements and the special consideration this appeared to give Anglo-Saxons, the committee found "agreement among migrants, settlement staff, researchers and experts that the ability to speak English is crucial to a number of aspects of short and long-term settlement ... as migrants who were unable to find employment acknowledged that lack of English diminishes prospects of successful settlement." The Government maintained the view that competence in English was an important indicator of settlement prospects, but was also adding "the ability to learn English" to the factors of assessment, as demonstrated, for example, by knowledge of other languages.[86] The new selection system came into effect on April 19, 1982.

One interesting minor change involved, as in the Canadian points system, the provision of extra points for applicants who settled in "designated growth areas," these areas to be decided in consultation with the states and territories and with relevant departments. The Minister also announced that the Employer Nomination Scheme and Business Migration Program, which were already in operation, and are self explanatory, had been reviewed and that some changes in policies and procedures were now under consideration. Finally, in another move which brought the Canadian and Australian systems closer together, the Minister said that, as part of the Department's policy to help people understand the decisions that affect them, they would now be given access to the Department of Immigration and Ethnic Affairs' instruction manual. In Canada, the immigration manuals of the Canada Employment and Immigration Commission were made available to the public in October 1979.[87]

The life and death of NUMAS is very instructive for immigration management. It was a selection system that had laudable objectives, particularly to improve consistency in immigrant selection; to ensure that selection was truly non-discriminatory and to ensure that assessments were based on *all* the factors relevant to settlement success. But it also had the major but unstated aim of achieving, as far as possible, a well-qualified, well-adjusted migration movement in the context of a universal, non-discriminatory immigration policy. It was thoroughly field-tested in Australia and overseas. It was originally approved, with its numerical weightings, by the Australian Population and Immigration Council. But as its ship came into port, it foundered on the twin rocks of family reunion and public hostility.

Family reunion, as we have seen, is one of the most complex issues of immigration management. NUMAS was not as lenient to family reunion as the present system is (i.e., the 1982 system as revised by the Hawke government), but it also had another strike against it. Lacking the political and human advantages of major improvements in family reunion, it was also unappealing in other more subtle ways. The name, the explicitness, the impression of over-careful weighing and measuring of qualities in migrants which are very hard to assess – all this worked against a favourable public reaction and even aroused, to some degree, a basic national antagonism. The fact is that qualities like "responsiveness, initiative, self-reliance, independence, presentation and adaptability" do have to be considered in the selection of migrants if the process is to have any real worth. Many Canadians and Australians, however, still clearly prefer to leave this aspect of selection to the discretion of the immigration officer and, in Canada at least, decently shrouded in mystery.

THE TRANS-TASMAN TRAVEL
ARRANGEMENT

Human traffic flows in large numbers to and fro across the Tasman Sea
which separates Australia and New Zealand. Since 1920 the free movement and interchange of their citizens of European descent, without passports or any form of immigration control, has been a basic feature of the
immigration policies of both countries. This mutual agreement, known as
the Trans-Tasman Travel Arrangement (TTTA), arrived at in 1920, included
citizens of Commonwealth countries of European descent, but did not
include New Zealand citizens of Asian, Polynesian, or mixed racial
descent who, while they did not require passports to travel to Australia,
had to obtain what was called "prior travel authority" to do so.

In the late sixties, the New Zealand authorities made several requests to
Australia for a review of these discriminatory procedures affecting New
Zealand citizens of non-European descent, but without success. In 1971,
the matter was explicitly reviewed by the McMahon cabinet, but it was
decided to retain existing controls on the entry of non-European New
Zealand citizens. The Whitlam government took a different line, however.
One of the first steps taken by Mr. Whitlam in January 1973, one month
after becoming Prime Minister, was to visit Wellington for discussions on
the subject with Norman Kirk, the Labour Prime Minister of New Zealand. As a result of this meeting, new reciprocal arrangements were introduced in March 1973. Under these arrangements:

1 Australian and New Zealand citizens could travel between the two countries without any travel documents except for the completion of outgoing and incoming passenger cards.
2 Citizens of either country could travel to Australia and New Zealand
   from other parts of the world without visas, provided they held valid
   passports.
3 Citizens of Commonwealth countries who had been granted permission
   to reside without restriction in either country and who were travelling
   directly between the two countries were not required to carry passports
   or visas.

The term "citizens" meant all citizens, regardless of origin. The reciprocal
arrangements included a commitment by both countries to review these
matters from time to time.

What has been called "the trans-Tasman drift of people seeking new
lives and better opportunities"[88] has produced over time a certain min-
gling of the white populations of Australia and New Zealand. Australia's

most recent census figures show that her present population of 16 million includes 177,000 New Zealanders, or 1.18 per cent. New Zealand's much smaller population of 3.2 million included, at the end of 1981, 43,089 Australians or 1.38 per cent. For some years, however, the drift has been very one-sided, with far more New Zealanders than Australians crossing the Tasman for temporary or permanent settlement on the other side. Though the recent world recession has been tough on both countries, New Zealand's economy suffered more and was hit harder by other international trends and developments, including Britain's decision to join the EEC. As a result, New Zealand has experienced a serious loss of valuable manpower, mainly to Australia, while Australia has had a worrying influx of New Zealanders competing with Australians for jobs. It was not until 1983-1984 that these numbers began to decline significantly.

Other serious problems have arisen in the 1970s, to plague Australia mainly, in relation to the Trans-Tasman Travel Arrangement. Under the TTTA, the route from New Zealand across the Tasman to Sydney or Melbourne, with its easy access and absence of normal immigration controls, has become a convenient back door into Australia for drug traffickers, criminals, and illegal immigrants of all kinds. This became an increasing source of concern to the Australian authorities in the mid-seventies and a regular subject for discussion with their New Zealand counterparts. From 1978 onwards, the ministers responsible for immigration in both countries began to hold regular twice-yearly meetings. At a meeting in April 1980 between Mr. Macphee and Mr. James Bolger, Minister of Labour and Immigration in the Muldoon government, it was agreed that officials would make a joint examination of the current state of trans-Tasman migration, the incidence of abuse and the possible means of eliminating it.

The principal abuses of the Trans-Tasman Travel Arrangement identified by the Australian Department of Immigration and Ethnic Affairs were the movement between the two countries of drug couriers and others involved in the drug trade under false identities; the ease of entry into Australia under false identities of persons representing a security threat to Australia; anonymous movement between the two countries for criminal purposes; the ease of circumventing normal immigration controls by entering New Zealand legitimately as a visitor and then adopting a false identity to secure permanent entry to Australia; and non-Commonwealth Pacific Islanders entering Australia claiming to be Maoris or of Tokelau, Niue or Cook Island origin.[89] No doubt as an outcome of these unrestricted opportunities, New Zealanders head the list in the proportional incidence of crime among migrant groups in Australia, with a record which has been described by the Department as "consistently worse than that for all other groups." Together with Yugoslavs, they are also the most likely to commit crimes of violence. In 1981 they constituted one half of Australia's criminal deportees.

During the last few years, Australia has been pressing for changes in the Trans-Tasman Travel Arrangement to permit a greater degree of control over this very free movement of people. New Zealand, on the other hand, has been reluctant to agree to any proposed change. Her position, firmly held by the former Muldoon government, has been that the TTTA is an important symbol of the close relationship between Australia and New Zealand and should be left as it is; and that it is not worth inconveniencing the honest traveller for "a few illegals and drug traffickers."

In April 1981, Australia moved unilaterally to introduce passport controls on travel between the two countries to become effective on July 1. In a statement to the House the Minister, Mr. Macphee, said that New Zealand had rejected an Australian proposal to adopt a common immigration entry and screening process to detect undesirables, partly on the grounds that it was too difficult to harmonize their respective immigration procedures sufficiently. Australia had therefore decided to introduce passport controls. During the past six weeks, the Minister said, surveys had shown that between 30,000 and 50,000 trans-Tasman travellers had no authoritative identification, such as passports or driver's licences, on arrival in Australia.

The Opposition supported this new policy. The ALP's spokesman on immigration, Mick Young, said that the tougher restrictions were "worth a try," even though it could not be guaranteed that all undesirables would be stopped from entering Australia. Australia was looked upon as a clearing house for smuggled drugs and the public would support moves to curtail this trade. He could not agree with the Prime Minister of New Zealand, Mr. Young said, that the move would damage relations between the two countries.

A year later, Australia and New Zealand began negotiations for a Closer Economic Relations Agreement (CER) which became effective on January 1, 1983. Under this agreement, Australia and New Zealand will progressively become a free trade area. According to Mr. Bolger, New Zealand's former Minister of Labour and Immigration who was one of the principal ministers involved in these negotiations, "If we did not have free movement of Australians and New Zealanders across the Tasman, it would have to be introduced to support the Closer Economic Relations Agreement." Clearly this very desirable free movement of people across the Tasman is likely to continue, and the new passport rule may well assist in helping to control it in a reasonable manner. Lack of a passport has rarely deterred serious criminals and drug traffickers, however, and it seems likely that this is not the last word on the difficult question of preventing illegal immigration and the criminal activities which often go with it from finding easy entry to Australia across the Tasman Sea.[90]

LABOR RETURNS TO POWER

In the last two chapters, we have examined the major immigration policies and programs of Canada and Australia, as they have developed through the critical years from the early seventies onwards. In the case of Australia, we began with the election of a Labor government under Gough Whitlam in December 1972. The ALP had been in opposition for 23 years, but enjoyed only a brief three years of power when it was defeated by the Liberal–NCP Coalition following the dramatic and painful constitutional crisis of the final months of 1975. We end, however, with the triumphant return of a Labor government in 1983 under a new, dynamic and popular leader – Bob Hawke, formerly President of the Australian Council of Trade Unions. This raised the question, therefore, as to whether this new Labor government would introduce major changes in Australia's immigration policy and management. By the end of 1984, important changes had been made in immigration priorities, with much less emphasis on immigration for development and much more on family reunion (with the family migration category in the Migrant Selection System enlarged). There were other changes too, as this government put its own stamp on some of the major policies and programs in this field, including refugee policy, citizenship, and multiculturalism. From 1985 onwards the Hawke government, clearly impressed with Australia's low fertility and prospect of population decline, significantly changed direction and opted for expansion in immigration.

As *The Economist* put it, after the 1983 election, "If you like odd men out, the fellow who swims against the tide and a general damn-your-eyes way of doing things, Australia since March 5th is your country and Robert James Hawke is your man."[91] Another noted journal observed, "To most Australians, though not to himself, Hawke is a larrikin: a bloke who drinks, chases women, gets on with the lads and tips his cap to nobody; much more in tune with how the bulk of male Australians like to see themselves than is the property-owning grandee Malcolm Fraser."[92] But Bob Hawke is also known as a skilled negotiator, a moderate democratic socialist, a growth man and a determined and clever politician. Son of a Congregational minister and a former Rhodes scholar, he is more middle class than working class, though a very talented trade union leader. As a major player on the Australian political stage for some years, Bob Hawke has inevitably had considerable involvement with national immigration policies. In relation to more specialized knowledge of this area of public policy, however, he was a member of the Immigration Advisory Council in the early seventies and of the Australian Population and Immigration Council (APIC) from 1976 onwards.

In a strategic decision made public on February 3rd, 1983, hours before Mr. Fraser announced a snap election for both Houses of Parliament for March 5th, Bill Hayden, the former leader of the ALP, a moderate, well-respected but uncharismatic politician resigned, recognizing the inevitable and making way for Bob Hawke. Mr. Hayden is now Minister for Foreign Affairs in the Hawke government. While leader of the Opposition, Hayden had called on several occasions for a thorough overhaul of Australia's immigration system, bearing in mind the current high levels of unemployment. NUMAS must be scrapped, he said, and a new family reunion program introduced which genuinely reunited families.[93] At the ALP's annual conference in July 1982, what the press called a "revamped migrant policy" had been adopted. It included the following key (but not very new) proposals:

1 To establish a national population council to consider and make recommendations on the relationship between population growth, immigration, the economy, and the quality of life.

2 To continue accepting refugees, but to initiate or support political settlements to ease their plight.

3 To develop a national language policy to extend and improve the teaching of English to migrants and their children and to encourage Anglo-Australians to learn a foreign language.

4 To conduct a review of Australian citizenship laws in view of the very large proportion of migrants – about one million – who have not become citizens.

5 To consult with the states to determine the level of future migrant intakes and the amount of federal funding required to enable state governments to provide adequate facilities.

6 To establish a tripartite committee of government, employers, and unions to deal with the problems faced by migrants.[94]

The policy also called for a future Labor government to establish closer links between the departments of Immigration and Employment. In a statement made at the same time, the then Opposition spokesman on immigration, Mick Young, said that family reunion would be the central theme of ALP policy and that, although the Department of Employment would be closely associated with immigration, the economic question would not be paramount. This must have afforded some relief to officials and others who feared that a new Labor government might break up the Department of Immigration and Ethnic Affairs and combine immigration with employment as Mr. Whitlam had done.

Finally, as an early indication of the thinking of the Hawke government in this area, we should look at its first major statement on Australian immigration policy and on the 1983–1984 immigration program, delivered in the House of Representatives by the new Minister for Immigration and Ethnic Affairs, Stewart West.[95] This was also the occasion for a classic encounter with the new Opposition spokesman on immigration John Hodges (the last of the three Ministers for Immigration and Ethnic Affairs in the Fraser government), which gave a clear warning of future differences on immigration policy between government and opposition.[96]

The Labor government's statement began with an endorsement of the nine basic principles of Australian migration policy outlined by Mr. MacKellar on June 7, 1978, which the new Minister listed in an abbreviated form. He went on to state that, in relation to the conflicting claims made for immigration (economically stimulating or simply adding to unemployment in times of recession), the Government would steer a middle course. The former government's estimate of migrant intake of between 115,000 and 120,000 for 1982–1983 had already been revised down to between 90,000 and 95,000. The figure for 1983–1984 would be held to a ceiling of between 80,000 and 90,000 with a major commitment to family reunion and refugees. Later, however, these estimates should be revised upwards again.

As well as his announcement of these revised annual levels, Mr. West had some interesting things to say on each of the Government's top priorities.

On family reunion, Mr. West said the Government intended to restructure the new points system to eliminate what they still felt were its more discriminatory features. The changes would include the removal of points awarded for knowledge of the English language and for occupational demand for family selection purposes, although they would be retained for arranged employment. The purpose of these and other changes, he said, was "to remove to some extent an inbuilt bias in favour of highly skilled English-speaking and financially well-off migrants." Ethnic communities had pointed out that, under the former government, "some people were more entitled to family reunion than others."

On refugees, the other major plank in the Labor government's migration policy, the Minister said that the Government reaffirmed its commitment to a refugee policy based on humanitarian considerations. This year, within an assisted intake of 16,000 refugees, a total of 12,200 refugees were expected from Indochina, 3,500 from Eastern Europe, only 100 from Central and South America and 200 from other regions. For 1983–1984, the Government proposed a ceiling of 20,000 refugees, together with greater diversification of refugee sources. It was unacceptable, Mr. West said, that only 100 out of 16,000 refugees in 1982–1983 should be from

Central and South America, when there were 300,000 refugees in Central America alone. Persons from totalitarian regimes in that part of the world were not adequately represented in Australia's humanitarian programs.

To achieve greater diversification of refugee sources, the Government proposed a flexible approach. Within an overall ceiling of 20,000 in 1983–1984, there would be approximately 15,000 assisted passage places for refugees plus a "special humanitarian component" of 1,000. This would include "a very approximate intake" of 10,000 Indochinese, recognizing the continuing reduction in the number of boat refugees; 2,500 East European refugees, recognizing the continuing reduction in the number of Poles seeking resettlement outside Europe; and 2,500 from other areas including Central and South America and the Middle East. In addition, there would be 2,000 unfunded refugee places in "contingency reserve" (a concept which Canada has been using for several years in its refugee planning), and 2,000 for the special humanitarian program intended for people in human rights difficulties, who might have family links with Australia but were outside the scope of assisted refugee entry. Finally, in relation to refugees, Mr. West said the Government would rigorously pursue their election commitment to seek political solutions to refugee situations.

Perhaps the most critical part of this speech, however, dealt with the recruitment of skilled workers overseas and reflected the ALP's strong views on this subject. Less reliance would now be placed, the Minister said, on the migration program as a source of skilled workers: "Skilled migration will continue to be needed to fill gaps for some time, but the Government will develop a manpower planning approach to ensure that economic recovery is not held back by skilled labor shortages and, conversely, that immigration does not become an alternative to Australian training and re-training programs, particularly for adults." In the meantime, the Government would continue to accept some skilled migrants in occupations in demand, and the Employer Nomination Scheme would also continue for the time being. This would probably bring some 2,500 workers to Australia in the next year. The Business Migration Programme, which was expected to bring some 2,000 business migrants and their families to Australia in 1983–1984 and had considerable potential to create employment and boost economic growth, would definitely be continued. These and other measures, the Minister said, had been designed "to lessen the impact of immigration on unemployment while still maintaining a commitment to family reunion and assisting refugees."

Among other points made in this important speech, the Minister said that there would be no change in the Trans-Tasman Travel Arrangements but that they would be closely monitored. The requirement that New Zealand citizens must produce a passport before entering Australia would remain. The Minister said his department was making "intensified efforts" to locate and remove illegal immigrants from Australia. It was estimated that between 50,000 and 60,000 illegal immigrants were already in Australia, with a possible 10,000 to 15,000 joining their ranks each year. "That is very serious," the Minister said, "in a situation of high unemployment when they have no right to stay here."

The former Minister of Immigration and Ethnic Affairs, John Hodges, replied to this statement for the Opposition, saying that there were matters here with which the Opposition concurred and matters with which they strongly disagreed. Speaking generally, Mr. Hodges said, "I believe that it can be fairly said, on the basis of the statement just given to the House by the Minister, that Australia now has a more authoritarian, a more rigid, a more discriminatory and certainly an anti-English-speaking migration policy." Notwithstanding the Government's assertion that it had sought a middle course, it had really put migration into reverse gear, Mr. Hodges said, and he produced arguments to show that in fact migrant intake should be increased in difficult times because it provided a major stimulus to the economy. The exchange clearly reflected, at least for the time being, the major differences which emerged since the late sixties between the ALP and the Liberal–NCP Coalition[97] on the uses and benefits of immigration.

On December 1, 1984, the Hawke government decided to go to the country in another general election, and was returned with a somewhat reduced majority. The Minister for Immigration, Stewart West, was then replaced by Chris Hurford, a graduate of the London School of Economics and a former accountant. Since their original election on March 5, 1983, this government has introduced other changes in immigration, citizenship, and multiculturalism. Their revised Migrant Selection System can be seen in Appendix 5. Changes made in the structure and management of the Australian Institute of Multicultural Affairs followed by the Institute's ultimate demise are discussed in Chapter 5. Among other improvements in settlement services, more money for the adult migrant education program and more grants-in-aid for ethnic organizations and trade unions have been provided. Migrant Access Centres, shop-front centres run by DIEA, are being established in all mainland state capitals to deliver "a co-ordinated and comprehensive information program" for new arrivals.

Differences of view continued between Government and Opposition on the uses of immigration in Australian economic development and on the composition of the immigration movement. A disturbing public debate, which is discussed in the final chapter, erupted in 1984 over the issue of Asian immigration. Later on, however, following the Hawke government's change of direction in 1985 and a change in the leadership of the Liberal

Party and Coalition, a greater degree of convergence appeared to be developing in this area between the Government and the L-NP, particularly with respect to Australia's future demographic needs. This will be discussed in more detail in Chapter 6.

CHAPTER FOUR

Refugees and Undocumented Migrants

REFUGEES

The critical years in immigration since 1972 have also been years of a world refugee explosion, when the estimated number of refugees in different world regions has risen dramatically, and when the operations and budget of the Office of the United Nations High Commissioner for Refugees (UNHCR) have expanded to become the largest of the major UN agencies. Within the short space of 10 years, and at about the same time during that period, both Canada and Australia have developed much more clearly defined refugee policies, and have accepted a fairly large number of refugees as a standing component of their annual immigration movements. This represents a major change in their response to the world refugee situation. At the same time, both countries have developed special programs for refugee sponsorship and refugee assistance. Both have responded very positively to one of the largest and most publicized of recent refugee movements, the remarkable Indochinese movement, which has acted in both countries, as it has elsewhere, as a major agent of change, requiring new policies and procedures and pre-empting resources on a large scale.

Since Canada and Australia have worked closely with UNHCR for many years and are active members of its executive committee of 41 states (elected by the UN Economic and Social Council from states with "a demonstrated interest in and devotion to the solution of the refugee problem"), and since public knowledge about this important international agency is very limited despite its size, we begin this chapter with a short discussion of UNHCR itself.

The Office of the UN High Commissioner for Refugees (UNHCR)

At its fourth session in 1949, the General Assembly of the newly formed

United Nations agreed in principle to the appointment of a High Commissioner for Refugees, as well as to the establishment of an office of the UN High Commissioner for Refugees to take effect from January 1, 1951. It was to succeed in a permanent sense two temporary, post-war relief and refugee rehabilitation organizations: the United Nations Relief and Rehabilitation Administration (UNRRA) established in December 1944, and the International Refugee Organization (IRO) which took over UNRRA's responsibilities on June 30, 1947 and closed down in February 1951. The statute of the new international agency, outlining the functions of the High Commissioner, as well as the location (Geneva), organization, and financing of his office, was adopted by the General Assembly on December 14, 1950. The High Commissioner's task was seen primarily as providing protection and assistance to refugees on a purely social and humanitarian basis. The High Commissioner was to report annually to the General Assembly through the Economic and Social Council. The administration expenses of UNHCR would be met through the UN budget.

Steps were also taken to draft a convention regulating the legal status of refugees. After a draft was prepared by a nine- man *ad hoc* committee, set up by the Economic and Social Council and chaired by the Canadian delegate, the matter was considered at a special conference of interested governments held in Geneva from July 2 to 25, 1951, in which both Canada and Australia took part. The outcome of this conference was that the United Nations Convention Relating to the Status of Refugees was adopted on July 28 of that year. Only 12 of the 26 governments attending the conference signed this document, however, and Canada and Australia were not among them. It took nearly three years before the first High Commissioner could secure the necessary number of ratifications to bring the Convention into force on April 22, 1954. Australia was one of these slightly tardy signatories to the Convention, appending her signature on January 22, 1954. Canada – reflecting a profound lack of interest and concern on the part of both Liberal and Conservative politicans of that day – was to wait for nearly 18 years before putting her signature to this document, despite continuing involvement in refugee matters and the admission of a considerable number of refugees.

The 1951 Convention was an important document; as amended some years later, it is still in use today. It consolidated previous international instruments relating to refugees and provided a clear statement of their rights as seen at that time. It also laid down minimum standards for the treatment of refugees without prejudice to the granting by states of more favourable treatment. Its provisions were to be applied to refugees without discrimination as to race, religion, or country of origin. It established the important principle of "non-refoulement," which sad to say is much violated today, stating plainly that "no contracting state shall expel or return (*refouler*) a refugee in any manner whatsover to the frontiers of territories where his life or freedom would be threatened on account of his race, religion, nationality, membership of a particular social group or political opinion." It provided for the documentation of refugees, including a refugee travel document in passport form. Among its most important provisions, the Convention established the following definition of a refugee. For the purposes of the Convention, the term "refugee" applies to any person who "as a result of events occurring before 1st January, 1951 and owing to well-founded fear of being persecuted for reasons of race, religion, nationality, membership of a particular social group or political opinion, is outside the country of his nationality and is unable or, owing to such fear, is unwilling to avail himself of the protection of that country; or who, not having a nationality and being outside the country of his former habitual residence as a result of such events, is unable or, owing to such fear, is unwilling to return to it."

The definition proved to have some serious inadequacies (not all refugees are outside their own country for example) and it certainly does not fit all refugee situations today. In the early years after 1951, however, its major inadequacy lay in the phrases: "As a result of events occurring before January 1, 1951 "and "as a result of such events." Within a few years of the framing of this definition, it was becoming increasingly clear that all refugee movements did not originate in World War II or its aftermath, and that refugees might well be a continuing feature of the international scene. As a consequence of this growing understanding of the refugee phenomenon in the post-war world, a short Protocol Relating to the Status of Refugees was prepared and submitted to the United Nations General Assembly in 1966. It eliminated the two restrictive phrases, making the Convention applicable to all refugees who came with the UNHCR mandate. Among a few other provisions, it also required "State Parties" to provide the Office of the High Commissioner with information and statistical data on the condition of refugees, the implementation of the Protocol, and the laws, regulations and decrees which are or may later be in force relating to the refugees. The General Assembly noted the Protocol and requested the Secretary-General to submit the text to states to enable them to accede. The Protocol was signed by the President of the General Assembly and by the Secretary-General on January 31, 1967.

Canada acceded to the 1967 Protocol as well as to the 1951 Convention on June 4, 1969. Australia acceded to the 1967 Protocol on December 13, 1973 while the Whitlam government was in office. One further development affecting both countries should be mentioned. An Executive Committee for UNHCR, whose principle function is "to advise the High Commissioner, at his request, in the exercise of his functions under the Statute of his office" had been established by the Economic and Social Council in April 1958. It had an initial membership of 24 states including

Canada and Australia who have remained members to the present day. The Executive Committee meets annually in full session in the early fall in Geneva. Canada and Australia send delegations of officials to these meetings. Representatives of voluntary organizations and other interested persons may attend as observers but, no doubt because of distance and expense, very few non-official Canadians or Australians actually do so.

We can now look back at the achievements and difficulties of UNHCR over more than 30 years. There is no doubt that it has been one of the most successful of international agencies, principally because it meets a critical need in international affairs and has been useful to a wide variety of countries at different times. In response to increasingly universal refugee problems, it has achieved – without too much strain – a remarkable degree of expansion from a small European-based and oriented agency with a budget of under half a million dollars, to a world-wide organization with representatives in 52 countries, a large staff in Geneva, and an overall budget of nearly $400 million. It has been internally peaceful, embracing an increasingly wide membership without strife. It has succeeded over the years in mildly pacifying or reassuring the Soviet Union and its allies about the need for international refugee management. It has established very good relations with African states, where the largest number of refugees are still to be found. In superpower and regional conflicts of various kinds, it has managed to remain in the background. In addition, UNHCR has always had a highly-motivated and hard-working staff, which has established a considerable and widely accepted degree of professionalism and expertise in the refugee field. In more than a quarter of a century of humanitarian effort, it has protected, assisted, and often saved the lives of many millions of refugees.

Today UNHCR operates in all continents and has been getting closer to universality. Recently the Soviet Union, as well as most of the countries of Eastern Europe, have been showing a definite interest and concern in its programs. Despite its many achievements, and like all international agencies, UNHCR has always been subject to criticism from the international community. There are strong voices today, particularly in the United States (which provides about one third of UNHCR funding), urging the creation of a new kind of international refugee agency, or simply doing without one altogether. More realistic criticisms have focused on the need to modernize UNHCR management and administration procedures (now under way); the need to study the root causes of refugee movements and to find durable solutions to them (a "Fund for Durable Solutions" has been created by the High Commissioner); and the need to establish what has been called "equal burden-sharing" among countries of first asylum and permanent settlement. In addition, a more equitable distribution of resources among refugee movements has been urged, as well as the need for a more intelligent and longer-term system of funding to permit a greater degree of forward planning, and more operational capacity and efficiency. The Canadian and Australian delegations to UNHCR have shown a strong interest in all these matters. To-day, with ever larger refugee movements, funding is a very serious problem.

The International Organization for Migration (IOM)

Canada and Australia have been closely associated with a smaller, but very important, international organization concerned with migrants and refugees, known until 1980 as the Intergovernmental Committee for European Migration (ICEM), then as the Intergovernmental Committee for Migration (ICM) and, since November 1989, as the International Organization for Migration (IOM). IOM is located in Geneva and works closely with UNHCR, often helping refugees who do not qualify under UNHCR's definition of a refugee and do not therefore come within the High Commissioner's mandate. It has developed valuable programs to assist developing countries, mainly in Latin America, in "the transfer of technology through migration." These programs include the Selective Migration to Latin America Programme which involves the movement of highly skilled manpower to Latin American countries from Europe, as well as the Return of Talent Programme which involves the voluntary repatriation of badly needed professional and skilled workers from the developed to the developing world. Since the beginning of the Selective Migration Programme in 1964, thousands of professionals, technicians, and skilled workers have moved to Latin America; a smaller number have been repatriated under the Return of Talent Programme begun in 1974.

At the request of member governments, IOM provides migration services such as orientation, counselling, and language training. It has become expert in the organization of prompt and effective transportation, at significantly reduced cost. Its services are frequently enlisted by various UN agencies, including UNHCR, for the movement of victims of natural disasters and other crises, and for efficient low-cost transport of relief supplies. IOM also organizes regular seminars on immigration and international migration, providing a valuable international forum for governments, voluntary agencies, and scholars in this field. Since its foundation, IOM has assisted over 4 million migrants to settle in some 126 countries. In 1990, it had a membership of 36 governments, a further 18 governments with observer status, and missions and offices in 40 countries.

Canada and Australia were founding members of this organization which was created at a meeting in Brussels in December 1951. (The other 14 countries were Austria, Belgium, Bolivia, Brazil, Chile, France, the Federal Republic of Germany, Greece, Italy, Luxembourg, the Netherlands, Switzerland, Turkey, and the United States.) In view of the fact that the International Refugee Organization was about to close down, the representatives of 16 countries came together to try to find a practical solution to the still desperate European problem of the remaining millions of refugees and displaced persons uprooted by World War II. They founded ICEM, a voluntary intergovernmental committee to be financed by participating states. Its first and most urgent task would be to provide international assistance to individuals and families who wanted to emigrate from Europe, *irrespective of nationality or refugee status*, and for whom overseas settlement seemed the best prospect. It is important to note that the founding members did not limit the objectives of this new organization to the movement of European refugees and migrants only. They recognized the principle that "the international financing of European migration should contribute not only to solving the problem of population in Europe, but also stimulate the creation of new economic opportunities in countries lacking manpower."

Canada and Australia did not stand by the organization they had helped to found. Both withdrew as members of ICEM, Canada in 1962 and Australia in 1973, both for unconvincing and, as we can see now, short-sighted reasons. Both countries eventually returned to the fold, but only as observers, but Australia resumed full membership as of May 24, 1985, when a special session of ICM was held to admit Australia and Kenya as full members. Canada became a full member again at a special session of the now renamed IOM on May 23, 1990.

In the author's earlier study of Canadian immigration, *Canada and Immigration: Public Policy and Public Concern*, the reasons for Canada's withdrawal were described as follows:

The reasons given by the Diefenbaker government for Canada's withdrawal in 1962 were that ICEM's role was intended to be temporary and related to the refugee problem which was now under control; and that ICEM was taking an increasing interest in technical assistance which Canada felt was more properly the concern of the United Nations and other agencies. Mr. Howard Green, then Secretary of State for External Affairs, also suggested in Parliament that the cost of participation in ICEM was high, and while financial considerations were not the primary reason for Canada's withdrawal, it had become increasingly difficult to justify paying such a price for an organization of marginal use in Canada.[1]

Canada's annual contribution to ICEM from 1951 to 1962 was approximately US$215,000. Upon withdrawing, Canada continued to make an annual contribution to ICEM of $60,000 until 1965 when it was decided that this contribution should be channelled to UNHCR instead.

In the early summer of 1970, the Canadian Department of Manpower and Immigration's Advisory Board on the Adjustment of Immigrants approached the Minister of Manpower and Immigration, Alan MacEachen, to see whether there might be a possibility of Canada's rejoining ICEM as a full member. The Minister replied that he had looked into the question very thoroughly and was satisfied that Canada's original reasons for withdrawing remained valid. He provided a Department background paper which described these reasons as follows: the principal reasons for the establishment of ICEM had disappeared; the need for ICEM transportation facilities had diminished as commercial facilities had improved, and Canada rarely needed them; ICEM was becoming more and more involved in technical assistance programs in Latin America which External Affairs and Finance felt should be handled through the UN; and there was a danger in encouraging the continuation of an international organization concerned with migration "as this might lead to the introduction of immigration matters into an international forum which would be contrary to the principle that immigration is essentially a matter of domestic concern."[2] One final comment was made, namely that "Officers of External and Finance have expressed the view that there have been no developments which would justify reconsideration of our position with ICEM. These departments would be against any move designed to reinstate Canada as a member."[3] The paper is dated June 17, 1969.

Rather similar reasons were given by the Whitlam government for Australia's official withdrawal from ICEM which became effective on December 31, 1973, ICEM having been notified in a letter from the Prime Minister, in his capacity as Minister for Foreign Affairs, on March 7, 1973. In the House of Representatives on September 12, 1973, Phillip Lynch, former Minister for Immigration and then spokesman on immigration for the Opposition, asked the Minister for Immigration, Al Grassby, about Australia's proposed withdrawal. What were the reasons for it? Was the decision to withdraw approved by Cabinet? Was it a fact that Australia's withdrawal had been widely interpreted as a rejection by the Government of the concept that refugee migration is a common responsibility to be shared by the international community? Did the Minister recognize the importance of ICEM's role in promoting increased multilateral co-operation by serving as a forum for the discussion of common migration problems? Would the Government reconsider its decision?

Mr. Grassby replied that this decision was taken after consultation between himself and the Minister for Foreign Affairs (the Cabinet had evidently not been consulted). The Government considered, Mr. Grassby went on, that with the changing pattern of immigration into Australia and the Government's own initiatives in immigration policy, giving priority to family reunion and sponsored migration, it should attain self-sufficiency in respect of the movement of migrants; and that it was no longer appropriate for Australia to remain a member of ICEM ... In his letter to the then Director of ICEM, John F. Thomas, the Prime Minister said much the same thing. This letter and the Director's reply were made available to the Opposition and were published in Hansard. Mr. Whitlam also stressed the Labor government's new emphasis on family reunion and sponsored migration, and its desire to attain self-sufficiency in the movement of migrants from Europe. "My Government," he said, "considers, therefore, that with the changing pattern of immigration into Australia, it is no longer appropriate for Australia to remain a member of ICEM, and to participate in activities that are outside the scope of our own immigration objectives." He expressed his sincere gratitude for "all the services which your organization has extended during the period of Australia's membership."[4]

Since these decisions were taken, refugee movements have multiplied and the number of refugees needing assistance in many parts of the world has increased steadily. Emigration from Europe has continued at relatively high levels and Europe – far from having its refugee problems solved – has continued to produce a steady stream of refugees of its own, as well as receiving large numbers of non-European asylum seekers. UNHCR reported that the overall number of refugees in Europe at the end of 1981 was some 589,200, including considerable numbers of Poles and other Eastern European refugees, as well as asylum seekers from the Middle East, the Horn of Africa, and Afghanistan. During 1982, 37,120 refugees were resettled from European countries of first asylum, the majority going to Switzerland (1,096), the Federal Republic of Germany (1,196), Australia (5,628), and the United States (17,410). In 1984, according to UNHCR, there were more than 600,000 refugees in Europe and 103,500 asylum seekers arrived that year. By 1990, the latter had increased to 420,000.

The need for IOM's services by its member countries and by other international agencies has increased in proportion to these developments. The UN High Commissioner for Refugees, in his annual reports to the General Assembly and in speeches elsewhere, regularly thanks IOM for its assistance. In his report covering the period from April 1, 1981 to March 31, 1982, for example, he described this assistance: "The long-standing collaboration with the Intergovernmental Committee for Migration (ICM), especially concerning practical arrangements for the transportation of Indochinese and Latin American refugees accepted for resettlement in third countries, continued to prove of utmost value."[5] At the present time, UNHCR, IOM, and the International Council of Voluntary Agencies (ICVA) are collaborating in the operation of an International Refugee Integration Resource Centre. The purpose of this centre is to facilitate the exchange of information on refugee integration. A computer-based documentation centre has been established to gather, store, and disseminate information on all aspects of refugee reception, resettlement, and integration.

In conclusion it should be said that in withdrawing from ICEM membership, Canada and Australia, despite their good record in relation to refugees, reneged for the time being on their responsibilities to this useful international organization which they helped to found, and on the principle that refugee migration is indeed "a common responsibility to be shared by the international community." It is very good news, however, that both countries have now resumed full membership and will be playing an important part in the future development of this useful organization.

Refugee Movements since 1970

Refugees are a product of war, tyranny, political upheaval, hostility to minorities, and natural disaster, but primarily of war. Sometimes fleeing from air raids and battle zones, often caught between opposing forces; sometimes thrown out or frozen out of countries where they were once permanent inhabitants; sometimes escaping from tyrannical regimes against all odds; sometimes simply moving out, where they can, from countries where the future for themselves and their children looks bleak, refugees have been a striking phenomenon of modern times. They come individually, in families and groups, in a steady or intermittent stream which can last for some years, or in sudden chaotic movements. Mainly they come without possessions, without language skills, and without knowledge of the countries or territories where they will have to settle.

Since 1960, there have been 65 major wars on this planet in which more than 11 million people have died, not to mention innumerable minor clashes and conflicts involving the use of arms. More than a third of all the nations of the world have been involved in this kind of violence. As a consequence, in the seventies, there has been a veritable explosion of refugees with one refugee movement succeeding another and refugees needing help in all world regions. It is absolutely vital that there be international machinery to protect and assist these refugees, as well as countries where they can settle if necessary. Both Canada and Australia, with their vast territories and small populations, have been receiving countries of first rank for refugees in the post-war world.

In both countries, official refugee policies, as well as the recognition of refugees themselves and of refugee movements *as a phenomenon distinct from immigration*, have their origin in the years immediately after World War II when UNHCR and ICEM were founded. However, during the war itself and in the years immediately preceding it, both countries were asked to respond to a refugee problem of desperate and tragic dimensions – the plight of Jewish refugees inside Nazi Germany and in its occupied territories – and they responded very differently. The Mackenzie King government in Canada – ultra-cautious, anti-Semitic, hostile to refugees and to immigrants from non-traditional sources – resisted all pressures to help, and moved only slowly to admit displaced persons from Europe after 1945. A critical opportunity occurred in 1938, shortly after Hitler and his armies overran Austria, when President Roosevelt convened an international conference of 30 nations at Evian in France, to try to find solutions to the refugee problem. Canada accepted the invitation reluctantly and, like the majority of the participants, came away without making the smallest offer of help.[6] Australia, on the other hand, was one of the very few countries who did help. After the conference, Australia offered to accept 15,000 Jewish refugees from Germany and Sudetenland. During the 12 months before the outbreak of war in September 1939, 7,500 arrived in Australia. The rest did not get away.

Between 1945 and 1970, Canada and Australia were involved in only three major refugee movements: the huge movement of displaced persons in the years immediately after World War II, the Hungarian refugee movement in 1956–1957, and the Czech refugee movement in 1968. In the first case, Canada admitted some 186,000 displaced persons and Australia 170,000; in the second, the figures were 37,000 and 14,000 Hungarian refugees respectively; and in the third, 11,000 and 5,000 Czech refugees. In addition, both countries were involved in World Refugee Year in 1959–1960 with Canada admitting 3,508 refugees and Australia a less generous 67 families, although Australian voluntary agencies also brought in a number of disadvantaged and handicapped refugees. In assessing these numbers, we should remember how relatively small these two countries were immediately after World War II. Canada's 1951 census showed a population of 14,009,429 while Australia's 1947 census gave hers as 7,579,858. These large post-war movements of displaced persons and refugees made a significant contribution to the great population expansion, which was to take place in both countries in the fifties and sixties. They also brought human resources of a very high order to Canadian and Australian shores – skills and talents from the highly developed, industrialized countries of Europe for the labour force and for the arts and sciences, which were an invaluable acquisition during these years, as they were on a larger scale for the United States.

Apart from these three important movements, refugees were admitted to Canada and Australia on an individual, *ad hoc* basis during this period, although the numbers were quite substantial overall.[7] Their White Canada and White Australia immigration policies affected refugees as well as immigrants, although these policies came to an end, as we know, in 1962 for Canada and in 1973 for Australia. Voluntary agencies in Australia –

the Red Cross, Catholic Immigration, the World Council of Churches, the Lutheran World Federation, Jewish Welfare, and other, more recent organizations had a much freer hand than their Canadian counterparts in bringing in small groups and individual refugees, often those who were aged, ill, or otherwise handicapped.[8] While refugees were now recognized in both countries as a separate category of immigrants, neither country had an established refugee policy or programs or an established status for refugees. On the eve of important changes in this area, a Canadian delegate to the 1972 meetings of the Executive Committee of UNHCR explained the Canadian approach: "Refugees selected for admission to Canada are admitted in the same manner as other immigrants and, as such, are extended the same rights and responsibilities as other Canadian residents ... We feel that refugees desire to integrate as rapidly as possible and to continue to designate him as a refugee once he has been admitted to Canada may tend to make him the object of pity and well meant but unwanted charity ... Canada will continue to consider refugees for resettlement both as part of our normal immigration program and in response to special circumstances or situations which may arise."[9] As the refugee explosion of the 1970s transformed the scene, this well-meaning approach became wholly inadequate. There had to be, in Canada and Australia, special policies and programs for refugees, and there had to be a much greater outlay of government funds to manage them and to support refugee settlement. In addition, serious thought had to be given to the problem of refugee status.

The Ugandan Asian Refugee Movement

1972 was a critical year in many ways. As we have seen, it brought a Labor Government to power in Australia in December after 23 years in opposition; and in Canada a month earlier a very able and determined minister, Robert Andras, took over the portfolio of Manpower and Immigration. Before either of these events, however, the first of the major refugee movements of the seventies emerged suddenly on the international scene. On August 4, 1972, President Idi Amin of Uganda announced that all Asians holding British citizenship must leave the country within 90 days. This edict affected about 50,000 out of a total of some 80,000 Asians in Uganda, those who had opted to retain British citizenship when Uganda obtained its independence from Britain in 1962. The British government, which had been trying since 1968 to control and limit the potentially very large flow of Asians from East Africa where their situation was becoming increasingly precarious, quickly accepted its legal obligations towards the Ugandan Asians. But it tried first to bring pressure to bear on President

Amin to extend the 90-day limit. When this failed, Britain appealed to the member countries of the Commonwealth and other governments to accept at least some of the Ugandan Asian "expellees," as the Canadian government decided to call them. Official requests from Britain to this effect arrived in Ottawa and Canberra in mid-August. They received very different responses from the Canadian and Australian governments.

These were the enfeebled, final days of the McMahon government in Australia and the L-NCP Coalition was still reluctant to abandon the White Australia policy. The prospect of admitting some hundreds or even thousands of Ugandan Asian refugees did not look attractive and the British government received a cool reply. The Australian government offered to admit a small number of these refugees, but only under the strict criteria applying to non-Europeans. Eventually some 200 were admitted and later the numbers were increased slightly by the Whitlam government.

Canada, on the other hand, was no longer restrained by considerations of racial discrimination. It *was* restrained by concerns about unemployment and the possibility of an adverse public reaction. But the Trudeau Cabinet, still in its early idealistic, planning and development stage, was moved more strongly by the refugees' plight; the predicament of the British government; and the opportunity the crisis offered for helpful, international action, dear to the hearts of many if not all Canadian Liberals. After careful consideration, therefore, Prime Minister Trudeau announced on August 24, 1972 that Canada was prepared to admit Ugandan Asian refugees. A team of immigration officials, together with representatives from the departments of External Affairs and Health and Welfare, would proceed immediately to Kampala to assess the situation in terms of numbers and to carry out the necessary screening and processing of the refugees.

Thereafter the Canadian operation moved forward swiftly and effectively, leading in the end to the admission of 7,069 Ugandan Asian refugees. The number was not very large compared with Britain's 28,165 but it made a distinct contribution and must of course be seen in the context of Canada's regular immigration movement (122,006 immigrants in 1972 and 184,200 in 1973). However, it was Canada's imaginative and efficient management of her Ugandan Asian refugee movement which was impressive, consisting of a group of innovative measures which broke with the old ideas of the fifties and sixties. This paved the way for much better refugee management in the future and particularly for a more responsible role for government in refugee resettlement.

Several outstanding features of the Canadian Ugandan Asian operation should be mentioned: first, the swift selection and processing of the refugees in Canada's Kampala office[10] and the attractive and well-managed reception centre created at the Longue Pointe military base near Montreal. At this centre, the Ugandan Asians were looked after as they came off the charter flights, counselled in relation to employment and living conditions in Canada, provided with warm clothing and moved on very quickly to the province where they decided to settle. This first phase was the responsibility of the Department of Manpower and Immigration. The second phase fell to the Department of the Secretary of State where a small task force with a total budget of $90,000, provided out of the total sum allocated for the whole Ugandan Asian operation, created 11 reception and settlement committees (known as Ugandan Asian committees) in the principal Canadian cities and towns where the Ugandan Asians would be settling. These committees were provided with office space, a full or part-time staff person, and a budget for a six-month operation, although this was frequently extended with the aid of additional provincial and municipal funding. The committees were government-voluntary committees whose membership consisted of federal and provincial government officials, together with representatives of established voluntary agencies and Asian community organizations which were closely involved in the entire operation.

Everyone seemed to enjoy this exercise. The Ugandan Asian refugees, though still stunned from their sudden uprooting, seemed pleased and relieved by their reception in Canada. The Minister of Employment and Immigration, Bryce Mackasey, who appeared frequently at Longue Pointe to welcome the refugees personally, obviously enjoyed it immensely. Those who worked at Longue Pointe felt they had done a very good job, and the Ugandan Asian committees, which had responded warmly and creatively to the task, felt the same way. This atmosphere of good management affected everyone and raised the level at that point of community interest and participation in refugee problems and assistance.

A follow-up study carried out in 1973 by the Department of Manpower and Immigration[11] showed that six months after their arrival in Canada, some 82 per cent of the respondents in the survey were employed, with the number increasing to almost 89 per cent after one year. Over 50 per cent were satisfied with their earnings after six months, and this proportion increased to more than two thirds at the end of the year. After one year in Canada, three quarters of the respondents said that they were satisfied with housing conditions and the majority were satisfied with the health care, educational, recreational, and cultural facilities available to them. Some 90 per cent of those interviewed after one year believed that they were accepted in the community in which they lived and more than 9 out of 10 heads of household said that they intended to settle in Canada permanently, regardless of what happened in Uganda. While a year is far too short a period to assess successful permanent adaptation to a new society, these figures showed that the Ugandan Asians had at least made a very good start in their new life in Canada.[12]

After the Ugandan Asians came the Chileans. In this case Canada's performance was less impressive, although 6,990 Chilean refugees were eventually admitted. On September 11, 1973, only a year after the beginning of the Ugandan Asian exodus from Kampala, President Salvador Allende was murdered in a right-wing military coup in Chile. Repressive measures were immediately taken against his officials and supporters, many thousands of whom were imprisoned or executed. A small number, some 50 in all, took refuge in the Canadian Embassy in Santiago. The Canadian government was strongly urged by UNHCR, Amnesty International, the Canadian churches, and national and voluntary organizations including the Canadian Association of University Teachers, the Associations of Universities and Colleges in Canada, and the Canadian Association for Latin American Studies, to open its doors immediately to these Chilean refugees, many of whom were professionals and academics. But the Trudeau administration proceeded cautiously. No special intergovernmental selection team was flown to Santiago, no fleet of charter flights organized, no refugee reception centre created in Montreal or elsewhere, and there was none of the positive publicity that surrounded the Ugandan Asian refugee movement.

In fact, Canada's senior policy-makers were uncertain about the whole affair. They were undecided about Canada's position *vis-à-vis* the United States, which was clearly supporting the new military government; and they were nervous about the possibility of admitting hundreds of dedicated Marxist-Leninists who might – as some saw it – try to establish a revolutionary base in Canada. Nearly two months after the coup, several immigration officers were brought from Buenos Aires to Santiago with a mandate to set up an orderly process of refugee selection. Detailed security screening had been ordered, however, which slowed down the process of refugee selection, and the immigration team at the Embassy was small.[13] By the end of December 1973, only 184 applicants had received visas to enter Canada, and by the end of February 1975 only 188 Chilean refugees had been admitted.

As time went on, however, with pressure sustained in Canada on behalf of the Chileans by the same organizations, by the small Chilean community itself and by other Latin American community groups in Canada; and with much more international publicity concerning the true character of the new government in Chile and the true sequence of events in the *coup d'état* of September 1973, these numbers increased to the not unimpressive total, as we have seen, of 6,990. But it was refugee movement without fanfare, without official welcoming committees, and without much government involvement in resettlement.

The Indochinese Refugee Movement:
First Phase

In the early seventies Australia was much less involved with refugees than Canada, but very much closer to the war in Vietnam which was to generate one of the largest refugee movements in recent times. It was Prime Minister Menzies who had announced to Parliament on April 7, 1965 that Australia would provide an infantry battalion for service in Vietnam (as well as the other kinds of assistance – military advisers and equipment – already provided). At its peak, the Australian force consisted of 8,300 men and the total number of Australian military personnel who served in Vietnam was 46,852, including 17,424 national servicemen. Australian casualties in Vietnam totalled 494 killed and 2,398 wounded. Nearly all the Australian forces were withdrawn by the end of 1971.[14]

Nevertheless, the whole issue of the Vietnam war, the strong opposition of the Whitlam government to Australia's military involvement, the unexpected but overwhelming American defeat, and the exodus of refugees were all matters of fierce debate and contention in Australia during the Whitlam years. But after the fall of Saigon on April 29, 1975, when refugees began leaving, or trying to leave, in large numbers, a very direct question of the possible admission and resettlement of at least some of these refugees arose for Australia. This was just at the point when the situation of the Whitlam government was becoming very precarious, and when it was under constant attack from the opposition and from the media.

Refugees, however, were not on Mr. Whitlam's crowded agenda and they related awkwardly to some of his most urgent foreign policy concerns. Like the Canadian government, he had initially responded slowly and unenthusiastically to the Chilean refugee crisis in 1973; only 1,050 Chilean refugees were finally admitted to Australia, plus a number admitted under special humanitarian criteria. When a group of 2,500 Timorese refugees arrived in Darwin by boat in August-September 1975 having fled from East Timor, they were looked after in government hostels, but only given temporary status in Australia (partly due to uncertainty as to whether they might proceed to Portugal or eventually return home).[15] And in the case of Vietnam, since Mr. Whitlam strongly disapproved of the whole American military intervention, he obviously did not want to assist the Americans with a refugee problem which they themselves had helped to create.

The initial reaction of the Whitlam government to the fall of Saigon, therefore, and to the large numbers of refugees trying to leave Vietnam, was to maintain that the refugees being evacuated by the United States were solely an American responsibility. Those who left on their own were best cared for by UNHCR and other international relief agencies to which Australia would provide extra financial assistance. On April 22, 1975, the Prime Minister announced the categories of Vietnamese citizens who would be eligible for temporary entry to Australia. They included only the spouses and children of Vietnamese students presently living in Australia: the spouses and children of Australian citizens of Vietnamese origin, subject to the completion of Australian citizenship; and Vietnamese with a long and close association with the Australian presence in Vietnam, whose life was considered to be in danger (and whose applications would be considered on a case-by-case basis).

In the Senate, where the L-NCP continued to hold a majority of seats, the Standing Committee on Foreign Affairs and Defence investigated and reported twice on the Indochinese refugee movement, first in 1976 and then in 1982. Their first report was very critical of the early responses of the Whitlam government to the emergency evacuation of Vietnamese nationals from Saigon, and of the limited number of refugees the government was prepared to accept for resettlement in Australia.[16] The following are two excerpts from the Report:

It is apparent to the Senate Foreign Affairs and Defence Committee that the Australian government generally refused until the last moment to agree to use its transport resources to evacuate Vietnamese nationals from South Vietnam and Saigon. Indeed it appears in retrospect that the attitude was taken that it was the responsibility of individuals to escape as best they could, and only when they were out of Vietnam would the Australian government consider assisting refugees in coming to Australia. In addition, those refugees who were evacuated by the United States were regarded as coming under the responsibility of that country which, by its act of evacuation, had accepted full responsibility for the resettlement and rehabilitation of those refugees.

In view of the Committee's belief that the Australian government had been informed of the gravity and magnitude of the situation in South Vietnam some three weeks before the evacuation of the Australian Embassy, we are unable to come to any conclusion other than one of deliberate delay in order to minimize the number of refugees with which Australia would have to concern itself. In addition, we believe that the guidelines of 22 April were so narrowly drawn that very few refugees would qualify for entry to Australia. In all, 5,629 nominations were received, but only 542 approved – 355 for permanent residence and 187 for temporary residence.[17]

This was only the beginning, however. As the full dimensions of this refugee crisis came to be recognized, the Whitlam government in its few remaining months in office and the Fraser government which followed it after the election of December 2, 1975, admitted an increasing number of Indochinese refugees. On May 14, 1975, for example, in response to an urgent request from UNHCR, the High Commissioner was informed that Australia was willing to accept refugees from Hong Kong and Singapore for permanent settlement in Australia. On May 28, 1975 a team of Australian immigration officers left for Hong Kong to begin interviewing Vietnamese refugees; on June 19 the first group of 201 arrived in Sydney. On July 20, a similar team left for Singapore and Malaysia where a large group of refugees had landed and on August 9 the first group of these refugees arrived in Brisbane. On January 21, 1976, the new Minister for Immigration and Ethnic Affairs, Michael MacKellar, announced that a further 800 Indochinese refugees would be admitted to Australia, mainly from refugee camps in Thailand. A selection team left for Bangkok on February 2, 1976 and, as a result, 568 refugees were brought to Australia by chartered aircraft between March 19 and 24, 1976. This group comprised 279 Laotians, 228 Cambodians, and 61 Vietnamese refugees. In all, Australia admitted 1,037 Indochinese refugees during 1975–1976, the first large group of Asian refugees to be admitted. It was still less than three years since Gough Whitlam had so decisively dismissed the White Australia policy.

1976 was the year when another large refugee or quasi-refugee movement began for Australia and Canada, from Lebanon. Lebanese migration was looked after by immigration officers at the Australian embassy in Beirut up to the last week in March 1976. Open warfare in Beirut was escalating at such an alarming rate that all staff were evacuated and the embassy closed on March 28; in June a small Australian immigration office was established in Nicosia on the island of Cyprus. By the end of April 1977, more than 10,000 visas had been issued to Lebanese in Cyprus and an additional 2,753 in Australian immigration offices in Athens, Ankara, Cairo, Paris, and Damascus. The Canadian embassy in Beirut, however, managed to remain open and to process would-be Lebanese immigrants when it was feasible. A small office was opened at Jounieh just north of Beirut and applicants were also processed at Canadian immigration offices in Amman, Damascus, and Cyprus. A total of 11,010 Lebanese refugees were admitted to Canada between 1976 and 1979. This refugee movement continues on a small scale both to Canada and Australia.

Meanwhile in 1975, the Canadian government, although it had determinedly avoided military involvement in the war in Vietnam, was faced with the same difficult decision relating to Indochinese refugees as Australia, with the same obligation to help them through its UNHCR commitments. Immediately after the fall of Saigon, the Canadian government announced that Vietnamese and Cambodians in Canada as students or visitors could apply for landing, and could sponsor relatives from Indochina or from refugee camps under relaxed criteria. In May, a further announcement was made that 3,000 Vietnamese and Cambodian refugees without relatives in Canada would be admitted: 2,000 from evacuation camps in the United States and 1,000 from other countries.

However, the refugees who were evacuated by the United States, or who managed to leave by air or overland for the countries of Southeast Asia, were not the only concern of UNHCR and the receiving countries like Canada and Australia. It was the boat people – those who tried to leave by sea – who drew the attention of the media world-wide and excited the most sympathy from the international community. They were at risk from the weather and the high seas, from the unseaworthy and crowded boats in which they sailed, from the passing ships in the South China Sea which would not pick them up, from the Southeast Asian countries which would often not let them land, and from the pirates who robbed, raped, and killed them.[18] One third to one half of all the boat people may have died in these ways.

In October 1976, Canada agreed to accept 180 boat people and in August 1977, an additional 450. In January 1978, it was decided in Ottawa to establish a program in which 50 boat families a month would be admitted; in August 1978, 20 refugee families from Thailand were added to that number. In November 1978, 604 refugees stranded on the freighter *Hai Hong* who had been refused landing in Malaysia were airlifted to Canada.

Australia was faced with a rather different dilemma relating to the boat people. With a good boat, or with courage, determination, and good luck, they could cover the vast nautical distance between Saigon and Darwin and reach Australia's northern or northwestern shores. The first small boat with five Indochinese refugees aboard arrived in Darwin in April 1976; during the following year, six other boats came, bringing a total of 204 men, women, and children to Australia. All were accommodated in government hostels and given permanent status. By June 1979, a total of 51 boats carrying 2,011 refugees had reached northern Australia. By then, in March 1978, the Fraser government had established the Determination of Refugee Status (DORS) Committee. Of the boat people who arrived before this, 1,043 were approved for permanent residence; most of those who arrived later were granted refugee status by the DORS Committee.

These boat arrivals brought the Indochinese refugee movement right to Australia's door, arousing keen public debate and media attention. Some saw it as the beginning of a mass invasion by Asian hordes. Some (including several senior members of the ALP) were sceptical as to whether the boat people were genuine refugees; there was talk of rich Vietnamese buying their way out of Saigon and arriving with gold bars concealed on their persons. But while there were just a few of these, it was plain that the large majority arrived with nothing. Other Australians, including wharf-labourers in Darwin and some other trade unionists, protested about bringing in cheap labour at a time of high unemployment. Military experts drew attention in the media to the dangerous gap the boat arrivals revealed in Australia's northern defences. But there was also a surge of sympathy in Australia for these courageous and battered refugees, and many offers of help came from individuals and community organizations of all kinds. The Fraser government too stood firm on Australia's responsibilities towards the Indochinese refugees, whoever they might be.

The majority of Indochinese refugees admitted by Canada and Australia up to the end of June 1979 were not boat people, however, but mainly refugees from the large holding camps in Malaysia, Hong Kong, and Thailand. In all, Canada admitted 14,060 Indochinese refugees during this period and Australia 11,872. (In addition, Canada admitted 11,010 Lebanese and Australia approximately 13,000.)

Canada's New Refugee Policy

These major refugee movements, crowded together in the early to mid-seventies, made it plain to both Canadian and Australian politicians and officials that the old, *ad hoc*, case-by-case approach to refugee admission was now useless by itself; and that a clearly defined refugee policy was a necessity, if only to exercise some measure of control over this turbulent situation. They approached the task in different ways.

Canada, as we have seen, was involved from the fall of 1972 onwards, in a major effort to review its immigration, population, and related policies, with a view to creating a badly needed new immigration act. The new Act, which was passed in 1976 and came into force in 1978, contained a very useful package of measures which were to constitute the framework of Canada's refugee policy from then on. These measures, listed briefly in Chapter 2, will be examined in more detail here. This legislative framework consists of six elements:

1 It includes a commitment "to fulfil Canada's legal obligations with respect to refugees and to uphold its humanitarian tradition with respect to the displaced and the persecuted."
2 Refugees are treated in the Act as a *distinct admissible class* to be selected and admitted separately from immigrants.
3 The UNHCR definition of a refugee is incorporated in the Act through the use of the term "Convention refugee," signifying Canada's commitment to the principles underlying the UN Convention and Protocol.

4 At the same time, the Act allows the Government to designate special classes of refugees apart from Convention refugees, enabling it to deal with some special groups and movements of refugees on its own terms and to avoid the constraints of the UNHCR definition when necessary.

5 The Act establishes a legal process of "Refugee Status Determination" involving the creation of a Refugee Status Advisory Committee to advise the Minister on whether or not a claimant should be granted refugee status. The Act also establishes the basic rights of claimants within this process, which include the right of appeal to the Immigration Appeal Board if rejected by the committee, and of appeal to the courts if rejected by the Board. (This has now been amended. See pp. 192–93.)

6 The Act and Regulations also provide, as we have seen, new and much more flexible arrangements for refugee sponsorship, which were to prove very useful for the Indochinese refugee movement. Under these arrangements, a group of not less than five Canadian citizens or permanent residents of Canada, who are over 18 years of age and live in "the expected community of settlement," as well as a corporation (such as a voluntary agency) incorporated under Canadian or provincial laws with representatives in the expected community of settlement, may sponsor a Convention refugee and his or her accompanying dependents. The sponsor must, however, give a written undertaking to the Minister to make provision for the lodging, care, maintenance, and resettlement assistance for those refugees for one year.

Since the new Canadian Immigration Act became law, therefore, refugees have been selected according to whether they are Convention refugees or members of a special class of refugees designated by the Canadian government. There have been three special classes of refugees: (1) Political Prisoners and Other Oppressed Persons, (2) Indochinese, and (3) Self Exiles (ended in 1990); and an administrative procedure coming under the heading Special Measures which permits the admission of individual refugees who do not fit into the other categories. The only part of this new legal infrastructure which has not worked well has been the refugee status determination process, mainly because the flow of claims for refugee status both genuine and unfounded has become so large, while the process itself has been too slow and cumbersome to deal with it. Later we will look at the steps taken by the Canadian and Australian governments to deal with this problem which now exists on a world scale.

As an immediate expression of the decision, embodied in the Immigration Act, to separate immigrants and refugees in the immigration planning and admission process in Canada, a refugee plan was prepared in 1978 for inclusion in the Minister's Report to Parliament on Immigration Levels

Table 7
Canada: Refugee Plans, 1982 and 1983

	1982	1983
Indochina	4,000	3,000
Eastern Europe	6,000	3,000
Latin America and the Caribbean	1,000	2,000
Africa	500	1,000
Middle East	400	800
Other World Areas	100	200
Contingency Reserve	2,000	2,000*
TOTAL	14,000	12,000

Source: Canada Employment and Immigration Commission, Annual Reports to Parliament on Immigration Levels, 1982 and 1983.
*As one of several economy measures in this area, Cabinet approved funding for 10,000 refugees for 1983, but did not actually fund the contingency reserve.[19]

for 1979. The plan proposed a target of 10,000 refugees, comprising 5,000 Indochinese, 2,300 East Europeans, 500 Latin Americans, and 200 Convention refugees from other parts of the world, plus a contingency reserve of 2,000. This plan was quite literally washed away by the mounting tide of Indochinese refugees, which required emergency measures carried out in the main in 1979 and 1980. The next realistic plan was for 1981 when a target of 16,000 refugees was projected, including 8,000 from Indochina, 4,000 from Eastern Europe, 1,000 from Latin America and the Caribbean, 200 from Africa, 300 from other world areas, and a contingency reserve of 2,500, plus a projected total of 5,000 private sponsorships, making a total of 21,000. In 1981 a three year planning cycle was adopted for immigration planning with annual reviews and adjustments, but since the world refugee situation is so volatile, it was decided to retain an annual plan for refugees.

The 1982 and 1983 refugee plans were for reduced levels – 14,000 and 12,000 respectively – on the grounds that Canada had just admitted a very large number of Indochinese refugees and that the recession was still having a serious impact on the Canadian economy. The intake for 1982 and 1983 was to be distributed as shown in Table 7.

The refugee plan for 1984 and the future immigration levels were announced on November 1, 1983. The plan envisaged a refugee intake of 12,000 including a contingency reserve of 2,000. As mentioned earlier, before these refugee plans are formulated, there are consultations with voluntary agencies and ethnic community organizations, conducted in the main by the Commission's regional directors of immigration.

Even though they may sometimes be overwhelmed by events, the value of these annual refugee plans was stressed in the 1980 Levels Report: "The number and frequency of refugee crises has underlined the need for an annual refugee plan – a single instrument to govern most of Canada's ongoing refugee intake. A plan improves the ability of the UN High Commissioner for Refugees, the provinces and voluntary agencies to allocate resources and make arrangements for resettlement assistance, and facilitates closer co-operation with other agencies so that the resettlement, foreign policy and foreign-aid aspects of Canadian relief efforts can be part of an orderly whole. A plan can also be discussed during the annual consultations with the provinces on immigration levels."[20] The annual refugee plan is not intended to establish a ceiling for total refugee admissions. It refers to the number of refugees whose resettlement costs are underwritten by the federal government for that year. Other refugees may be sponsored by private sponsoring groups and organizations. The majority of Indochinese refugees admitted in 1979–1980 were privately sponsored. It is estimated that in 1990 there will be some 13,000 privately sponsored refugee admissions from abroad. These numbers are expected to increase.

Australia: Refugee Policy Defined

We return now to Australia and to the major changes in refugee policy and planning made by her governments in the seventies and early eighties. The Senate Standing Committee on Foreign Affairs and Defence, in its first report on the Indochinese refugee movement published in 1976 (discussed earlier in this chapter), made firm recommendations on refugee policy.[21] "In reaching the conclusion that Australia should be in a position to respond quickly and effectively to refugee crises," the committee said, "[we] consider it essential that there exist an approved and comprehensive set of policy guidelines together with the necessary administrative machinery to be applied to refugee situations. Such guidelines do not exist at present nor has the administrative machinery been established; their absence reduces our practical ability to respond to crises and in turn can become justification for not involving ourselves with particular situations."

The committee felt that this should be a matter of high priority for the Government and that although the guidelines should be formulated within the general context of Australia's overall immigration program, they must constitute a separate and identifiable component which caters specially for the sudden, and sometimes unforeseen, migratory movements of people as refugees." It should also be recognized, the committee said, that there was a place within Australia's refugee policy for "a regular and identifiable intake of refugees and displaced persons who do not meet the existing immigration criteria. This intake should constitute a significant part of our broad immigration target in any one year and should be subject to adjustment in emergencies." The government of the day should also be prepared to accept some "hard-core refugees," with inevitably increased costs.

The Senate committee also recommended the establishment of a standing interdepartmental committee on refugees "with responsibility for the overall forward planning and co-ordination of government activity with respect to all government matters," and an advisory body to be known as the Australia Refugee Policy Council, which would help the Government "to formulate an Australian policy on all aspects of refugee resettlement and to review and continually assess its implementation and effectiveness." The committee also made a number of recommendations relating to refugee resettlement, including the major one that "community response is an essential ingredient to the effective promotion of resettlement," that "an active participation of all sections of the community is called for."[22]

The Fraser government responded to these recommendations and to their own appreciation of the need for clearly defined immigration and refugee policies with reasonable speed. On May 24, 1977, the Minister, Michael MacKellar, made a major speech in the House outlining the Government's proposed "Refugee Policy and Mechanisms."[23] Unlike Canada's new refugee policies which were incorporated in her new Immigration Act 1976 and therefore "anchored in law," the new policies and programs announced by Mr. MacKellar were mainly administrative in character. (They did include a short statement of principles, the first of which closely resembles the commitment to refugee assistance incorporated in Part 1 of the new Canadian Immigration Act.) Short of a new migration act this administrative approach was probably inevitable. As we have seen, Australia's Migration Act 1958, with some later minor amendments, vested complete authority and discretion in the hands of the Minister. A major revision of the act would not take place for another twelve years.

Mr. MacKellar outlined four principles on which his government's approach to refugees would be based and thus far, they have not been challenged or amended by the Hawke government.

1 Australia fully recognizes its humanitarian commitment and responsibility to admit refugees for resettlement.
2 The decision to accept refugees must always remain with the Government of Australia.
3 Special assistance will often need to be provided for the movement of refugees in designated situations or for their resettlement in Australia.
4 It may not be in the interest of some refugees to settle in Australia. Their interests may be better served by resettlement elsewhere. The Australian government makes an annual contribution to the UNHCR which is the main body associated with such resettlement.

It was the Government's view, Mr. MacKellar said, that the acceptance and settlement of refugees should be a continuous process – a point made by the Senate committee – beginning with "a quick and decisive response to international crises and concluding, after what may be a long and difficult path for the refugee, with successful integration into the Australian community." He also announced the creation of a Standing Inter-Departmental Committee on Refugees to advise the Minister; the establishment of a separate interdepartmental committee to deal with the question of refugee status determination (the DORS Committee set up on March 16, 1978); the strengthening of the Refugee Unit of the Department of Immigration and Ethnic Affairs; the re-establishment of formal relations with the Intergovernmental Committee for European Migration (ICEM) through observer status;[24] and the resumption of the practice of posting an Australian immigration officer to UNHCR in Geneva.

Mr. MacKellar also said the Government would consider "proposals from the Minister for Immigration and Ethnic Affairs for designating refugee situations and appropriate responses to them," a proposal not unlike the provision for "designated classes" of refugees in the Canadian Immigration Act. In addition, he said voluntary agencies were to be encouraged "to participate and indicate periodically or as the need arises the extent of the assistance they can provide." Early consideration would be given to refugees who were the subject of "adequate sponsorship by appropriate voluntary bodies." Again, this is evidence of a marked similarity in the evolution in both Canada and Australia of a more formal relationship, a new kind of partnership, between government and the voluntary sector in the sponsorship and resettlement of refugees.

Finally, Mr. MacKellar said his statement was intended as "a declaration of a comprehensive refugee policy and the establishment of administrative machinery to put it into effect." He believed there would be few in the House who would not support a commitment for Australia to play the most effective role possible in refugee resettlement. The Government was committed to this view, in the belief that there was "a community willingness to assist the dispossessed and displaced from overseas in a sensible and realistic way to seek sanctuary and a new life in Australia."

The Indochinese Refugee Movement:
Second Phase

Canada and Australia's new refugee policies and programs were in place not a moment too soon. The first phase of the Indochinese refugee movement, which began with the fall of Saigon in April 1975, and had seemed of such dramatic size, was in fact only a prelude to a much larger exodus which gathered force in the following years and reached crisis proportions in 1979.

The flow of boat people from Vietnam to the major countries of first asylum in Southeast Asia increased from 5,833 in July 1978 to 53,133 in June 1979. At the same time, there were major movements of refugees overland. An estimated 160,000 ethnic Chinese from Vietnam fled to China overland in 1978, while large numbers of refugees from Laos, Kampuchea and Vietnam sought refuge in Thailand. By the end of June 1979, there were 153,000 Indochinese refugees in camps in Thailand, 74,800 in Malaysia, 42,900 in Indonesia, 64,000 in Hong Kong and 9,800 in other countries of first asylum, making a total of 350,000 refugees in boat and land camps. Between 1975 and 1978, total UNHCR expenditures on assistance to Indochinese refugees had increased five-fold, exceeding by far its expenditures in all other parts of the world. Its regional office in Kuala Lumpur had become the largest and busiest of all offices outside Geneva.[25]

The world was watching this large and growing refugee movement – almost nightly on television in all states with access to this form of communication. Vivid scenes of the plight of the Indochinese refugees on the high seas, and in the often primitive and overcrowded early refugee camps, were brought into the homes of millions of viewers. This undoubtedly raised the "refugee consciousness" of many publics among the member nations of UNHCR and increased their willingness to help, although it may have had precisely the opposite effect within the countries of Southeast Asia, where it probably increased the sense of alien threat and intrusion. Whatever its overall effect, intensive media attention introduced an unpredictable element of rising and falling public interest in refugee matters, often unrelated to real need; of concern with short-term solutions; and of an almost exclusive focus on the major refugee movement of the day. This may have been the most dramatic or most publicized refugee situation, but it did not equal the vast numbers of refugees in Africa, for example, who were then needing help. In Canada and Australia, television coverage of the exodus of the Indochinese refugees undoubtedly helped to overcome distance and indifference, and to increase the number of volunteers who came forward to help with the largest refugee movement either country had known since the end of World War II.

Alarmed by the ever-increasing numbers of Indochinese refugees arriving in the Southeast Asian countries of first asylum in 1978–1979, which he described as assuming "the proportions of an appalling tragedy," the UN High Commissioner for Refugees, Paul Hartling, tried to increase the number of places for resettlement and to seek other solutions. In December 1978, he convened a "Consultative Meeting with Interested Governments on Refugees and Displaced Persons in Southeast Asia" – an idea proposed by Australia at the October 1978 meeting of UNHCR's Executive Committee. The meeting produced a substantial increase in resettlement places, and in pledges of financial aid, but it was not enough. Seven months later, on July 20 and 21, 1979, a much larger meeting was convened in Geneva by the then UN Secretary General, Dr. Kurt Waldheim. It was attended by representatives of 66 nations, 27 of which were represented at ministerial level. Canada's chief representative was Flora MacDonald, Secretary of State for External Affairs in the Progressive Conservative government which had just come to power, while the Australian delegation was led by Michael MacKellar. Unexpectedly, the Socialist Republic of Vietnam sent its Deputy Foreign Minister, Phan Hien, and other officials.

In a major speech for the United States, which received warm applause, Vice President Walter Mondale reminded those present of another critical conference on refugees which had had an impressive attendance, but had ended in failure – the infamous Evian Conference of 1938 – and he warned his audience of the dangers of failing on this occasion. Among other practical measures to relieve the situation in Southeast Asia, he urged the creation of transit centres for at least 250,000 refugees where they could await processing or acceptance by third countries; and he indicated strong American support for any efforts which might be made by the Vietnam government to try to stop the flow of boat people from Vietnam "for a reasonable time," a form of moratorium which was then being negotiated. He announced that President Carter would ask Congress for an extra US$105 million for UNHCR for the immediate future and US$20 million towards the creation of transit centres. He also said the President had ordered the US Navy to send extra ships into the South China Sea to help "the drowning and the desperate," and long range Navy planes to fly patrols over it to locate refugees in distress.

The outcome of this very successful conference was that offers of resettlement places for the following 12-month period increased from 125,000 at the end of May to 260,000 in July, with a further 11,000 coming in after the July meeting. There were major additional financial contributions from a number of governments for UNHCR operations, and contributions for the establishment of "a fund to provide durable solutions" to which the United States contributed US$20 million for the first year. From that point on, steps were taken to establish transit centres at sites offered by the Philippines and Indonesia.[26] Shortly before the conference, on May 30, 1979, UNHCR officials had negotiated a "memorandum of understanding" with the Vietnam government, consisting of a seven point program for the orderly departure of family reunion and other humanitarian cases from Vietnam. Although the moratorium which was agreed on in Geneva with

Table 8
Leading Countries of Admission of Indochinese Refugees, 1975–1985

Country	No.
U.S.A.	583,049
People's Republic of China	262,853
Canada	98,424
France	97,827
Australia	96,262

Source: UNHCR

the Vietnamese officials did not bring the flow of boat people to an end, it did bring about a dramatic decrease in the number of refugees leaving Vietnam by boat, and in the caseload of boat refugees in the countries of first asylum. It had no effect on the outflow of refugees overland.[27]

Canada and Australia have been among the five countries admitting the largest numbers of Indochinese refugees, the other three being the United States, the People's Republic of China, and France. Table 8 shows the numbers of Indochinese refugees admitted by all these countries from the fall of Saigon in 1975 to June 30, 1985.

Canada and Australia have been among the countries that have made the largest per capita contributions to international refugee aid agencies. They also lead the world in the number of refugees admitted from all regions during the post-war period compared with the size of their populations.[28]

The figures given here for Indochinese refugee admissions for all five of the major countries of resettlement are unlikely to be final. Refugee movements seldom end tidily and for some years after the main movement is over, relatives, latecomers, orphans, the sick, and the handicapped continue to arrive under programs of one kind or another. But this refugee movement is not even over yet. Refugees packed into overcrowded, ramshackle boats are still leaving Vietnam, although in much smaller numbers; passing ships are still failing to come to their aid; and Thai pirates are still preying on them. As of June 30, 1985, according to UNHCR, there were still 160,339 Indochinese refugees in camps in Southeast Asia awaiting resettlement, including 121,776 land refugees and 38,563 boat refugees. Six years later, the exodus – although smaller – still continues.

How did Canada and Australia, with populations of 26 and 17 million respectively, manage and absorb these very large influxes of refugees which have not yet come to an end – much larger in terms of population size than the more than half a million Indochinese refugees who have gone to the United States thus far? They did it (and are still doing it) by making good use of existing resources and experience and by mobilizing the community, as recommended by Australia's Senate Committee and as urged on governments for years by the voluntary sector in both countries.

Canada made good use of the provisions of her new Immigration Act 1976, which became effective in 1978. On December 7, 1978, regulations were introduced establishing an "Indochinese Designated Class" and setting forth in detail the circumstances in which a group of five individuals or a corporation could sponsor members of this class, as provided for in the Act. As more and more refugees got out of Vietnam in small boats, or left Laos, Kampuchea, and Vietnam overland in the early months of 1979, it was clear that Canada would have to do more than admit the rather limited number of Indonesian refugees included in her first annual refugee plan, presented in the fall of 1978. The situation was complicated by an approaching federal election held on May 22, 1979, and narrowly won by the Progressive Conservatives under Joe Clark. On July 18, 1979, just before the Geneva conference, the short-lived Clark government announced that up to 50,000 Indochinese refugees would be accepted by Canada by the end of 1980 – a figure which was increased by 10,000 on April 2, 1980 after the Liberals had been returned to power on February 18. As head of the Canadian delegation in Geneva, Flora MacDonald presented Canada's 50,000 offer to the conference in ringing tones, challenging other countries to follow the Canadian lead and roundly condemning Vietnam for its brutality and flagrant abuse of human rights.

The Clark government also announced on July 18 that a Canadian Foundation for Refugees would be established – an organization about which the succeeding Trudeau government was less than enthusiastic[29] – to receive contributions from Canadians who wished to help Indochinese refugees but were unable to join a sponsoring group. At the same time, a Special Refugee Task Force was created within the Canada Employment and Immigration Commission to manage Canada's Indochinese refugee movement. It did this very efficiently, this time co-ordinating all phases of the program from selection overseas to resettlement in Canada. A real moment of inspiration came, however, with the idea of a matching formula, as a way of encouraging the voluntary sponsorship of refugees and thereby adding to the numbers who could be admitted. Originally proposed by the churches and voluntary agencies, the idea was taken up enthusiastically by Flora MacDonald and Ron Atkey, the Conservative Minister of Manpower and Immigration, both eager to find new policies and approaches that would impress the Canadian public and the international community.

The matching formula consisted of a pledge made by the Clark government, before the Geneva conference, to bring in one government-assisted refugee for every refugee sponsored by the voluntary sector. The target of 50,000 Indochinese refugees would be made up of 8,000 originally projected under the first refugee plan, plus 21,000 privately sponsored refugees and 21,000 government-assisted refugees. It was an attractive proposition and the voluntary sector became firmly attached to it. As laid down in the Act, private sponsors were required to support and care for these refugees for only one year (or until they were self-sufficient, whichever came first), which was not too daunting financially for a group of five or a corporation. The prospect of getting two refugees for one, however, was very appealing and the Canadian public responded warmly and quickly to it. More than 7,000 private groups and organizations, representing many thousands of individual Canadians, sponsored Indochinese refugees. Of the 60,000 refugees planned for in 1980 who came in over a period of 18 months, 26,000 were government-assisted and 34,000 were privately sponsored.

The matching formula undoubtedly helped to create and sustain the great surge of enthusiasm and desire to help which these figures represent, but the Clark government did not stand by it for long. Private sponsorships came in much faster than expected; the target of 21,000 was reached in four months, with the prospect that the overall level of 50,000 would soon be exceeded. The Government was also becoming concerned about costs, having somewhat overreached itself with a large pledge of $15 million for Cambodian relief. It was also concerned that there might be some public backlash if more than 50,000 Indochinese refugees were accepted. In December 1979, therefore, much to the wrath of the churches and voluntary agencies, the Minister, Ron Atkey, announced that a new policy would be adopted, that the 50,000 target would be firmly adhered to and that it would be filled, so to speak, by the still abundant offers of private sponsorship. It was evident that the matching formula would no longer apply.

The days of the Clark government were numbered, however. Its sudden defeat in the House on December 13, 1979 brought to an end any serious controversy there might have been on this issue. During its campaign for the federal election on February 18, 1980, the Liberal Party promised to reinstate the matching formula. While they did not precisely do this on their return to power, they did devise, in consultation with the voluntary sector, an acceptable ongoing program for the Indochinese refugees. Canada's overall target would be increased to 60,000 and no limit would be placed on the number of private sponsorships, which by then were probably passing their peak. There was no apparent public backlash when this policy was announced.

The same sense of satisfaction and success that had occurred with the Ugandan Asian refugee movement in 1972–1973 could be felt in Canada among the officials and volunteers who took part in this major phase of the Indochinese refugee movement. The official review of the 1970–1980 program issued by the Canada Employment and Immigration Commission summed it up euphorically by saying:

Never before had Canada been involved in a refugee movement which arose so dramatically or persisted in such large numbers for so long. Never had the distances been so vast, the cultural differences so pronounced. Never had groups of Canadians, motivated by conscience and a determination to relieve mass suffering, become so personally involved; and never before had they joined with their federal and provincial governments in a formal partnership to provide a new homeland for refugees.[30]

It could be pointed out, of course, that they had not often been asked to do so. However, the success of private sponsorship on this occasion undoubtedly made a strong impression on government. The CEIC review goes on to say that "the main lesson of the Indochinese program is that voluntary sponsorship works – and that it works exceedingly well, [providing] a better and more personal base for refugee settlement, self-sufficiency and integration."[31] The new Liberal Minister of Manpower and Immigration, Lloyd Axworthy – not a man given to extravagant statements – speaking in the House shortly after the election, paid tribute to his predecessor who had initiated this refugee program and the program of matching grants. "What we have witnessed in Canada over the past years," he said, "in terms of the enormous outpouring of generosity by private Canadians through church organizations and voluntary organizations, is one of the great success stories in this country."

Australia did not make as dramatic an offer at the Geneva conference as Canada did, but by June 30, 1981, she had resettled 51,780 Indochinese refugees, including 43,393 Vietnamese, 5,050 Laotians, and 3,276 Kampucheans.[32] Her reliance on community involvement and assistance has been less than Canada's because she possesses an invaluable resource for the initial accommodation, orientation, and language training of migrants and refugees – her migrant hostels now known as migrant centres which were referred to earlier. As of June 30, 1983, there were 13 active Commonwealth migrant centres, several of which the author has visited. There are five migrant centres in New South Wales (Endeavour, Westbridge, East Hills, Cabramatta, and Fairy Meadow – the last two offering non-residential services only); four in Victoria (Midway, Enterprure, Eastbridge, and Wittona), and one each in Queensland (Wacol), South Australia (Pennington), West Australia (Greylands), Northern Territories (Tamarind) and Tasmania (Mount Saint Canice). As of the end of June 1983, 77 per cent of centre residents were refugees – 65 per cent from Indochina and 12 per cent from Eastern Europe. Ten of these hostels have a residential capacity of between 600 and 900 migrants at one time, and the two smaller ones (Tamarind and Mount Saint Canice) between 50 and 70.

An ancient recollection – deriving from the early difficulties of Australia's migrant hostels after World War II – lingers on in immigration circles in Canada, to the effect that hostels for immigrants and refugees are more trouble than they are worth; and that virtue always lies in getting new arrivals out into the community as soon as possible. Neither of these propositions has ever been valid. Hostels are expensive and must be well run, but they have great advantages. They permit intensive, initial language training and orientation courses to be provided for large numbers of immigrants or refugees, and in a very direct way they ease the first stages of adjustment to a new society. When immigrants and refugees disappear into the community as they do in Canada, it is hard to reassemble them; many never get the language training and orientation to Canadian life which they badly need.

On October 29, 1979, an alternative method of caring for refugees involving direct participation and responsibility by the community was announced by the then Minister, Michael MacKellar. Under the Community Refugee Settlement Scheme (CRSS), which is similar to the Canadian system of private sponsorships then in full swing, refugees are moved directly into the community where they are cared for by a variety of community groups: churches, service clubs, ethnic community organizations, families or individuals who have offered to provide a range of practical assistance. The community groups are supported by government grants which are not, however, intended to cover all the costs involved. All the states and territories gave their approval to this scheme which has now been extended to include, among others, East European, Latin American, and disadvantaged refugees. CRSS groups may now also sponsor family reunion cases on behalf of the families in their care. The first group of Indochinese refugees to be resettled under this scheme arrived in Whyalla, South Australia on February 13, 1980. By 1982–1983, more than 400 groups had taken part in the CRSS, and by October 1983, 6,355 Indochinese refugees and 983 East European refugees had arrived in Australia under the scheme. These are much smaller numbers of refugees than those who came in under Canada's system of private sponsorships, but they must be seen in the context of the much larger numbers who were accommodated in Australia's migrant centres.[33] Apart from the CRSS, the Australian community has been involved in the Indochinese and other recent refugee movements in a variety of other ways, mainly through voluntary agencies and ethnic community organizations, including "hosting" or friendship schemes for refugees and their families to ease the transition from the migrant centres into the community. Speaking at the annual meeting of the International Catholic Migration Commission in Geneva in

October 1982, a senior official of Australia's Department of Immigration and Ethnic Affairs said: "We are having to look again at the role of community organizations, humanitarian and philanthropic organizations of a voluntary character in this process [of refugee resettlement]. It may be that in the coming years we are going to have to enter into a more vigorous partnership with community groups ... Now this does not in any direct way affect the level of our refugee program, but I think that in the coming years it will increasingly be a factor in our thinking."[34]

The second report of Australia's Senate Standing Committee on Foreign Affairs and Defence on the Indochinese refugee movement was introduced in the Senate on November 15, 1981 and tabled in 1982.[35] This time the committee had been asked to look at the Indochinese refugee situation and Australia's role in assisting the refugees, with particular reference to the Report of the Committee on Australia and the Refugee Problem tabled in the Senate on December 1, 1976. The committee's major conclusions, which contrast sharply with the generally critical nature of their 1976 report, are as follows:

From the evidence received, the committee considers that the settlement of Indochinese refugees is progressing well. The committee commends the results achieved through a combination of efforts by the Commonwealth and state governments, voluntary groups and the refugees themselves. Settlement of Indochinese refugees has been a significant domestic issue, although the committee received little evidence of resentment or indifference. The general acceptance by the Australian community of different racial and cultural backgrounds is gratifying. The committee concludes that overall, positive measures have been introduced to assist refugee resettlement and they are a constructive response to what was envisaged in the recommendations of the Committee's 1976 report ...

The committee also concluded that "Refugee issues have become an important element in Australia's bilateral relations, in particular with the countries of Southeast Asia," and that "their impact on Australia's multilateral policy is considerable." The committee believed that refugee problems would continue to affect international affairs for years to come and that Australia's standing in the world would, in part, be determined by its policies in relation to refugees. "The formulation of a refugee policy accompanied by comprehensive administrative guidelines is a welcome and vital element of Australia's role in refugee issues," the committee said, and added:

It is essential that the policy and program resulting from it are understood and accepted at the international level and by the Australian community. This is an important task for Australia's representatives overseas and for the Government, in co-operation with the involved non-government sector at home. The immigration policy is an integral part of Australia's relations with many countries and the refugee policy is increasing in prominence within the policy. Therefore the possible effects of the refugee policy on Australia's relations with its migrant source countries must not be overlooked.[36]

This sound advice applied to Canada as well as to Australia and with equal force. To an extent so far unrecognized by most Canadian politicians and senior bureaucrats, and certainly by her academic community, immigration and refugee policies are the very substance of international relations and should be treated accordingly.

There have been other, lesser, developments during these critical years in which refugees have become such an important part of the immigration policies and programs of both Canada and Australia. In the latter half of 1981, for example, Australia developed what are known as "Special Humanitarian Programs" (SHPs) which correspond in some respects to Canada's "Designated Classes" under the Immigration Act 1976, and have the same objective of avoiding the restrictions of the UNHCR definition of a refugee. Those accepted under these programs are generally required to demonstrate that they have (1) close relatives in Australia; or (2) close former ties with Australia; or (3) a strong and well-established community in Australia which is able and willing to provide all necessary settlement support. There is at present a global SHP (which includes a Soviet-Jewish SHP which has existed for some time), and an East Timorese SHP introduced in October 1980. A number of Polish nationals detained in Poland on account of their involvement with the Solidarity movement have been resettled in Australia under the Special Humanitarian Program. Another development which should be mentioned is that both countries, after prolonged and difficult negotiations with Hanoi, now have their own programs of orderly departure for relatives in Vietnam wishing to join family members now in Canada and Australia.

We turn now, however, to a major aspect of refugee policy which has become a critical issue in the international community today, namely, refugee status determination. Thus far it appears to have caused relatively few problems in Australia, but a very complex and difficult situation in Canada, making an interesting contrast in two entirely different ways of approaching this complicated question.

Refugee Status Determination

As the world refugee situation became more critical in the early seventies, and as the opportunities for emigration or temporary employment in other countries became more restricted with the onset of the world recession, it was quickly perceived within the commerce of migration and by many would-be migrants who lacked the qualifications or family connections to be accepted in receiving countries that refugee status was a very desirable objective. Minority groups, large and small, also began to see refugee status in another country as a possible way of escape from their own disadvantaged or dangerous situations, while unscrupulous lawyers and commercial agents saw it as a way into countries of first asylum or permanent settlement for their clients. As a result, there has been a quite remarkable escalation in claims for refugee status in a wide range of countries, nearly all of them parties to the 1951 United Nations Convention relating to the Status of Refugees and/or the 1967 Protocol. Many of these claims are "manifestly unfounded" as they are described in legal language. Many are difficult, borderline cases which deserve compassionate consideration but do not fit well into established categories. Many require for their determination a really well-informed and up-to-date appreciation of the political situation in the many countries from which the claimants come. All of these factors make the process of refugee status determination very difficult.

The UN Convention and Protocol do not specify the precise procedures which should be used to determine refugee status. It is left to the contracting states to devise systems of their own and these systems vary widely. In France, for example, the competent authority for determining refugee status is the Director of the Office for the Protection of Refugees and Stateless Persons, an autonomous body attached to the Ministry of External Relations. He is assisted by a council, consisting mainly of government officials, which advises him on matters of general policy relating to the determination of refugee status. Appeals against negative decisions may be brought before a special appeals commission whose decisions may be appealed on questions of law to the Conseil d'État. In Britain, the competent authority for determining refugee status is the Home Secretary. Claims are processed in the first instance by the Refugee Section of the Home Office Immigration and Nationality Department. Appeals against a negative decision may be made to a government adjudicator, with the possibility of further appeals to the Immigration Appeal Tribunal and to the courts. In Sweden, the competent authority is the National Immigration and Naturalization Board whose decisions may be appealed to the government itself within three weeks from the day the Board's decision is communicated to the claimant. In the United States, the competent authority is the District Director of the Immigration and Naturalization Service (INS) in the area where the claim for refugee status is made. The District Director is required in all cases to seek an advisory opinion from the Bureau of Human Rights and Humanitarian Affairs in the Department of State.

Some countries, including Canada, have been swamped with claims for refugee status during the last few years and large backlogs have developed. In early 1984 the backlog of claims for refugee status at the District Director level in the United States was 165,000 including the claims of 115,000 Cubans and 5,000 Haitians. In West Germany, which has been faced with an avalanche of claims, applications pending before the Federal Office for the Recognition of Foreign Refugees were 33,000 in 1982 and an estimated 200,000 in 1983, even after extensive modifications had been introduced in the system. In Canada, the number of persons seeking refugee status increased from some 500 claims in 1977 to 6,792 in 1983–1984.[37] By the end of 1988, there was a backlog of over 60,000 refugee claimants and the numbers were to go even higher.

Australia created a straightforward system of refugee status determination, with one level of decision-making and only one possibility of appeal. Canada, on the other hand – striving for fairness and attempting to meet her legal obligations under the UN Convention in full – created, through the provisions of her Immigration Act 1976, an immensely complicated system with several levels of decision-making and at least two major avenues of appeal. It was described by one legal authority as a system "riddled with anomalies, inconsistencies and other shortcomings which have demonstrated that it is both cumbersome and susceptible to abuse,"[38] and by another in the following terms: "There are two striking features of [Canada's] refugee-claims procedure. One is its complexity, the other is its imcompleteness. The process is filled with inquiries and examinations, determinations and redeterminations, applications and appeals. Yet a refugee claimant can go through the whole system without ever having been heard by anyone deciding on or advising on his claim. He may never have a chance to respond to any objections that are made to his claim."[39]

Although it could be criticized for limited review and appeal possibilities, the Australian system of refugee status determination seemed nonetheless to be simple and effective. It relied on a high quality of decision-making, and did not appear to be susceptible to much abuse. The competent authority for determination of refugee status was the Minister for Immigration and Ethnic Affairs. Applicants applied first to the immigration authorities in their state of residence. They were then interviewed under oath by a senior immigration officer and a transcript of the interview made available to the Minister, to the applicant, to the UNHCR Representative in Australia, and to the DORS (Determination of Refugee Status) Committee. The DORS Committee was composed entirely of senior officials from the departments of Immigration and Ethnic Affairs (Chairman), Prime Minister and Cabinet, Foreign Affairs, and Attorney General, with the UNHCR representative attending as an observer. After considering the case, the committee made a recommendation to the Minister who took the final decision. There was no right of appeal, but the Minister could refer any case back to the Dors Committee in the light of additional information. From its first meeting on March 11, 1978 until June 30, 1986, the Committee Considered 2,200 applications, but recently applications have been increasing and this system has been changed (see pp xxvi/xxvii).

The Canadian system, embodied in the Immigration Act 1976 with some additional procedural changes, was far more complicated. The competent final authority was also the Minister of Employment and Immigration, but there were many stages through which a claim to refugee status could pass, sometimes taking as long as three years, if not longer. One of the principal conclusions in one of several studies of this process was that "the laborious procedures imposed by the Act, together with a dramatic increase in claims, have created serious delays in the disposition of cases, with repercussions throughout our system of immigration enforcement."[40]

The two most recent Liberal ministers of Employment and Immigration in Canada prior to the 1984 federal election, Lloyd Axworthy and John Roberts, both initiated studies with a view to improving this system, if not reorganizing it. In September 1980, Lloyd Axworthy's Task Force on Immigration Practices and Procedures produced its report, "The Refugee Status Determination Process." The report focussed almost entirely on the rights of applicants, the need for fairness and, as the task force described it, "the operation of the process within the existing legislative context." They made some valuable recommendations including the need to establish the independence of the Refugee Status Advisory Committee; the need to give more weight to the principle of "the benefit of the doubt"; and the urgent need to provide applicants with an oral hearing as part of the primary determination stage. But the task force failed almost entirely to address the central problem of delays, backlogs, and the general unworkability of the system, which they evidently felt would require major amendments to the Immigration Act. They did manage one central recommendation in this regard, however, presented with a minimum of explanation and detail: "The Immigration Act should be amended to replace the present refugee determination process with a central tribunal which would hear and determine refugee claims. If such a full hearing process is established at the first level of refugee determination, the concept of a redetermination should be eliminated."[41]

When John Roberts became Minister of Employment and Immigration in the summer of 1983, he called on a member of the task force, Ed Ratushny, Professor of Law at the University of Ottawa (who had recently been involved in an important study of illegal migrants in Canada[42]) to explore the matter further. The Ratushny report, "A New Refugee Status Determination Process for Canada," was presented to the Minister in May 1984. It analysed the problem very clearly and, unlike its predecessor, dealt directly with the issues of delay and abuse of the system. Its major conclusion was that the existing refugee status determination process had serious shortcomings which must be addressed as quickly as possible. Considerable momentum for reform already existed, according to Professor Ratushny. What was needed now was "to crystallize the specific form which legislative changes should take and generate sufficient public support to establish the political will to act."[43]

The Ratushny report examined a number of possible models for a reconstructed refugee status determination process for Canada, appearing to favour a very good proposal made to the Canada Employment and Immigration Commission by a group known as the Concerned Delegation of Church, Legal, and Humanitarian Organizations. The core of this proposal was the recommendation that the Refugee Status Advisory Committee should be reconstituted as the Refugee Review Board with final decision-making authority subject only to judicial review in the Federal Court. The Minister, John Roberts, then called upon a friend and well-known Toronto author and citizen, Rabbi W. Gunther Plaut, to study these materials and to produce at least two possible models for a responsible and efficient refugee status determination process, from which government could finally choose.

In the meantime, the number of refugee claimants was escalating rapidly, as we have seen. In December 1986, more than 3,000 people entered Canada to make refugee claims. In the first six weeks of 1987, more than 6,000 claims were made. It was estimated that of the 18,000 refugee claimants in 1986, two thirds were not genuine refugees and that a large majority had come at the instigation of or with the help of commercial operators. In the face of this situation, the Conservative government finally decided to act decisively. On May 5, 1987, the then Minister of Employment and Immigration, Benoît Bouchard, tabled a Bill to establish a new refugee determination process for Canada and to amend the Immigration Act 1976 accordingly. It came into force on January 1, 1989.

The Act creates a new independent body: the Immigration and Refugee Board. The new Board has two sections – an Immigration Appeal Board to deal with immigration matters and a Convention Refugee Determination Board to deal with refugee claims. The new system provides a number of safeguards for the individual, including the right to legal counsel and legal aid (provided where necessary). Every refugee claimant arriving in Canada will first be seen by a panel of two people: one a member of the Refugee Board and the other an immigration adjudicator. Their decisions may be appealed by leave to the Federal Court on questions of law, jurisprudence, and perverse or capricious interpretations of fact.

Claimants with refugee status elsewhere and claimants arriving from safe third world countries who have a reasonable opportunity to claim protection there will be returned to those countries but a unanimous decision is required. People with an arguable claim are referred to the Refugee Board for an oral hearing which is held before two members of the Board. A unanimous decision is required to reject a claim. Claimants accepted by the Board can apply for landing. Under this new system, it is hoped that claims will be processed in months instead of years as before. The major problem for the Board, however, has proved to be the accelerating number of claims.

The whole question of refugee status determination, and the very different approaches taken initially by Australia and Canada to the need to devise a workable and acceptable system of refugee status determination, illustrates as well as anything can one of the basic, ever-present dilemmas of immigration and refugee management. This is the conflict between the need for every sovereign state "to maintain the integrity of its borders," as Professor Ratushny puts it, and consequently of its immigration laws; and the need to give a fair hearing and sympathetic consideration to the claims of the unqualified and disadvantaged who are not part of regular immigration and refugee movements. The basic premise of the Australian system is clearly that maintaining the integrity of Australia's borders and laws comes first, whereas Canada, as part of an immigration law which sought to be just and equitable, has leant over backwards to be fair to individual applicants (even though the system has not been perfect in that regard), at the expense of developing an efficient but still equitable system which can handle an increasing flow of applications with reasonable speed. A balance must obviously be struck, but we should bear in mind that the integrity of the borders and laws of Australia and Canada may be more difficult to maintain in the fairly near future.

We have seen how important refugees have become within the larger field of immigration policy and management in Canada and Australia – taking up a bigger share of the annual immigration movement, absorbing more resources, requiring more policy development, and involving the community to a much greater degree than before. This is likely to continue and may well increase. It is estimated that there are now at least fifteen million refugees on all continents, a substantial number of whom require re-settlement. The Indochinese refugee movement will certainly not be the last major refugee movement. Today, the main focus is again on Africa where drought, desertification, and civil war are creating refugee problems of disastrous proportions. According to UNHCR, there were also 3 million Afghan refugees in Pakistan and 2 million on Iran in 1990.

Both Canada and Australia have impressive records in relation to refugees in the post-war period and their performances in this field have been very similar. Tables 9 and 10 show the separate movements or major

Table 9
Canadian Refugee Programs, 1947-1984

Special Refugee and Humanitarian Movements		No. of Refugees
1947-1952	Post-war European Movement	186,150
1956-1957	Hungarian Movement	37,194
1968-1969	Czechoslovakian Movement	11,943
1970	Tibetans	228
1972-1973	Ugandan Asians	7,069
1973-1979	Special South American Program	6,990
1975	Cypriots	700
1975-1978	Special Vietnamese/Cambodian Program	9,060
1976	Kurds from Iraq	98
1976-1977	Angola/Mozambique Returnees	2,100
1976-1979	Lebanese	11,010
1979-1984	Indochinese Movement	90,000

Source: Canada Employment and Immigration Commission

Table 10
Australia: Refugee Arrivals, January 1945-June 1984

Top 14 Source Nationalities	No. of Refugees
Polish	74,973
Vietnamese	70,492
Hungarian	26,185
Latvian	19,241
Cypriot/Lebanese	17,389
Czechoslovakian	15,276
Ukrainian	14,464
White Russian (from China)	13,292
Kampuchean	11,052
Lithuanian	9,906
Laotian	6,519
Timorese	5,479
Estonian	5,329
USSR*	4,791
Total all nationalities	418,870

Source: Department of Immigration and Ethnic Affairs.
*Jewish refugees from the Soviet Union.
Note: These are estimated figures only. A breakdown of about 90,000 East European refugees arriving between 1954 and 1982 is not available.

groups of refugees admitted by the two countries from 1945-1947 to 1984. Few outside government are aware of how closely they remain in touch in this area – meeting annually (if not more often) at the meetings of UNHCR's Executive Committee and as members once more at IOM meetings; sharing documentation (annual reports, ministerial statements, news releases, task force and specialist reports); and communicating by telephone and telex when necessary. All of this is supplemented by frequent mutual visiting by politicians and senior officials. It is not surprising that their refugee policies and programs have become very similar. It remains for the advisory bodies, non-governmental organizations, and concerned individuals in the world of refugees to find ways to overcome the vast physical distance which still separates them.

UNDOCUMENTED MIGRANTS

Undocumented migration is now a widely accepted international term for illegal migration or immigration, although for domestic purposes Canada and Australia continue to use the latter – Canada referring in her official documents to "illegal immigrants" and Australia to "illegal entrants and overstayers." Although much of this kind of immigration *is* illegal, much of it hardly merits that description, so that undocumented (or irregular) migration seems both a kinder and more appropriate term. In 1975, the General Assembly of the United Nations recommended that all UN bodies use the expression "migrant workers in an irregular situation or without documents."[46]

Undocumented migration is a major phenomenon in the world today, affecting many countries. It ranks on a level with the three other current forms of international migration: migration for permanent settlement, refugee movements, and temporary migration. There is a great deal of confusion and misunderstanding about it, many people believing that the problem can always be solved by firm government action. It is more realistic, however, to say that in democratic societies it can be controlled and reduced to some extent, but that it will probably be with us always as the reverse side of legitimate migration and refugee movements. And it has been with us always, as mankind has striven to go where life may be better, with or without permission. Today, however, undocumented migration has been vastly increased by improved communications and by the increasing disparities between rich and poor nations. This raises the question whether we now need forms of international monitoring, protection, and assistance (if not regulation), similar to those which we have tried to provide for refugees over the past 70 years.

It should be noted that the undocumented migrant and the claimant for refugee status are in very similar situations and can often be, at different times, the same person. An undocumented migrant can sometimes achieve entry via refugee status, while the claimant for refugee status who is turned down often becomes one of the army of undocumented migrants.

Fairly extensive international discussion of this problem has taken place in the last few years, but little collective action has resulted beyond resolutions and recommendations. Further action would require a level of collaboration between developed and developing countries which, unfortunately, appears unattainable at present. The major features of this international consultative effort so far have been first, the adoption in 1975 by the ILO (International Labour Office) of two instruments relating to "clandestine or illegal migration," Convention No. 143 and Recommendation No. 151, which relate mainly to the prevention and elimination of clandestine or illegal immigration and the abuses associated with it. They relate also to the protection of the basic human rights of all migrant workers, and to the need for collaboration between the countries of origin and the countries of employment. Next came the unsuccessful efforts of the EC (European Community) between 1974 and 1978, to co-ordinate the policies of its member countries on illegal immigration. It was hoped to achieve increased collaboration in this area, adequate sanctions against the traffic in clandestine workers and other abuses, and the protection of the rights of all workers. A directive on illegal immigration was drafted by the EEC Commission in the fall of 1976. This was then considered by the European Parliament which suggested some amendments which were incorporated in April 1978. Some six months later, however, the revised draft was put aside by the EEC Council, because of serious differences of opinion among member countries on all the main issues.

Thirdly, and most recently, the United Nations has been attempting to draft a Convention to protect the rights of all migrant workers and their families. A resolution was passed in the General Assembly in December 1978 requesting the Secretary General to explore the possibility of drawing up such a Convention with member states, in collaboration with the specialized agencies, particularly the ILO. The General Assembly decided to establish, in its fall 1980 session, a working group open to all member states which would prepare the draft Convention. Several drafts were submitted, including one prepared by a group of Mediterranean and Scandinavian countries in 1981 which was accepted as a basis for discussion. The principle (and at present distinctly Utopian) objective of this submission was that the Convention should provide for the creation of a worldwide system of collaboration to eliminate illegal migrations, suppress abuses of migrants, and lay the foundations of a scheme gradually to reabsorb remaining groups of illegal migrants.[47] After four years' work, the Working Group has produced a draft Convention. At the time of writing, this was being considered by the UN Economic and Social Council.

In April 1983, the Intergovernmental Committee for Migration (ICM) convened a seminar in Geneva on the theme of "Undocumented Migrants or Migrants in an Irregular Situation." The seminar was attended by 55 governments, including Canada and Australia, and more than 60 non-governmental organizations and social and demographic research institutes. It was part of a regular series of seminars organized by ICM on the adaptation and integration of immigrants. In his opening remarks, ICM's Director, Dr. James L. Carlin, said, "In convening this seminar, ICM shares the widespread concern that the present adverse economic conditions are contributing to the global upsurge of irregular migration and consequently, are making migrants more vulnerable to discrimination and abuses, including at times neglect of their human rights." Irregular migration, he said, while not a new phenomenon, was affecting national government policies, regional interests, and international relations; and it tended to inspire negative attitudes towards normal migration – a very important point. To a great extent today, migration is "intra-regional and flows from developing countries with rapidly growing populations and underemployment to countries with developed and rather more sophisticated economies."[48]

The seminar produced some interesting papers on undocumented migration (listed in the Bibliography). It also arrived at a number of useful conclusions and recommendations. It was recognized, for example, that undocumented migration is mainly spontaneous and is due to a number of specific causes, identified as: (a) the absence or inadequacy of migration laws and regulations; (b) the complexity of existing laws and regulations, as well as the difficulty of obtaining the necessary documentation for legal immigration; (c) quotas and restrictive legislation adopted by certain receiving countries; (d) ignorance of existing migration legislation, due to low levels of education, insufficient information, and difficult access to official sources of information and documentation; (e) in certain regions, the ignorance or non-recognition of national frontiers where these divide economic, social, and ethnic communities; (f) the demand by certain unscrupulous employers for cheap, irregular manpower; and (g) illegal labour-force trafficking by employers and intermediary agents.

On the question of "regularization of status" (which usually means amnesty) the conference participants believed that, while it may provide a solution to a particular problem, "constant repetition of this process will be self-defeating, in that it will encourage further illegal entry and stay in the country, in the expectation of yet further regularization." It was strongly held, therefore, that "solutions should be sought in bilateral co-operation between receiving and sending countries and at the multilateral level, where appropriate, in different regions of the world." It is worth quoting the recommendations of the conference in full, because of the importance and universality of undocumented migration today:

1 Every effort should be made by countries of origin and receiving countries to eliminate illegal labour force trafficking. Governments should also exert greater control over employers to prevent illegal hiring and its negative effects.

2 Governments should be invited to collect more relevant data on undocumented migration, as well as undertaking more research studies in this

area, and should make this available to international organizations.

3 Steps should be taken, at both national and international levels, to ensure that migrants in an irregular situation enjoy their fundamental human rights. This should not, however, imply a *de facto* recognition of the legality of their status.

4 Governments should take appropriate measures to foster greater public understanding of the problems of illegal migrants and the acceptance of humane solutions.

5 Efforts should be made at an international level to define an appropriate legal framework for co-operation between countries of origin and receiving countries, aimed at solving the problems of illegal migrations.

6 The objectives of such co-operation should be to prevent illegal flows of migrants, to deal humanely with the problems of existing illegal migrations, and to ensure that, as a long-term goal, all migrations take place through legal and controlled channels.[49]

The effects on an individual or a family of trying to make a living in a foreign country without any kind of official status are well known and, to a remarkable degree, universal in character at least among industrialized countries where there is evidence on the subject. These effects were listed in one of the papers delivered at the seminar. A foreign worker in an irregular situation, it was claimed, (1) receives lower wages than a worker in a regular situation; (2) never has any social security coverage; (3) in the event of any claim concerning labour matters, cannot apply to any official body – trade union, labour court, etc. – precisely because he is in breach of the law; (4) performs unhealthy or dangerous work without adequate protection or safety; (5) is obliged to live in very poor conditions, both as regards housing and with respect to integration in society, because of various factors such as ignorance of the language, low level of culture, etc.; (6) frequently lives apart from his family; reunification is very difficult and has to be achieved, if at all, by illegal methods. Consequently the education of his children will also be affected by this irregular situation.[50] Another paper described the condition of migrants in an irregular situation as "trapped in a position of permanent inequality."[51]

The Australian Experience

In contrast to the international community, where the pressures for action are weak, individual countries which have experienced large inflows of undocumented migrants and have many living within their borders, have attempted in the last few years to establish a greater degree of control over this form of migration and unofficial settlement. They have introduced stricter laws relating to it and have experimented with different forms of regularization. France, West Germany, the United Kingdom, Belgium, the Netherlands, Argentina and more recently the United States have all tried amnesties in recent years. Canada and Australia, protected at least until recently by distance, ocean barriers, and, in Canada's case, the appeal of a very affluent and climatically more attractive nation to the south, are among the countries that have moved or are moving towards greater control and have tried different forms of regularization. Both countries estimated the numbers of undocumented migrants in their midst in 1983–1984 as about 50,000. The majority were thought to be overstayers.

It has been suggested that countries which have a significant number of undocumented migrants within their borders are faced with three choices: to deport or expel them, to regularize their status, or to disregard their presence.[52] Canada and Australia have used all three of these approaches, as well as several others. During the period under discussion, Australia's first encounter with a serious problem of immigration control was very similar to the problem of the "hole in the dyke" left by Canada's 1967 Immigration Regulations and a new appeal system, discussed in Chapter 2. It came through the Easy Visa Scheme, mentioned in Chapter 3, introduced in October 1973 – with the best of intentions – by the then Minister for Immigration Al Grassby. It was intended to promote and facilitate more visits to Australia by relatives, tourists, and others, by reducing to a minimum the formalities involved in acquiring a visa. Within a few months, however, to quote the 1976 Annual Review of the Department of Immigration and Ethnic Affairs, "it became clear that the system was being abused to a substantial degree by people whose reason for coming was not a bona fide visit but rather to seek work and/or to settle in Australia. The number of visitors admitted under the Easy Visa Scheme and not complying with conditions of entry (which prohibited employment) reached such unacceptably high levels that it became necessary first to suspend the system in certain countries and then, in January 1975, to abolish it completely."[53] Since January 1, 1975, all persons coming to Australia for settlement or temporary stay from all countries, with the exception of New Zealanders and certain other exempted persons, have been required to obtain visas.

A year later, on January 26, 1976, the Fraser government offered the first of what were to be two important amnesties to "prohibited immigrants who were overstayed visitors at the end of 1975."[54] 8,614 applied during the amnesty period, which ran from January 26 (Australia Day) to April 30, 1976, and they came from a remarkable range of countries – 82 in all. The most important countries of origin were Greece (1,282), Britain (911), Indonesia (748), China (643), Turkey (466), Fiji (438), Hong Kong (363), Italy (339), the United States (283), and Tonga (264), with smaller numbers from other countries in Europe, the Middle East, Asia, and Latin America. If nothing else, this episode shows how rapidly the word about opportunities for migration spreads within the international community today. It is interesting to note that, following this amnesty, there was a significant increase in visitor travel to Australia, and in the number who failed to depart at the end of the agreed period of their visit, indicating that they too had hoped to benefit from an amnesty.[55] When announcing the amnesty in Perth on January 5, 1976, the Minister, Michael MacKellar, made a point of saying, as he did on several other occasions, that the amnesty "should be understood by all to be seeking to rectify a situation not of our making. It will not be repeated.[56]

The 8,614 undocumented migrants who applied during the 1976 amnesty, most of whom were accepted, were not a great haul. Four years later, the Fraser government tried again, this time with a bigger campaign and a more carefully developed strategy. In the meantime, undocumented migration or illegal immigration as it was called had been increasing in Australia as it had everywhere in the seventies. In 1978, the Department of Immigration and Ethnic Affairs reported: "there has been a significant increase in the number of people who seek to enter by illegal means. In 1977–1978 organized attempts to do this involved the use of visa and other immigration stamps forged overseas, false passports and abuse of the direct transit facility. As a result, immigration control officers, particularly at airports, faced many difficulties in maintaining proper controls without also increasing the time required to clear large numbers of tired and impatient passengers ... Attempts to circumvent immigration entry control by malpractice, subterfuge or seeking discretionary decisions in 1977–1978 reached a level not previously experienced in Australia."[57] At the same time, the deportation of prohibited immigrants located in different parts of Australia increased significantly in these years from 395 in 1973–1974 to 1,102 in 1978–1979, of whom the large majority were overstayers.

On June 7, 1978, the Minister announced major changes in immigration policies and procedures (discussed in Chapter 3) which included new regulations relating to change of status in Australia. As mentioned earlier, the possibility of changing from temporary to permanent status when already in a receiving country is a critical issue in immigration and is closely related to problems of illegality. This possibility was withdrawn in Canada in 1972, except in special cases, as part of the Liberal government's efforts to control and reduce the major illegal immigration movement of the early seventies which led to Canada's Adjustment of Status Program (or amnesty) in the same year. Mr. MacKellar's new regulations of 1978 also closed off this possibility, except for what were then felt to be a harmless and deserving group, namely spouses and dependent children of Australian residents; refugees with valid entry permits; aged parents who would have qualified for admission if they had applied overseas; and private students who were able to satisfy the normal criteria for migration. Two years later, however, on the occasion of the Fraser government's second amnesty, change of status within Australia would be made still more difficult.

In 1980, the Government made three important moves to control and reduce undocumented migration from overseas and illegal settlement within the country. Ian Macphee had now replaced Michael MacKellar as Minister for Immigration and Ethnic Affairs. On June 19, 1980, Mr. Macphee announced the immediate introduction of a Regularization of Status Programme, in effect an amnesty, which became widely known as ROSP and is described below. He also introduced two bills in the House in the fall of that year, a Migration Amendment Bill 1980 and an Immigration (Unauthorized Arrivals) Amendment Bill 1980, both of which came into force in January 1981. The purpose of the first bill was "to restrict by law the categories of immigrants eligible to be granted permanent status subsequent to their arrival in Australia." Outside certain categories (spouses, unmarried children, or aged parents of an Australian citizen or other permanent resident; refugees; certain persons holding temporary entry permits with permission to work in Australia who meet migration criteria; and other persons holding temporary entry permits where there are strong compassionate or humanitarian grounds involved), all persons, the Minister said, "who break the law by overstaying their visas and refusing to leave will be deported." This meant – and it was a very important change in the law – that the Minister no longer had absolute discretion in law to grant resident status to visitors and persons in Australia without permanent resident status. Thus the process of securing status when in Australia illegally, described by Mr. Macphee when he introduced this bill in the following terms, would become much more difficult:

People unable to meet Australia's normal immigration requirements have continued to come to Australia as visitors and subsequently to seek resident status, frequently enlisting the support of members of Parliament, the media, ethnic communities and other voluntary organizations. Such changes of status have been against Government policy but were legally possible. Many thousands of people who could not satisfy normal migration policy requirements deliberately overstayed and remained illegally. Often years later such persons would seek change of status arguing that they had become so integrated in the Australian community that they must be deemed to be constitutent members of it.

Cases involving more than 20 consecutive appeals to the Minister or to the

Department against a refusal to approve permanent residence were not uncommon, Mr. Macphee said. In some instances, the number of individual representations ran into the hundreds.[58]

The second bill introduced by Mr. Macphee, the Immigration (Unauthorized Arrivals) Amendment Bill 1980, was a direct outcome of the Indochinese refugee movement – then at its height – and of the arrival of small boats carrying refugees to Australian shores. As we have seen, there was much talk in Australia at that time about the illegal traffic in refugees, and the high prices paid by some refugees to leave Vietnam and the high profits made by some of those who transported them. The bill was intended, Mr. Macphee said in his speech to the House on its second reading, "to deter ships owners, masters, crew, agents and charterers from bringing people without visas or other proper prior authority to travel to Australia." It applied to travel by air as well as by sea, and made it an offence punishable by a fine of up to $100,000 or 10 years imprisonment or both (quite harsh penalties) for the operators, including crew members of aircraft and ships, to bring into Australia more than five "relevant persons." A relevant person was one who was not an Australian citizen, did not hold a visa or a return endorsement for travel to Australia, or had not been exempted by the Minister from the necessity of obtaining a visa or return endorsement. Essentially the bill was directed against "rackets involving the clandestine importation of illegal immigrants flouting the laws of the country of entry." Such ventures, the Minister said, "may involve the carriage of people secreted in ships and aircraft crossing national borders. Their motivation is greed and the returns can be large."

In his speech to the House Mr. Macphee quoted some recent examples of the commercial traffic in refugees: "Towards the end of 1978 five large freighters filled with Vietnamese arrived in ports of South East Asia. The *Southern Cross* sailed into Indonesian waters, the *Hai Hong* arrived off Malaysia, the *Huey Fong* and the *Sky Luck* showed up in Hong Kong and the *Tung An* went to the Philippines. Each carried between 1500 and 3000 passengers who had paid to leave their homeland with the sanction of their government." Genuine refugees, he said, had nothing to fear in seeking assistance from the Australian government. The Government saw this bill, however, as an essential part of maintaining immigration controls, and believed that it would provide an effective deterrent to the operators of vessels who might consider bringing unauthorized persons to Australia.[59]

If the law was amended to make change of status in Australia very difficult (except in the few permitted categories), and if strong measures were taken to deter the handlers of unauthorized migrants, something had to be done also about the many illegal entrants and overstayers known to be in the country already, who had not come forward in very large numbers during the 1976 amnesty. Existing controls were clearly not adequate to the task and there were obvious political advantages to be derived from clearing the matter up, at least to a substantial extent. Therefore it was decided to try again. This was the rationale for ROSP, the Regularization of Status Programme introduced on June 19, before the two bills discussed above received their first reading in the House.

The Regularization of Status Programme – Australia's 1980 Amnesty

The Regularization of Status Programme (ROSP) was a six-month amnesty which ran from June 19 to December 31, 1980. It applied to people in Australia without permanent resident status and there legally or illegally, who had arrived in Australia before January 1, 1980 and who wished to remain in the country permanently. People who were still lawfully in Australia, but, who had previously applied for permanent resident status and whose applications had been refused or were still under consideration, could reapply or request that their current applications be considered under ROSP. All applicants and all members of their immediate families, in Australia or overseas, would have to meet health and character requirements for migration. They would have to have been of good character before coming to Australia and while in Australia. In addition, the applicants and all members of their immediate families must have a genuine intention to reside permanently in Australia. ROSP did not apply to overseas students or to foreign diplomats, their employees or members of their families, or to those who had been ordered deported under the Migration Act at the time the program was announced.

In his official announcement, the Minister said that it was the Government's firm intention that the incentive for illegal immigration should be eliminated, and that this would be done by "precluding by law the grant of permanent resident status to persons who had flouted Australian immigration requirements." And he went on to make the important point that this would mean in effect that there could be no future amnesties without a change in the Migration Act, and that this would require the concurrence of both houses of Parliament. It would thus be difficult for future governments to embark on further amnesties.[60]

ROSP was organized in much the same manner as Canada's 1973 Adjustment of Status Program (described in Chapter 2), although there were significant differences between the two programs. The Department of Immigration and Ethnic Affairs described the workings of ROSP:

The Department conducted a large-scale campaign to ensure that those eligible took advantage of ROSP ... The campaign was assisted by publicity in all sections of the media. It included public presentations by the Minister of permanent residence papers to applicants ranging from young, overstayed, working holiday-makers to a 95-year-old ship deserter (who "missed his ship" in 1908), conferences at which the Minister explained the scheme to ethnic community and media representatives, a ROSP radio week in 48 languages on two ethnic and five public broadcasting stations across Australia and news releases, posters and a monthly broadsheet "ROSP News." The campaign was supported by some advertising in metropolitan, provincial and ethnic newspapers. Task Forces of departmental officers made personal contact with ethnic groups and community organizations, and all regional offices of the Department made special arrangements to handle inquiries from individuals assisted, when necessary, by the Telephone Interpreter Service.[61]

Within eight days of its announcement, Department officers received more than 7,000 inquiries about ROSP. In the full six month period, 11,042 applications covering about 14,000 people of nearly 90 nationalities were received at the Department's offices around Australia. Once again only a small number were rejected. Among the applicants, 43 per cent had come from Europe, including Britain and Northern Ireland; 33.7 per cent from Asia; 9.6 per cent from the Americas; 7.5 per cent from Oceania; 5.1 per cent from the Middle East; and 1.1 per cent from Africa.[62]

In a study of ROSP carried out for the International Migration for Employment Branch of the ILO, published in 1982, Desmond Storer concluded that "as far as the general Australian community and the more established ethnic groups were concerned, ROSP was largely successful. These groups supported ROSP and could find little to criticize." However, he had reservations about the more recent minority groups from Asia, the Pacific Islands, and the Middle East who, he felt, were not reached or involved in ROSP effectively. In relation to the media, Storer wrote, "the Australian media gave strong support to the programme"; and to public reaction, "our review of the Australian media response to ROSP indicates widespread support for the aims and conditions of ROSP. The whole program seemed to be remarkably free from wide public controversy ... and it is generally considered to have been a success." On the practical aspects of amnesty management, he felt that the Australian government did very well and developed procedures that were "well worth emulating." If another amnesty were held in Australia, his suggestions for improvement would include the appropriation of more financial resources, greater involvement of "grass-roots ethnic community organizations," a "more open planning period" in which procedures could be tested, and a publicized system of appeal in which judgements on problem cases would be subject to public scrutiny.[63]

Canada Seeks New Solutions

Canada's 1973 Adjustment of Status Program was described in Chapter 2 because it provided such a dramatic beginning to the very creative period of immigration management from 1972 to 1976 under Robert Andras; and because it gave a definite impetus to the major review of immigration policies and programs Andras initiated, which led to the new Immigration Act 1976.[64]

The style of the two amnesty programs was similar. The Australians had, of course, all the information available on Canada's Adjustment of Status Program (and no doubt on other recent amnesties), as well as their own earlier experience to go on. There were minor differences in management. The Canadian program, for example, was run by a small task force and the Australian with a senior immigration official acting as co-ordinator. The major difference, however, was money. The Canadians spent much more on their program,[65] and this was reflected in a much more extensive advertising and publicity campaign. The Canadian program was also much shorter: 60 days compared with six months for ROSP, and this made it easier to sustain the necessary sense of drama and urgency. Both ministers (Bob Andras and Ian Macphee) worked exceptionally hard to make their programs a success and both programs had all-party support. But the political atmosphere in Canada in 1973 was much less contentious than it was in Australia in 1980, and Opposition MPs seemed to fling themselves into the task of helping the Canadian Adjustment of Status Program more enthusiastically.

Amnesties may not produce very large numbers of undocumented migrants, but they undoubtedly serve a very useful political purpose. They demonstrate the government's serious concern as well as firm determination to do something about the problem; and also its ability to make a generous gesture towards the excluded which will please many groups in society. There are, however, more than three ways in which states can try to deal with undocumented migration, in addition to deportation, regularization, and acceptance of those already there. They can, for example, tighten or loosen immigration regulations and controls, making it more difficult to enter or easier, perhaps, for families to reunite. And they can study the problem in a serious and well-publicized way, thereby giving the impression at least that they are gathering valuable evidence on the subject and are seriously attempting to find the best solution. The latter is the route chosen by Canada's Liberal government in the early eighties.

Because of the world recession and high unemployment in the late seventies, when anxieties and resentment about immigration, legal and illegal, always increases, the problem of undocumented migration and the presence of many such migrants in Canada, began to rear its head again towards the end of that decade. In the spring of 1982, the Minister of Employment and Immigration, Lloyd Axworthy, asked his Canada Employment and Immigration Advisory Council "to undertake a study of illegal immigrants in Canada, analyse the origins and extent of the problem, and provide him with suggestions." In November of the same year, the Council produced an alarmist and unhelpful report, based on very inadequate research, reflecting the fact that no single member of the Council at that time had any real knowledge or expertise in the field of immigration.[66]

The Council concluded that illegal immigration was a major problem which, unless addressed by the Government of Canada, would "reach proportions that will be extremely difficult to control." It accepted an estimate of 200,000 illegal immigrants in Canada at that time, suggesting, however, that this number was probably on the low side. (The Council's wholly unqualified Immigration Committee, which was responsible for the report, had paid one visit to the United States where it had automatically accepted a current and inflated estimate of 10 million illegal immigrants in that country.) The report spoke also of "curative and preventive measures" as well as of "solutions." It recommended, among other things, that illegal immigrants then in Canada should be given legal resident status after a phased, six-year probationary program administered by the Government with the help of non-governmental community agencies. It did not say how these illegal immigrants should be identified. It also wished to see tighter control at ports of entry and stiffer enforcement measures within Canada, including "the more active seeking-out of illegal immigrants" by the Canada Employment and Immigration Commission. The report was interesting only because, in all probability, it really reflected the views of the one third of the Council's membership drawn from the trade union movement, where anxieties about high unemployment and the possibility of illegal immigrants flooding the labour market were acute at that time.

The estimate of 200,000, the unrealistic six-year probationary program, and the aggressive approach to enforcement were unacceptable to the Liberal government and a way had to be found to lay the report tactfully aside. Without actually saying that he disapproved of it, although he was known to do so, the Minister, Lloyd Axworthy, called on an old friend and well-known Vancouver lawyer, W.G. Robinson, QC, "to co-ordinate further dialogue and analysis" on this problem, appointing him as his special adviser on December 21, 1982. "The sensitive issues raised by the Council's report," Mr. Axworthy said, "warrant the broadest possible study and public consultation." Mr. Robinson in turn called on Ed Ratushny, Professor of Law at the University of Ottawa and now Director of its Human Rights Research and Education Centre, to help him in this endeavour. (Both had been members of Mr. Axworthy's Task Force on Immigration Practices and Procedures, established in September 1980, with Mr. Robinson as Chairman, which had produced in November 1981 the report on the refugee status determination process discussed in the last chapter.[67])

Mr. Robinson and Professor Ratushny presented the Minister with two reports. The first, largely the work of Professor Ratushny, was described as a discussion paper and entitled *Illegal Immigrants Issues Paper*.[68] Submitted to the Minister on February 15, 1983, its stated purpose was to explore further some of the issues raised in the Advisory Council's report and "to take issue with some of the Council's conclusions." The second report, which appears to have been mainly the work of Mr. Robinson with Professor Ratushny acting as Chief Counsel and Director of Research, was submitted in June 1983 and is entitled *Illegal Migrants in Canada*. In his letter to the Minister which accompanied the report, Mr. Robinson said that it was written "with a view not only to recommending specific courses of action which you might adopt, but also to providing a broad elaboration of the background and issues which might offer a useful starting point for ongoing discussion of the problem.[69]

Both these reports were very useful, and they maintained the discussion of illegal immigration in Canada on an intelligent, rational, and humane level. We will examine each in turn, noting particularly the recommendations made to the Minister in the second report. We will then look at the response of government and at subsequent events.

The *Illegal Immigrants Issues Paper* quietly demolished the assumptions and proposals of the Advisory Council, including the notion that there were more than 200,000 illegal immigrants in Canada at that time (1982). It analysed the difficulties presented by the Council's proposed six-year "conditional settlement program," and suggested that this proposal did not really differ from a general amnesty to which there were many objections. The paper discussed the question of border control, quoting a recent study of deportable aliens in the Toronto area which showed that 77 per cent were single and between the ages of 20 and 25; 5 per cent had children in Canada; 95 per cent had entered the country legally; 83 per cent had arrived by air; 88 per cent were granted stays of three months or less upon arrival; 66 per cent were employed (mostly in maintenance, janitorial, and domestic work in hotels, restaurants, manufacturing, and other industrial employment); and the major countries of origin were the United States, Jamaica, Guyana, and Portugal. According to the author of the study, "these figures are at least consistent with the view that most illegal immigrants in Canada are young, single men and women who enter lawfully as visitors but overstay to take advantage of better economic opportunities than are available in their home countries.[70]

The paper then discussed law enforcement in Canada with respect to illegal immigrants, contrasting the "proactive enforcement" advocated by the Council with the "reactive" enforcement policy then in place. This reactive policy, while not passive, sought to operate at an acceptable level of enforcement activity. (At that time, the Canada Employment and Immigration Commission had more than 100 immigration officers investigating illegal immigration on a full-time basis, with many more working on it part-time.) The paper warned against the dangers involved in a proactive approach, which might well involve the "targetting" of certain groups in Canada, including visible minorities; infiltration and raids on these ethnic communities; and spot checks in hotels and factories where the presence of illegal immigrants was suspected, all of which would have a negative effect on community relations. Finally, the paper deals with the prosecution of employers who knowingly employ illegal aliens, the problem of making the social insurance number (SIN) card system more secure, and the possibility of extending Canada's visitor visa requirements.

The Issues Paper was skilfully written in the form of a discussion – raising issues, suggesting implications and consequences. No firm conclusions were drawn. These were left to the final report, the plan being to distribute this discussion paper widely and elicit public response before conclusive recommendations were made to the Minister.

Mr. Axworthy tabled the final report, *Illegal Migrants in Canada*, before the Standing Committee of the House of Commons on Labour, Manpower and Immigration on June 29, 1983, saying that he thought it was one of the most valuable documents on an immigration problem in recent years.[71] We cannot explore all the findings of this fairly lengthy report, but the following are some of its most important recommendations. They were made after a general discussion in the text intended to show the complexity and universality of the phenomenon of illegal migrants. Mr. Robinson recommended that:

1 The figure of 50,000 should be accepted as a "working figure" for the estimate of the maximum number of illegal migrants in Canada.
2 The Canada Employment and Immigration Commission should make public its current estimate of the number of illegal migrants in Canada at least every three years in the Annual Report to Parliament on Immigration Levels, together with a description of the steps being taken to deal with the problem.
3 The Minister and other representatives of Canada should emphasize that it is not government policy to adopt programs of general amnesty in future and this message should be included in the literature given to immigrants overseas.
4 Discretionary power to land long-term illegal residents had been vastly

under-utilized and a mechanism should now be provided to deal with this problem on a continuing basis. The following criteria should be established for the discretionary landing of illegal migrants: (a) the length of time the candidate has remained illegally in Canada (with a minimum of five years for eligibility); (b) the absence of conviction for serious offences (with immigration-related offences distinguished from criminal offences); (c) the circumstances leading to the decision to become illegal and to continue in that status; (d) present and future capacity for successful establishment and integration into Canadian society; (e) the presence of immediate, extended, and *de facto* family ties in Canada; (f) the presence of children and particularly children born in Canada; and (g) the situation in the applicant's home country.

5 Improvements could be made in border control, including as a long-term goal the establishment of a comprehensive electronic system of entry and exit controls, with linkage to all immigration posts abroad.

6 Under the Immigration Act, a visitor visa is required for entry into Canada from any country unless that country is specifically exempted from the visa requirement. In practice, approximately 80 countries are covered ... The Government should undertake a major review of the list of visa-exempt countries and, in the absence of compelling reasons, should remove all countries except the United States.

7 Canada should continue with an essentially "reactive" enforcement policy, with certain improvements.

8 The area of employment provides one of the most fertile areas for enforcement in relation to illegal immigrants ... Higher priority should be given to the application of the existing employer sanction provisions under the Immigration Act, and greater efforts should be made to increase the security of the SIN card system.

9 The national headquarters of the Canada Employment and Immigration Commission should assume a greater leadership and co-ordinating role in relation to enforcement policy, including preventive measures and the establishment of prosecution priorities.[72]

The Liberal government accepted a number of the recommendations in the Robinson report, but not all of them. The Government invented its own version of Mr. Robinson's interesting mechanism for the discretionary landing of long-term illegal residents, which was to be applied on a one-time basis, rather than as a more permanent feature of Canada's immigration system as it was obviously intended to be. In addition, no significant changes were made in Canada's visa requirements or in the list of visa-exempt countries, although a few countries have been removed from the list. It is interesting that Australia has had no qualms about imposing universal visa requirements, which are evidently a great help in controlling illegal migration. But Canada has been very nervous about this (even with a permanent exemption for the United States), worried, as Mr. Axworthy said to the Standing Committee, about its consequences for her political, trade, international, and bilateral relations.[73]

The Liberal government's official response came in two stages. First, Mr. Axworthy announced to the Standing Committee on June 29 that he accepted the figure of 50,000 as the maximum number of illegal immigrants in Canada, and agreed with the report on the question of amnesties (which, he said, were a "band-aid approach" to the problem of illegal immigration), and on continued use of a reactive enforcement policy. He intended to take a series of measures in response to the Robinson report. They consisted of: (1) a case-by-case review against definitive criteria of the cases of long-term illegal migrants, with all decisions denying landing to be reviewed automatically by a committee of senior officials; (2) more dialogue between immigration officials and the public on illegal immigration – information on this question would be included from then on in the Annual Immigration Levels Report to Parliament; (3) pilot projects to develop more effective border controls; (4) an electronic system of entry and exit controls to be developed as a long-term goal; and (5) stricter enforcement of the employer sanctions in the Immigration Act. On the matter of the expanded use of the visitor visa, Mr. Axworthy said that he would shortly be presenting to Cabinet a proposal to review the present list of visa exemptions, and to recommend that immediate action be taken to withdraw the exemption for certain countries. On August 4, a five-member committee of senior immigration officials was established in Ottawa, under the interim chairmanship of the Deputy Minister, Gaetan Lussier, to review cases of long-term illegal residents in Canada.

On August 12, 1983, John Roberts succeeded Lloyd Axworthy as Minister of Employment and Immigration. In November he announced that his former Parliamentary Secretary and Member of Parliament, Rémi Bujold, would now take over the chairmanship of the Minister's review committee on long-term illegal migrants in Canada. Illegal residents who had been living in Canada undetected for five years or more, and had established themselves successfully, could apply to the committee – either in person or anonymously through a third party – for a review of their status. Cases detected through regular enforcement activities were also eligible to apply. This was a one-time program, the new Minister said, and the cut-off date for applications was March 30, 1984. The criteria in case-by-case evaluations would be the same as those recommended by Mr. Robinson, with the addition of "assets and liabilities, employment history and work skills."

The cut-off date for this program was extended three times: to August 31, 1984 and then to January 3 and July 3, 1985. The program itself has since been terminated. While it did not attract a large number of applicants, it probably attracted enough to make the effort worthwhile. As of August 17, 1984, there were 2,259 cases before the committee, of which 976 had been approved, 114 refused and 169 referred for further investigation. In another initiative, John Roberts announced on March 12, 1984 that as of March 14, 1984, nationals of Guyana, Jamaica, Peru, and Guatemala would require visas to visit Canada. At the same time, he announced that citizens of Israel would no longer require visas. "About 40,000 Israelis visit Canada annually," he said, "and since we are experiencing virtually no control problems, we have included Israel on our visa-exempt list." This list was reviewed regularly and amended as necessary.[74] Other recent changes have involved the removal of Sri Lanka and Bangladesh from the visa-exempt list in September 1981 and the removal of India a month later, mainly because of the large number of Sikhs then seeking refugee status in Canada on what were felt to be very inadequate grounds. Canada's visa-exempt list has thus become a system of rewards and punishments. Would it not be better to require visas for visitors from all countries, with the exception of the United States, as the Robinson report recommended?

Canada's most recent effort to control or reduce the flow of undocumented migrants consists of a Deterrents and Detention Bill designed "to stop abuse of the refugee determination system through firm deterrent measures." It is intended to work together with the new refugee status determination system discussed earlier in this chapter. The bill was tabled in the House of Commons on August 11, 1987 was approved and received Royal Assent on July 23, 1988. It came into effect in stages, on August 12 and October 3, 1988, and January 1, 1989. It gives the government power to:

- substantially increase penalties for smugglers and their accomplices, including the imposition of 10-year jail sentences and fines of $500,000;
- impose heavier fines and penalties on transportation companies that bring undocumented people to Canada, with fines of $5,000 for each undocumented passenger;
- detain people who arrive without proper documentation until their identities can be established;
- remove people who pose a criminal or security threat. They will be detained until they can be removed from Canada.

Australia after ROSP

After the ROSP amnesty, in 1981 the Fraser government made a deliberate effort to strengthen immigration controls and to take firmer measures against illegal migrants and overstayers. No further changes were to be made in these procedures until the introduction of new Immigration Regulations by the Hawke government in December 1989. (See Preface.) During the last year of Liberal-National Party government, as we have seen, John Hodges was Minister for Immigration and Ethnic Affairs, replacing Ian Macphee who became Minister for Employment and Industrial Relations in a major Cabinet reshuffle in May 1982 – a promotion which put him into the Inner Cabinet. Shortly thereafter, on September 5, Mr. Hodges announced a "crackdown on working visitors." Entry conditions were to be tightened for certain temporary residents admitted to Australia with permission to work, and the numbers of working holiday-makers would be reduced. Australian labor market trends, the Minister said, aggravated by worldwide recession, "leave no room for looseness in applying controls intended to protect the Australian community". About 100,000 visitors now went to Australia each year for three months or more, and recent official estimates suggested that as many as one third breached entry conditions by taking jobs.[75] During 1982–1983, 2,640 illegal immigrants left Australia as a result of these measures. Of this number, 939 left voluntarily, 960 left under supervision (an increase of 116 per cent over the figures for 1981–1982) and 741 were deported – a 39 per cent increase over the previous year.[76]

We have seen that in Canada the Robinson report on illegal migrants recommended more dialogue between immigration officials and the public on illegal immigration; and that the Minister responded by saying that information on this subject would now be included in the Annual Report to Parliament on Immigration Levels. It should be noted that Australia's Department of Immigration and Ethnic Affairs has for some time done an excellent job of providing information to the public on illegal migration, and on the whole area of enforcement. This information has been available in the Department's annual review which first appeared in 1976 – information denied to the Canadian public in an accessible form for many years. Since that date, each annual review has contained a section on the "Control of Entry to Australia" (called "The Immigration Screen" in the 1983 Review), where detailed information is provided on international passenger movement to Australia, legislative changes, control procedures, deportation statistics, immigration detention centres (with photographs), and what is called "immigration malpractice." The latter describes the investigation of immigration rackets, use of false identities and passports, sale of fraudulent documents, simulation of refugee status, and the like. The many merits of this annual review will be discussed further in the final chapter.

During the past few years, Canada and Australia have gained valuable experience in the control of undocumented migration, and more understanding of the phenomenon itself. They have discovered at first hand the limitations of amnesties (which both have announced will no longer be used), and both are moving towards more sophisticated electronic control systems at ports of entry, linked to their overseas immigration offices. Nevertheless, it seems evident that, although not of crisis proportions now, the problem of undocumented migration will continue, particularly for stable, affluent countries like Canada and Australia and for those with very long land or sea borders which are difficult and expensive to police. More serious difficulties with undocumented migration may lie ahead, however, if the striking disparities between an affluent developed world with minimum population growth and a seriously overcrowded, undernourished developing world are allowed to continue. For the undocumented migrant, of deliberate or less deliberate intent, things are getting tougher. In the future, it will require greater ingenuity and greater determination to enter a foreign country without official status or documents and stay there. The most hopeful prospect for all those involved in this field lies in forms of international monitoring, regulation, and collaboration. But these are very slow in coming.

CHAPTER FIVE

Multiculturalism

Multiculturalism as an area of public policy can be defined as the official recognition by governments, expressed in legislation and/or in speeches and programs, of the many different ethnic origins of their present populations, combined with the stated intention to protect and assist those who are not members of the founding majority or charter groups. It emphasizes cultural freedom, social justice, and equality of opportunity for all within the existing political system. This policy was adopted by both Canada and Australia in the early seventies for the same reasons and with the same objectives, but with rather different means of implementation developed over the subsequent years.[1]

These moves reflected a growing political awareness of the increasing ethnic diversity of the Canadian and Australian peoples, due mainly to the immigration and refugee policies and programs of the post-war period; and to the need, of the political parties in power, to control and benefit from the changing and expanding nature of their domestic political environment. They were also a direct response to the present liberal climate of opinion within the democratic international community with respect to human rights, and particularly the rights of minorities, which has emerged out of the ending of empires, the proliferation of newly independent countries, the rise of small nationalisms, and the pre-occupation with ethnicity of the post-war period thus far. Multiculturalism as a national policy is also an inevitable outcome of the broadening base of immigrant recruitment by Canada and Australia during this period, as well as of the adoption of universal, non-discriminatory immigration policies by Canada in 1962 and by Australia in 1973. Canada's 1981 census showed that 43.5 per cent of her population was of British origin, 28.9 per cent of French origin, and 27.6 per cent of all other origins combined. In Australia, of course, the percentage of the population which is of British origin is far higher – about 77 per cent.

A great deal has been written about multiculturalism in recent years as if it were entirely divorced from politics. Nothing could be further from the truth. As the Canadian and Australian experience of the last few years clearly shows, multiculturalism is a highly political phenomenon, involving the development of a special relationship between government and ethnic communities. At the same time, it is difficult to handle politically because there is no very clear place for it in a liberal democratic society, which already has established values and traditions over exactly the same territory, that is, values relating to citizenship, justice, equality, political participation, and human rights generally, and which embraces, above all, the principle of universality and not the principle of particularism. It is also difficult to implement in constructive and practical ways, since the potential field for action is so extensive, and the rhetoric often implies far larger projects than are financially or administratively feasible. Political parties too feel a strong need to put their own impress on it and multicultural policies and programs (particularly the latter) are likely to change to some extent with each change of government.

While multiculturalism in Canada and Australia represents a genuine effort on the part of the majority to achieve a greater degree of equality and social justice for all citizens, it is nevertheless an artificial creation taking the form of a broad government-supported and financed interest group or coalition of ethnic communities, the financing making it much easier to control. Thus far at least, it has not been a movement which is, to any substantial extent, self-generated and spontaneous, or which has strong roots in the community in a collective sense. Multicultural policies and programs are therefore inevitably seen as an element of political strategy on the part of the party in power, and questions can be raised about the degree of freedom possible for the leaderships of these communities within such a dependent relationship. The relationship itself and the environment which it creates, while providing a much improved degree of access to the senior levels of government for ethnic communities, may also prove to be a political cul-de-sac, isolating their active members from mainstream politics.

As well as suspicion about its uses as a political tactic, multiculturalism also arouses a more fundamental opposition or anxiety particularly in high places, and it is interesting to see how similar this opposition is in both Canada and Australia. It exists not among the general public which, at least so far, probably has very little knowledge of or concern about multiculturalism, but among some senior politicians, public servants, and members of influential interest groups in both countries. It does not take the form of outright hostility to multiculturalism, but of serious reservations on the subject and a firmly-held belief that this area of public policy should be kept well under control.[2] It is not difficult to see why this is so.

Since multiculturalism has no well-defined limits and involves a new relationship between government and ethnic communities whose dimensions are not yet very clear, it appears to some of those involved in government to pose a vague threat to the democratic system. It is seen as leading away from the open, individualistic systems to which Canadians and Australians are accustomed, and towards the kind of political system in which the cake has to be sliced very carefully among powerful and competing groups. There is a perceived threat also that society is being reshaped in a minorities image and that resources are being spent in areas of only marginal need.

Within this sector of public opinion the question is also asked whether multicultural programs in effect strengthen separateness among ethnic communities? Is cultural heritage being emphasized now at the expense of Canadian and Australian identity and of commitment to these societies as a whole, and is that in the interest of ethnic communities in the long run? Is there in all this multicultural effort an undue emphasis on rights and benefits with inadequate attention to contribution? Do multicultural programs really reach or benefit the mass of immigrants of many different national origins whose primary concern, as always, is with a better life and new opportunities for themselves and their children?

Ethnic communities and the organizations that speak for them are essentially interest groups which perform an important role in modern democratic societies. They are neither more nor less noble or effective than other interest groups are, and they vary widely in their effectiveness and desire to serve their own communities. They have not, in the past, shown great capacity in Canada or Australia for effective inter-group collaboration, nor very much interest in migrants or refugees from communities other than their own, except when provided with the facilities and means to do so by governments (as in the case of large refugee movements). They suffer from all the problems faced by other interest groups which do not have particularly large, well-to-do, and politically influential memberships, namely leadership, fund raising, attracting and holding a reasonably-sized membership including the young, and working out strategies and programs which best serve their interests. They also suffer from a natural and inevitable brain drain out into the main community. Much of their younger talent does not wish to be permanently identified with or confined within an ethnic community, although some are willing to be active on a part-time or intermittent basis. Others wish to be completely free to pursue the rewards and opportunities offered by mainstream society.

Mainly because of these problems, ethnic communities and organizations have tended to have conservative management. Only a very few achieve large, active memberships and some sociologists have questioned whether they can be regarded as "communities" in any real sense.[3] Many multicultural programs involve the leadership and activists of these groups rather than the uninvolved proletariat. Politicians have always exaggerated the possibility of buying or winning the so-called "ethnic vote." While some goodwill may be gained, it seems clear that ethnic communities today do not respond to such persuasion by delivering a sizeable number of votes. They are far more likely to respond favourably to what they feel is good, stable, and positive government for society as a whole.

The most important fact about immigrants in this context, and one which is frequently overlooked in the literature of multiculturalism and ethnic affairs, is their primary motive for migrating. It is fair to say that the majority of immigrants, including a great many of those who are sponsored by their families, do not uproot themselves and leave their native land in order to lead the same kind of life in a foreign country. They go primarily, as millions have gone in past migrations, to better their condition and to take advantage of the opportunities, hoped-for rewards, and future promise of their new country for themselves and their children. In our concern for the status of minorities and anxiety to encourage respect for many different ethnic origins, it is easy to forget this important fact. In other words, a great many immigrants look forward to becoming Canadians or Australians. The preservation of cultural heritage is a lesser concern and for them the whole concept of multiculturalism can be confusing.

As we know, some ethnic communities provide a form of shelter and temporary safe haven for newcomers. Some immigrants stay within the shelter of their own communities throughout their lives. Many behave quite differently. Similarly, some immigrants feel more at ease if advised and helped by people of their own ethnic origin. Others, particularly those from totalitarian countries or countries with deep political divisions, are suspicious of their own compatriots and prefer to use community services. Some immigrants take great pleasure in becoming Canadian or Australian as soon as possible, however superficial an adjustment that may be. Others take much longer to make adjustments of any kind. For this reason, a variety of helping agencies and services are needed in the field of settlement. Their main purpose should be to help immigrants to live and work comfortably in their new environment, to become familiar with the services and benefits it provides, and gradually to feel part of the community itself.

MULTICULTURALISM IN CANADA

Canada invented multiculturalism as a national policy in 1971, and Australia borrowed the idea soon afterwards. In many ways, multiculturalism in Canada is a new name for an old activity, namely the long-standing efforts of the federal Citizenship Branch to encourage harmonious community relations in Canadian cities, and to protect and assist ethnic groups. This small branch of government was created within the Department of the Secretary of State during World War II. It became part of Canada's new Department of Citizenship and Immigration in 1950, and in 1966 was moved back to the Department of the Secretary of State when Citizenship and Immigration was dismantled to make way for a new Department of Manpower and Immigration. In addition, the Province of Ontario, in which at least half of Canada's post-war intake of immigrants has settled, had its own Citizenship Branch since 1959 (now part of Ontario's Ministry of Citizenship) which has pursued similar objectives.[4] The major differences between these activities and the policies and programs now associated with Canada's official policy of multiculturalism within a bilingual framework, announced by Prime Minister Pierre Trudeau in October 1971, lie in the much higher priority accorded to this area of public policy; in the increased though still not very substantial funding provided for it; and in the creation of a cabinet post for a Minister of State responsible for Multiculturalism, as well as a national consultative council to advise him.

The Liberal government probably had two major reasons for its 1971 decision to give much higher priority to this area of public policy. The first related to the deliberations and reports of the Royal Commission on Bilingualism and Biculturalism, 1963–1969, which was created by the Pearson government to recommend "what steps should be taken to develop the Canadian Confederation on the basis of equal partnership between the two founding races, taking into account the contribution made by other ethnic groups." During the course of its deliberations, the Commission received representations from several of the major ethnic groups who were fearful that the latter part of the Commission's mandate and their own contribution to Confederation might be ignored. The Commission did address this question, however, and their fourth and final report was entitled *The Cultural Contribution of the Other Ethnic Groups*. It recommended that much higher priority, attention, and support be given to these groups, provided this was done in the context of Canada's two charter groups and two official languages.[5]

The second reason relates to the Liberal government's awareness of the increasing numerical strength within Canada's population of groups of non-British and non-French origin, and their undoubted electoral importance at a time of possible long-term changes in the Liberal Party's sources of electoral support. The party's traditionally strong support in Quebec (which would, in fact, never be challenged while Pierre Trudeau was Prime Minister) could be threatened, as some saw it, by the newly modernized, development-conscious, independent-minded Quebec then emerging. It was essential, therefore, to confirm the party's hold on another important element in its traditional coalition of supporters – Canada's major ethnic communities and the vote they were believed to deliver. Any major over-dramatic move in this direction might offend their Quebec supporters, however, so new policies and programs in this field had to be developed with caution. Some authorities on federalism in Canada have wondered why any government would introduce these policies at such a precarious stage in federal-provincial relations, and at the very difficult period in relations with Quebec following the October crisis of 1970.[6]

In any event, the Trudeau government took the decision to establish multiculturalism as a national policy, to appoint a minister to look after it – as much to control and manage this area of public policy in the interest of the Liberal Party as to develop it in a Canadian sense – and to provide him with a limited, innocuous set of programs and a small budget with which to implement them. The initial budget in 1972–1973 was $5,154,000, which was increased to $10,132,600 in 1973–1974. It was not considered necessary to create a new ministry for multiculturalism; a small Multiculturalism Directorate within the Department of the Secretary of State was felt to be adequate. The initial phase of implementation was entrusted to the now large and active Citizenship Branch. It was thought that a sufficient show of support had been made for the non-English and non-French-speaking groups in Canada, while the limited nature of the policies and programs in multiculturalism would ensure that they would not be seen as a threat in Quebec. This analysis proved to be wrong on both counts.

To emphasize these political considerations is not to deny the presence of a more idealistic approach to multiculturalism on the part of some of the politicians and bureaucrats who introduced it. It was there, but only to a limited degree, and certainly no significant changes in the political system were ever contemplated as an outcome of these new policies and programs. One change, however, did take place. From this point on, the political rhetoric relating to ethnicity in Canada changed significantly. The old political speech about the rich and variegated fabric of Canadian society, used frequently by politicians of all parties before this time, became an idealistic statement about multicultural Canada, a society to which all had contributed and from which all would receive due recognition and reward.

As we have seen, the Prime Minister announced the government's policy of multiculturalism within a bilingual framework in October 1971. In his statement to the House – his only major speech on this subject during his entire period in office (1968–1984) – Mr. Trudeau said: "We believe that cultural pluralism is the very essence of Canadian identity. Every ethnic group has the right to preserve and develop its own culture and values within the Canadian context. To say we have two official languages is not to say we have two official cultures, and no particular culture is more 'official' than another. A policy of multiculturalism must be a policy for all Canadians." The government, he said, had accepted and endorsed the recommendations and spirit of Book IV of the Report of the Royal Commission on Bilingualism and Biculturalism. It believed that the time was overdue for the people of Canada to become more aware of the rich tradition of Canada's many cultures, and wished to ensure that this cultural diversity would continue. The policy of multiculturalism within a bilingual framework would have four major objectives which he described as "preserving human rights, developing Canadian identity, strengthening citizen participation, reinforcing Canadian unity and encouraging cultural diversification within a bilingual framework."

The policy itself was to be based on four principles, defined in the following way:

1 The Government of Canada will support all of Canada's cultures and will seek to assist, resources permitting, the development of those cultural groups which have demonstrated a desire and effort to continue to develop, a capacity to grow and contribute to Canada, as well as a clear need for assistance.
2 The government will assist members of all cultural groups to overcome cultural barriers to full participation in Canadian society.
3 The government will promote creative encounters and interchange among all Canadian cultural groups in the interest of national unity.
4 The government will continue to assist immigrants to acquire at least one of Canada's official languages in order to become full participants in Canadian society.

Six programs were planned to implement the policy: (1) multicultural grants; (2) a cultural development program; (3) funds for the writing of ethnic histories if requested by ethnic groups; (4) funds to support Canadian ethnic studies; (5) additional funds for the teaching of Canada's official languages; and (6) programs by the federal cultural agencies – the National Museum of Man, the National Film Board, National Library, and Public Archives – to set the record straight, so to speak, by reflecting more effectively Canada's many cultural traditions and the contribution of Canadians of non-British and non-French origin to Canadian development.[7]

Further, in May 1972, in a speech in Winnipeg, the Prime Minister announced the decision to create a national advisory council on multiculturalism. In November 1972, Dr. Stanley Haidasz, MP, of Toronto, a well-known Liberal and active member of the Polish community in Canada, was appointed Minister of State responsible for Multiculturalism. In May 1973, the Canadian Consultative Council on Multiculturalism was created with 101 members representing 47 ethno-cultural backgrounds. The council held its first meeting in October of that year.

Most of these policies and programs were very inadequately thought out by those who were responsible for them, and barely explained at all to the Canadian public. Prime Minister Trudeau assumed no responsibility for this, as if the gesture itself had been enough, and no serious effort was made by any senior politician to define multiculturalism in a Canadian context. As a result, major expectations were aroused, particularly among Canada's older ethnic groups, which were never fulfilled. At the same time, no special effort was made to explain to the politicians and people of Quebec how multiculturalism and Canada's official policy of bilingualism were supposed to fit together, or how these new policies related to her two founding peoples. Inevitably, despite their limited nature, they aroused deep and immediate hostility in Quebec. The root of this hostility lay in the concept of multiculturalism itself in which all ethnic groups are seen as equal, thus de-emphasizing if not contradicting the central historical and political fact of the two founding peoples of Canadian Confederation.

The first sign of this hostility, which soon developed into firm opposition to multiculturalism in any but a very restricted sense, came quickly. In reply to the Prime Minister's October 7, 1971 letter informing him of the federal government's intentions in this field, Premier Robert Bourassa of Quebec said that he had "serious misgivings about the principle of the multicultural policy" which, he said, clearly contradicted the mandate of the Royal Commission on Bilingualism and Biculturalism as defined by the Government of Canada. The basic premise of the commission had been the equality of the two founding peoples of Canadian Confederation, with Confederation taking the form of a bilingual and bicultural society, with due regard for the contribution of the other ethnic groups and for the steps to be taken to safeguard this contribution. To dissociate culture from language, as the Government had done in its statement to the House on multiculturalism, seemed to him a questionable basis on which to found a policy.

Premier Bourassa also pointed out that, for some years, the Government of Quebec, through its Department of Immigration, had been providing similar programs, such as subsidies to ethnic groups and language courses. It was imperative, therefore, to reach some understanding in order to avoid duplication and to safeguard Quebec's jurisdictional rights which were involved in most of the projects the Prime Minister was putting forward. "You will have gathered," the Premier said, summing up, "that Quebec does not accept your government's approach to the principle of multiculturalism."[8]

One of the best statements on Quebec's view of multiculturalism is still to be found in a paper presented at the Second Canadian Conference on Multiculturalism in 1976 by a well-known sociologist, Professor Guy Rocher of the University of Montreal. Following are two short extracts from the paper:

It is of course true that the number of ethnic groups making up the population of Canada has increased markedly in recent decades, and that ethnic groups in Canada have demonstrated a welcome cultural vitality. It is accordingly perfectly conceivable that this sociological multiculturalism in Canada should be recognized, and a policy formulated to help ethnic groups give this country the benefit of their cultural resources.

However ... while multiculturalism is a sociologically valid concept in Canada, it has no meaning politically. In my view it is clear that, from a political standpoint, Canada is a country defined by a twofold culture, anglophone and francophone, and it is the interplay of political forces between these two great "societies," to use the expression in the preliminary report of the Royal Commission on Bilingualism and Biculturalism, that will determine the future of this country.[9]

Other critical voices at this conference, which the author attended, warned of the danger of cynical manipulation of multiculturalism by political parties; pointed out that such a small budget could only mean tokenism; and suggested that French-English duality was enough for any nation to cope with "without enshrining the whole world's diversity within our history and our borders."[10] Apart from these comments and a few warning voices from Quebec and Manitoba, however, comment on the whole was very favourable, as it had been when the Prime Minister made his announcement. At that time, the leaders of the opposition parties, the Progressive Conservatives and the New Democratic Party, firmly supported the new policies and programs in the House. Outside Quebec, the press was cordial, with one major exception – Toronto's *Globe and Mail*, hardly a friend of the Liberal Party. After observing multiculturalism for a year or two, the *Globe* described it as "a leap into emptiness" and as a move "intended solely to persuade those Canadians of other than French and English mother tongues that they would not be neglected while Ottawa pushed ahead with official biculturalism and bilingualism. In short, a bribe – to buy off opponents of bi-and-bi – and a bribe of rather cynical dimensions."[11]

It is clear from their subsequent management of this area of public policy, and the limited funds which they devoted to it, that the Trudeau government never intended multiculturalism to be a policy departure of great significance. It was seen simply as a public gesture of goodwill, as well as a proper recognition of the continuing contribution of many cultures to Canadian society. At the same time, it was also seen from the beginning as a set of policies and programs which would serve a useful political purpose in helping to ensure the continued support of ethnic groups for the Liberal party. At the back of it, however, as Premier Bourassa and others rightly sensed, lay the Trudeau concept of one Canada in which there was no special place for Quebec as a province unlike the others, a bilingual Canada but one in which the best opportunities for the people of Quebec lay within the nation as a whole. The strength of Quebec's opposition to multiculturalism was under-estimated by the Trudeau government, which also failed to consider the possibility that ethnic groups might expect more from multiculturalism than the government intended – more than updated rhetoric and the promise of respect for cultural heritage – that they might, in fact, expect significant political change to emerge from it. It was a failure of political sensitivity on both counts which had serious consequences.

Following the Prime Minister's announcement of October 1971, the senior officers of the Department of the Secretary of State's Citizenship Branch were actively engaged in putting the six planned multicultural programs to work. They were also grappling with the problem of public participation in the multicultural field – public participation then being a favoured approach of the still young Trudeau administration. It was obvious that there had to be some; and so they conceived a strange brainchild, the idea of a consultative council of 100 members (a parliament without power), large enough to include representatives from all the active ethnic groups and from all the major and minor regions of Canada. When the author, who was there at the time, protested that a much smaller council – say of 30 to 40 or less – would be a far more effective consultative body, and would have some chance of developing a sense of common purpose and providing the Minister with good advice, she was told by the Assistant Deputy Minister in charge of these activities that consultation was not really the prime objective of the exercise. What a 100-man council would do, he said, would be to provide the government with 100 channels of communication out to the ethnic communities on government policies and programs, as well as 100 ways of getting feedback. With these objectives, it is not surprising that more than a few dedicated Liberal Party workers – of diverse ethnic origins of course – found themselves members of the new Consultative Council appointed in May 1973.

We can look back now on some 15 years of multiculturalism under Liberal management, allowing for the nine-month Tory interregnum of 1979,[12] and attempt to assess its successes and failures.

Nine Ministers (including three Tories) have held this portfolio since Dr. Haidasz' appointment in November 1972. Only one of these ministers, Jim Fleming (March 3, 1980 to August 12, 1983), tried to give the whole multiculturalism program some shape and focus, not necessarily pleasing several of the largest ethnic groups in the process. (Mr. Fleming was rather unceremoniously removed from this office in Prime Minister Trudeau's last major Cabinet reshuffle in order, it is said, that a promising Liberal backbencher might get some Cabinet experience.) The 1973–1974 budget of $10 million was cut in half in the mid-seventies, due to hard economic times, it was explained. As a result mainly of Mr. Fleming's efforts, the budget was restored to its former level, and increased slightly to $13.6 million in 1983. Today, the budget has been increased by approximately one third.

There were four chairmen of the Canadian Consultative Council on Multiculturalism which can without more ado be written off as a failure. It has at last been replaced by a much smaller body, partly at the urging of the council itself. This was first announced by Jim Fleming on July 25, 1983. Appointments to the new council, now called the Canadian Multiculturalism Council (CMC), were announced by his successor, David Collenette, on November 14, 1983. The council now has 60 members.[13]

The CCCM was defeated from the beginning by several factors. First it was crippled by its impossible size and unwieldy character; and secondly by the very mixed motives of the Trudeau government in relation to it, among which a serious intention to consult the council and to take its advice on important questions was conspicuously absent. Thirdly, the CCCM suffered, as did most advisory councils under the Trudeau administration, from the heavy burden of the Liberal Party's patronage arrangements, under which talent and experience counted for much less than Liberal Party affiliation. Fourthly, in common with other advisory councils, the CCCM suffered from another striking failure of this government, namely the failure to make proper use of Canada's academic talent on these advisory bodies, positively ignoring in this case some of her eminent academic specialists on multiculturalism. Most of all, perhaps, the CCCM suffered from the general confusion about the status and uses of multiculturalism in Canadian politics – what was it meant to achieve and which constituency was it primarily intended to serve?

The CCCM and CMC, together with the small Multiculturalism Directorate of the Department of the Secretary of State (now upgraded to department status) have been the principal institutions created at the federal level in the field of multiculturalism so far, although a parliamentary Standing Committee on Multiculturalism was established in 1985. At one point, the federal government did consider the possibility of establishing a national institute on multiculturalism or on Canadian ethnic studies, but this idea was rejected. As we shall see, the creation of this kind of institution as a source of well-informed, independent advice to the government, as well as to promote research and writing in this field, is the route which Australia followed at the outset in her effort to manage this area of public policy in a reasonable and productive way. This policy was changed by the Hawke government, however, which has brought multiculturalism under the direct supervision of the Prime Minister.

The initial Liberal design for multiculturalism was defective in another way which should be mentioned. Because of the fragmentation of immigration management in Canada after 1966, discussed in Chapter 2, and the division of responsibilities for the short- and longer-term settlement of immigrants between the departments of Manpower and Immigration and Secretary of State, multiculturalism was completely divorced at the outset from the field of immigration policy and management and it remains so to this day. It was thus deprived of a unique source of strength and vitality, as well as the opportunity to contribute to and to be involved in a very important and related area of public policy.

Early in 1983, Jim Fleming, still Minister of State responsible for Multiculturalism, issued a statement in the form of a letter which was widely circulated, reviewing what he felt were the achievements and recent developments in this area. He mentioned that the budget had been increased to $13.6 million and that he would continue to press for more adequate funding. Substantial funds had been provided for ethnocultural organizations over the past decade, he said, in what were now called the Group Development and Cultural Integration programs, for development purposes and for "the integration of Canadians of all cultural origins into the mainstream of society." The Heritage Languages program was currently providing the funds for heritage language classes, run by ethnocultural groups in after-school hours, for some 90,000 children across Canada; and a first national Conference on Heritage Languages had been hosted by Multiculturalism Canada in Saskatoon in July 1981 with some encouraging subsequent developments. In addition, funding was being provided for 48 multicultural centres across the country designed to bring people of all ethnocultural backgrounds together.

The Minister then spoke of achievements in the arts and in ethnic studies and research. He felt that a solid base for the ethnocultural folk arts had been established over the last decade. In many major centres, the folk arts had become self-sustaining and even profit-making and much greater use was being made now of film, theatre, and television. In the field of ethnic studies and research, a great many projects had been funded by Multiculturalism Canada. One of the most successful programs had been the Generations Series, books on individual ethnocultural groups. Histories had been published of the Scots, the Portuguese, the Arabs, the

Greeks, the Japanese, the Norwegians, the Poles, and the Hungarians. Three others – on the Croatians, the Chinese, and the Ukrainians – would appear within the next few months. In addition, under the University Endowment Assistance Program, chairs had been established in Hungarian, Ukrainian, Mennonite, and Acadian studies and several others were now under consideration.

Attention must also be given, Mr. Fleming said, particularly in harder economic times, to initiatives which reduce cultural tension and barriers, and to efforts to increase the sensitivity of mainstream institutions to cultural diversity. "I believe that for the principles of multiculturalism to be fully realized," he said, "it is essential that we take our message beyond the minority ethnocultural communities, and that we sensitize all Canadians." He also described a relatively new and important departure for Multiculturalism Canada, a program to combat racism. One of the first moves in this program was the convening of a National Symposium on Race Relations and the Law, held in Vancouver in April 1982. A special Race Relations Unit had also been established within the Multiculturalism Directorate. Later that year, Mr. Fleming was instrumental in establishing a Special Committee of the House of Commons on Participation of Visible Minorities in Canadian Society, which reported in March 1984.[14] The Minister's final point in this public statement was to emphasize that, as of April 1982, the multicultural nature of Canada had been entrenched in her Charter of Rights and Freedoms. The pertinent sections were: "*Section 15(1)* Every individual is equal before and under the law and has the right to the equal protection and equal benefit of the law without discrimination and, in particular, without discrimination based on race, national or ethnic origin, colour, religion ... *Section 27* This Charter shall be interpreted in a manner consistent with the preservation and enhancement of the multicultural heritage of Canadians.[15] To some commentators, Section 27 seemed a rather minimal achievement; others felt relieved that at least the expression "the multicultural heritage of Canadians" was now in the constitution.

Interviewed in Toronto in December 1983, Mr. Fleming said he felt a good deal had been achieved during his three and a half years with this portfolio, chiefly in changing the government's approach from the "ethnic hand-out and food fair policy" of earlier years to one which emphasized multiculturalism for the whole society, not just as a way of placating ethnic groups and getting their votes. Money had been spent on good programs rather than on simply keeping ethnic organizations alive, and there had been much more emphasis on inter-group relations of which the multicultural centres, which were mainly small and outside the big cities, were a good example. For the future, he thought multiculturalism would remain a concern and activity of the federal government because there was a need for it, but not as a major factor or influence in politics. It would be "generalized" and, having got it into the Charter of Rights, which had not been easy to get through Cabinet he said, it would be institutionalized further and would become an established part of society's thinking and approach to community relations.[16]

It might be mentioned here that, as indicated in the Minister's statement, one of the principal beneficiaries of the Trudeau government's multicultural policies and programs has been Canada's academic discipline of sociology, for which they have created a bonanza of remarkable proportions. Since grants became freely available for ethnic research after October 1971, there has been what one commentator described as an "explosion of academic research into ethnicity." Between 1971 and 1982, 88 scholarly works on cultural minorities were published in Canada, plus at least 10 collections of papers on Canadian ethnic groups and ethnic relations. In 1973, the Canadian Ethnic Studies Association was founded with the aid of funding from the Multiculturalism Directorate. The Association has gone on to develop, in collaboration with the Research Centre for Canadian Ethnic Studies at the University of Calgary, a new scholarly journal, *Canadian Ethnic Studies*, which is published three times a year, and has also organized some biennial conferences in different cities and provinces, all with the aid of multicultural grants. A number of other academic associations and research centres in ethnic studies, too numerous to mention here, have also been founded, and many academic conferences and seminars have been held. Only a very few academics from disciplines other than sociology have taken part in this remarkable academic exercise.[17]

Most of the scholarly work in this area has involved studies of individual ethnic communities and ethnic relations, in addition to some useful survey research which is always acceptable to governments. Immigration, which despite the objections of several of Canada's older ethnic groups, is critically related to multiculturalism, has been all but ignored. A civilized, sometimes keenly felt, internal, debate about the nature of multiculturalism – the only one in Canada – expressed mainly in journal articles and conference papers, has taken place among Canadian sociologists and several other academic specialists in recent years. With only a few notable exceptions, however, this debate reveals a considerable ignorance of or disinterest in its political dimensions; and among this academic fraternity, hardly anyone has taken to the hustings, so to speak, to proclaim the virtues of multiculturalism to a wider audience.

Further developments in the institutionalization of multiculturalism in Canada took place in the late eighties. On December 1, 1987, a bill "for the preservation and enhancement of multiculturalism in Canada" received its first reading. This bill, which is now law, provides a firm legislative base for Canada's multicultural policies and programs. In 1988, The Prime Minister announced that a new full Department of Multiculturalism and Citizenship would be created, and a year later enabling legislation (Bill C-18) was introduced.

MULTICULTURALISM IN AUSTRALIA

Some form of multiculturalism as a national policy probably became inevitable in Australia when the Whitlam government deliberately brought the White Australia policy to an end in November 1973. As we have seen in Chapter 3, however, opinion was by no means unanimous in Australia on the wisdom of that move, although it was accepted afterwards by many with evident relief. Nevertheless, some Australian politicians, like their Canadian counterparts, were becoming aware at that time of a new factor in the political equation – not of overwhelming importance perhaps but enough to merit attention – namely the increasing number and potential political influence of the Australians of non-British and non-Irish origin. Inevitably, the major ethnic groups in Australia were becoming larger and their leaderships more politicized, articulate, and difficult to ignore. The ethnic vote, if such there was, could be an important electoral factor in areas with high concentrations of immigrants like Sydney and Melbourne. The post-war or late post-war international climate, referred to earlier, of small nationalisms, strong ethnic and community attachments within larger societies, and emphasis, at least theoretically, on human rights was having its effect on Australia also.

The Whitlam government did not explicitly espouse a policy of multiculturalism, but it paved the way for it. As we have seen, it was the first Australian government to respond to these international trends in a significant way, and the first to show a real concern for Australia's image among Third World countries, particularly in the Pacific region. Mr. Whitlam himself spoke of Australia as "a multicultural nation" and his first Minister for Immigration, Al Grassby, both as Minister and later as Commissioner for Community Relations, espoused the cause of multiculturalism with characteristic enthusiasm. It fell in perfectly with his natural inclinations towards equality and with his natural hostility towards the concepts of a superior British charter group, or of a majority and minorities, or of a mainstream society into which other smaller tributaries would flow. From this point on, as a colourful, able, and humorous speaker much in demand, he preached the cause of a new multicultural Australian nation with equal rights and opportunities for all citizens, whatever their ethnic origin.

During what proved to be its final year of office, the Whitlam government, as we have seen, had made the first tentative moves towards the creation of an ethnic broadcasting service in Australia. A committee was established to run two experimental ethnic radio stations in Sydney and Melbourne, initially for a trial period of 13 weeks, and eventually on a permanent basis. The Sydney station began broadcasting in seven languages on June 9, 1975; its counterpart in Melbourne opened on June 23 with programs in eight languages.

It was the Fraser government, however, coming to power in December 1975 after Labor's overwhelming defeat, which gave shape and structure to multiculturalism in Australia. A few months earlier, as discussed in Chapter 3, the Liberal–Country Party Coalition, led by Malcolm Fraser, had made a major statement on immigration and ethnic affairs which included the following cautious commitment to multiculturalism: "The Liberal and National Country Parties recognize the special needs of migrant peoples in this country ... They are committed to the preservation and development of a culturally diversified but socially cohesive Australian society, free of racial tensions and offering security, well-being, and equality of opportunity to all those living here."[18]

On coming to power, the LNCP was dismayed to find that they had hardly any "ethnic contacts" and very little idea as to who the ethnic group leaders in Australia really were. They felt that the Labor Party, with its initial moves in this area and its multicultural rhetoric, had stolen a march on them and had moved a fair way towards capturing the ethnic vote. They therefore set about repairing this situation. As we have seen, Michael MacKellar, the Fraser government's first Minister for Immigration and Ethnic Affairs, is credited with selling multiculturalism to the Prime Minister and Cabinet, both as a step in the right direction for Australia and as a means of re-directing the ethnic vote towards the LNCP.

The Fraser government took a number of major decisions in the field of multiculturalism, some of which were described in Chapter 3. During his first year in office, Mr. MacKellar, together with the Minister for Post and Telecommunications, announced that the federal government would assume responsibility for maintaining a permanent ethnic broadcasting service. Ethnic broadcasting advisory bodies would be set up at the national and state levels. In January 1977, the government established the Australian Ethnic Affairs Council (AEAC), effectively replacing the former Immigration Advisory Council which had been active during the period of Labor government. The new 24-member council (it was later reduced to 15 members) was to advise the Minister on all matters affecting the integration of immigrants into the Australian community, on the promotion and development of harmonious relations within the Australian society, and on measures to encourage understanding of migrant cultures. Ethnic broadcasting was taken a stage further in February when a National Ethnic Broadcasting Advisory Council was created, with state ethnic broadcasting advisory committees to be set up initially in New South Wales and Victoria. In August, it was announced that a new Special Broadcasting Service would be created, linking and drawing advice from the council and committees on the broadcasting needs of ethnic communities. And in the same year, as responsibility for migrant welfare, migrant adult education, information, and other functions were being reintegrated into the Department of Immigration and Ethnic Affairs, a new Ethnic Affairs Branch was added to develop policies on migrant integration and "to foster understanding of migrant cultures and harmonious relations within the community." The branch became responsible for AEAC, providing it with all the necessary services and support.

There were three other important developments: The Galbally Review of Post-Arrival Programs and Services for Migrants, the Government's acceptance of its recommendations, and their subsequent implementation, all of which has had very important implications for multiculturalism; the creation of an Australian Institute of Multicultural Affairs (whose life would prove to be very short); and an unsuccessful attempt to create an Independent and Multicultural Broadcasting Corporation (IMBC). The latter proposal was defeated in the Senate, mainly on the grounds that the creation of a separate radio and television broadcasting service was not the right way to handle ethnic broadcasting in Australia. As we have seen in Chapter 2, the Galbally Review put major emphasis on the concept of multiculturalism in present-day Australia, as well as on the involvement of ethnic organizations and agencies in the delivery of services for migrants, and on the need for multicultural education programs in the schools to encourage "a multicultural attitude in Australian society." As we have seen also, the implementation of these and other recommendations proceeded very rapidly.

Looking back now, it seems evident that the whole Galbally exercise has been approved in Australia as a major effort to improve services and programs for migrants; to involve ethnic groups in the provision of these services and programs; to promote multicultural education in the schools and in the community generally; and to help to establish the concept of Australia as a multicultural society; and all of it done with considerable speed and dispatch. At the same time, there have been criticisms and reservations, some of them at a very senior level.

One of these criticisms concerns what appeared to some Australians to be the almost blatant use of multiculturalism by the Fraser government as a political instrument. The Government seemed determined to achieve as much as possible in this area very quickly (even "instant multiculturalism"); and to secure the firm support and involvement of ethnic communities while there was time, i.e., before a predicted swing back to the Australian Labor Party. To those who have a rather idealistic view of multiculturalism and hope that this is a philosophy which will be embraced by the whole of Australian society, the Fraser government's very determined drive and pragmatic approach in this area were disturbing. These critics did not want multiculturalism to become a political battleground in which the two major parties, with their strong ideological differences, compete for minority support.

Another substantial criticism relates to two basic principles of the Galbally Report: the desirability of involving ethnic groups in the delivery of services to migrants, and the principle of self help for individuals and groups in the settlement process. On the latter question, the Galbally Report said, "Our recommendations in this area are directed to the encouragement and development of self help among the ethnic communities, because we believe that they can meet the welfare needs of migrants more effectively than government agencies. At the same time we propose a reduction in the Commonwealth's direct involvement in the delivery of welfare services to migrants and an extension of its capacity to provide support and consultancy services." Both these principles, however, lay the foundation for a network of special services for migrants and tend to encourage separateness in service delivery among ethnic groups. They run counter to the principle of universality and to the idea that migrants will adjust to a new society more quickly if they are encouraged to make early use of the services available to the whole community. Some members of the Fraser government itself, as well as some senior public servants, had real anxieties on this score.

One other important dimension of the efforts of the Fraser government in the field of multiculturalism should be mentioned. This is the attempt to define multiculturalism in an Australian context, to promote community discussion of it, and to make multicultural policies and programs widely known in Australia. We will look first at these developments and then at the response of the Hawke government, from the spring of 1983 onwards, to the L-NP's brand of multiculturalism and particularly at the Labor government's determined effort first to reshape and reorganize the Australian Institute of Multicultural Affairs and later to dismantle it.

Defining Multiculturalism

Although Canada has continued to fund conferences and studies in this area, Australia has made a much greater effort to define multiculturalism and to define it in the context of her own society and political system. This is mainly due to the fact that her governments have assembled the talent and provided the forums from which to do it, namely her advisory councils. In August 1977, the Australian Ethnic Affairs Council (AEAC) which had been established some seven months earlier, produced a submission on the Australian Population and Immigration Council's Green Paper, *Immigration Policies and Australia's Population*, discussed in Chapter 3. The submission was entitled *Australia as a Multicultural Society*. In June 1979, the two Councils, APIC and AEAC, produced a joint discussion paper on this question entitled *Multiculturalism and its Implications for Immigration Policy*. In part, this was a response to the first document which had been felt to be too theoretical and rather idealistic. It had been written in fact by two sociologists: the Chairman of AEAC, Professor George Zubrzycki, mentioned in Chapter 3, a distinguished scholar of Polish origin at the Australian National University in Canberra who has been an able and courageous advocate of multiculturalism in Australia from the beginning; and Dr. Jean Martin of ANU who was a distinguished scholar in the sociology of migration, and who acted as consultant to the AEAC.

In April 1981, as we have seen, the two councils were disbanded, mainly for financial reasons, and a new joint council was created called the Australian Council on Population and Ethnic Affairs (ACPEA). In May 1982, at the request of the Minister, Ian Macphee, the council's Ethnic Affairs Task Force, chaired by Professor Zubrzycki, produced a third policy discussion paper entitled *Multiculturalism for all Australians: Our Developing Nationhood*. To prepare this document, the Ethnic Affairs Task Force carried out extensive public consultations on multiculturalism with the help of the Department of Immigration and Ethnic Affairs. A number of briefs were received, community leaders and experts were consulted, and public meetings and seminars were held in Sydney, Melbourne, Brisbane, Launceston, and Perth.[19]

All three papers stress the changing nature of Australian society as the outcome of "migration policies that in thirty years have changed our predominantly Anglo-Australian population into an ethnically diverse one," as AEAC's 1977 paper puts it. "The scale and diversity of immigration since World War II," says the 1979 APIC/AEAC paper, "have brought about a major change in the composition of the Australian population. Nearly three million of us were born outside Australia, of whom slightly more than half come from non-English-speaking countries. Furthermore, over 600,000 of our Australian-born population are the children of foreign-born mothers. The cultural impact of this shift in the ethnic balance of the population has been of major significance." Repeating these facts, the 1982 ACPEA paper stresses the extent to which they highlight Australia's demographic and cultural diversity. "This diversity," the paper says, "and the fact that Australia's future is increasingly being linked with Asia and the Pacific, make it imperative that we look where we are going as a people."[20]

All three papers see multiculturalism as an important national policy for Australia, although its full meaning and implications had still to be established. In its preamble, the APIC/AEAC paper stressed the basic political requirement for the new policy:

The Councils express a conviction that development of multiculturalism should take place within the framework of existing democratic parliamentary institutions and with due regard to social and political rights and obligations. The statement recognizes that multiculturalism is dynamic, and will inevitably lead to new social patterns and administrative structures and practices. Such innovations need not require the loss of features that are traditional and valued in Australia, nor are they likely to do so. While there is much scope in multiculturalism for fresh and rewarding approaches to social organization, changes should take place in a way that will support and strengthen the democratic system of government.

The final ACPEA paper outlines the four basic principles which, in the council's view, are essential for a successful multicultural society: social cohesion; respect for cultural identity and awareness of Australia's cultural diversity; equal opportunity and access for all Australians; and equal responsibility for, commitment to, and participation in Australian society. Multiculturalism is for all Australians and applies as much to the Anglo-Australian majority as it does to other ethnic groups. At the same time, it is urged that to make multiculturalism successful, "minority groups with a non-English-speaking background must not flourish on the margin and at the expense of the total Australian society, but must be orientated to it."[21]

Of the three discussion papers, only the 1979 APIC/AEAC paper realistically explored the problems associated with multiculturalism for migrants and for the whole society. It raised the question, for example, whether creating a network of ethnic organizations and formalizing group differences would adversely affect national unity, questioning a statement in the earlier AEAC paper that "... in a cohesive multicultural society, national loyalties are built on ethnic loyalties," a very debatable proposition. The 1979 paper also touches on the operation of ethnic groups as interest groups which, as it points out, can sometimes be a response to the desire of governments to deal with them in a systematic and orderly way. Here the paper concludes: "... the emergence of ethnic lobbies is a legitimate development, providing they do not place themselves beyond or above the one Australian nation of which they are a part. The danger of abuse will be minimized to the extent that the established Australian community opens its political parties, professional organizations and other institutions to newcomers – and indeed goes out of its way to invite their participation."[22]

Apart from these few paragraphs, however, none of the three papers (no doubt partly because they were all submitted directly or indirectly to a minister in the Fraser government) examines the politics of multiculturalism, including the critical element of the complex relationship between government and ethnic groups, and the major concern of political parties, in and out of office, to secure their support. Nor is there any real discussion of the present or potential sources of opposition to or disinterest in multiculturalism in Australian society. With these elements missing, there is a certain feeling of political unreality about each of the three discussion papers, thoughtful and liberal though they are.

Since then, the political dimension of multiculturalism in Australia has been illustrated in the clearest possible way by the actions of the Hawke government since coming to power in March 1983, in relation to the L-NP-created Australian Institute of Multicultural Affairs.

The Hawke Government and AIMA

The close association of the Chairman of the Australian Institute of Multicultural Affairs (AIMA), Frank Galbally, and its director, Petro Georgiou, with Prime Minister Fraser and his government was well-known in Australia. To some extent, this made all the operations of the Institute suspect. When, in addition, the Institute carried out one or two special assignments for Mr. Fraser at a high level of priority and with considerable speed, the impression that it was simply an adjunct to the Prime Minister's department was confirmed. The new Labor government was unlikely to tolerate the continuation of this kind of management, or to hesitate to put its own stamp on this new institution.

On July 24, 1983, within four months of assuming office, the Labor government, in the person of the Minister for Immigration and Ethnic Affairs, announced that a Committee of Review had been established to consider whether AIMA had been efficient and effective in meeting its statutory objectives and functions; and whether any changes in objectives, functions, or administrative arrangements were desirable. The Chairman of the Committee of Review was Dr. Moss Cass of Melbourne, who had been a member of Mr. Whitlam's Cabinet and subsequently Opposition spokesman for the ALP on immigration and ethnic affairs. The other three members had all been associated with the ALP in different ways. The Committee was asked to report to the Minister by November 1, 1983, i.e., in little over three months. It was assisted in this endeavour by a secretariat of sixteen, plus ten researchers and two consultants.[23]

The Committee's report for the Minister, produced in November, 1983, was a damning indictment of AIMA and its Fraser-appointed management. Whatever AIMA's failings had been, however, the report could hardly be praised for objectivity. The authors seemed to look only for evidence of inadequacy and adverse opinions among those whom they consulted. No allowance whatsoever was made for the fact that AIMA was only three years old and was still in what one of its member described in evidence as the formative stages. Nothing, apparently, could shake the conviction of the Committee that AIMA and all its works were a disaster.

The general conclusion of the Cass report was that AIMA had been neither effective nor efficient in fulfilling its charter, which was to address itself to the central issues of multiculturalism in Australia. There were other criticisms. The Committee of Review concluded that there were serious shortcomings in the quality of the research carried out by AIMA and in total output relative to expenditure. In addition, it was widely believed in the community, they said, that the Fraser government set the agenda for the Institute, although in fact only two research projects had been undertaken at the Government's request. The public perception of AIMA had been of "an elitist, politically partisan organization with too close links with the power structure to enable it to retain any degree of objectivity and independence." The academic community, too, had been highly critical of the Institute's "organizational practices in research and its high-handed mode of operation." AIMA's efforts in community education and dissemination of information had also been unimpressive, the Committee said, while its record in promoting harmonious community relations, one of the principal objects of its charter, was non-existent "despite evidence of increasing prejudice and discrimination in Australian society." Finally, in all its activities, AIMA had tended to work alone and had failed to collaborate with other agencies working on similar issues. The Committee's report, a major indictment of AIMA on almost every front, made four major recommendations:[24]

1 AIMA should be replaced by a new independent statutory authority known as a "Commission," located within the portfolio of the Minister for Immigration and Ethnic Affairs. The Commission should be accountable to Parliament through the Minister.
2 A Standing Committee on Ethnic and Community Relations should be established, by resolution of the House of Representatives, which should examine all reports from the new Commission and make recommendations for action on any proposals arising from these reports or elsewhere.
3 The Commission, as a national structure, should act with due regard to the interests and concerns of the states and territories and involve them actively in its work. The Commission should relate to the three levels of government including State Ethnic Affairs Commissions and community groups, and be empowered to act as a national co-ordinating body in the field of multicultural affairs.
4 Participation of and consultation with the community should be integral elements of all the activities of the Commission.

The report made a number of other detailed recommendations relating to the objectives, functions, and powers of the new Commission; its membership, management, and committee structure; the role and responsibilities of its chief executive; and its basic tasks in community education, information, support of cultural heritage, and the development and funding of research in the multicultural field.[25]

The Hawke government responded cautiously to these proposals. In a statement to the House on December 8, the Minister for Immigration and Ethnic Affairs stated that the Government had accepted two of the Committee's recommendations: that the report itself be tabled in the House and that extensive consultations be undertaken on it. But the Government would maintain an open mind on the proposed new Commission, the Minister said, until the consultations had been completed and all the options regarding the future of AIMA had been studied. An Interim Council would be appointed which would undertake those consultations and report to the government on the report and its recommendations.[26]

The new Interim Council, duly appointed by the Minister, took over from the former Council of AIMA on December 20–22, 1983. It consisted of nine members: an acting chairman, Dr. Kenneth Rivett, a well-known professor of economics at the University of New South Wales in Sydney, who had been a leader in the Immigration Reform Group in Australia in the sixties and early seventies and was an authority on immigration and refugee issues; AIMA's Director, Petro Georgiou; Dr. Moss Cass, Chairman of the Committee of Review; Professor George Zubrzycki who had been a member of the original AIMA Council, and five other members. The composition of the Interim Council was in itself a conciliatory gesture on the part of the Hawke government.

Meanwhile, the original AIMA council and, of course, AIMA's management did not take these developments lying down. On December 17 they issued a reply to the Report of the Committee entitled *Response to the Report to the Minister for Immigration and Ethnic Affairs of the Committee of Review of the Australian Institute of Multicultural Affairs*. The response was as categorical in its views as the report of the Committee of Review had been: "The foundation Council of the Institute believes that the conclusions reached by the Committee are not supportable and that consequently the recommendation for abolishing the Institute has no basis."

The reply drew attention to the fact that those appointed to undertake the review had already publicly criticized the Institute, and that the Chairman of AIMA had advised the Prime Minister and the Minister for Immigration and Ethnic Affairs in July of his doubts whether the review would be fair and impartial. AIMA's main contention, however, was that the

Committee of Review had entirely failed to meet the first requirement in its terms of reference, namely to consider and report to the Minister on "whether AIMA has been efficient and effective in meeting its statutory objects and functions." In relation to the report itself, the AIMA response commented that its methodology was unsound; it abounded with major errors; key conclusions were at odds with evidence cited within the report itself, or available elsewhere; and generalized allegations made by unnamed individuals were offered as facts.

The claim that the Institute had been unhelpful and secretive and had not provided appropriate assistance to the Committee, made much of in the Report of the Committee of Review, was also refuted. The remainder of the AIMA response consisted of a case-by-case rebuttal of the many claims and statements in the Committee's report which the Council considered untrue or misleading.[27]

The Minister asked the new Interim Council to report to him by April 16, 1984, and to provide a distillation of the community's views as well as its own recommendations. At its first meeting in December, the Council decided that "it would concentrate on the recommendations of the Committee of Review rather than look at assertions and counter-assertions about the past." It did not, therefore, evaluate the first and most critical part of the committee's report, nor did it mention the AIMA response. It did, however, permit itself one comment: "Council records also that it has found no evidence to suggest any lack of devotion by [AIMA] staff to the cause of multiculturalism, nor any lack of concern about those sections of the ethnic communities which are most disadvantaged."

Between December and April, teams of Interim Council members held extensive public consultations in all eight of Australia's capital cities and in Geelong, Newcastle, Townsville, and Wollongong. In addition, they held more than 60 private meetings, with 55 of AIMA's Council members; representatives of the Federation of Ethnic Communities Council of Australia and nine Ethnic Communities' Councils; the chairmen and members of two Ethnic Affairs Commissions; senior officers of several State Ethnic Affairs Departments and many other groups and individuals including most of the staff of the Institute. More than 100 written submissions were received from Commonwealth and state departments and agencies and from voluntary organizations. All this evidence was carefully and methodically analyzed. The outcome was a set of recommendations to the Minister that were fairly close to those of the Committee of Review:

1 There should be a new act of Parliament establishing an independent statutory authority to be known as the Australian Commission for Multicultural Development.

2 The objects of the Commission should be (a) to promote a just, equitable, and harmonious Australian society based on mutual knowledge and esteem, and on an appreciation of Australia's ethnic and cultural diversity and its contribution to Australian life ... and (b) to provide advice to the Commonwealth government on social policies and any other issue relating to object (a). The diverse cultures referred to above include the cultures of the Aboriginal peoples who form an integral part of the multicultural Australian society.

3 The Commission should report to Parliament through the Prime Minister who should consider appointing a "Minister Assisting the Prime Minister for Multicultural Development," and who should also consider designating the Minister for Immigration and Ethnic Affairs as that minister.

4 At least one House of Parliament should consider establishing a Standing Committee on Multicultural Development which could request reports from the Commission and would examine all reports of the Commission.

These recommendations were presented to the Minister on April 13, 1984, in the form of a report entitled appropriately *Looking Forward: A Report on Consultations concerning the Recommendations of the Committee of Review of the Australian Institute of Multicultural Affairs*. The Hawke government, however, did not accept the major proposals of the Committee of Review or the Interim Council. In an important and judicious speech in the House of Representatives on October 11, 1984, the Minister, Stewart West, said that the Government had decided "to retain the Australian Institute of Multicultural Affairs as a statutory body active in multicultural affairs ... [but] to expand its objectives and functions, reorder work priorities, and achieve greater public visibility of, and openness in, AIMA's operations." The Government saw no advantage in turning the Institute into a Commission, but they did accept some of the recommendations in the two reports: the need for a broader mandate for AIMA; more consultation and co-operation with "departments, authorities and agencies at the three levels of government and with community groups, voluntary agencies, the media and employer, employee and other organizations", and the definite inclusion of Aboriginal affairs within the concerns of the Institute.

Mr. West noted that "The AIMA Council has reported widespread support for the general ideals of a multicultural society, and the overwhelming consensus of opinion expressed in the consultations was that an authority with distinct multicultural responsibilities within such a society was essential." He also said the Government did not accept the need for any change in the "portfolio arrangements for AIMA," and believed that the present close relationship between AIMA and the Department of Immigration and Ethnic Affairs was a very desirable one. Nor did the Government accept a recommendation that AIMA should have a direct role in combatting prejudice and discrimination and should have "handling powers on discrimination matters." These powers, the Minister said, were solely the statutory responsibility of the Human Rights Commission, which would become the Human Rights and Equal Opportunity Commission with a Commissioner for Racial Discrimination. Finally, the Minister said a bill to amend the Australian Institute of Multicultural Affairs Act would be introduced during the autumn sittings. The five-year term of appointment of the present director of AIMA was due to expire on January 31, 1985. The position would shortly be publicly advertised.[29]

AIMA did not survive for very long, even with these changes, the Hawke government evidently deciding that multiculturalism must be brought under closer control. On December 6, 1986, it was announced that the Institute of Multicultural Affairs would be disbanded and replaced by an Office of Multicultural Affairs within the Department of the Prime Minister and Cabinet. And on March 13, 1987, the Prime Minister announced the creation of an Advisory Council on Multicultural Affairs to report to him and to the then Minister for Immigration and Ethnic Affairs, Mick Young. It was a sad day for some of those who had been closely involved with AIMA and believed in the advantages of having a strong, independent-minded research institute in Australian multiculturalism. But others, particularly within the public service, are said not to have mourned its departure and to believe that the voice of multiculturalism in Australia would be stronger under the present arrangement.

MULTICULTURALISM REVIEWED

These, then, were the first uncertain years of multiculturalism as a national policy in Canada and Australia. In both countries, they confirm the fact that the political dimensions of multiculturalism are all-important and must be studied by those who are concerned with this subject. Governments have created and will continue to control this area of public policy. While they have accorded a certain degree of priority to it, however, they have spent relatively little money on it so far, compared with other social policies and programs. For this reason, the size of the budget in Canada and Australia for multiculturalism in its various forms will continue to be an important indicator of its political status. At the same time, political parties – whether in or out of office – while proclaiming in party platforms and speeches a wholly objective devotion to this cause, will continue to try to ensure that this devotion will result in increased support for their party at the polls.

It is interesting that the Mulroney government, which has made some important improvements in Canada's multicultural policies and programs, strongly emphasized its support for multiculturalism during the months leading to the federal election of September 4, 1984. The following is an extract from a report in the *Globe and Mail* of June 4, 1984 entitled "Mulroney Pledges PCs to 5-point stand on Multiculturalism":

Progressive Conservative Leader Brian Mulroney has told a cheering crowd the Tory Party will no longer allow itself to be called the Party of White Anglo-Saxon Protestants. It stands for multiculturalism.

His speech Saturday night to more than 2,000 people at a banquet in a downtown Toronto hotel capped a highly successful day-long conference on multiculturalism, the first time the Conservatives have attempted a conference of this size on this topic anywhere in Canada.

The participants, many of whom were newly-minted Tories, the very people the party is counting on to make a breakthrough in Toronto-area ethnic communities in the next election, came away impressed that the Conservatives are genuine in their intentions this time.[30]

Mr. Mulroney told his audience that multiculturalism was no less important than bilingualism and biculturalism and that there were nine million Canadians whose roots were neither English nor French. Multicultural diversity, he said, was an absolutely indispensable part of Canada's national identity and to reject it was to reject the essence of this society. Unity did not depend on uniformity. It depended on shared experiences, shared values, mutual respect, and mutual goals. He then outlined a five-point program which he said his party intended to implement: (1) changes in the hiring policies of the federal government to encourage the upward mobility of racial and cultural groups in the public service; (2) the provision, in collaboration with other levels of government, of services in non-official languages in neighbourhoods where numbers warrant it; (3) more funds for official language training to help new Canadians; (4) more funds for heritage language classes and cultural retention studies; and (5) greater efforts to stamp out racism "wherever it rears its ugly head."

These were useful proposals, but they could not be described as radical new departures. Nevertheless, they were warmly applauded at this special conference and the Tories were rewarded on September 4 by some impressive victories in the Toronto ridings.

We have looked at the political face of multiculturalism in Canada and Australia where it has very similar features and evokes similar concerns and uncertainty. But we should also look at its other face which is far more often on display. There is no question that an official policy of multiculturalism can be a civilized and civilizing factor in national and community development. In Canada and Australia, there has also been a welcome spin-off effect at the provincial/state and city levels, where a number of ethnic advisory councils, commissions, and committees now exist. One or two provinces and states have been particularly innovative and successful in this field. In general, it is fair to say that in both countries today there is widespread acceptance of the need to change public attitudes towards ethnic diversity, to develop forms of multicultural education at all levels, and to establish a widespread understanding and respect for a full range of ethnic origins and heritage. The need for equality, equal opportunity, and full participation for citizens of all ethnic origins is widely accepted also, although the means of achieving them are not very clear as yet. It has been stressed in both countries too that the positive message implied in this policy should reach the whole community, and that multiculturalism should not simply be a private conversation and process of bargaining between government and ethnic communities in which wider issues play no part, even though reaching the community as a whole is one of the more difficult problems of implementation.

Given all of this, however, there is still quite firm resistance in Canada and Australia to the idea that multiculturalism should lead to major changes in the political system, or to major changes in the law, except in the area of human rights. It is important, therefore, to consider in realistic terms what multiculturalism is and what it is not.

Multiculturalism in these two countries does not mean any degree of power-sharing with ethnic communities, as the leadership of several of Canada's older ethnic groups hoped it might. Although it may help in a general way, it will not, as a set of programs with a small budget, necessarily lead to equity and social justice for all, as Australia's Committee of Review felt it should, because this is a task for the whole of government. In addition, multiculturalism will never convince the founding peoples of Canada and Australia, the British and (in Canada's case) the French and their many assimilated members of other origins, to abandon their hard-earned and long-enjoyed political status and to regard themselves as part of a fraternity of ethnic groups, nor should it try to do so. The national identities of Canada and Australia, their historical evolution as independent democratic nations, and the contemporary societies which their now very diverse peoples have helped to create, are far more important, it should be said, than ethnic origins and the retention of ethnic cultures. The native peoples of Canada and Australia too – the Indians and Inuit of Canada and the Aborigines of Australia – while they may wish to have access to multicultural programs, are much more likely to find their own way politically, as indeed they are already doing. Large claims for multiculturalism which fail to come to terms with its political and financial limitations in these and other areas, serve only to disturb and alienate many of its potential supporters.

The true mission of multiculturalism and the real sense in which it is "a policy for all Australians" and for all Canadians, is the civilizing one of helping to create a more just, tolerant, and caring society, and of providing some of the modern concepts and new political language with which to do this. One of the most important contributions which multiculturalism can make to this cause today is in the field of race relations. This very important question will be discussed in the final chapter.

CHAPTER SIX

Canadian and Australian Immigration Today

It is hoped that this study will show how very similar the immigration experiences of Canada and Australia are, and how important immigration has been and still is in their population growth and national development. As we have seen, their responses to its major problems and difficulties have also been very similar, growing more alike since the early seventies. The general public, and even the informed public in both countries, are probably unaware of the remarkable degree of communication and exchange of information that goes on all the time between Canada and Australia at the political and bureaucratic level – we might call it the Canada-Australia watch – despite the immense distances that separate them. At the outset of this study, the author approached the Canadian High Commission in Canberra and the Australian High Commission in Ottawa, to see whether they could provide examples of this regular interchange of information in different areas of public policy. The response of the Canadian and Australian High Commissioners was identical. Impossible, they said, the traffic was simply too heavy. It would require a document of great length because the High Commission's facilities of telephone, telex, cable, and the like were in such frequent use for this purpose – someone in Ottawa or Canberra always wanted to know something. A new piece of legislation or any major development in public policy in either country, they said, unleashed quite a flood of inquiries.

The central fact of very similar management of immigration and its related policy areas by Canada and Australia tells us a great deal about immigration itself and the difficulties it presents for governments. Although, as we have seen, it has been distinctly higher on the national agenda in Australia where it has been treated, except during the Whitlam years, as an important policy area in its own right, there is no doubt that immigration is seen by politicians and the public in both countries as both a benefit and a threat. It is also obviously tolerated much more freely in good times than in bad. Family or personal experience of immigration, recent or sometimes stretching a long way back, inclines the public to believe, in good times, that immigration can have great advantages, bringing in energetic, enterprising, and creative people in all walks of life – the kind of people who built Canada and Australia. At the same time, immigration also carries indefinable threats which become worse in harsh economic times – threats, for example, of the loss of jobs to newcomers or of the takeover of neighbourhoods by ethnic communities. There are perceived threats too of subtle changes in society, involving the introduction of different political, religious, and social values, and ways of life which are disturbing to the established residents and against which they feel powerless.

Immigration also carries special threats of a larger and smaller kind for politicians which are identical in Canada and Australia and are rarely mentioned in public. These are the threats of innumerable, time-consuming interviews and phone calls and endless correspondence on individual immigrant cases, as well as the steady demand for attendance at a great many ethnic group functions and the importance of distributing these favours equitably. There is also the essential requirement of continuous public tolerance and the dangers, at times, of frankness when difficulties occur; politicians are aware too of the degree to which a small problem in this area can be blown up in the media out of proportion to its real consequence, and prove very damaging to political reputations. It is not surprising, therefore, that both Bob Andras and Michael MacKellar, when responsible for immigration in the 1970s, found, that their respective cabinets were lacking in enthusiasm and concern for this particular field of public policy. Cabinet members wanted immigration to be well-managed. Otherwise they preferred not to hear about it.

THE PROBLEMS OF MANAGEMENT

There is no doubt that immigration itself is very difficult to manage, involving as it does a host of individual decisions on the part of the receiving country and of would-be immigrants, and great uncertainty and unpredictability on the demand side. This unpredictability has increased in recent years because of the incidence of large refugee movements and a steady rise in undocumented migration. Immigration is also an area in which the control of volume is critical, and fairness very difficult to achieve, in a world where a compassionate case can be made for almost every would-be immigrant, overstayer, and refugee. The post-war period in Canada and Australia has been increasingly characterized by efforts to find better and more open ways of making decisions relating to volume; and to institute appeal systems and use devices like amnesties and formal case review procedures, in an attempt to achieve fairness in marginal cases, or in the case of the long-term undocumented migrant.

At about the same time, we have become less innocent in recent years about the commerce of migration, and the exploitation of immigration and its avenues of entry by criminal and irresponsible elements. It has become very clear that any loopholes inadvertently left in the law, any gestures of goodwill towards friendly states, or any schemes to make the immigration process less complicated will probably be exploited almost immediately. We have seen examples of this in the fate of Al Grassby's Easy Visa Scheme, in the uses made of the Trans-Tasman route into Australia, and in the advantage taken in Canada of the change of status provision in the 1967 Immigration Regulations and simultaneous creation of an independent Immigration Appeal Board. We have also seen that both Canada and Australia believe that they have quite large numbers of illegal immigrants within their borders, despite amnesties and other control measures, and are faced continuously with the problem of how to deal with them without harassing them in a manner unacceptable to the public. Today, therefore, immigration involves an elaborate and sophisticated policing function which may relate at any one time to a very serious security problem, to drug trafficking, to the prevention of illegal entry, to document fraud, to the apprehension of undocumented migrants, or simply to petty crime in an immigration context.

For these reasons and because immigration, however competently and prudently handled, touches the most fundamental of political concerns – the well-being, development, and security of the state – we can expect that the national government will play a paramount role in its direction and management; and this has been the case in Canada since 1867 and Australia since 1900. Although the Australian states have played a much more important part in immigration than the Canadian provinces, at least until recently, and have been consulted and involved throughout the post-war period, they have remained (as the Canadian provinces are) subordinate to the federal government in this field. The processes of Commonwealth-state and federal-provincial consultation in immigration, however, are now becoming increasingly alike.

In his statement on "Immigration Policies and Australia's Population" of June 7, 1978, the Minister for Immigration, Michael MacKellar, announced that in the new system of immigration planning over a three-year period, state governments would be consulted on the level and content of each triennial program and on the annual revision of the program. State governments would also be able to initiate their own nomination schemes for the recruitment of immigrants to meet state needs. Today, conferences of Commonwealth and state ministers take place twice a year in Australia. The first of these yearly meetings, which usually takes place in April, provides an opportunity for the states to express their views on the social, demographic, and manpower factors relating to the number of migrants to be admitted during the following three years. Prior discussions on these matters take place between Commonwealth and state officials. The discussions are wide-ranging and include migrant settlement and community relations. These arrangements have not changed under the Hawke government. At a meeting of Commonwealth and state ministers held in April 1984 in Brisbane, for example, the ministers or their representatives agreed that the present non-discriminatory policies, as well as the Labor government's emphasis on family reunion and the diversification of refugee sources, should continue. They also discussed the possibility of a moderate increase in the skilled labour and business migration programs, the present arrangements for the recognition of overseas qualifications, Commonwealth support for state initiatives in migrant education and welfare services, the provision of language services, and the Migrant Resource Centre Program and Migrant Centre accommodation.[1]

The Canadian system is designed in a different way but has the same effect, although there is probably less face-to-face contact between ministers or senior officials and the agenda is more limited. As we have seen in Chapter 2, consultations with the provinces are an important and mandatory feature of Canada's annual immigration levels planning process and take place – as in Australia – in the first few months of the year. In addition, there are federal-provincial immigration agreements with seven of the ten provinces (Quebec, Saskatchewan, Newfoundland, Nova Scotia, New Brunswick, Prince Edward Island and Alberta), requiring continuing consultation and co-operation in the areas of immigration, demography, and employment. In the case of Quebec, which was the first province to sign an immigration agreement with the federal government, a Joint Committee on Immigration was established under the most recent agreement. Quebec's right to select foreign nationals who wished to settle permanently or temporarily in the province, and therefore to establish a Quebec presence in certain overseas immigration offices (or to have her own immigration offices overseas) was also recognized. These arrangements will probably be changed, however, because of the new constitutional explorations now in progress. Consultations with all the provinces are conducted by the regional representatives of the Canada Employment and Immigration Commission located in each provincial capital, except in the case of Quebec, where the Joint Committee is under the co-chairmanship of an assistant deputy minister from the ministry responsible for immigration in Quebec, and the Executive Director of the Immigration Group in the Canada Employment and Immigration Commission, at least so far.

Governments, therefore, play a very important leadership role in immigration in both Canada and Australia, and have probably been well ahead of public opinion in this field throughout the post-war period, which accounts in part for their caution and anxieties relating to it. The state of public opinion in immigration is very difficult to assess. Public opinion polls, with their known limitations, are of particularly doubtful value in this area, since most members of the public simply do not have enough information about immigration intake, distribution, or source countries to make a reasonable judgement. In addition, the questions asked often do not permit or encourage any appreciation of long-term national needs. Nevertheless, they are all we have. In its 1984 Review, Australia's Department of Immigration and Ethnic Affairs reported that post-war public opinion polls show that:

- *In 1945* only 10 per cent of those polled supported Italian migration
- *In 1947* 48 per cent were opposed to acceptance of displaced persons from Europe.
- *In 1948* 47 per cent favoured retention of the White Australia policy
- *In 1952* 52 per cent thought that there were too many migrants coming to Australia.
- *In 1958* 63 per cent favoured a cut in the then migration level.

- *In 1959* 31 per cent favoured retention of the title "White Australia"
- *In 1966* 62 per cent thought that anything higher than the then level of Asian migration (1,000) was too high
- *In 1970* 50 per cent thought that anything higher than the then level of Asian migration (3,000) was too high
- *In 1975* 50 per cent thought that Asian migration levels were too high.[2]

Similar poll results can be found in Canada. In a supplementary study to the 1975 Green Paper on Immigration Policy, Nancy Tienhaara analysed post-war Gallup polls on immigration and concluded that: "the Gallup polls of the post-Second World War period demonstrated that although there was a narrow margin of support for the idea that Canada needed immigrants in 1947, the majority of Canadians since 1952 at least have believed that Canada does not need immigrants. Today [1974], as in 1952, the Gallup polls show that only about one third of Canadians think Canada needs new immigrants, while more than half are opposed, and the remainder are undecided." On the question of refugees, she concluded that they elicited more support in Canada than immigrants did. Even here, however, "a majority of Canadians can be expected to oppose an increased intake of refugees except when an avalanche of publicity on the dire need of the refugees themselves offsets considerations of self-interest in favour of humanitarianism ..."[3]

In his study *Canada and the Indochinese Refugees*, published in 1982, Howard Adelman concluded that government policy was far ahead of public sentiment in responding to this refugee movement, and that, with only a few important exceptions, it had provided the leadership required. Adelman quotes various polls to show that a majority of Canadians was always opposed to increasing the intake of Indochinese refugees, even when there was intensive media coverage of the refugees' sufferings.[4] As we saw in Chapter 4, many Australians also showed considerable hostility to the boat people when they began to arrive on Australia's northern shores. Yet a great many Canadians and Australians eventually responded very generously to the needs of the Indochinese refugees in one of the largest refugee movements either country has ever had. It is a mistake to think, however, that public opinion generally in Canada and Australia is liberal in matters of immigration and refugee policy. Government leads the way and cautiously brings the public along with it.

THE POLICY-MAKING PROCESS

If government plays the principal role in determining immigration and refugee policy, do other institutions and organizations have at least some input in the process? Has Parliament, for example, played an important part in the evolution of immigration and related policy areas in Canada and Australia, and has it exercised some check on the Executive in this field? In both countries there have been relatively few major debates on immigration during these years. Rather, Parliament has been the place for ministerial statements on the subject, usually taking the form of reports on the current situation or on proposed policy changes, followed by comments from party spokesmen. It has also been the place for questions on particular programs, which often elicit useful information. The absence of vigorous debate of a continuing kind through the post-war period can be accounted for, at least in part, by the fact that Australia had a bipartisan immigration policy until the advent of the Whitlam government; and Canada has had a "tripartisan" immigration policy (i.e., supported by the three major parties) all through this period. In Australia, however, parliamentary discussion of immigration has become more vigorous and more contentious in the last few years. The lack of a detailed knowledge of the field – essential in immigration – must also inhibit the participation of many backbenchers. Few of those without a known immigration connection or special interest in this area ever take part.

Has parliamentary control been exercised through the committee system? Since 1968, Canada has had a Standing Committee on Labour,

Manpower, and Immigration which examines the relevant annual estimates and all important ministerial statements, reports, and proposed
policy changes, but its area of concern is so large that it can devote only a
limited amount of time to immigration. This committee also suffers from
the same fragmentation of immigration management discussed in Chapter
2: important sectors of this field are completely outside its jurisdiction.
Australia does not even have a standing parliamentary committee on
immigration, although both major parties have their own parliamentary
immigration committees. There is nothing in the Canadian and Australian
parliamentary systems that approaches the keen scrutiny of immigration
legislation and active involvement in policy-making in immigration of the
congressional committees in the United States.

Political parties in Canada and Australia have obviously exercised a
major influence on policy-making in immigration while in power, but they
have rarely done so in opposition. Until the election of the Mulroney
government, opposition parties in Canada have raised few objections to
the major policy developments of the last few years, and few constructive
proposals have emerged from the opposition benches. Questions might be
raised, for example, about the number of refugees to be admitted, the
possibility of extending an amnesty deadline, the current figures for deportation or minister's permits, or a contentious individual case, but hardly
any fundamental criticism of immigration policy or management has been
made in recent years. We saw how harmoniously the all-party members of
the Special Joint Committee of the Senate and the House of Commons on
Immigration Policy worked together in their examination of the Green
Paper in 1975, and in their recommendations to government on future
immigration policy. This confirms the substantial degree of agreement
among Canadian political parties on the basic features of immigration
policy and management.

It will be interesting to see whether this degree of consensus will endure
for long under the Mulroney government with its huge majority, particularly if this government is obliged to make difficult decisions about Canada's population prospects and the need for higher annual levels of immigration (discussed later in this chapter). Will the two opposition parties,
Liberal and New Democrat, fighting for a leading role in the House, see
immigration as a fruitful point of attack? Or will a comfortable all-party
consensus continue to prevail? Since Canada's present demographic problem – the prospect of future population decline due to continuing low
fertility – is a serious one, it seems likely that the "tripartisan" approach
to immigration will continue, with only minor differences. At present,
however, the only clear fact is that the Mulroney government itself is
taking this problem very seriously.

In Australia, whose politics have a far stronger ideological component, the situation has been very different since the bipartisan approach to immigration began to break down from the late sixties onwards, and sharp differences began to appear. Mr. Whitlam, for example, took a very different view of immigration from that of his Liberal predecessors, and initially the Hawke government seemed to be establishing a clear position on immigration which differed considerably from that of the L-NPC. Bipartisanship in immigration policy became an issue in itself, and both the Government and the Opposition accused the other of departing from it. During the long period in office of the Fraser government, however, there was a good deal of agreement on immigration and related policies and programs, most notably on the management of the large Indochinese refugee movement. The Australian Labor Party was deeply suspicious of NUMAS, of the Galbally Review of Post-Arrival Programs and Services for Migrants, and of the creation of the Institute of Multicultural Affairs, with Mr. Galbally and Mr. Georgiou in leading roles. There was also a gathering conviction on the part of the ALP that the L-NPC stood for numbers, for the recruitment of too many skilled workers from overseas – threatening the jobs and opportunities of Australian workers – and for a lack of dedication to family reunion. They also suspected that the Fraser government consistently preferred the traditional sources of migrant recruitment, even in the context of the accepted nondiscriminatory immigration policy.

At the outset, the central features of the Hawke government's immigration policy, as expressed by the Prime Minister and his first Minister of Immigration and Ethnic Affairs, Stewart West, appeared to be as follows:

a. Australia's non-discriminatory, universal immigration policy remains in force and must not be tampered with.
b. Immigration is not needed today for population growth.
c. Immigration is not needed as a major supplier of skilled labor. Australian workers must be trained to meet current labor force needs.
d. The major purpose of immigration today should be to serve a social and humanitarian purpose, emphasizing family reunion and the admission of refugees who should be drawn from a wider area of need.
e. The government is committed, however, to the continued development of the Business Migration Program with the specific objective of introducing new and improved business technology, the creation of jobs, and the stimulation of exports.
f. Management, i.e., the Department of Immigration and Ethnic Affairs, should remain unchanged.
g. A National Population Council should advise the Government on population and immigration matters.
h. Multiculturalism should remain an important national policy provided

that the political influence of the Fraser government and Fraser "cronyism" are removed.

In October 1984, the Liberal – National Party Coalition produced its first policy statement on immigration in opposition.[5] The statement affirmed the nine basic principles of immigration policy announced in the national Parliament on June 7, 1978 by the Minister for Immigration and Ethnic Affairs, Michael McKellar, and later endorsed by the Hawke government (see Appendix 2). Additional elements were then added including support for multiculturalism; recognition of the desire of ethnic communities for full participation in all aspects of Australian political, economic, and cultural life; support for migrant services but with more emphasis on the use by migrants of community-based services (it was the Galbally Review which had urged the delivery of migrant services by ethnic organizations); and special emphasis on English language training. There were two contentious matters in this rather plain policy document, which did not produce any new thinking in this area. First there was an early statement that "In the opinion of many, successful migration policies hold the key to the future of this nation, including contributing to the revitalisation of our economy by increasing the size of our domestic market and adding skills in short supply." Second, there was the following statement on racial discrimination, which should be seen in the context of the unexpected national debate on Asian immigration provoked by Professor Blainey which had taken place a few months earlier. The statement reads:

We believe that racial discrimination within Australia cannot be tolerated. Australia has avoided the problems often encountered in other countries. To ensure this is sustained, we will continue to work for a policy which has broad community support. We believe this requires:

Our migration program to have as an important objective the maintenance of an integrated Australian community in which core Australian democratic and social values are preserved.

Administration of the migration program with sensitivity about the pace at which the community can integrate immigration flows.

A balance of categories which properly reflects a balance between Australia's own interests, our international responsibilities, our support for the family reunion program, the employment needs of Australians, and the short- and long-term needs for migrants with skills and capital.

In a news release issued on October 18, 1984, the Minister, Stewart West, made some scathing comments on this L-NP policy statement. The Coalition, he said, had taken nearly a year to produce a "non-policy" and a document without any specific figures or targets. The statement also implied that "economic migration" should be significantly increased. "This," he said, "would mark a return to the Coalition policies of 1981–1982 when they brought in large numbers of skilled workers, which was a disaster for the Australian labor force and for the migrants themselves." This policy could only be implemented by a significant increase in the migration program as a whole, or by cuts in the family reunion program which would cause suffering to all migrant communities in Australia. The Government, Mr. West said, welcomed statements by the Coalition that it rejected racial discrimination and was in favour of a bipartisan approach to immigration policy but there was nothing in the document just released which gave any substance to these statements. It was simply a "shoddy compromise" between the forces of disrepute and the forces of decency in the Liberal Party.[6]

We can conclude that the spirit of bipartisanship in immigration policy was at a low ebb during these early years of the Hawke administration. After two years in office, however, a remarkable change took place in this government's thinking on immigration policy. Clearly impressed with the seriousness of Australia's future demographic problems, the Hawke government has had second thoughts and has once again opted for expansion and the traditional Australian use of immigration for population growth and economic development. This change may well bring a return to bipartisanship in immigration, and there is some evidence that this is already happening. We will discuss the government's statement in Parliament on this change of direction later in the chapter.

Meanwhile, one other potentially important element in the policy-making process in immigration in Canada and Australia should be considered. Interest groups are always believed to exercise a considerable influence on immigration policy-making, particularly by those outside the system. The range of potentially influential groups has included business and labour as front runners during the post-war period, while a host of national organizations, ethnic groups and ethnic group coalitions, the churches, and the more established voluntary agencies have brought up the rear. Established or ad hoc organizations involved in the protection of civil rights as well as bodies such as the RSL (Returned Soldiers and Sailors Imperial League of Australia) and the Royal Canadian Legion have sometimes contributed to an immigration debate. How much actual influence has this diverse collection of interest groups really had on immigration policy?

In Canada, until recently, it is fair to say that the influence of the major interest groups on immigration policy has been very limited and, where it has occurred, has lain much more in the *perception* of their views by politicians and officials than in any direct impact. At the same time, the influence of national organizations, ethnic groups, and voluntary agencies has been minimal, except in the area of family reunion (where their representatives have sometimes touched off an ever sensitive political response) and occasionally in relation to refugees. The creation of the Canada Manpower and Immigration Advisory Council and its advisory boards in 1967, the Canadian Consultative Council on Multiculturalism in 1973, and the Canada Employment and Immigration Advisory Council (designed to reflect the views of business and labour) in 1977 could have provided a legitimate means to convey the views of the larger and some of the smaller interest groups to government and to see that they were discussed. But the Trudeau government, which created two out of three of these advisory councils, did not when it came down to it, really want or value that kind of advice and always held it at arm's length.

Nevertheless, the same government did introduce the Immigration Act 1976 which established a mandatory and, to government, more congenial process of annual consultation on immigration levels. In this process, as we have seen, more than 100 national organizations are consulted annually and many more provincial and local organizations are invited to give their views at the regional level. There is also an annual consultation with organizations and groups concerned with refugee policy and settlement. Business and labour as well as a few of the larger national organizations and ethnic groups are able to prepare well-researched briefs which are taken into account; the voluntary agencies and smaller ethnic organizations at least get a hearing. This is, of course, a more manageable and controllable way of taking advice than via advisory councils.

There is no doubt that consultation on immigration and related policies with the concerned public (and here and there with the general public) and with it documentation of a much more detailed and attractive kind took a great leap forward in both countries in the mid-seventies. In Australia, this process probably began with the National Population Inquiry whose principal report was submitted to the Minister for Labor and Immigration in January 1975; in Canada it began with preparations for the Green Paper on Immigration Policy tabled in the House of Commons one month later.

In the matter of interest group impact, Australia has had the inestimable advantage throughout the post-war period of having two effective advisory councils in immigration: the Immigration Planning and Immigration Advisory councils and their successors. These councils could certainly convey the views of business, labor, and the community in general to government, and their advice has been valued. The Immigration Planning Council, 1949–1974, (Canadian politicians and officials should note) always had direct access to the Cabinet. Its members were distinguished, senior representatives of business, labor, and other walks of life in Australia. The council, which worked closely with the Department of Immigration (the Secretary of the Department was always an *ex officio* member), advised the Minister on the immigration program for the coming financial year and on longer-term economic and demographic trends and their implications for immigration. In tabling a special report from the council, "Australia's Immigration Programme for the Period 1968 to 1973," on September 10, 1968, the then Minister for Immigration, B.M. (Billy) Snedden, thanked the council for their valuable report which he said would be given wide distribution. "The members of the Planning Council," the Minister said, "are all very busy men who occupy positions of leadership in various spheres of activity. They have devoted a great deal of time to the preparation of this report and they have produced a document which adds considerably to our knowledge of the problems we must face and solve if immigration is to continue to be the vital force in our national development that it has been during the last two decades."[7]

When the L-NCP Coalition was returned to power in 1975, it reconstituted the Australian Population and Immigration Council (APIC) created by the Whitlam government a year earlier. As we have seen in Chapter 3, APIC was a very distinguished council, and it was chaired for the first time by the Minister, Michael MacKellar. This arrangement continues today, and the National Population Council, created by the Hawke government, is also chaired by the Minister. Some might object that this ministerial presence diminishes the independence of the council, but this has not been the case, with APIC or with its successor ACPEA (the Australian Council on Population and Ethnic Affairs) or with the present council. The simple fact is that talent and a natural independence of mind are rarely constrained in this way, even if the wish to constrain them were there which was not the case.

During two long visits to Australia in 1977–1978 and 1980–1981, the author was fortunate in being made an honorary member of APIC, and being able to attend most of the meetings of the whole council and some of its committee meetings. There was no comparison between the level of discussion and constructive contribution of APIC and the operations of the Canada Manpower and Immigration Council and its advisory Board on the Adjustment of Immigrants of which she had earlier been a member, or of the Canada Employment and Immigration Advisory Council whose proceedings she has been able to observe or study. The essential difference – and it is a very important one – lies in the relationship between the advisory council and government. In Australia, APIC was a senior partner in policy-making and was both trusted and very well-informed. The Canadian advisory councils in this field have not been trusted by government, have not operated at a sufficiently senior level, and, so far, have not been allowed to play any significant role. Another important factor is the quality and talent of the membership. With only a few exceptions, Canada has simply not used her best talent in the service of this important area of public policy, as Australia has done, and has failed conspicuously thus far to appoint academic specialists to these councils.

In a field where it is not easy to make a constructive contribution to policy-making and where government anxieties about political repercussions and representations are acute, an advisory council can serve a very useful purpose. If given the opportunity to do so, it can provide advice to government in a much more sustained, thorough, and better informed way, covering a wider range of issues, than any once-a-year consultation can achieve. By working closely with an immigration department and having continuous access to a high level of information in this area, council members acquire a thorough knowledge of immigration, its management, and problems which can be useful to the community in many ways, on and off the council. An advisory council can also perform a valuable function as a principal spokesman for immigration, an area of public policy that has no political influence and no specific interest group of its own. In the Canada-Australia watch, therefore, Canada should take much more note of Australia's long and successful experience with advisory councils in immigration.

RECENT IMMIGRATION PROGRAMS

During the last few years, both Canada and Australia reduced their intake of immigrants drastically in response to the recent world recession and its impact on their economies and levels of unemployment. In Australia, the reduction was also due to the Hawke government's initial belief that immigration should not be a major supplier of skilled labour, and that a large annual intake of immigrants was undesirable. As of December 1984, the seasonally adjusted unemployment rate in Canada was 10.8 per cent and in Australia 8.5 per cent. In 1983, Canada admitted 89,157 immigrants including refugees, and in 1983-1984, Australia admitted 69,805. A glance at the immigration statistics in Appendix 1 will show how low those levels are for the post-war period.

Both countries reduced immigration by cutting down their intake of what Canada calls "independent immigrants" and Australia "skilled labor migration," that is, those who have no relatives to sponsor them and are admitted by virtue of their skills and talents. There were also reductions in the more distant relative categories. In both countries, the closer family and refugee categories – the most politically sensitive areas – remained as they were or were only slightly reduced. Canada achieved this recent reduction in intake by what was called a "Restriction on Selected Workers" regulation introduced on May 1, 1982, which specified that only selected workers with some form of arranged employment were eligible for admission. This regulation had a dramatic effect. In 1981, there were 21,172 landings in this part of the immigration movement. In 1982 there were 18,143 but in 1983, they amounted to only 6,439.[8]

Australia also used the device of requiring a job offer to reduce the numbers of her Category C family migrants (brothers, sisters, and non-dependent children). In February 1984, the Minister, Stewart West, together with the Minister for Employment and Industrial Relations, Ralph Willis, also announced new plans "to reduce the reliance on skilled migrant workers." The essence of the strategy, they said, was "to change the balance between domestic and overseas skilled labor supply for the long-term benefit of existing workers and the community at large." Both ministers emphasized that it would in no way impinge on the Government's commitment to maintain the priority it had accorded to family and refugee migration.[9]

These substantial reductions in the numbers of independent immigrants or skilled labour migrants meant that it was very difficult if not impossible to be admitted to Canada or Australia in the early 1980s *unless* one had relatives (and preferably close relatives) there, or a job offer, or an occupation in very special demand, or unless one was a refugee or could successfully claim refugee status. The category of immigrants with skills and talents has always been regarded in Canada and Australia (and in the United States) as a valuable element in immigration, from which some of the most creative and enterprising immigrants have come, but at that time a great many were being excluded. By contrast, both Canada and Australia – in what has always been an area of friendly competition – were then putting enthusiastic emphasis on enhanced business migration programs. These programs do not produce large numbers, but they do produce significant if not very large infusions of capital, new technology, and it is hoped, additional employment-creating capacity.

The essential features, then, of Canadian and Australian Immigration up to the end of 1984 comprised (1) major emphasis on close family and refugee migration; (2) substantial reductions in the admission of skilled immigrants; (3) a major emphasis on business migration programs; and (4) no emphasis at all on immigration for population growth, or for future population maintenance, or to help achieve a more balanced age distribution within the Canadian and Australian populations. As we shall see, however, there is every sign now that this period of restricted immigration in both countries, far from being a permanent condition as some have suggested, is coming to an end.

Tables 11 and 12 give a profile of the immigration movement to Canada in 1983 and to Australia in 1983–1984, to illustrate the effect of these restrictions. Of Canada's immigrants, 38.3 per cent came from Asia and the Pacific; 27.3 per cent came from Europe including the United

Table 11
Canada: Landings by Class, 1983

	No.
Family Class	48,698
Convention Refugees	4,100
Designated Class (Refugees)	9,867
Assisted Relatives	9,867
Retired	2,094
Entrepreneurs	1,865
Self-Employed	4,360
Independent	13,176
TOTAL	89,157

Source: Canada Employment and Immigration Commission

Table 12
Australia: 1983–1984 Immigration Program

	No.
Family Migration	
Sub-categories A and B[a]	22,673
Sub-category C[b]	14,066
SUB-TOTAL	36,739
Skilled labor and business migration	
Skilled labor	4,189
Employer nominees	3,067
Business migrants	1,453
Independent migration[c]	136
Special Eligibility[d]	443
SUB-TOTAL	9,288
Refugee and Special Humanitarian Programs	15,485
Old Policy[e]	838
TOTAL	62,350[f]

Source: Australia, Department of Immigration and Ethnic Affairs
Notes
(a) Spouses, dependent children, retired parents, and parents of working age in certain conditions.
(b) Brothers, sisters, and non-dependent children.
(c) This category provides for the admission of a limited number of outstanding applicants of obvious benefit to Australia who are not eligible for consideration in other categories.
(d) New Zealand citizens plus people with special creative and sporting talents, and self-supporting retirees.
(e) People visaed in 1983–1984 but who were approved under the policy in force before April 19, 1982.
(f) Australia records visaed migrants (62,350 in 1983–1984) and settler arrivals (69,805). The program is defined by the number of visas issued. Settler arrivals represent the actual impact of the program.

Kingdom; 17.6 per cent came from the Americas excluding the United States; 8.3 per cent came from the United States; and 8.3 per cent came from Africa and the Middle East. Possibly temporarily, because of the large Indochinese refugee movement, the Asia and Pacific region has supplanted Europe as the principal source of Canada's immigrants; but numbers from that region have been growing steadily recently, as well as from the Americas excluding the United States. Following a well-established pattern in provincial distribution during the post-war period, just over 40,000 immigrants, or almost 45 per cent of the total movement in 1983, were destined for Ontario, 18.4 per cent went to Quebec, and 16.2 per cent to British Columbia. Alberta received 12 per cent of the total movement, the three Prairie provinces had a combined total of 18.4 per cent, and the four Atlantic provinces a total of just under 2 per cent.[10]

According to their region of last residence, 25,324 of the settler arrivals in Australia in 1983–1984 came from Asia (these numbers reflect the Indochinese refugee movement); 13,624 came from Britain and Ireland; 6,072 from Northern Europe, 4,774 from Southern Europe; 3,561 from the Middle East; 3,237 from Africa; 3,060 from the United States and Canada; 2,061 from Central and South America; and 8,092 from Oceania. In relation to distribution among states and territories, 25,916 or 37.1 per cent of these migrants were destined for New South Wales; 18,350 or 26.3 per cent for Victoria; 8,663 or 12.4 per cent for Queensland; 8,761 or 12.6 per cent for Western Australia; 5,134 or 7.4 per cent for South Australia; and less than 2 per cent each for Tasmania, the Northern Territory, and the Australian Capital Territory.[11]

POPULATION OUTCOME: ETHNIC ORIGINS IN THE 1980S

Canada today has a more ethnically diversified population than Australia, chiefly because of her two founding peoples and the much larger numbers of Europeans who entered Canada in the late 19th and early 20th centuries. Because of this, Canada had more experience of ethnic diversity and of larger non-majority, ethnic communities at an earlier stage. Proximity to the United States has contributed to this experience, but often in conflicting ways – demonstrating the dangers and evils of racial conflict and racial discrimination, but at the same time emphasizing the advantages of homogeneity. Despite this ethnic diversity and longer experience of ethnic difference, which may result in more tolerant attitudes and less potential hostility towards new ethnic communities and visible minorities today, Canada – as we have seen – discriminated against non-white immigrants from the late 19th century onwards with the same determination as Australia and for the same reasons, only seeing compelling reasons to change 11 years earlier. Neither country, we have to note, was prepared even to think about a universal, non-discriminatory immigration policy until full national independence, a reasonably well developed political system, adequate citizenship legislation, and really encouraging economic prospects and the confidence which goes with them, had been achieved. This came only after World War II.

We will now look at the immigrant element and ethnic composition of the Canadian and Australian populations as shown in the 1981 Census in each country. Statistics Canada reports that on census day, June 3, 1981, there were 3.8 million immigrants in Canada,[12] making up 16 per cent of the total population – higher than the percentage in the United States (5 per cent) but lower than in Australia (20 per cent). Among the people identified as immigrants at the time of the 1981 census, close to a third, 1.15 million, had come to Canada in the past decade and another quarter had arrived between 1960 and 1971. In all, about 85 per cent had arrived since World War II. Overall, more than 6 in 10 had come from Europe, although this varied by period of immigration. The largest percentage of immigrants from Great Britain, Scandinavia, Poland, Austria, and the USSR had come before 1961. The countries of Northern and Western Europe accounted for half the immigrants who arrived in that period; Southern Europe, 17 per cent, Eastern Europe and the U.S.S.R., 20 per cent, and the United States another 8 per cent. Very few who had come before 1961 were from Third World countries. Just 3 per cent were from Asia and 1 per cent from countries in the Caribbean and Central and South America. All of Africa accounted for less than half of one per cent.

By the 1960s, however, mainly because of the change to a universal, non-discriminatory immigration policy in Canada's 1962 Immigration Regulations, the pattern of source countries was moving away from Northern and Western Europe towards Southern Europe, Asia, the Caribbean, and Central and South America. Although Great Britain remained the single most important source, 3 out of 10 of the immigrants who had come during this decade were from Southern Europe. The most spectacular increases, however, were for immigrants from Asia, the Caribbean, and Central and South America, whose shares of the total rose to 12 per cent and 8 per cent respectively. Between 1971 and 1981, immigrants from these areas have represented even larger proportions of all arrivals. The 1981 count of the 1.15 million who had come after 1970 showed that 33 per cent were from Asia and 16 per cent from the Caribbean and Central and South America. The proportion from Africa was only 5.5 per cent, but this marked a considerable increase over the 0.4 per cent of those who had arrived before 1961. Europe remained the principal source of immigrants, however, although it only represented just over 34 per cent of those who had come between 1971 and 1981. Not quite 14 per cent came from Great Britain, although it was still the leading source of immigrants. There was a major decline in the number of immigrants from Eastern Europe and the USSR, who represented only 3 per cent of the arrivals in this decade. The United States, on the other hand, gained a little, rising to 8.5 per cent of the 1971–1981 immigrants.

Tables 13 and 14 show the number of immigrants from the 10 leading

Table 13
Canada: Ten Leading Countries of Birth of Immigrants: Before 1961, 1961–1970, and 1971–1981

Before 1961

Country of birth	*No.*	*% of Total Immigrants*
Great Britain	524,900	29.8
Italy	214,700	12.2
United States	136,900	7.8
Poland	118,000	6.7
U.S.S.R.	112,600	6.4
Netherlands	112,400	6.4
Federal Republic of Germany	107,200	6.1
Yugoslavia	39,000	2.2
German Democratic Republic	28,400	1.6
Austria	28,300	1.6
Immigrants from ten leading countries as a percentage of all immigrants who arrived before 1961		80.8

1961–1970

Country of birth	*No.*	*% of Total Immigrants*
Great Britain	195,300	21.1
Italy	141,000	15.2
United States	67,000	7.2
Portugal	57,300	6.2
Greece	40,700	4.4
Yugoslavia	33,200	3.6
Federal Republic of Germany	31,400	3.4
India	28,200	3.0
Jamaica	23,600	2.5
France	19,100	2.1
Immigrants from ten leading countries as a percentage of all immigrants who arrived during the 1961–1970 period		68.7

1971–1981

Country of birth	*No.*	*% of Total Immigrants*
Great Britain	158,800	13.8

Table 13 (continued)

United States	97,600	8.5
India	75,000	6.5
Portugal	66,400	5.8
Philippines	55,300	4.8
Socialist Republic of Vietnam	49,400	4.3
Hong Kong	42,200	3.7
Italy	29,100	2.5
Guyana	27,500	2.4
Immigrants from leading countries as a percentage of all immigrants who arrived during the 1971–1981 period		52.3

Source: 1981 Census of Canada

Table 14
Canada: Immigration by World Area, 1981–1983

	1981		1982		1983	
	Landings	%	Landings	%	Landings	%
Africa and the Middle East	10,254	8.0	9,859	8.1	7,606	8.5
Asia and the Pacific	45,716	35.5	38,459	31.8	34,171	38.3
Americas (excl. USA)	15,783	12.3	17,196	14.2	15,687	17.6
USA	10,559	8.2	9,360	7.7	7,381	8.3
Europe (incl. UK)	46,299	36.0	46,156	38.1	24,312	27.3
Not stated	7	–	117	0.1	–	–
TOTAL	128,618	100.0	121,147	100.0	89,157	100.0

Source: Canada Employment and Immigration Commission

countries of birth as a percentage of all immigrants who arrived in Canada before 1961 and during the 1961–1970 and 1971–1981 periods; and immigration to Canada by world area, 1981–1983.

There have been substantial changes in recent years in the sources of Canadian immigrants, particularly between 1971 and 1981. Not only have the sources changed, they have become more diverse. The 1981 census showed that 80 per cent of the immigrants who had arrived before 1961 came from only 10 countries. The 10 leading countries between 1971 and 1981 accounted for only 57 per cent of the immigrants during those years.[13]

Today, approximately 43.5 per cent of Canada's population is of British origin, 28.9 per cent of French origin, and about 27.5 per cent of other

Table 15
Canada: Population by Ethnic Origin, 1981

Total Population	24,083,495
Native Peoples	413,380
Status Indians	266,420
Non-Status Indians	47,235
Inuit	23,200
Métis	76,520
European Origins	20,762,025
British	9,674,250
French	6,439,100
German	1,142,365
Italian	747,970
Ukrainian	529,615
Netherlands	408,235
Scandinavian	282,795
Jewish	264,020
Polish	254,485
Portuguese	188,105
Balkans (including Yugoslavia)	129,075
Hungarian	116,395
Czecho-Slovakia	67,700
Spanish	53,540
Finnish	52,315
Baltic	50,300
Russian	49,430
Belgian	42,270
Austrian	40,630
Swiss	29,805
Romanian	22,485
Maltese	15,440
North and South American Origins	530,930
American (Birthplace)	312,000
Caribbean	81,605
Latin America	117,555
Haitian	15,295
African Origins	45,215
Asian and African Origins	830,930
Indo-Pakistani	196,390
Asian Arab	50,140
Lebanese	27,320
Armenian	21,155
North African Arab	10,545
Egyptian	9,140
Far East Asian Origins	407,085
Chinese	289,245
Indo-Chinese	43,725
(Burmese, Cambodian, Laotian, Thai)	
Japanese	40,995

Table 15 (continued)

Vietnamese	31,360
Korean	22,095
Pacific Islands Origins	80,340
Philippine	72,630

Source: 1981 Census of Canada
Note: Demographers point out that changes in procedures for the 1981 census, allowing for multiple ethnic origins, have affected the comparability of 1981 and earlier ethnic census data for single ethnic origins. The 1981 estimates for single ethnic origins are likely to underestimate the totals that would have been obtained had the 1971 census procedures been retained. In general, data on ethnic origin must therefore be interpreted with caution, particularly for groups that have experienced considerable mobility over long periods of time and others which have emigrated to Canada from North and South America and particularly from the Caribbean. This may also apply to some of Canada's native peoples.

origins. Although immigrants constitute a higher proportion of Australia's population today (20 per cent to Canada's 16 per cent) Australia is in fact far more homogeneous than Canada. In a detailed study based on 1976 census material and published in 1979 with a supplement in 1981, Charles Price, Australia's well-known social historian and demographer, estimated that Australians of British origin represented 76.95 per cent of the population.[14] Table 15, taken from 1981 census material, shows Canada's population by ethnic origin, giving the major and medium-sized groups only.

Australia's non-Aboriginal population was primarily of British origin until after World War II. Before that, only about one tenth of the settlers had come from other countries. After the end of the war, however, there were major increases in immigration from European countries as we have seen. By 1961 there were 228,296 Italian-born immigrants in Australia, 109,315 of German descent, 102,083 from the Netherlands, 77,333 from Greece, and 49,776 from Yugoslavia. The percentage of the population born in Australia fell from 90.8 per cent in 1947 to 80.5 per cent in 1971, while the percentage of European-born rose from 8.6 per cent to 17.2 per cent. The numbers of Asian-born, although increasing, were only a very small percentage of the population, 1.3 per cent, in 1971. By 1978, however, as a result of the Whitlam government's decision in 1973 to abandon the White Australia policy and the increasing number of Asian refugees, the Asian-born element in the population had increased to 2 per cent of the population. The foreign-born element comprised 20 per cent of the population, of which 40 per cent were of British origin and 40 per cent of European origin. The most rapidly increasing birthplace group since 1970 has been New Zealanders with a population in Australia of 183,200 in 1981.[15] Figure 1 and Tables 16 and 17 show Australia's source countries 1947–1981; birthplaces of the Australian population, 1947–1981; and ethnic origins of the Australian population, 1961–1978.

Figure 1
Australia: The Changing Face of Immigration

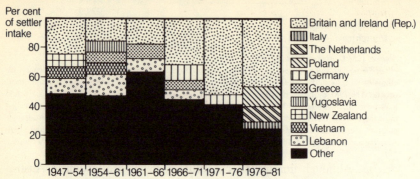

Source: Department of Immigration and Ethnic Affairs, Australian Immigration Consolidated
Statistics, various issues.

Major birthplace groups, 1981 (per cent)

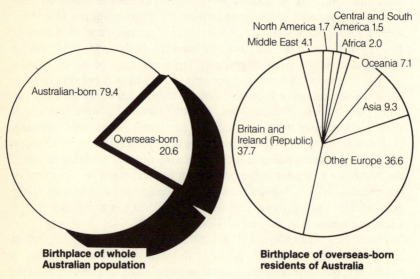

Source: Australian Bureau of Statistics and Department of Immigration and Ethnic Affairs.

Table 16
Australia: Birthplaces of the Population

Birthplace	1947	1961	1971	1981
Australia	6835171	8729406	10176320	11758411
New Zealand	43610	47011	80466	183200
Total*	6880367	8780173	10266431	11951761
Europe				
England	381592	556478	842032	918250
Scotland	102998	132811	159292	156300
Wales	11864	16898	230996	24850
Ireland†	44813	50215	63770	69800
Italy	33632	228296	289476	2833300
Germany	14567	109315	110811	1113950
Poland	6573	60049	59700	60950
Netherlands	2174	102083	99295	98800
Greece	12291	77333	160200	150550
Malta	3238	39337	53681	58700
Yugoslavia	5866	49776	129816	153600
Baltic States	1822	24487	26482	23500
Hungary	1227	30553	24160	28700
Soviet Union	4976	29546	27660	28600
Czechoslovakia	1484	12132	16602	16600
Austria	4219	23807	23941	23450
Total*	651606	1596212	2196478	2299800
Asia & Pacific				
Islands				
India, Pakistan				
Bangladesh &				
Sri Lanka	8610	17599	39960	63959
China	6404	14486	17601	27550
Cyprus	681	8576	13267	24050
Other Asia	8401	38395	96398	329041
Total*	24096	79056	167226	444600
Africa				
Egypt	803	16287	28226	31550
Union of				
South				
Africa	5866	7896	12655	27800
Total*	7537	28559	61935	61500
America				
United States	6293	10818	*30035	33700
Canada	4061	5990	12838	18250
Total*	11691	14538	55752	99200
GRAND TOTAL	7579358	10508186	12755638	14854861

††Published census figures except for 1981 which is based on an analysis of 1981 census topic by Dr. C. A. Price.
†Includes Northern Ireland. Republic of Ireland and undefined Ireland.
*Includes groups not specified.

Table 17

Ethnic Origins of the Australian Population, 1861–1978[1] (in percentages)

ORIGIN	1861[2]	1891[2]	1947	1978
English	42.457	47.137	50.878	45.37
Scottish	12.371	13.516	14.692	12.25
Irish	22.090	24.814	22.798	17.62
Welsh	1.254	1.487	1.578	1.39
Channels etc.	.201	.263	.263	0.22
Total British	78.373	87.217	90.209	76.85
Italian	.065	.205	.935	4.17
Greek	.035	.063	.300	2.35
Maltese	.004	.007	.086	.82
Spanish	.043	.106	.130	.54
Portuguese	.017	.026	.024	.14
Albanian	–	.002	.023	.03
Other Sth.	–	.002	.004	.01
Estonian	.001	.002	.017	.06
Latvian	.004	.014	.023	.18
Lithuanian	.004	.017	.023	.10
(Total Baltic)	(.009)	(.033)	(.063)	(.34)
Bulgarian	.002	.003	.011	.02
Czechoslovak	.009	.022	.043	.18
Hungarian	.009	.017	.036	.39
Polish	.115	.233	.317	.95
Rumanian	.004	.017	.025	.07
Russian, Ukraine	.026	.077	.200	.47
Serb. Croat, Slovene	.017	.081	.200	1.55
Macedonian	–	.001	.032	.15
Total East Europe	.191	.484	.927	4.12

ORIGIN	1861	1891	1947	1978
Egyptian	.001	.001	.003	.19
Turk	.001	.002	.003	.18
Lebanese-Syrian	.004	.091	.118	.60
Other West Asia[3]	.001	.003	.005	.04
Armenian	.001	.001	.005	.09
Assyrian	–	–	–	.05
Total W. Asian	.008	.098	.134	1.15
Afghan	.001	.017	.014	.01
Indian	.130	.242	.078	.18
Pakistani	.009	.036	.011	.02
Bangladeshi	.002	.002	.002	
Sri Lankan	.007	.031	.010	.07
Total Sth. Asian	.149	.328	.115	.28
Burmese	–	–	.001	.03
Thai	–	–	.001	.02
Indo-Chinese	–	–	.001	.06
Malay	.003	.013	.016	.07
Indonesian	.002	.008	.006	.04
Filipino	.002	.011	.006	.04
E.Timorese	.001	.001	.003	.01
Total S.E. Asia	.008	.033	.034	.27
Chinese	2.842	1.593	.223	.27
Japanese	.001	.020	.008	.04
Korean	–	–	.001	.02
Other Asian	–	–	–	.01
Total	2.843	1.613	.232	.34

Danish	.246	.452	.412	.41
Norwegian	.074	.210	.218	.17
Swedish	.172	.397	.398	.30
Finnish	.017	.035	.056	.13
(Scandinavian)	(.509)	(1.094)	(1.084)	(1.01)
Austrian	.017	.045	.108	.31
German	3.741	4.205	3.936	4.07
Dutch	.112	.120	.216	1.53
French	.342	.422	.417	.47
Belgian	.026	.037	.041	.07
Swiss	.101	.142	.145	.17
Other Nth.	.005	.029	.025	.05
Total Nth. Europe	4.853	6.094	5.972	7.68
African	.020	.027	.021	.09
American	.003	.004	.014	.04
Pacific Islander	.037	.302	.070	.12
Total	.060	.333	.105	.25
Aborigine, T.S.I.	13.351	3.389	.770	1.00
TOTAL	100.000	100.000	100.000	100.000
Numbers (000's)[4]	1348.1	3279.5	7709.4	14263.1
European	83.581	94.206	98.610	96.71
Non-European	16.419	5.794	1.390	3.29

Source: Charles A. Price, "The Ethnic Composition of the Australian Population", Table 4.6 in *Australian Immigration, a Bibliography and Digest*, (ed. Charles A. Price), No. 4, 1979, Department of Demography, Australian National University, Canberra, p. A96.

Notes:

1. Australian-born descendants, and persons born in the Americas, Asia, Africa and Oceania are distributed between ancestral ethnic groups. Jewish persons are in ancestral countries of birth. Descent calculated by averaging paternal and maternal lines of descent – ethnicity estimated from birthplace origins.

2. Birthplaces not shown in 1861 and 1891 censuses have been extracted from "Other Asia," and similar categories by using details on naturalization records.

3. Western Asia includes Asia west of Afghanistan and south of Russia.

4. Totals for 1861, 1891 and 1947 differ from published census totals as they include estimates for Aborigines.

FUTURE PROSPECTS FOR IMMIGRATION

Although immigration and particularly the incidence of refugee movements are always unpredictable, it seems probable that the changes in
source countries which we have seen in Canadian immigration since 1962,
and in Australian immigration since the early seventies, are likely to continue in the foreseeable future. Increasing proportions of immigrants to
both countries are likely to come from Asia and the Third World, the
regions of rapid, continuing population growth where the demand to
migrate will probably be very high. It seems likely also that, primarily for
four major reasons, Canada and Australia will continue to admit immigrants – probably in quite substantial numbers – for some time to come.
These reasons are:

1 The real prospect for both countries, as for other developed, industrialized countries, of future population decline – perhaps starting a little
earlier in Canada than in Australia – and the need for increased immigration beginning very soon now, in order, at least to maintain existing
population levels or to achieve limited population growth after the turn of
the century.

2 The continuing belief by many Canadians and Australians (in good
economic times) that immigration is still an important factor in national
development and prosperity.

3 The distinct probability that, unless political and economic co-operation of a much more developed and effective kind takes place between the
affluent, industrialized part of the world and an increasingly over-popu-
lated and often impoverished Third World (in which about 75 per cent of
the world's population now lives), we and our children are going to see a
very considerable out-migration from the latter. With the increasing movement of undocumented migrants towards the more prosperous cities and
regions of the world, this has in fact already started. Countries of immigration like Canada and Australia, with stable political systems, a high
standard of living, and apparently endless living space, may well have to
find ways of coming to terms with it.

4 The effect of climatic change. As a result of the rapid increase of
carbon dioxide, as well as other elements in the atmosphere, due to human
interference, scientists are predicting a major warming trend in the earth's
climate which, they believe, has already started.[16] This will bring with it
warmer temperatures at all times of the year right across Canada, which
would be higher in the higher latitudes. At the same time, substantially
increased rainfall is predicted for some parts of Australia beginning in the
fairly near future. If these remarkable climatic changes take place, as

predicted, it could mean that both countries could support distinctly larger populations in the future.

Demographers agree today that, barring unexpected developments, most developed, industrialized countries, including Canada and Australia, are now set on a course leading to population decline in the next century. The well-known American demographer, Leon Bouvier, writes:

Sometime around 1973, a momentous new demographic phenomenon began to unfold throughout most of the developed world – fertility fell below the level of 2.1 births per woman needed to replace the population in the long run and *remained there* ... Actual population size did not begin to fall immediately in the early seventies ... because all of these nations experienced a rise in their fertility rate after World War II; some for just a few years; others like Australia, Canada and the United States for 10 to 15 years ... Never before in modern history has fertility been so low in so many countries for such a long period as has been the case since 1973. And as of 1984, the rate in most developed countries shows no evidence of climbing back to the point where population growth, or at least population replacement, can be assured over the long run.[17]

Major demographic changes have been taking place in the developing world as well. A dramatic fall in mortality after the end of World War II in Asia and Latin America, though not in Africa, combined with fertility rates which remained very high, has created a tremendous momentum for population growth. In many developing countries today, the percentage of the population under the age of 15 is close to 50 per cent.

Canadians and Australians are used to the idea of population growth, indeed they have expected it. Efforts to establish strong lobbies for "zero population growth" in both countries, following the publication of Paul Ehrlich's *The Population Bomb* in 1968, quickly petered out.[18] A sense of ease seems to come with the possession of very large territories, however inhospitable parts of them may be. This implies that a larger population can always be accommodated somewhere within this vast domain, and that it would be unnatural to put limitations on its growth. Today, however, the fertility rates for Canada and Australia stand at 1.6 and 1.8 respectively. Until recently, immigration levels, as we have seen, have been very low. Difficult decisions are being taken now by both countries in relation to population and immigration policy, in light of the prospect of future population decline.

Australia's demographic situation is slightly more encouraging than Canada's. In both countries, however, the population is ageing at a similar rate. In Australia, with an average annual net migration gain of 75,000, higher than at present, the median age is likely to rise from 29.6 years in

1981 to about 38.2 years in 2021. In Canada, the median age was close to 30 in 1981 and will probably be close to 40 in 2021.[19]

In the mid-eighties in Canada, the prospect of future population decline has begun to cause some alarm, mainly in government circles. The Mulroney government has started to respond to it and the opening moves are being made in what may soon become a wider public discussion in Canada on this serious national problem. In Quebec, where the fertility rate declined to 1.45 births in 1983 (the lowest in Canada), a National Assembly committee has recently held special hearings on the demographic situation. In the background paper Future Immigration Levels, tabled with the Annual Report to Parliament in November 1984, the issue was raised for the first time in Canada in very explicit terms. The paper pointed out that constant net immigration of 50,000 (net immigration here means gross immigration minus emigration) currently estimated by Statistics Canada at 50,000 per annum) and constant fertility at 1.7 would, for example, result in the following developments:

- from the year 2001 onward, the contribution of net immigration to total annual population growth would exceed the contribution from natural increase (births minus deaths);
- from the year 2015 onward, net immigration would be the only positive contributor to Canadian population growth because natural increase would be negative (deaths would exceed births thereafter); and
- from the year 2021 onward, net annual immigration of 50,000 would be exceeded by natural decrease, and the total Canadian population would have begun to decline.

The paper then presented five population outcomes for Canada, between 10 and 50 million, showing the combinations of fertility and net immigration needed to produce stable populations of these sizes over a long period of time. It concludes that:

- assuming a continuation of current fertility (1.7) and net immigration of 50,000 per year, the eventual stationary Canadian population would be slightly above 10 million;
- to maintain the current level of Canada's population at about 25 million, if fertility remained constant at 1.7, net annual immigration to Canada would have to more than double, to about 125,000, for the long term; and
- assuming constant fertility of 1.7, each additional 50,000 immigrants would add about 10 million to the stable Canadian population.

The paper emphasizes that "assuming current trends continue, the rest of this century will be the last period of any robust demographic growth in Canada. The following 20-year period (2000-2020) will be greatly influenced by the demographic events of 1980-2020. Were fertility to stay at or below current levels and annual net immigration to be held to a minimum of 50,000, growth would diminish; decline would begin by about 2020. Lower net immigration would advance the timetable and move the onset of decline closer to the year 2001."[20]

A recent study of Canadian fertility by Anatole Romaniuc of Statistics Canada entitled *Fertility in Canada: From Baby-boom to Baby-bust*, presents a similar view of Canada's demographic future and of the important role which immigration is likely to play in it. While not discounting the possibility that Canada's fertility rate may still be subject to "the swings which seem characteristic of modern society," Dr. Romaniuc believes that these swings are likely to be of smaller amplitude than in the past. His conclusion on the implications for immigration policy is as follows: "The current regime of low fertility, and the consequent ageing and slowdown of growth in the Canadian population, are creating an historically new situation which may affect long-term immigration strategies. Indeed if the fertility rate does not increase substantially and if population growth is a national goal, then large-scale immigration is clearly the alternative. In order to ensure a population growth of 1 per cent per year, the number of immigrants would have to be gradually raised to reach 275,000 by the end of the century ... If the total fertility rate were to drop to 1.4 births, the number of immigrants required, according to Dr. Romaniuc, might reach 325,000 by the year 2000. Even if the fertility rate went up to 2.2 births, the number of immigrants would have to be raised as of the year 2000 to at least 200,000 per annum. Figure 2, taken from Dr. Romaniuc's study, illustrates this analysis.

These demographic facts and projections present Canadian politicians (who have hardly ever discussed population questions with the Canadian public) and particularly the Mulroney government with some very difficult problems. At present, as we have seen, Canada has no population policy, no administrative structure within the federal public service with sufficient authority and sufficient resources to implement one, and, unlike Australia, no advisory body on population. The most difficult problems, however, relate first, to the long-overdue education of the Canadian public in population issues, and especially in the difficult choices that will have to be made from now on in relation to much higher levels of immigration; and secondly, to the real involvement of the provinces in demographic decision-making and future immigration planning of a much more complex and difficult kind. It will be interesting to see during the next few years whether this urgent matter of long term national survival gets the high priority it requires from the Canadian governments.

Figure 2

Canada: Immigration Required to Achieve, in the Long Run, a Stationary
Population of Specified Size for Canada, Assuming a Constant Level of Sub-
replacement Fertility.

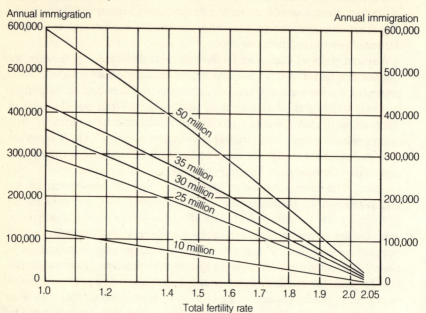

Source: Employment and Immigration Canada, *The Role of Immigration in Determining Canada's
Eventual Population Size*, Ottawa, June 1983

For the present, however, the Mulroney government is approaching this
question cautiously through further investigation and research, while
embarking on moderate initial increases in immigration levels. As we have
seen in Chapter 2, a major, two-stage review of current immigration policies and programs, including a good deal of public consultation, was
started on November 19, 1984. In addition, the Minister of National
Health and Welfare, Jake Epp, was asked in his capacity as Chairman of
the Cabinet Committee on Social Development, to undertake "a separate
assessment of the linkage between immigration levels and future demographic needs and of the economic and social implications of the future size,
rate of growth and structure of the Canadian population." This Demographic Review which began in the fall of 1985 is expected to be completed
early in 1989.

The Hawke government in Australia has taken a rather more direct
approach. In 1985, when announcing forthcoming immigration levels in
Parliament, the Minister for Immigration, Chris Hurford, made a plain

statement explaining the serious problems of population decline and age-ing that face Australia as a result of her low level of fertility – "currently 10 per cent below the long-term population replacement level with little chance of recovery."[21] Immigration, he said, must now be seen in the context of Australia's population and economic development needs. The Government was concerned to "awaken Australia's interest in and appre-ciation of the population dimension." Its vision for the future was one of "managed, gradual expansion of the migration program." An admissions program of 95,000 was planned for 1986–1987 which represented a "mod-est initial increase" over the expected outcome of 89,000 for 1985. But for the next two years, the Government had set indicative planning levels of 110,000 and 125,000 respectively. Subject to community support, these levels could represent "a return by managed steps to historical intake levels of 160,000 to 170,000 or about 1 per cent of the population of that time," the Minister said.

On the question of long-term population options for Australia, the National Population Council had advised him, Mr. Hurford said, that:

If it were decided that Australia's population by the year 2000 should be about 19 million, then that outcome would be achieved by an average annual immigration program of 120,000, or if it were decided that there should be a population target of some 30 million by the year 2038, the 250th year of European settlement of this continent, then such an outcome could be reached with an average annual migrant intake of 160,000. Both outcomes could be achieved by manageable progressive increases in recent levels of immigration to intakes comparable to those experi-enced in the 1940s and 1960s when the population base and Australia's absorption capacity was substantially less than it is now or will be in the future.

This speech represented a significant change of direction in immigration policy for the Hawke government and the ALP. Among its interesting features the most critical was the statement that, although many Austral-ians and Australian opinion leaders have subscribed to it, "the populist view that during periods of high unemployment or economic downturn immigration is disadvantageous to the employment prospects of Austral-ians seeking to enter the labour market" is mistaken. Recent research had shown that immigration has contributed positively to economic growth and development and, even in the very short term, does not adversely affect the employment prospects of the Australian resident population. "Our understanding must be," the Minister said, "that immigrants care-fully selected create more jobs than they take." The Government was therefore creating a new category of immigrants to be called the "Indepen-dent and Concessional Category," (Concessional meaning concessions under the points system for family members eligible for admission in this category) in order to attract a wider range of people with the potential to contribute to Australia's economic and social needs. This new category is similar to the Independent category in the Canadian system, which is now being re-activated.

These actions of the Canadian and Australian governments speak for themselves. Among other things, they confirm that immigration and population will be critically important areas of public policy in both countries for the foreseeable future.

COMMUNITY AND RACE RELATIONS

If we envisage the possibility of much larger numbers of immigrants entering Canada and Australia in the fairly near future, and coming in substantial proportions from developing countries, how acceptable will that be to the general public in both countries? The answer will depend to a considerable extent, of course, on the degree to which these publics have been consulted and involved in the difficult process of national decision-making on population maintenance or growth in the years ahead. It will also depend on economic circumstances, and particularly on what will probably be very different employment conditions in both countries in the near future. It may depend, as we have seen, on the possibility of favourable climatic change and the degree of optimism that may generate. And it will depend, of course, on the state of international relations, particularly between developed and developing nations, and the degree to which the Pacific region, for example, becomes, as expected, a vital centre of world political and economic activity. What indications do we have now from the present state of community and race relations in Canada and Australia which might provide some enlightenment in this area?

A sudden storm blew up in Australia in March 1984 over the issue of Asian immigration. It started in the country town of Warrnambool in Victoria where the well-known Australian historian Geoffrey Blainey of the University of Melbourne addressed a gathering of Rotarians. Among other things, he is reported to have said that the pace of Asian immigration was now well ahead of public opinion, and that the continued entry of Asians at the present rate could "weaken or explode" the tolerance extended to immigrants over the past 30 years. At the same time, a new Gallup poll on immigration was published in Australia, producing the now standard result (in Australia and Canada), within a small range, that 62 per cent of the Australian community disapproved of the increasing proportion of immigrants coming from Asia, while 64 per cent believed that the total number of migrants admitted during the current year was too large.[22]

Meanwhile, Professor Blainey's comments set off a furious storm involving government and opposition: banner headlines, special editorials, and a flood of letters to the editor in the press; prime time attention on television and radio; minor racist organizations having a field day and anti-Asian slogan painters and graffiti writers in their element. It has all been described as "a rough free-for-all lasting well over three months."[23] Professor Blainey elaborated his views on immigration in subsequent articles in *The Age* and *The Herald* (March 30 and April 4, 1984) and probably on other occasions, as well as in a particularly unpleasant small paperback entitled *All for Australia*. His views included considerable doubts about the effectiveness of multiculturalism as a national policy in Australia, and the consistent presentation of Asian immigration as a threat, without any regard for the international environment of migration today, or for Australia's place in the Pacific region, or for the facts of Asian immigration and settlement in Australia – an immigrant community which, as we have seen, represents only 2 per cent of the population. It was also implied that Australia will always prefer immigrants from the traditional sources, the United Kingdom and Europe.

In terms that were very pejorative to Asian immigrants and refugees, Professor Blainey also claimed that Asian immigrants present problems for Australia because of their "lack of experience in democracy." In this regard, he mentioned two special concerns: that Asians have no experience of democratic practices, procedures, and beliefs in such areas as religious tolerance or civil liberties, and that Asians could place a strain on Australia's democratic institutions by "creating tensions," or being the source of tensions created by others. In these matters, it might be pointed out that comments like these not only reveal a profound ignorance of the immigration process itself and all the allegiances it creates, but completely fail to appreciate why a great many immigrants have come to Australia in the first place. Professor Blainey also appears to be unaware of the established fact that every wave of immigrants and every refugee movement, whether from traditional sources or not, inevitably creates some tensions in the host community. Except in unusual circumstances, it takes time – although less time today than it once did – for the host community to accept these newcomers wholeheartedly or with reasonable tolerance. Irresponsible comments like Professor Blainey's delay that acceptance, and cause pain and anxiety among immigrants and refugees themselves, thus holding back their adjustment to their new society.

Early in this short, sharp national debate on Asian immigration in Australia provoked by Professor Blainey, the L-NP entered the fray, unwisely, many Australians felt, because it helped to give the controversy a national dimension and also helped to legitimize, to some extent, Professor Blainey's point of view. The L-NP in fact used the incident, which should have been forgotten, as the occasion for an attack on the Hawke government's immigration policy. In a debate in the House on May 10, 1984, which hinged on the question of whether Asian migration was increasing at the expense of migration from the United Kingdom, Ireland, and Europe, Andrew Peacock, then Leader of the Opposition, accused the government of:

- failing to establish a proper "balance and mix of immigrants" in Australia's annual immigration program, as he said the Fraser government had done;
- presiding over a major shift in the sources of migrants, away from the UK, Ireland, and Europe and towards Asia;
- cutting back too far in the number of migrants coming to Australia in the skilled labour, business migration, and other categories, which reduced the number of UK, Irish, and European migrants;
- failing to consult community groups about these decisions, as the previous government had scrupulously done, and only consulting ACTU (the Australian Council of Trade Unions).

Finally, while proclaiming the Opposition's total commitment to a universal, non-discriminatory immigration policy, Mr. Peacock stated, "It is our contention that a balance, a mix and a proper composition in our migrant programs is essential to ensure the stability and the fabric of Australian society."[24]

It is a clear indication of the significance of this unexpected national debate that the Prime Minister himself decided to intervene. In a strong speech in the House on the same day, Mr. Hawke said: "Over the past few days, powerful emotions have been unleashed in this country and in this Parliament over the issue of immigration. We in this place have a particular responsibility to ensure that what we do and say on this matter is judicious, calm and constructive. There is a risk that if the debate on immigration loses touch with facts and departs from a civilized approach, racism and racial intolerance could be promoted to the detriment of our national unity and our basic values. I know I speak for this Government, for the Australian Labor Party and for the overwhelming majority of Australians in rejecting racial intolerance and in calling for a measured and humane discussion of these issues ..." The Prime Minister went on to state plainly that the cutbacks in immigration had been introduced by his government because of a level of unemployment unprecedented in the post-war era; and that the proportion of settlers, excluding refugees, coming to Australia from Europe, the United Kingdom, and Ireland was still higher than from any other area, despite a decline in migrant applications from that region. After refuting several other charges made by the Leader of the Opposition, and providing statistics to prove his points, the Prime

Minister came to the question of "balance": "This Government does not consider that a balance or mix in our migration program determined on racial grounds can have any place in our society. It categorically rejects the discriminatory concept of quotas which is implicit in what the Leader of the Opposition has said in recent days about increasing the number of European migrants. It also categorically rejects any proposals to introduce covert discrimination through differential standards in selection criteria." The Opposition, Mr. Hawke said, had paid lip-service to the concept of bipartisanship but, by its behaviour, had sought to undermine it. It was nonsense to claim, as the Opposition had done, that the Government was departing from a bipartisan immigration policy by running a "pro-Asian and anti-British" immigration program. However, it was not too late, Mr. Hawke said, to restore decency and common sense to the discussion, and he appealed to the Leader of the Opposition "to put an end to this debate as a party political dispute and in particular to dampen down the racial overtones which it can so easily assume." Finally, he said: "Is there anyone in this place who wants to see discrimination reintroduced into our immigration policies, with all the tragic social damage and conflict which that would bring to this great country? Does anyone here want to see Australia turn its back on those in our region who have known anguish and human suffering? Do we want to see Australia lose its reputation as a tolerant, open-hearted country which can hold its head high in the world? I know where the Government stands on this matter. I would like to believe that the Opposition stands with us."[25]

This recent episode in Australian political life has been described by Australian commentators, in the press and elsewhere, in various ways: as a demonstration of "old bigotries and old hang-overs" and an attempt to divide one Australian from another on racial grounds; as a "last gasp" view of Australia, a temporary phenomenon, "a sort of momentary fever"; and as an "uninformed, emotive and politically motivated debate." Senator Don Chipp, leader of the small parliamentary group of Australian Democrats, whose mild comments on Australia as a multiracial society caused a somewhat similar storm in 1972, said that he deplored the politicization of the debate, which had been "inflamed by intemperate remarks based on ill-considered advice coming from inaccurate information." "I do not believe that those who have provoked and continued this debate are necessarily racist," he said. "The danger is that the consequence of their inflammatory rhetoric and unsubstantiated argument is that they will encourage those underground elements of racism and prejudice that are looking for publicity and support."[26]

There has been no comparable national debate on immigration intake in Canada or on the proportion of immigrants coming from non-traditional sources which, as we have seen, is certainly increasing; and, given the common approach to immigration by the three major political parties and their common concerns in this area, it is unlikely, at least at present, that a debate of this kind would ever reach the floor of the House. But Canada is certainly not without blemishes as a multiracial society. She has her fair share of the racial antagonisms present in every political community and, in Don Chipp's words, of underground elements of racism and prejudice looking for publicity and support. Incidents of physical violence against visible minorities occur from time to time in her major cities. As in Australia, the polls do not indicate majority approval of immigration or of refugees. There is plenty of evidence of discrimination against visible minorities in employment, housing, and other areas, and of inadequate participation by these minorities in Canadian society so far, even though the overall climate is liberal.[27]

Does all this mean that, in the face of what will probably be some adverse public reaction in both countries from time to time, Canadian and Australian immigration policy will be modified in future to limit the entry of immigrants from Asia, for example, or from other non-traditional sources? In the author's view, this is very doubtful. Both Canada and Australia have made remarkable progress in the area of non-discrimination and universality in immigration policy in recent years and are very unlikely to turn back. Nor could their present international roles and image sustain such a move. In addition, the forces of change and the pull and prospects of future economic development are far too strong. The growing economic strength of the Pacific region and its increasing influence in world politics mean that both Canada and Australia will want to be increasingly involved in that region. Already Canada's trade with the Pacific area is more extensive than with the Atlantic and it appears that this trend is accelerating rapidly.[28] The present Prime Minister of Australia and his two immediate predecessors have repeatedly emphasized that Australia must be a partner in Pacific development. Most important, perhaps, the demographic factors discussed in this chapter are likely to be of increasing significance from now on. It is fair to say, therefore, that the "old bigotries and old hang-overs," of the kind we have described here, while they may create sudden storms, are unlikely to play any significant part in the future development of immigration policy in Canada and Australia.

One other point might be mentioned. Immigration to Canada and Australia during the post-war years, when very large numbers of immigrants and refugees of many national origins have been admitted, to the extent combined with natural increase of a doubling of their populations, has been a remarkably successful and peaceable process. Sociologists who try to measure degrees of adaptation to a host society rarely isolate and consider the most important adaptation of all – adaptation to the political system. This may not be difficult for immigrants and refugees who come from similar democratic societies, but could conceivably be difficult for those who come from countries with totalitarian governments of one kind or another, or with less developed political systems. But it is quite evident that this has not been the case. None of the phenomena of political discontent, or individual or group political ambitions, which might threaten the political system in Canada and Australia have occurred. It is true that some inter-group feuding and rivalries have been imported, but they have hardly affected the host societies. Some hopes for the recovery of lost homelands have been harboured, but without any base in the real political world. The truth is that there have been no riots, no breakaway political parties, no charismatic immigrant leaders, no real militancy in international causes, no internal political terrorism so far and only the isolated, individual case of a threat to national security.

Past and present critics of immigration, who express fears about immigrants and refugees who lack experience of democracy, forget how strong the appeal of democratic government and democratic societies has always been. Immigrants who have the energy to migrate, and refugees the strength to survive, are not children; they recognize a good, stable political system when they see one. Experience in Canada and Australia shows that they are much more likely to be somewhat fearful of change in their adopted country than to want to rock the boat in any way. In addition to the millions who have come in hope of a better life and wider opportunities for themselves and their children, a great many have come to Canada and Australia precisely because they are free, democratic societies, and a great many refugees find in that freedom and democratic way of life the real compensation for their earlier hardships and sufferings.

Appendixes

Immigration and Population Statistics

Table 18
Canada: Immigration by Calendar Year, 1852–1989

1852	29,307	1887	84,526	1922	64,224	1957	282,164
1853	29,464	1888	88,766	1923	133,729	1958	124,851
1854	37,263	1889	91,600	1924	124,163	1959	106,928
1855	25,296	1890	75,067	1925	84,907	1960	104,111
1856	22,544	1891	82,165	1926	135,982	1961	71,689
1857	33,854	1892	30,996	1927	158,886	1962	74,586
1858	12,339	1893	29,633	1928	166,783	1963	93,151
1859	6,300	1894	20,829	1929	164,993	1964	112,606
1860	6,276	1895	18,790	1930	104,806	1965	146,758
1861	13,589	1896	16,835	1931	27,530	1966	194,743
1862	18,294	1897	21,716	1932	20,591	1967	222,876
1863	21,000	1898	31,900	1933	14,382	1968	183,974
1864	24,779	1899	44,543	1934	12,476	1969	161,531
1865	18,958	1900	41,681	1935	11,277	1970	147,713
1866	11,427	1901	55,747	1936	11,643	1971	121,900
1867	10,666	1902	89,102	1937	15,101	1972	122,006
1868	12,765	1903	138,660	1938	17,244	1973	184,200
1869	18,630	1904	131,252	1939	16,994	1974	218,465
1870	24,706	1905	141,465	1940	11,324	1975	187,881
1871	27,773	1906	211,653	1941	9,329	1976	149,429
1872	36,578	1907	272,409	1942	7,576	1977	114,914
1873	50,050	1908	143,326	1943	8,504	1978	86,313
1874	39,373	1909	173,694	1944	12,801	1979	112,096
1875	27,382	1910	286,839	1945	22,722	1980	143,117
1876	25,633	1911	331,288	1946	71,719	1981	128,618
1877	27,082	1912	375,756	1947	64,127	1982	121,147
1878	29,807	1913	400,870	1948	125,414	1983	89,157
1879	40,492	1914	150,484	1949	95,217	1984	88,239
1880	38,505	1915	36,665	1950	73,912	1985	84,302
1881	47,991	1916	55,914	1951	194,391	1986	99,219
1882	112,458	1917	72,910	1952	164,498	1987	152,098
1883	133,624	1918	41,845	1953	168,868	1988	161,992
1884	103,824	1919	107,698	1954	154,227	1989	192,001
1885	79,169	1920	138,824	1955	109,946		
1886	69,152	1921	91,728	1956	164,857		

Source: Canada Employment and Immigration Commission

Table 19
Canada: Summary of Principal Components of Canada's Population,
1861–1981

| | Intercensal Years Data | | | | Population at End of Decade | |
Period	Births	Deaths	Immigration	Total	Canadian Born	Foreign Born
	.000	.000	.000	.000	.000	.000
1861–1871	1,369	718	183	3,689	3,064	625
1871–1881	1,477	754	353	4,325	3,722	603
1881–1891	1,538	824	903	4,833	4,189	644
1891–1901	1,546	828	326	5,371	4,672	699
1901–1911	1,931	811	1,759	7,207	5,620	1,587
1911–1921	2,380	988(1)	1,612	8,788	6,832	1,956
1921–1931	2,415	1,055	1,203	10,377	8,069	2,308
1931–1941	2,294	1,072	150	11,507	9,488	2,019
1941–1951	3,186	1,214	548	14,009(2)	11,949	2,060
1951–1961	4,468	1,320	1,543	18,238	15,394	2,844
1961–1971	4,063	1,360	1,429	21,568	18,273	3,295
1971–1981	3,589	1,647	1,447	24,083	20,216	3,867

Source: Canada Employment and Immigration Commission, Immigration Statistics, 1984.
(1) Excludes extra mortality associated with World War 1, estimated at 120,000.
(2) Includes Newfoundland which had a population of 361,416 in 1951.

Table 20
Australia: Settler Arrivals, 1959–1960 to 1989–90

1959–1960	105,887	1975–1976	52,748
1960–1961	108,291	1976–1977	73,189
1961–1962	85,808	1977–1978	75,732
1962–1963	101,888	1978–1979	68,749
1963–1964	122,318	1979–1980	81,271
1964–1965	140,152	1980–1981	111,900
1965–1966	144,055	1981–1982	118,000
1966–1967	138,676	1982–1983	93,000
1967–1968	137,525	1983–1984	69,805
1968–1969	175,657	1984–1985	77,510
1969–1970	185,099	1985–1986	92,590
1970–1971	170,011	1986–1987	113,540
1971–1972	132,719	1987–1988	143,470
1972–1973	107,401	1988–1989	145,115
1973–1974	112,712	1989–1990	121,227
1974–1975	89,147		

*1959–1960 was the first year when settler arrivals (i.e., the permanent movement) were recorded
separately.

Figure 3
Australia: Annual Migration, 1860–1973

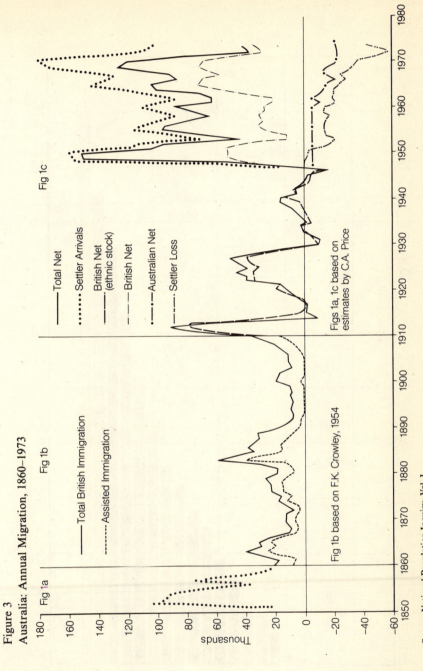

Fig 1a   Fig 1b   Fig 1c

—— Total Net
•••••• Settler Arrivals
—— British Net (ethnic stock)
––––– British Net
–•–•– Australian Net
–••–••– Settler Loss

—— Total British Immigration
----- Assisted Immigration

Figs 1a, 1c based on estimates by C.A. Price

Fig 1b based on F.K. Crowley, 1954

Thousands

180 160 140 120 100 80 60 40 20 0 -20 -40 -60

1850 1860 1870 1880 1890 1900 1910 1920 1930 1940 1950 1960 1970 1980

Source: National Population Inquiry, Vol. I

Figure 4
Australia's Population, 1788–2000

MILLIONS   MILLIONS

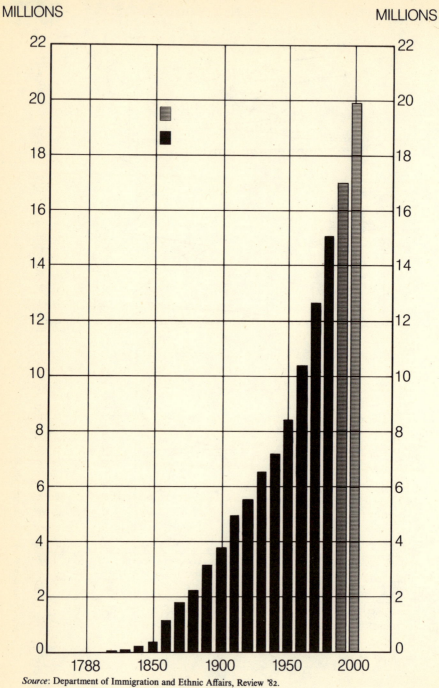

Source: Department of Immigration and Ethnic Affairs, Review '82.

Objectives and Principles of Immigration Policy

CANADA
Immigration Act 1976, Part I
Canadian Immigration Policy

Objectives

3 It is hereby declared that Canadian immigration policy and the rules and regulations made under this Act shall be designed and administered in such a manner as to promote the domestic and international interests of Canada recognizing the need

(a) to support the attainment of such demographic goals as may be established by the Government of Canada from time to time in respect of the size, rate of growth, structure and geographic distribution of the Canadian population;

(b) to enrich and strengthen the cultural and social fabric of Canada, taking into account the federal and bilingual character of Canada;

(c) to facilitate the reunion in Canada of Canadian citizens and permanent residents with their close relatives from abroad;

(d) to encourage and facilitate the adaptation of persons who have been granted admission as permanent residents to Canadian society by promoting cooperation between the Government of Canada and other levels of government and non-governmental agencies in Canada with respect thereto;

(e) to facilitate the entry of visitors into Canada for the purpose of fostering trade and commerce, tourism, cultural and scientific activities and international understanding;

(f) to ensure that any person who seeks admission to Canada on either a permanent or temporary basis is subject to standards of admission that do not discriminate on grounds of race, national or ethnic origin, colour, religion or sex;

(g) to fulfill Canada's international legal obligations with respect to refugees and to uphold its humanitarian tradition with respect to the displaced and the persecuted;

(h) to foster the development of a strong and viable economy and the prosperity of all regions in Canada;

(i) to maintain and protect the health, safety and good order of Canadian society; and

(j) to promote international order and justice by denying the use of Canadian territory to persons who are likely to engage in criminal activity.

AUSTRALIA

Principles of Immigration Policy

Department of Immigration and Ethnic Affairs, Review '83

1 The Australian government alone decides who can enter Australia.

2 Migrants must provide some benefit to Australia, although this will not always be a major consideration in the case of refugees and family members.

3 The migrant intake should not jeopardize social cohesiveness and harmony in the Australian community.

4 Immigration policy and selection is non-discriminatory.

5 Applicants are considered as individuals or individual family units, not as community groups.

6 Suitability standards for migrants reflect Australian law and social customs.

7 Migrants must intend to settle permanently.

8 Settlement in closed enclaves is not encouraged.

9 Migrants should integrate into Australia's multicultural society, but are given the opportunity to preserve and disseminate their ethnic heritage.

Organization Charts

Figure 5
Organization Chart, Canada Employment and Immigration Commission, 1991

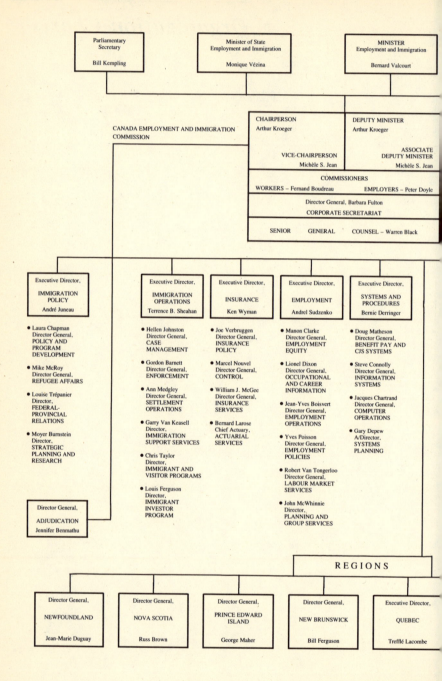

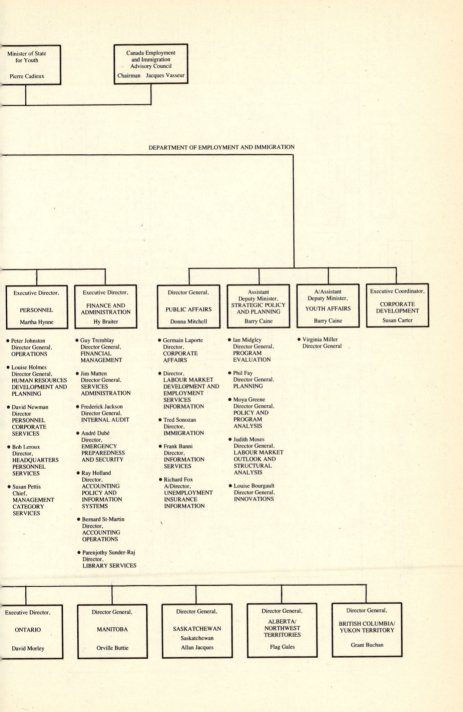

Figure 6
Organization Chart, Australian Department of Immigration, Local Government and Ethnic Affairs 1991

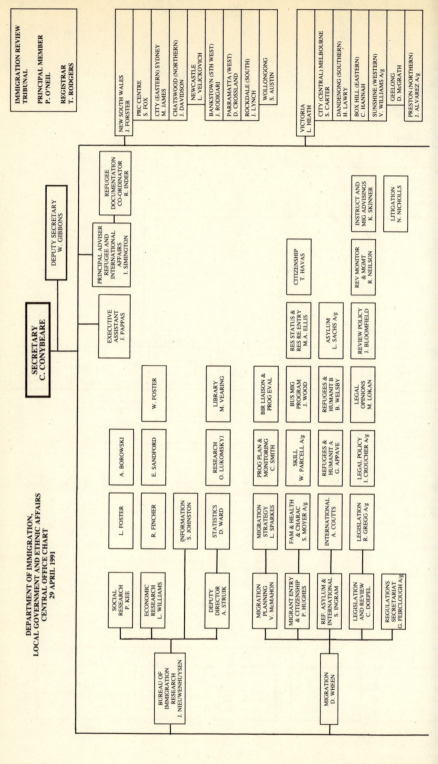

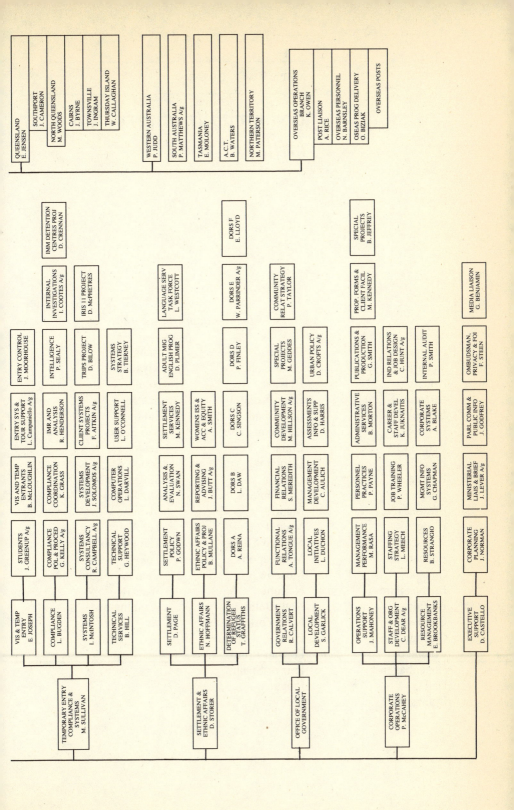

QUEENSLAND
E. JENSEN

SOUTHPORT
J. CAMERON

NORTH QUEENSLAND
M. WOODS

CAIRNS
J. BYRNE

TOWNSVILLE
J. INGRAM

THURSDAY ISLAND
W. CALLAGHAN

WESTERN AUSTRALIA
P. JUDD

SOUTH AUSTRALIA
P. MATTHEWS A/g

TASMANIA
E. MOLONEY

A.C.T.
B. WATERS

NORTHERN TERRITORY
M. PATERSON

OVERSEAS OPERATIONS
BRANCH
K. OWEN

POST LIAISON
A. RICE

OVERSEAS PERSONNEL
N. BARNSLEY

OSEAS PROG DELIVERY
O. BIZIAK

OVERSEAS POSTS

IMM DETENTION
CENTRES PROJ
D. CRENNAN

INTERNAL
INVESTIGATIONS
I. COOTES A/g

IRIS II PROJECT
D. McPHETRES

ENTRY CONTROL
J. MOORHOUSE

INTELLIGENCE
P. SEALY

TRIPS PROJECT
D. BILOW

SYSTEMS
STRATEGY
B. TIERNEY

ENTRY SYS &
TOUR SUPPORT
L. Campaniello A/g

IMR AND
ANALYSIS
R. HENDERSON

CLIENT SYSTEMS
PROJECTS
F. AITKIN A/g

USER SUPPORT
L. O'CONNELL

VIS AND TEMP
ENTRANTS
B. McLOUGHLIN

COMPLIANCE
POL & PROCED
K. GRASS

SYSTEMS
DEVELOPMENT
J. SOLOMOS A/g

COMPUTER
OPERATIONS
L. DARVILL

STUDENTS
J. GREENUP A/g

COMPLIANCE
POL & PROCED
G. KELLY A/g

SYSTEMS
CONSULTANCY
R. CAMPBELL A/g

TECHNICAL
SUPPORT
G. HEYWOOD

VIS & TEMP
ENTRY
E. JOSEPH

COMPLIANCE
L. BUGDEN

SYSTEMS
I. McINTOSH

TECHNICAL
SERVICES
B. HILL

TEMPORARY ENTRY
COMPLIANCE &
SYSTEMS
M. SULLIVAN

LANGUAGE SERV
TASK FORCE
L. WESTCOTT

ADULT MIG
ENGLISH PROG
D. PLIMER

SETTLEMENT
SERVICES
M. KENNEDY

WOMENS ISS &
ACC & EQUITY
A. SMITH

ANALYSIS &
EVALUATION
N. SWAN

REPORTING &
ADVISING
J. BUTT A/g

SETTLEMENT
POLICY
P. GODWIN

ETHNIC AFFAIRS
POLICY & PROJ
B. MULLANE

DETERMINATION
OF REFUGEE
STATUS
T. GRAFFITHS

SETTLEMENT
D. PAGE

ETHNIC AFFAIRS
N. HOFFMANN

SETTLEMENT &
ETHNIC AFFAIRS
D. STORER

DORS F
E. LLOYD

DORS E
W. PARRINDER A/g

DORS D
P. FINLEY

DORS C
C. SINGSON

DORS B
L. DAW

DORS A
A. REINA

COMMUNITY
RELAT STRATEGY
P. TAYLOR

SPECIAL
PROJECTS
M. GEDDES

URBAN POLICY
D. CROFTS A/g

COMMUNITY
DEVELOPMENT
M. HILLSON A/g

ASSESSMENTS
INFO & SUPP
D. HARRIS

FINANCIAL
RELATIONS
S. MEREDITH

MANAGEMENT
DEVELOPMENT
C. AULICH

FUNCTIONAL
RELATIONS
A. TONGUE A/g

LOCAL
INITIATIVES
L. DUCHON

GOVERNMENT
RELATIONS
R. CALVERT

LOCAL
DEVELOPMENT
S. GARLICK

OFFICE OF LOCAL
GOVERNMENT

PROP FORMS &
CLIENT FACIL
M. KENNEDY

PUBLICATIONS &
PRODUCTION
G. SMITH

IND RELATIONS
& JOB DESIGN
C. HUNT A/g

INTERNAL AUDIT
P. SMITH

ADMINISTRATIVE
SERVICES
B. MORTON

CAREER &
STAFF DEVEL
K. JUKNAITIS

CORPORATE
SYSTEMS
A. BLAKE

PERSONNEL
PRACTICES
P. PAYNE

JOB TRAINING
P. WHEELER

MGMT INFO
SYSTEMS
G. CHAPMAN

MANAGEMENT
PERFORMANCE
M. RASA

STAFFING
STRATEGY
L. MEECH

RESOURCES
B. STRANGIO

OPERATIONS
SUPPORT
J. MAHONEY

STAFF & ORG
DEVELOPMENT
C. DEAR A/g

RESOURCE
MANAGEMENT
E. BROOKBANKS

CORPORATE
OPERATIONS
P. McCAHEY

SPECIAL
PROJECTS
B. JEFFREY

MEDIA LIAISON
G. BENJAMIN

OMBUDSMAN,
PRIVACY & FOI
F. STEEN

PARL COMM &
PUBLIC INFO
J. GODFREY

MINISTERIAL
LIAIS & BRIEF
J. LEVER A/g

CORPORATE
PLANNING
J. NORMAN

EXECUTIVE
SUPPORT
D. CASTELLO

Overseas Immigration Offices, 1991

CANADA

Overseas Immigration Offices, 1991

Abidjan	Dublin	Rabat
Ankara	Guatemala	Riyadh
Athens	Helsinki	Rome
Atlanta	Hong Kong	San Jose
Bankok	Islamabad	Santiago
Beijing	Kingston	Sao Paulo
Belgrade	Lima	Seattle
Berne	Lisbon	Seoul
Bogota	London	Singapore
Bonn	Los Angeles	Stockholm
Boston	Madrid	Sydney
Bridgetown	Manila	Tel Aviv
Brussels	Mexico City	The Hague
Bucharest	Minneapolis	Tokyo
Budapest	Moscow	Vienna
Buenos Aires	Nairobi	Warsaw
Buffalo	New Delhi	Washington
Cairo	New York	
Chicago	Paris	
Colombo	Port-au-Prince	
Copenhagen	Port of Spain	
Dallas	Prague	
Damascus	Pretoria	

AUSTRALIA

Overseas Immigration Offices, 1991

Ankara
Athens
Auckland
Bankok
Beijing
Belgrade
Berne
Bonn
Buenos Aires
Cairo
Chicago
Copenhagen
Colombo
Damascus
Dublin
Edinburgh
Geneva

Hanoi
Hong Kong
Jakarta
Kuala Lumpur
Lisbon
London
Los Angeles
Madrid
Manchester
Manila
Mexico City
Moscow
Nairobi
New Delhi
New York
Osalca
Paris

Port Moresby
Pretoria
Rome
San Francisco
Santiago
Seoul
Singapore
Stockholm
Suva
The Hague
Tokyo
Toronto
Vancouver
Vienna
Warshaw
Washington

Immigrant Selection Systems

CANADA

The following is a summary of the Canadian points system which was introduced in 1967, amended in the Immigration Regulations of 1978 and revised in 1985.

Table 21

Canada: Immigration Selection Criteria: A Summary of the Points System

Factors	Criteria	Max. Points	APPLICABLE TO: self-employed	entre-preneurs	assisted relatives	others
1. Education	One point for each year of primary and secondary education successfully completed.	12	●	●	●	●
2. Specific Vocational Preparation	To be measured by the amount of formal professional, vocational, apprentice-ship, in-plant or on-the-job training necessary for average performance in the occupation under which the applicant is assessed in item 4.	15	●	●	●	●
3. Experience	Points awarded for experience in the occupation under which the applicant is assessed in item 4 or, in the case of an entrepreneur, for experience in the occupation that the entrepreneur is qualified for and is prepared to follow in Canada.	8	●	●	●	●
4. Occupational Demand	Points awarded on the basis of employment opportunities available in Canada in the occupation that the applicant is qualified for and is prepared to follow in Canada.	15	●		●	●
5. Arranged Employment or Designated Occupation	Ten points awarded if the person has arranged employment in Canada that offers reasonable prospects of continuity and meets local conditions of work and wages, providing that employment of that person would not interfere with the job opportunities of Canadian citizens or permanent residents, and the person will likely be able to meet all licensing and regulatory requirements; or the person is qualified for, and is prepared to work in, a designated occupation and meets all the conditions mentioned for arranged employment except that concerning Canadian citizens and permanent residents.	10				●
6. Location	Five points awarded to a person who intends to proceed to an area desig-nated as one having a sustained and general need for people at various levels in the employment strata and the necessary services to accommodate population growth. Five points subtracted from a person who intends to proceed to an area designated as not having such a need or such services.	5	●	●		●
7. Age	Ten points awarded to a person 18 to 35 years old. For those over 35, one point shall be subtracted from the maximum of ten for every year over 35.	10	●	●	●	●
8. Knowledge of English and French	Ten points awarded to a person who reads, writes and speaks both English and French fluently. Five points awarded to a person who reads, writes and speaks English or French fluently. Fewer points awarded to persons with less language knowledge and ability in English or French.	10	●	●		●
9. Personal Suitability	Points awarded on the basis of an interview held to determine the suitability of the person and his/her dependants to become successfully established in Canada, based on the person's adaptability, motivation, initiative, resourceful-ness and other similar qualities.	10	●	●	●	●
10. Relative	Where a person would be an assisted relative, if a relative in Canada had undertaken to assist him/her, and an immigration officer is satisfied that the relative in Canada is willing to help him/her become established but is not prepared, or is unable, to complete the necessary formal documentation to bring the person to Canada, the person shall be awarded five points.	5	●	●		●

* Members of the family class and retirees are not selected according to these criteria; Convention refugees are assessed against the factors listed in the first column but do not receive a point rating.

Table 22
Canada: Selection Criteria for Independent Immigrants:
The Points System (Revised in 1985)

	Units of Assessment	
Factor	Previous	Revised
Education	12 maximum	12 maximum: no change
Specific Vocational Preparation	15 maximum	15 maximum: no change
Experience	8 maximum	8 maximum: no change
Occupation	15 maximum: "O" an automatic processing bar	10 maximum: "O" an automatic processing bar
Arranged employment	10: 10 unit penalty if not obtained	10: no penalty if not obtained
Location	5 maximum 5 unit penalty if designated as not in need	eliminated
Age	10 maximum: 10 units if 18 to 35 years. If over 35, one unit subtracted for each year up to 45	10 maximum: 10 units if 21 to 44 years. Two units subtracted per year if under 21 or over 44
Knowledge of French and English	10 maximum: Five units to a person who reads, writes, and speaks English or French fluently; 10 units if fluent in both languages	15 maximum: up to 15 units for fluency in official language(s)
Personal Suitability	10 maximum	10 maximum: no change
Levels Control	N/A	10 units maximum: set at 5 to start
Relative	5	eliminated
TOTAL	100	100
PASS MARK	50	70
Bonus for Assisted Relative Applicants	15–30	10 if accompanied by an undertaking of assistance

Source: Canada Employment and Immigration Commission.

Total and Pass Mark

Under both the previous and revised systems, the maximum number of units of assessment which may be awarded is 100. The pass mark under the previous system was 50; the pass mark under the present system is 70. The higher pass mark is intended to ensure the selection of highly qualified applicants. The 10-unit bonus for applicants with relatives in Canada means that they will need a minimum of 60 units of assessment to be successful, provided that they – like applicants without relatives – are awarded at least one unit of assessment under the Occupational Demand factor.

Minimum Number of Units of Assessment Required

The minimum number of units of selection ("points") required under the immigrant selection criteria is usually expressed as 50. This requirement applies to two of the "Independent" categories: *Self-employed Persons*, and *Other Independent Immigrants*. *Entrepreneurs* must be awarded 25 units of selection out of a possible maximum of 75. *Assisted Relatives* must be awarded the minimum number of units of assessment indicated below, out of a possible maximum of 70.

Table 23
Canada: Units of Assessment Required for Assisted Relatives (Max. 70)

Type of Relationship	Citizenship Status of Relative in Canada	Minimum units of Assessment Required
Brother, sister, grandfather, grandmother, father, mother, son, daughter, unmarried niece or nephew under 21	Canadian citizen	20
	Permanent resident	25
Aunt, uncle, grandson, granddaughter, married niece or nephew, niece or nephew 21 or over	Canadian citizen	30
	Permanent resident	35

AUSTRALIA

Migrant Selection System, 1988

Australia's migrant selection system has been extensively revised following the report of the Committee to Advise on Australia's Immigration Policies (CAAIP) in 1988. There are now three major migration streams: Family, Skill, and Humanitarian, as well as a small special eligibility category. A revised points selection system has been developed by a working party of the National Population Council which applies to a Concessional Family Class and an Independent Entry Class. Control over volume is maintained through the use of a floating pass mark and a system of "capping" by the Minister of part of these two category streams if there is an excessive demand for places. The following is a sample score card.

Table 24
Australia: Migrant Selection System

Working out your points score

You would need to get 95 points in the Independent Entrant Class or 85 points in the Concessional Family Class for an application to be considered.

Concessional Family Class applicants may score point under Skill, Age, Relationship, Citizenship, Settlement and Location. They are NOT scored on the Language Skills factor.

Independent Entrant Class applicants may only score points under Skill, Age and Language Skills.

Concessional Family Class and Independent Entrant Class

EMPLOYABILITY FACTOR

Skill
The qualifications and experience listed in this factor relate to the qualifications and experience you would need to have to work in your *usual occupation* in Australia. Your qualifications will be examined by the appropriate assessing authority. To achieve the points set out below, your qualifications:
– must be assessed as equivalent to the Australian qualification level listed below, and
– must be relevant to your usual occupation.

Occupations in Australia that require:	*POINTS*
• Trade certificate/degree (acceptable), with sound continuous relevant experience, and included on Priority Occupation List *(see next page)*	75
• Trade certificate/degree (acceptable), with sound continuous relevant experience	70
• Trade certificate/degree (acceptable), with limited experience	60
• Diploma (acceptable), with sound and continuous relevant experience	55
• Diploma (acceptable), with limited experience	50
• Trade certificate/degree/diploma (recognised overseas and requiring only minor upgrading, which must be available in Australia), with sound, continuous relevant experience	35
• Trade certificate/degree/diploma (recognised overseas and requiring only minor upgrading, which must be available in Australia) with limited experience	30

- Other post secondary school qualifications or equivalent experience   30

- Secondary school completion   20

- Four years secondary schooling   10

- Less than four years secondary schooling   0

Additional points

Points for skill are also awarded to applicants who have acceptable qualifications but who do not have relevant work experience. Your qualifications, which will be examined by the appropriate assessing authority, must be equivalent to the Australian qualification listed below.

Graduates who have a:
- Degree/trade certificate/diploma (acceptable) awarded up
  to 12 months prior to application   45

- Degree/trade certificate/diploma (acceptable) awarded more
  than 12 months prior to application with experience in a
  semi-skilled or unskilled occupation   40

Age	POINTS	Age	POINTS
18 to 29 years	30	40 to 49 years	5
30 to 34 years	20	Less than 18 or more	
35 to 39 years	10	than 50 years	0

Independent Entrant Class Only

Language Skills	*POINTS*
• Proficient in English (able to speak, read and write English well)	15
• Reasonably proficient in English but some training required	10
• Bilingual in languages other than English, or only limited English	5
• Extensive English training required	0

Concessional Family Class Only

RELATIONSHIP FACTOR	*POINTS*
If you are the	
– Parent of your sponsor	15
– Brother, sister, non-dependent child of your sponsor	10
– Nephew or niece of your sponsor	5

CITIZENSHIP FACTOR

If your sponsor has been an

– Australian citizen for five years or more	10
– Australian citizen for less than five years	5

SETTLEMENT FACTOR

If your sponsor (or the spouse of your sponsor) has been
in continuous employment in Australia (including self-employment)
for the last two years   10

NOTE: Points will not be awarded if the sponsor has been in receipt of unemployment or special benefit
for more than one month in total in the last two years.

LOCATION FACTOR

If your sponsor has lived in a State or Territory designated area
for the last two years *(refer to the Designated Area List
on the back page)*   5

TOTAL POINTS ....

Note:

- Usual Occupation *is the job you are doing at present or a job which you have done during the last
  two years. You would be expected to have worked in that job continuously for a total period of NOT
  LESS THAN six months during the last two years.*
- Sound and continuous relevant experience *means you would be expected to have worked in your usual
  occupation for at least three years immediately prior to the time of your application.*
- Limited experience *means you would be expected to have worked in your usual occupation for at
  least six months, but for less than three years.*
- For reasons of space, the priority occupation list on the reverse side of this score card has been omitted.

Immigration Appeal and Refugee Status Determination Systems

CANADA

A new system of immigration appeal and refugee status determination was introduced on January 1, 1989. This involved the creation of a board to be called the Immigration and Refugee Board (IRB). The Board consists of two distinct divisions: the Convention Refugee Determination Division and the Immigration Appeal Division. The Refugee Division deals exclusively with the determination of refugee claims. The Appeal Division is a court of record and hears a range of immigration appeals, including appeals from permanent residents of Canada and holders of valid visitor's visas who have been denied entry to or ordered removed from Canada, and appeals from Canadian citizens and permanent residents who have sponsored applications by close family members wishing to immigrate to Canada that have subsequently been refused by a visa officer.

The Immigration and Refugee Board is Canada's largest administrative tribunal with over 120 full-time members in the Refugee Division and about 22 in the Appeal Division. Both Divisions may take on as many part-time or additional full-time members as they require. The IRB is headed by a Chairman who is the chief executive officer of the Board, with a Deputy Chairman for each Division. The Board has its national headquarters in Ottawa and five regional offices located in Montreal, Toronto, Winnipeg, Calgary, and Vancouver.

Refugee Determination System

A request for refugee status can be made at any port of entry to Canada. A person who is already in Canada can make a claim at any Canada Immigration Centre or at the beginning of an immigration inquiry. The refugee determination process now takes place in two stages. *Stage One* consists of an initial hearing before an adjudicator and a member of the Refugee Division. After consideration by the adjudicator of any issues relating to admissibility or violations of the Immigration Act, an initial review of the claim takes place. First the *eligibility* of the claimant is considered. People who are not eligible for consideration as a Convention refugee include:

- those with refugee status in another country;
- those coming to Canada from a "safe third country";
- previously rejected claimants not out of Canada for more than 90 days;
- persons convicted of serious crimes; and
- known war criminals and security threats.

If either the adjudicator or the IRB member decides that the claimant is eligible for consideration, the initial hearing then considers any evidence that would establish whether or not the claim has some credible basis. This "credibility" evidence includes the human rights record of the claimant's country of origin as well as previous Refugee Division decisions on nationals of the same country. If the claim is rejected by both members of the initial hearing panel and the claimant is in violation of the Immigration Act, then action is taken to remove the claimant from Canada. If the claim is accepted by either of the panel members, it is referred immediately to a full hearing before the Refugee Division.

Stage Two consists of a Refugee Determination Hearing which takes place before a panel consisting of two members of the Refugee Division who are required to make a final decision on the claim. Only one member of the panel is required to decide in favour of the claimant for refugee status to be confirmed. Following a favourable conclusion of the hearing, the claimant may apply for and receive landed immigrant status in Canada.

The Right to Appeal

The claimant is entitled to appeal a negative decision to the Federal Court of Justice throughout all stages of the refugee determination process. Leave must be obtained from a Federal Court judge to initiate such a review, however, which may only relate to questions of law or "capricious" findings of fact. The Federal Court will not consider the merits of the refugee claim.

AUSTRALIA

A new system of review for immigration decisions was announced on December 8, 1988 and introduced in 1989. It consists of a statutory two-tiered system of review. The first tier is an independent review of decisions by a special unit in the Department of Immigration, Local Government and Ethnic Affairs called the Migration Internal Review Office, which is independent of the primary decision-making areas. The second tier consists of an independent Immigration Review Tribunal established under the amended Migration Act 1958 and empowered to consider cases on their merits and make the final decision. Under sections 115 and 137 of the Migration Act, the Minister is empowered to set aside decisions after each review stage to make a decision that he or she thinks is in the public interest and is more favourable to the applicant (who must have a right of review). If such a ministerial decision is made, it must be reported to Parliament. An appeal may be made to the Federal Court by the applicant for review or by the Minister on any question of law resulting from any decision of the Tribunal. Fees are charged for each tier of review, with a lower fee for the first tier.

The members of the Immigration Review Tribunal are appointed by the Governor-General and consist of a Principal Member, who is the Executive Officer of the Tribunal, a number of senior members, and a number of other full or part-time members. Members hold office for a period not exceeding five years and may not be appointed after reaching the age of 65.

Refugee Status Determination

A new system for determining claims for refugee status and humanitarian stay in Australia was announced on October 26, 1990 and came into effect on December 10. Significantly larger resources are being provided to speed up decision making on refugee status applications, whose numbers are increasing. The new system has three stages: (1) a primary stage when applications are assessed and decisions made quickly on refugee status, (2) a review stage where there are negative assessments at the first stage, and (3) a third stage where there are clear grounds for humanitarian stay but where refugee status is not recommended. Ministerial approval will then be required for temporary entry on humanitarian grounds. Applicants who are granted permission to remain in Australia on humanitarian grounds by the Minister receive a four-year temporary entry permit on the same conditions as a refugee.

A Refugee Status Review Committee has been established for the review stage, replacing the existing Determination of Refugee Status (DORS) Committee. It includes a representative of the Refugee Council of Australia, as well as representatives of the Department of Immigration. Local Government and Ethnic Affairs (Chair), the Department of Foreign Affairs and Trade, and the Attorney General's Department. A representative of the United Nations High Commissioner for Refugees attends in an advisory capacity.

Australia's Telephone Interpreter Service

AUSTRALIA

Telephone Interpreter Service

The Telephone Interpreter Service (TIS) is one of the most innovative, practical, and successful of the settlement services provided for migrants by the Commonwealth government. Operated by the Department of Immigration Local Government and Ethnic Affairs, TIS provides interpreting, information, and referral services by telephone to non-English speaking migrants, to assist them in their dealings with government authorities, members of the professions, voluntary agencies, and other organizations. In special circumstances, the attendance of an interpreter may be arranged.

Migrants with a communication problem can be linked with an interpreter speaking any one of more than 70 languages. Special facilities allow three-way conversations among inquirer, interpreter, and a third party, such as a hospital, solicitor, or government official.

The Telephone Interpreter Service was introduced in February 1973 in Sydney and Melbourne. It now extends to all capital cities, as well as to Wollongong, Newcastle, Albury/Wodonga, Shepparton, Geelong, the La Trobe Valley, Whyalla, Launceston, and Burnie. Figure 7 shows the total number of calls received, the main languages used, and the type of assistance requested in 1988–89.

Figure 7
Australia's: Telephone Interpreter Service Calls, 1988–89

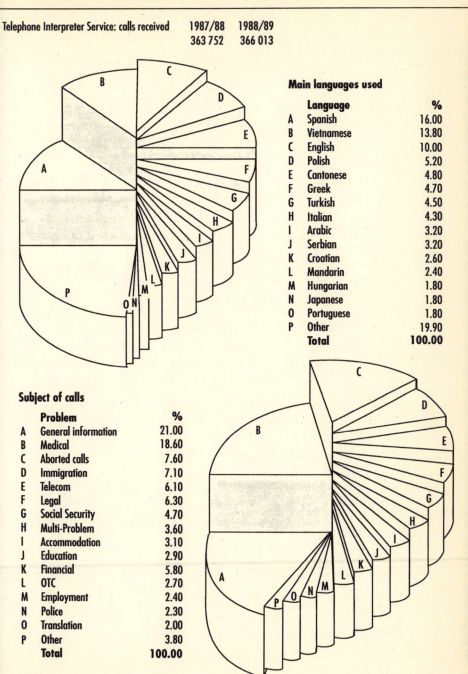

Telephone Interpreter Service: calls received

	1987/88	1988/89
	363 752	366 013

Main languages used

	Language	%
A	Spanish	16.00
B	Vietnamese	13.80
C	English	10.00
D	Polish	5.20
E	Cantonese	4.80
F	Greek	4.70
G	Turkish	4.50
H	Italian	4.30
I	Arabic	3.20
J	Serbian	3.20
K	Croatian	2.60
L	Mandarin	2.40
M	Hungarian	1.80
N	Japanese	1.80
O	Portuguese	1.80
P	Other	19.90
	Total	**100.00**

Subject of calls

	Problem	%
A	General information	21.00
B	Medical	18.60
C	Aborted calls	7.60
D	Immigration	7.10
E	Telecom	6.10
F	Legal	6.30
G	Social Security	4.70
H	Multi-Problem	3.60
I	Accommodation	3.10
J	Education	2.90
K	Financial	5.80
L	OTC	2.70
M	Employment	2.40
N	Police	2.30
O	Translation	2.00
P	Other	3.80
	Total	**100.00**

Notes

1 *See* John W. Dafoe, *Clifford Sifton in Relation to his Times* (Toronto: Oxford University Press, 1931); Sir Clifford Sifton, "The Immigrants Canada Wants," *Macleans Magazine*, April 1, 1922, reprinted in Howard Palmer, ed., *Immigration and the Rise of Multiculturalism* (Toronto: Copp Clark, 1975); James B. Hedges, *Building the Canadian West: The Land and Colonization Policies of the Canadian Pacific Railway* (New York: Macmillan, 1939); and Harold M. Troper, *Only Farmers Need Apply* (Toronto: Griffin House 1972).

2 Immigration statistics were not very reliable in those days, but the figures usually given are 961,000 immigrants from Britain, 784,000 from the United States, and 594,000 from continental Europe.

3 Canada's 1911 census gave the following population figures for the major European groups in Canada:

Austrian	44,000	Netherlands	56,000
German	403,000	Polish	34,000
Hungarian	12,000	Russian	44,000
Italian	46,000	Scandinavian	113,000
Jewish	76,000	Ukrainian	75,000

Source: Warren E. Kalbach, "Growth and Distribution of Canada's Ethnic Populations 1871–1971," in Leo Driedger, ed., *The Canadian Ethnic Mosaic: A Quest for Identity*, (Toronto: McClelland and Stewart, 1978).

4 Troper, *Only Farmers Need Apply*, Chapter 2. "Machine and Personnel."

5 Sir Clifford Sifton, "The Immigrants Canada Wants." *Macleans Magazine* had asked Sifton "to put in the shape of a short article ... the substance of some remarks which he made a short time ago to the Toronto Board of Trade on the subject of immigration."

6 Dafoe, *Clifford Sifton in Relation to his Times*, p. 140.

7 Hedges, *Building the Canadian West*, pp. 132–39.

8 *See* Troper, *Only Farmers Need Apply*, Chapter 7, "Closing the Door: The Issue of Negro Immigration," and Robin W. Winks, *The Blacks in Canada: A History* (Montreal: McGill-Queen's University Press, 1977).

9 Dafoe, *Clifford Sifton in Relation to his Times*, p. 492.

10 House of Commons Debates, 54, April 12, 1901, p. 2939, quoted in Troper, *Farmers*, p. 22.

11 *See* Charles A. Price, *The Great White Walls are Built: Restrictive Immigration to North America and Australasia 1836–1888*, (Canberra: Australian National University Press, 1974); Myra Willard, *History of the White Australia Policy to 1920* (Melbourne: Melbourne University Press, 1947); W. Peter Ward, *White Canada Forever: Popular Attitudes and Public Policy Towards Orientals in British Columbia* (Montreal: McGill-Queen's University Press, 1978); and Harry Con, Ronald Con, Graham Johnson, Edgar Wickberg, and William E. Wilmott, *From China to Canada: A History of the Chinese Communities in Canada* (Toronto: McClelland and Stewart, 1983).

12 Price, *The Great White Walls are Built*, Chapter 3.

13 Price, *The Great White Walls are Built*, p. 58.

14 Bathurst *Free Press*, June 22, 1858 and September 1, 1858, quoted in Price, p. 81.

15 Price, *The Great White Walls are Built*, Chapter 10, and W. Peter Ward, *White Canada Forever*, Chapter 1.

16 Willard, *History of the White Australia Policy*, p. 17.

17 Willard, *History of the White Australia Policy*, Chapter 4.

18 Price, *The Great White Walls are Built*, p. 197.

19 George Reid, Premier of New South Wales, in the Legislative Assembly. Parliamentary Debates, 1896, *History of the White Australia Policy*, vol. 85, p. 3948, quoted in Willard, p. 108.

20 Russel Ward, *A Nation for a Continent: The History of Australia 1901–1975*, (Richmond, Victoria: Heinemann Educational Australia, 1977), p. 30.

21 Russel Ward, ibid., Chapter 1, and Manning Clark, *A Short History of Australia*, Revised Edition (New York: Mentor Books, New American Library, 1969), Chapter 10.

22 Willard, *History of the White Australia Policy*, pp. 184–85.

23 Frank Crowley, ed., *A New History of Australia*, (Melbourne: Heinemann Australia, 1977), pp. 297–98.

24 An Immigration Reform Group began meeting at Melbourne University in 1959. The group produced a set of recommendations on a more liberal immigration policy, which was published in a book entitled *Immigration: Control or Colour Bar?* in 1962, and in other publications later on. Asso-

ciations for immigration reform were organized in mainland states during the sixties.

25 W. Peter Ward, *White Canada Forever*, Chapter 4.

26 W. Peter Ward, Ibid., p. 66.

27 Mackenzie King held hearings to assess the degree of damage in the Vancouver riot and settle the question of compensation. The Japanese were awarded $9,000 and the Chinese, who sustained the most damage to property, $26,000.

28 W. Peter Ward, *White Canada Forever*, p. 83.

29 W. Peter Ward, Ibid., Chapter 5.

30 See H. and R. Con, Johnson, Wickberg, and Wilmott, *From China to Canada*, chapters 9 and 10.

31 Freda Hawkins, *Canada and Immigration: Public Policy and Public Concern*, Second Edition (Montreal: McGill-Queen's University Press, 1988), pp. 94–95.

32 During the nineteenth century, it is estimated that Britain was involved in close to one half of all the world's commercial transactions and owned more than one third of the world's shipping. She has been described as "the main propelling force behind an economic revolution which was transforming the world," making a major contribution to the industrialization of Europe and the United States. *See* C.J. Bartlett, ed., *Britain Pre-eminent: Studies of British World Influence in the Nineteenth Century* (London: Macmillan, 1969).

33 Willard, *History of the White Australia Policy*, p. 190.

34 Legislative Assembly, New South Wales, Public Documents 5/88, p. 4782, quoted in Price, p. 256.

35 J.M. Roberts, *The Pelican History of the World* (London: Penguin Books, 1980), Book 5, Chapter 4.

36 *See* an excellent paper on this subject by Carl Berger, University of Toronto, entitled "The True North Strong and Free," in Peter Russell, ed., *Nationalism in Canada* (Toronto: McGraw-Hill (Canada), 1966).

37 R.L. Borden, MP, *The Question of Oriental Immigration*, speeches delivered in 1907 and 1908; quoted in W. Peter Ward, *White Canada Forever*, p. 75.

38 Willard, *History of the White Australia Policy*, p. 119.

39 Early in 1904, Australia had reached an agreement with the Government of Japan, and in 1912 with the Government of China, which provided for the entry into Australia of merchants and their families, assistants for Asian businesses established in Australia and students.

40 Hedges, *Building the Canadian West*, pp. 357–62.

41 Charles A. Price, *Migrants in Australian Society*, a paper given at H.R.H. The Duke of Edinburgh's Third Commonwealth Study Conference, Australia, 1968.

42 Russel Ward, *A Nation for a Continent*, p. 141.

43 *See* Joy E. Esberey, *Knight of the Holy Spirit: A Study of William Lyon Mackenzie King* (Toronto: University of Toronto Press, 1980) and C.P. Stacey, *A Very Double Life: The Private World of Mackenzie King* (Toronto: Macmillan, 1976).

44 Kenneth McNaught, *The Pelican History of Canada* (Toronto: Penguin Books, Revised Edition, 1976), p. 232.

45 John Holmes, "Nationalism in Foreign Policy," Peter Russell, ed., *Nationalism in Canada* (Toronto: McGraw-Hill, 1966), p. 207.

46 McNaught, *The Pelican History of Canada*, p. 255.

47 Commonwealth Parliamentary Debates, August 2, 1945, vol. 184, p. 4911, quoted in Colm Kiernan, *Calwell: A Personal and Political Biography*, Melbourne: Nelson, 1978), p. 120.

48 The Hon. Hubert Opperman, MP, Minister for Immigration, "Australia's Immigration Policy on the Admission of Non-Europeans" from a speech delivered in Canberra on May 28, 1966, *Migration News*, Journal of the International Catholic Migration Commission, no. 1, Jan–Feb. 1967, p. 6.

49 Commonwealth Immigration Planning Council, *Australia's Immigration Programme for the period 1968 to 1973* Report to the Minister of State for Immigration, the Honourable B.M. Snedden QC, MP, tabled in the House of Representatives, September 10, 1968.

50 *See* Freda Hawkins, *Canada and Immigration: Public Policy and Public Concern*, a study of Canadian immigration policy and management during this period.

51 *See* Warren E. Kalbach, *The Effect of Immigration on Population*, Supplementary Study to the Green Paper on Immigration Policy, Department of Manpower and Immigration (Ottawa: Supply and Services Canada, 1975).

52 *See* Freda Hawkins *Canada and Immigration: Public Policy and Public Concern* pp. 101–06, for a detailed account of the provisions of the Immigration Act 1952.

CHAPTER TWO

1 The following are four excellent studies of the Trudeau years: Christina McCall-Newman, *Grits: An Intimate Portrait of the Liberal Party* (Toronto: Macmillan of Canada, 1982); George Radwanski, *Trudeau* (Toronto: Signet Books, Macmillan of Canada, 1979); and Richard Gwyn, *The Northern Magus* (Toronto: McClelland and Stewart, 1980); and Stephen Clarkson and Christina McCall, *Trudeau and Our Times* (Toronto, McClelland and Stewart, 1990).

2 Interviews with Mr. MacEachen, Mr. Mackasey, and with senior officials.

3 The author had a series of interviews with Mr. Andras between 1976 and 1979, and had other opportunities to talk to him as a member of the

Department of Manpower and Immigration's Advisory Board on the Adjustment of Immigrants.

4 *See* Freda Hawkins, *Canada and Immigration: Public Policy and Public Concern.* "Immigration Within Manpower," pp. 338–46. The Economic Council of Canada in its Eighth Annual Review (September 1971), in part an examination of Canadian manpower policies, made the following comments (p. 88): "But, in our view, while immigration *is* an instrument of manpower policy – one that is used, on a continuing basis, as a labour market adjustment program – it is also far more than that, having widespread and fundamental implications for social and economic development in this country."

5 Minister of Manpower and Immigration, 1965–1968.

6 Andras, interview, April 1, 1977.

7 *See* the author's article, "Canada: The Unintended Amnesty," *Migration Today*, vol. 5, no. 3, June 1977, from which some of the material in this section is taken. See also David S. North, "The Canadian Experience with Amnesty for Aliens: What the United States Can Learn," study supported by the Ford Foundation (Washington, D.C.: Center for Labor and Migration Studies, New Transcentury Foundation, 1979).

8 Immigration Adjustment of Status Regulations, P.C.,1973–2313, July 31, 1973.

9 Canada, House of Commons Debates, June 30, 1973.

10 Ibid.

11 Ibid.

12 Amnesties have become one way of handling the problems of illegal or undocumented migration. Australia, Britain, France, Belgium, Argentina, and The Netherlands all had amnesties of various kinds in the seventies. In the United States, an amnesty is being offered to illegal immigrants under the Immigration Reform and Control Act of 1986.

13 North, "The Canadian Experience with Amnesty for Aliens" pp. 40–45.

14 Andras, House of Commons, June 20, 1973.

15 Canada, House of Commons Debates, September 15, 1973.

16 Freda Hawkins, *Canada and Immigration: Public Policy and Public Concern,* (first published in 1972); David Corbett, *Canada's Immigration Policy* (Toronto: University of Toronto Press, 1957).

17 A phrase of the Chairman of the Canadian Immigration and Population Study. The author was a consultant to the CIPS, and had many opportunities to talk to its staff.

18 *See* Freda Hawkins, *Canada and Immigration: Public Policy and Public Concern,* pp. 159–62.

19 Montreal *Gazette,* April 10, 1975.

20 *Green Paper on Immigration Policy* (Ottawa: Information Canada, 1975). Now available from the Department of Supply and Services, Ottawa.

21 *See* Bibliography for a full list of these studies.

22 *See* Chapter 3.

23 The Hon. Robert Andras, Minister of Manpower and Immigration, *Statement on Tabling the Green Paper on Immigration Policy*, House of Commons, February 3, 1975.

24 The Australian Population and Immigration Council was amalgamated with the Australian Ethnic Affairs Council to form the Australian Council on Population and Ethnic Affairs, but the latter had only a short life. After the election of the Hawke government in March 1983, it was replaced by the National Population Council. On March 13, 1987, the Prime Minister announced the creation of an Advisory Council on Multicultural Affairs which would report to him and to the then Minister for Immigration and Ethnic Affairs, Mick Young.

25 Special Joint Committee of the Senate and the House of Commons on Immigration Policy, *Report to Parliament*, Ottawa: Information Canada, 1975 (Department of Supply and Services). The author made an individual submission to this committee, attended a number of its hearings, and talked to the co-chairmen and most of the committee members.

26 Minutes of Proceedings and Evidence of the Special Joint Committee of the Senate and the House of Commons on Immigration Policy, First Session, Thirteenth Parliament, 1974–1975.

27 Peter Dobell and Susan d'Aquino, *The Special Joint Committee on Immigration Policy 1975: An Exercise in Participatory Democracy*, Behind the Headlines (Toronto: Canadian Institute of International Affairs, vol. 34, no. 6, 1976), pp. 24.

28 Frequent reference was made to a well-intentioned but unfortunate paragraph on page 12 of Volume 1 of the Green Paper, in which Canada's increasingly multiracial immigration movement and the response of Canadian society to it are discussed in very oblique terms.

29 Minutes of Proceedings and Evidence of the Special Joint Committee of the Senate and the House of Commons on Immigration Policy, Issue no. 4, April 9, 1975, pp. 12–14.

30 Interview, House of Commons, June 29, 1976.

31 Minutes of the Standing Committee on Labour, Manpower and Immigration, House of Commons, April 28, 1981.

32 Minutes of Proceedings and Evidence of the Special Joint Committee of the Senate and the House of Commons on Immigration Policy, Issue no. 4, April 9, 1975, pp. 10–11.

33 This idea has often been discussed but never implemented. It was considered as a possibility by the Clark government in 1979. In 1977, however, the Department of Manpower and Immigration and the Unemployment Insurance Commission were amalgamated to form the Canada Employment and Immigration Commission and immigration became part of an

even larger organization with a strong employment orientation. In 1981, the Foreign Branch of the Immigration Division was transferred to the Department of External Affairs. For further discussion of these developments, see this chapter and Chapter 6.

34 The Immigration Act 1976 does contain two provisions of this kind (Part 3,19 (1) (b) and 27 (1) (f)), but they are couched in terms that are less harsh than those in the 1952 Act. There are also far more liberal arrangements for special inquiries and appeals, and deportation procedures are more flexible under the new Act.

35 The term "Red Tory" refers to a small, informal group of well-known members of the Progressive Conservative Party in Canada which has also included the former Minister of Employment and Immigration, Flora MacDonald, the former Chief Commissioner of the Canadian Human Rights Commission and former M.P., Gordon Fairweather, and the present Secretary of State for External Affairs, Joe Clark. This group has been more progressive in its views and more inclined to support state intervention in the economy, and a state-supported system of social security and welfare services, than other members of the party. Some see this as an expression of a traditional Tory sense of obligation towards the less fortunate members of society, as well as a sense of what is needed to preserve the established social order.

36 Department of Manpower and Immigration, *Green Paper on Immigration Policy*, Volume 1, Immigration Policy Perspectives, p. 4.

37 Ibid., Volume 3, *Immigration and Population Statistics*, Part 2.

38 Ibid. The other assumptions were as follows: A single mortality assumption was used. On the basis of an analysis of recent experience in Canada and other countries, a further moderate decline in mortality was projected over the next 15 years. Expectation of life at birth was assumed to rise from its level of 68.8 years for men and 75.2 years for women in 1966 to 70.2 years and 78.6 years respectively in 1986. Future trends in fertility were regarded as extremely uncertain given the wide fluctuations of the past 50 years. A continuation of the steep decline of recent years, or a baby boom of post-war proportions were considered unlikely. Fluctuations within a narrower range were therefore postulated and three alternative assumptions were used in the projections, ranging between a gradual decline to 1.8 births per women and a gradual rise to 2.6 births per women in the late 1970s or early 1980s. (The four projections included in Volume 3 of the Green Paper also provided population figures for each of the provinces and territories; these have not been included here.)

39 Warren E. Kalbach, "The Effect of Immigration on Population," Supplementary Study to the Green Paper on Immigration Policy (Ottawa: Department of Manpower and Immigration, 1975). Jacques Henripin, "Immigration and Language Imbalance," Supplementary Study to the

Green Paper on Immigration Policy (Ottawa: Department of Manpower and Immigration, 1975). (Both studies may be obtained through the Department of Supply and Services, Ottawa).

40 See *Green Paper on Immigration Policy*, Vol. 1, p. 7.

41 *The Effect of Immigration on Population*, ibid., pp. 39–40.

42 *Demographic Objectives for Canada*, document prepared by the Demographic Policy Secretariat, Department of Manpower and Immigration, Ottawa, 1975.

43 Interview with the Hon. Robert Andras, Minister of Manpower and Immigration, June 28, 1976.

44 Interviews with the Hon. Rod Logan, Minister of Labour and Manpower, and Dr. Douglas C. Stanley, Deputy Minister, Department of Labour and Manpower, Fredericton, New Brunswick, March 18, 1977.

45 Conversation with the Deputy Minister, Ministry of Culture and Recreation, Government of Ontario, Toronto, November 17, 1979.

46 *See* notes for a speech by the Hon. Robert Andras, Minister of Manpower and Immigration, to the Sales Club of Toronto, February 10, 1976, press release, Office of the Minister of Manpower and Immigration, Ottawa.

47 Two years later, on November 24, 1978, Mr. Andras was appointed Minister of State for Economic Development and President of the Board of Economic Development Ministers.

48 The term "governor-in-council" means, in plain terms, the Governor General acting on the advice of the Cabinet.

49 *See* Freda Hawkins, *Canada and Immigration: Public Policy and Public Concern*, pp. 329–33.

50 During the period leading up to the publication of the Green Paper, Bob Andras, then Minister of Manpower and Immigration, told the author that the Cabinet was most unwilling to provide more money for immigrant services. It was pointless to ask them, he said. They believed that any additional services that might be required should be provided by the provinces.

51 Government of Canada, news release, April 1, 1981.

52 *See* Freda Hawkins, *Canada and Immigration: Public Policy and Public Concern*, Index: Sponsored Movement and Sponsorship Issue.

53 *See* Bibliography for a list of the Council's reports on aspects of immigration.

54 Employment and Immigration Canada, *Background Paper on Future Immigration Levels*, November 1984, p. 7.

55 *See* Bibliography.

56 Christopher Taylor, "New Directions in Canadian Immigration Policy: The Role of Planning," The Population Association of America, Annual Meeting, Pittsburgh, April 14, 1983.

CHAPTER THREE

1 In his autobiography *Trial Balance*, Dr. H.C. Coombes, a well-known Australian public servant and an adviser to the Whitlam government, wrote, "It is difficult already to recall the excitement, the euphoria which possessed many Australians when the Labor Party was returned in December 1972. Like many others, I had in the years after the death of Chifley felt cheated by the rejection of the war-time promises of a better world for the 'common man,' saddened by the increasing selfishness and materialism of our society, shamed by our subservicence to American power and our participation in the Vietnam War, and above all disillusioned by the slow death of the casual, tolerant, egalitarian image Australians had of themselves and their society. But how different it suddenly seemed. We felt we had again a Government motivated by the same spirit that had illuminated Chifley's 'light on the hill,' which had enabled Curtin to speak bluntly to Churchill in the interest of Australian security. We had a Prime Minister of world stature – intelligent, literate and eloquent who within a few weeks had begun to express in the councils of the world what was best and most characteristic of the Australian Way." H.C. Coombes, *Trial Balance* (Melbourne: Macmillan, 1981), pp. 307–8.

2 The author had several conversations with Mr. Whitlam on the subject of immigration: first a long and very helpful interview in his office in Sydney in February 1978, and later at University House in Canberra in 1980 on the campus of the Australian National University, where he was a Visiting Fellow.

3 Quoted in the Prime Minister's Foreign Policy Statement, House of Representatives, Canberra, May 24, 1973.

4 Ibid.

5 "Bi-partisanship in Immigration Policy," an Address by the Hon. A.J. Forbes, MC, MP, Minister for Immigration, 44th Annual Summer School, University of Western Australia, Perth, January 27, 1972 (Canberra: Department of Immigration).

6 "The Evolution of a Policy," statement by the Hon. Phillip Lynch, MP, Minister for Immigration (Canberra: Australian Government Publishing Service, March 1971).

7 "An Australian Immigration Policy," an address by the Hon. A.J. Forbes, MC, MP, Minister for Immigration, North Sydney Federal Electoral Conference (Canberra: Department of Immigration, July 31, 1972).

8 Canada, 1971 Immigration Statistics, Department of Manpower and Immigration, Ottawa.

9 See *The Guardian*, July 19, November 18 and November 12, 1970, and January 8 and 9, 1971.

10 Department of Immigration.

11 *See* J.D.B. Miller and Brian Jinks, *Australian Government and Politics*, 4th Edition (London: Duckworth 1971), pp. 67–77 and James Jupp, *Party Politics: Australia 1966–81* (Sydney: George Allen and Unwin, 1981), Chapter 7, "Australian Labor Ideology."

12 Sydney, February 6, 1978. These views should be seen in the context of Mr. Whitlam's general distrust of the public service, and his evident desire to rearrange it and to experiment with new structures. *See* Weller and Smith, "The Rise and Fall of Whitlam Labor: The Political Context of the 1975 Elections," in *Australia at the Polls: The National Elections of 1975*, Howard R. Penniman, ed., (Washington D.C.: American Enterprise Institute for Public Policy Research, 1977) and Elaine Thompson, "The Public Service," in *From Whitlam to Fraser*, Allen Patience and Brian Head, eds. (Melbourne: Oxford University Press, 1979).

13 Interview with Dr. Peter Wilenski, Sydney, February 7, 1978.

14 Interview with Mr. Whitlam, February 5–6, 1978. The author also discussed the matter with Mr. Clyde Cameron who became Minister for Labor and Immigration in June 1974. Mr. Cameron said that the possibility of a merger of the departments of Labor and Immigration *was* discussed at this early stage, but was rejected as too heavy a load for one minister. Later when the two departments were amalgamated, some of Immigration's major responsibilities had been transferred to other departments. Interview, May 30, 1978.

15 Don Chipp and John Larkin, *Don Chipp: The Third Man* (Melbourne: Rigby, 1978), Chapter 13.

16 As one example only, the *Canberra Times* wrote on June 4, 1972, "Mr. Arthur Calwell is a wasting asset, alike to the Australian Labor Party and to the nation. Like some dinosaur preserved into the modern age, from time to time he raises his voice to bellow his dismay at the bewildering spectacle about him. His latest outburst is an exercise not in political debate, but in a form of cheap rhetoric born on Victoria's goldfields and Queensland's canefields a century ago, despicable from its inception and of relevance today only as an example of the lengths to which some people go to peddle alarmism and their own irrational prejudice."

17 *See The Review*, May 6, 1972.

18 Among many studies of this period in Australian politics, *see* the following for a detailed account and assessment of the achievements and problems of the Whitlam government: Graham Freudenberg, *A Certain Grandeur: Gough Whitlam in Politics* (Melbourne: Macmillan 1977); Howard R. Penniman, ed., *Australia at the Polls*, particularly Chapters 2 and 3; Patience and Head, eds., *From Whitlam to Fraser*; James Jupp, *Party Politics*; Geoffrey Sawer, *Federation Under Strain: Australia 1972–75* (Melbourne: Melbourne University Press, 1977); Gareth Evans, ed., *Labor and the Constitution, 1972–75* (Melbourne: Heinemann, 1977); E. Gough Whitlam, *The Truth of the Matter* (Ringwood (Vic): Penguin, 1979); and

Sir John Kerr, *Matters for Judgment* (Melbourne: Macmillan, 1978).

19 A.J. Grassby, *The Morning After*, foreword by Gough Whitlam (Canberra: Judicator Publications, 1979).

20 Tabled in the House of Representatives on October 11, 1973.

21 *See* Appendix 5 for a description of the Canadian points system and of Australia's present Migrant Selection System.

22 The Committee on Social Patterns had just completed a two-year enquiry into the departure of settlers from Australia. *See* Immigration Advisory Council, Committee on Social Patterns, *Inquiry into the Departure of Settlers from Australia*, Final Report (Canberra: Department of Immigration, October 11, 1973).

23 Mr. Whitlam explained to the author in one interview that, in addition to his belief that the Department of Immigration was a very inadequate department with entrenched racist views, he simply had no one in the Cabinet who could take Al Grassby's place.

24 This is reminiscent of events in Canada in December 1965 when the Department of Citizenship and Immigration died a sudden death, to be replaced almost immediately by a new Department of Manpower and Immigration. Hardly anyone in the old department was informed. *See* the author's study, *Canada and Immigration: Public Policy and Public Concern*, pp. 150–56.

25 Hansard, House of Representatives, July 30, 1974. Clyde Cameron had for some time considered himself a natural choice to head a combined Ministry for Labor and Immigration, and in December 1972 issued a press release describing himself as "Minister for Labor and Immigration – elect." The ALP caucus, however, elected Al Grassby as the first Labor Minister for Immigration.

26 The Hon. Clyde Cameron, Minister for Labor and Immigration, press statement, Canberra, October 2, 1974.

27 Interview with the Hon. Clyde Cameron, Minister for Labor and Immigration, by Alan Ramsey and Kenneth Randall, *New Accent*, Canberra, August 2, 1974.

28 Freudenberg, *A Certain Grandeur*, p. 355.

29 Interview, May 30, 1978.

30 Professor W.D. Borrie, CBE, is now Emeritus Professor of Demography at the Australian National University.

31 *National Population Inquiry, First Report*, vol. 1, introductory chapter, "The Terms of Reference and their Interpretation."

32 National Population Inquiry, First Report, volume 2, p. 711.

33 Ibid., pp. 711 and 741.

34 Ibid., p. 742.

35 Ibid., pp. 711–24.

36 Ibid., pp. 724–25.

37 National Population Inquiry, First Report, p. 746.

38 The Hon. Clyde Cameron MP, Minister for Labor and Immigration, news release, February 2, 1975.

39 Senator James McClelland, Minister for Labor and Immigration, news release, September 5, 1975.

40 The election results were as follows: *House of Representatives*: Liberal–NCP 91, ALP 36. *Senate*: Liberal–NCP 36, ALP 27, Independent 1. The Fraser government won the next two elections (1977 and 1981) but lost control of the Senate in 1981. It was finally defeated by a revitalized Labor Party under a new leader, Bob Hawke, who won a landslide victory on March 5, 1983.

41 John Edwards, *Life Wasn't Meant to be Easy: a Political Profile of Malcolm Fraser* (Sydney: Mayhem, 1977), Chapter 2.

42 Interview, August 25, 1977.

43 The Public Service Board is the body in Australia which acts as the central personnel authority and management improvement agency for the Australian Public Service.

44 Australia, *The Commonwealth Government and the Urban Environment* (Canberra: Australian Government Publishing Service, 1978).

45 In the interview already referred to with the Hon. Michael MacKellar, Minister for Immigration and Ethnic Affairs, 1975–1979, Mr. MacKellar said that he would have liked to get population "well and truly in from the beginning," but was afraid of being too explicit about this in case other departments might get hold of it.

46 Department of Immigration and Ethnic Affairs, *Review 1978 A Review of Activities to June 30, 1978* (Canberra: Australian Government Publishing Service, 1978).

47 *See* the author's earlier study, *Canada and Immigration: Public Policy and Public Concern.*

48 Cameron Hazelhurst and J.R. Nethercote, eds., *Reforming Australian Government: The Coombes Report and Beyond* (Canberra: Australian National University Press, 1977), Introduction, p. 1.

49 Interview with Lady Heydon, Canberra, September 1, 1977.

50 This view is reflected in the following comment from the introduction to the Department's 1979 annual review which contains a brief review of management problems: "People joining the Department tend to make it a career decision. There has been relatively little movement to other departments. That does maintain the Department's functional expertise. On the other hand, until recently, the character of the Department's work offered insufficient training and experience in major financial management, in the gamut of parliamentary and legal business, in aspects of general office management and in applied research." Department of Immigration and Ethnic Affairs, *Review 1979* (Canberra: Australian Government Publishing Service, January 23, 1978).

51 Interview, Canberra, January 23, 1978.

52 *See* Department of Immigration and Ethnic Affairs, *Reviews 1981* and *1983*.

53 Joint Management Review, *Immigration Functions Related to Control and Entry*, 2 vols. (Canberra: Department of Immigration and Ethnic Affairs, July 1978). In writing this section of the book the author had the benefit of some very useful discussions with Mr. Casselman.

54 *See* Freda Hawkins, *Canada and Immigration: Public Policy and Public Concern*, pp. 102–05, for a discussion of the effect of the wide powers of discretion given to the Minister of Citizenship and Immigration under Canada's Immigration Act 1952.

55 The *Australis*, the last liner carrying migrants to Australia, docked in Melbourne on December 15, 1977. She was carrying 650 assisted migrants.

56 Minister for Immigration and Ethnics Affairs, news release, DIEA 19/76, March 30, 1976.

57 Ibid.

58 Ibid.

59 The author was made an honorary member and consultant to APIC while in Australia and attended almost all its full council meetings, as well as a number of committee meetings.

60 For most of this period, Professor W.D. Borrie, formerly Director of the National Population Inquiry, was Chairman of APIC's Migration Committee. This point was made in his report.

61 Australian Population and Immigration Council, *Immigration Policies and Australia's Population, a Green Paper* (Canberra: Australian Government Publishing Service, 1977).

62 An internal task force within the Department of Immigration and Ethnic Affairs, headed by the First Assistant Secretary, was in charge of this policy review.

63 The Hon. M.J.R. MacKellar, MP, Minister for Immigration and Ethnic Affairs, "Australia's Immigration Policy," Australian Government Publishing Service, Canberra, 1978.

64 *See* Chapter 4 for a further discussion of the Trans-Tasman Travel Arrangement.

65 The British Immigration Act 1971, introduced by the Heath government, created the category of "patrials" for those who would have an automatic right of entry into Britain, and "non-patrials" for those whose entry would be restricted. Patrials were those who could claim at least a distant family connection with Britain. This Act was superseded by the British Nationality Act 1981 which abolished the concept of patriality.

66 Employment and Immigration Canada, *Annual Report to Parliament on Immigration Levels 1981*, p. 33.

67 Joint Management Review, vol. 1, pp. 4-74.

68 The Administrative Review Council was established under the Administrative Appeals Tribunal Act 1975, together with the Administrative Appeals Tribunal. The council is an advisory body making recommendations to the Attorney General, designed to provide citizens with the most effective way of obtaining a review of adverse administrative decisions; and to improve the quality of decisions that affect the interests of citizens. The Administrative Appeals Tribunal, with which the council is directly concerned, is an independent tribunal which reviews decisions made by Commonwealth ministers, authorities, and officials. At that time, it was empowered to review decisions made by the Minister for Immigration and Ethnic Affairs under three sections of the Migration Act only: Section 12, Deportation of aliens convicted of crimes; Section 13, Deportation of immigrants in respect of matters occurring within five years after entry; and Section 48, Directions by the Minsiter that a person shall not act as an Immigration Agent. By mid-summer 1978, only a very small number of cases had been initiated.

69 The Commonwealth Ombudsman is appointed under the Ombudsman Act 1976 with authority to investigate complaints, and to initiate inquiries concerning administrative actions of departments and prescribed authorities, and to make reports regarding those investigations. He is not authorized to investigate actions taken by a Minister, but may review the advice and recommendations given to the Minister.

70 MacKellar, *Australia's Immigration Policy*, p. 11.

71 *Migrant Services and Programs*, Report of the Review of Post-Arrival Programs and Services for Migrans (Canberra: Australian Government Publishing Service, 1978).

72 Ibid., pp. 3-4.

73 Department of Immigration and Ethnic Affairs, *Review '81* (Canberra: Australian Government Publishing Service, 1981, p. 18).

74 Australian Institute of Multicultural Affairs, *Evaluation of Post-Arrival Programs and Services*, Melbourne, May 1982.

75 Ibid., pp. 8-9.

76 Ibid., p. 12.

77 Ibid., p. 8.

78 The Immigration Survey of 1973 actually replaced a proposed "longitudinal survey" of migrant experiences (i.e., a survey conducted through the first few years of a mgirant's settlement in Australia), which was announced by the Department of Immigration in 1970. This would have followed the lines of the Canadian Longitudinal Study on the Economic and Social Adaption of Immigrants, started by the Canadian Department of Manpower and Immigration in 1969, whose Director, Dr. E. Ziegler, visited Canberra in June 1970. After Dr. Ziegler's visit, the Department of

Immigration sent their senior officer in charge of immigration research to Ottawa in the fall of 1970, to examine the Canadian Longitudinal Study more closely and to work out an Australian version of it. But when, on his return, the Commonwealth Bureau of Census and Statistics was consulted, it recommended that a "cross-sectional survey of the migrant population" would be preferable; this was carried out in 1973. The Canadian Longitudinal Study consisted of three separate surveys of large groups of immigrants selected in 1969, 1970, and 1971. The results of the first survey were published as part of the Green Paper on Immigration Policy in 1975. The results of the second and third surveys, which did not differ greatly from those of the first, were reviewed by the Department in 1973–1974, but never published.

79 Immigration Advisory Council Committee on Social Patterns, *Inquiry into the Departure of Settlers from Australia*, report on the 1973 Immigration Survey (Canberra: Australian Government Publishing Service, 1973): Australian Population and Immigration Council, *A Decade of Migrant Settlement*, report on the 1973 Immigration Survey (Canberra: Australian Government Publishing Service, 1976).

80 The SSAS factors were as follows:
Part A (Economic Factors): age, employment, occupational skills, physical, age or other factors, availability of employment, experience, employment record, knowledge of English, financial aspects (income, assets, funds for transfer to Australia); *Part B (Personal and Social Factors)*: attitude to migration, expectations, responsiveness, initiative, self-reliance and independence, presentation (appearance, personal hygiene, speech, behaviour), family unity, community, sport and cultural interests, and convictions (if any). In Part B the questions applied to the spouse and children as well as to the applicant.

81 Professor Jerzy (George) Zubrzycki, CBE, Professor of Sociology at the Australian National University (now retired) is a well-known and influential figure in Australian immigration. He became Chairman of the former Australian Ethnic Affairs Council in 1977 and was a member of the Council of the former Institute of Multicultural Affairs. He has written on a wide range of subjects in immigration and ethnic affairs (see Bibliography). While in Ottawa during the academic year 1973–1974, he studied Canadian selection procedures, took part in discussions relating to the preparation of Canada's Green Paper on Immigration Policy, and attended meetings of the then Advisory Council on the Adjustment of Immigrants of which the author was a member. Professor Zubrzycki reported his findings on Australia's Structured Selection Assessment System to the Social Studies Committee of the Australian Population and Immigration Council.

82 From a leaflet on NUMAS produced by the Department of Immigration and

Ethnic Affairs in September 1979 for use in immigration offices and else-where.

83 *Canberra Times*, June 24, 1980.

84 Interview, Canberra, August 29, 1980.

85 Minister for Immigration and Ethnic Affairs, news release, Canberra, March 6, 1981.

86 Minister for Immigration and Ethnic Affairs, Statement to Parliament, Canberra, October 29, 1981.

87 Ibid., and *Review '82*, Department of Immigration and Ethnic Affairs, 1981–1982, p. 52. Australia now has a *Freedom of Information Act* which became law on December 1, 1982. This Act extends the right of the public to access to official information possessed by public authorities of the Commonwealth by (1) making internal rules and procedures available to the public; (2) giving a right of access to official documents of ministers and departments; (3) giving an opportunity to amend personal records on official files that are incomplete, incorrect, out of date, or misleading; and (4) providing for internal and external review of decisions made under the Act.

Canada has an *Access to Information Act* which became effective on July 1, 1983. The first two schedules of this Act constitute an Access to Information Act and a Privacy Act. The purpose of the first is "to extend the present laws of Canada to provide a right of access to information in records under the control of a government institution in accordance with the principles that government information should be available to the pub-lic, that necessary exceptions to the right of access should be limited and specific and that decisions on the disclosure of government information should be reviewed independently by government." The purpose of the second schedule is "to extend the present laws of Canada that protect the privacy of individuals with respect to personal information about them-selves held by a government institution and that provide individuals with a right of access to such information."

88 *See* "The Grass is still Greener for Some," an interesting article by John Coomber in the *Canberra Times* of December 29, 1982.

89 New Zealand recognizes a special responsibility towards the peoples of the South Pacific. Inhabitants of the Cook Islands, Niue and the Tokelaus are New Zealand citizens and can move the New Zealand freely.

90 Information in this section on the Trans-Tasman Travel Arrangement comes from a series of interviews with DIEA officials in 1980, from Depart-ment documentation, and from reports and articles in the *Canberra Times* for April 28, 1981, September 27, 1982, November 2, 1982 and December 29, 1982.

91 *The Economist*, "Bob Hawke's Australia: A Survey," August 6, 1983, p. 3.

92 *The London Observer*, "Australia's Hawke Takes Wing," article reprinted in the Toronto *Globe and Mail*, February 21, 1983.

93 As one example of Mr. Hayden's views on this subject, see the *Canberra Times*, September 14, 1981.

94 *The Australian*, "The ALP National Conference," July 6, 1982.

95 Stewart West is a former trade unionist who was born on March 31, 1934 at Forbes, New South Wales. His family moved to Wollongong in 1941 and he was educated at Wollongong High School. After leaving school, he became in turn a bank officer, a steel worker, and a waterside worker, and became President of the South Coast Branch of the Waterside Workers Federation in 1972. He was elected to the House of Representatives in a by-election in October 1977 and has been re-elected in 1980 and 1983.

96 Parliamentary Debates, House of Representatives, Australia's Immigration Policy and Program, May 18, 1983, pp. 662–66.

97 On October 16, 1982, in line with New South Wales, Victoria and Queensland, the National Country Party dropped "Country" from its title. From then on, the party became known as the National Party at the federal level and the coalition became the L-NP.

CHAPTER FOUR

1 Freda Hawkins, *Canada and Immigration: Public Policy and Public Concern*, p. 20.

2 Letter from the Minister of Manpower and Immigration to the Chairman of the Advisory Board on the Adjustment of Immigrants, June 1, 1970. Department of Manpower and Immigration, Background Paper, "The Intergovernmental Committee for European Migration," June 17, 1969.

3 A further explanation for the third reason was offered later on in the paper: "ICEM's current activities range from helping individual migrants or refugees to assisting member governments in the development of migration programs. Insofar as the development of migration programs is concerned, ICEM has been concentrating on Latin America, with the United States as the main driving force and financial backer. The U.S., of course, is primarily interested in strengthening the economic and skilled manpower resources of Latin American countries and makes use of ICEM recruitment facilities in connection with technical co-operation programmes of the O.A.S."

4 Hansard, House of Representatives, September 12, 1973, pp. 931–33.

5 UN Economic and Social Council, Second Regular Session 1982, *Report of the United Nations High Commissioner for Refugees*, May 14, 1982, p. 60.

6 For a full account of Canada's lack of response to the plight of Jewish refugees and of Canadian attitudes during this period, see Dirks, *Canada's*

Refugee Policy: Indifference or Opportunism? (Montreal: McGill-Queen's University Press, 1977), Chapters 3 and 4, and Abella and Troper, *None is Too Many: Canada and the Jews of Europe 1933–1948* (Toronto: Lester and Orpen Dennys, 1982).

7 Canada, for example, admitted 29,512, refugees on an individual basis between 1959 and 1979.

8 *See* Charles Price, "Immigration Policies and Refugees," *International Migration Review*, vol. 15, Spring–Summer 1981.

9 Quoted in Gerald Dirks, *Canada's Refugee Policy: Indifference or Opportunism?* (Montreal: McGill-Queen's University Press, 1977).

10 It is true that this produced a very good-looking, well-qualified group of individual refugees and families (including a number of elderly people), and that Canada was later criticized for taking "the cream of the crop." Can we really expect immigration officers to do otherwise, unless there is some kind of planned sharing effort on the part of the countries involved in relation to the less well-qualified and the handicapped?

11 Department of Manpower and Immigration, *Ugandan Asian Expellees: The First Twelve Months in Canada* (Ottawa: Canada Employment and Immigration Commission, April 14, 1977).

12 For more detailed information on Canada's Ugandan Asian refugee movement, see the author's article "Uganda Asians in Canada," *New Community*, Journal of the British Community Relations Commission (now the Commission for Racial Equality), vol. 11, no. 3, Summer 1973.

13 Canada's temporary immigration office in Kampala had had a staff of 42. In a brief submitted to the Canadian government in October 1974 by a number of concerned organizations, including the Canadian Council of Churches, the Canadian Labour Congress, the Confederation of National Trade Unions, Amnesty International and Oxfam, the following statement was made: "Canada has reacted reluctantly and slowly to the refugee situation created by the coup and its aftermath ... Expressed humanitarian concern by the Canadian government has been contradicted by the lengthy processing and excessive security interrogations." Quoted in Gerald Dirks, *Canada's Refugee Policy*.

14 *See* Frank Frost, "Australia's War in Vietnam 1962–1972," in *Australia's Vietnam, Australia in the Second Indochina War*, Peter King, ed. (Sydney: George Allen and Unwin, 1983), p. 57, and Michael Sextan, *War for the Asking: Australia's Vietnam Secrets* (London: Penguin Books, 1981).

15 Since 1975, a tragic conflict has continued in East Timor in which many Timorese have died or become refugees. For several centuries, the island of Timor, some 400 miles northwest of Australia, was divided between the Dutch in the western half and the Portuguese in the east. While West Timor, together with other parts of the Dutch East Indies, became the Republic of Indonesia in 1949, East Timor remained under Portuguese

rule. This continued until the April 1974 revolution in Portugal, following
which her overseas territories were finally decolonized. But in 1975, civil
war broke out in East Timor between rival factions with different views on
her future. When the left-wing, anti-Indonesian liberation movement Fretelin (Revolutionary Front for Independence) was gaining the upper hand
and had proclaimed an independent Democratic Republic of East Timor,
Indonesian forces invaded on December 7, 1975. In August 1976, East
Timor was officialy incorporated in Indonesia. Fretelin's resistance continued, however, and has been supported by a majority of the UN member
states. Nevertheless, a number of states, including Australia and New Zealand, have given official recognition to the incorporation of East Timor in
Indonesia – although not to the arbitrary methods used – on the grounds
that an independent state would not be viable, that Fretelin has known
pro-Communist sympathies, and that such a state might be a potential
source of instability in the region.

The number of casualties and refugees resulting from this conflict have
been difficult to estimate. Indonesian figures indicate that by 1980, some
60,000 people had died in East Timor as a result of the civil war or starvation, and that some 25,000 had fled to West Timor and about 5,000 to
Australia. Today the guerrilla war between Fretelin and the Indonesian
Army continues, and Timorese refugees and their relatives are still being
admitted to Australia.

16 Senate Standing Committee on Foreign Affairs and Defence, *Australia
and the Refugee Problem: The Plight and Circumstances of Vietnamese
and other refugees* (Canberra: Australian Government Publishing Service,
1976).

17 Ibid., pp. 20 and 24.

18 Piracy continues. The United Nations High Commissioner for Refugees
stated in 1984 that since 1980 he had received reports of 1,376 murders of
boat people, 2,283 rapes and 592 abductions of women whose fate is now
unknown. Anti-piracy efforts by the Thai government (many pirates are
known to be Thai fishermen), coupled with the diminishing refugee traffic,
have reduced the number of incidents. It is believed that some Thai local
authorities, hoping to discourage the flow of refugees, are still avoiding
vigorous action however. (*Globe and Mail*, Toronto, June 8, 1984).

An anti-piracy program was introduced in 1981, through an agreement
between the Thai government and 11 donor countries, which involved sur-
veillance of a large area of the South China Sea by aircraft and patrol
boats. UNHCR reports that, in 1982, 64 per cent of the boats had been
attacked by pirates during their voyage, but that the percentage dropped
to 53 per cent in 1983 and to 36 per cent in 1984.

19 Employment and Immigration Canada, *Annual Report to Parliament on
Immigration Levels 1983*, p. 23.

20 *Levels Report*, 190, p. 20.

21 Ibid., pp. 89–98.

22 The Hon. M.J.R. MacKellar, MP, Minister for Immigration and Ethnic Affairs, "Refugee Policy and Mechanisms," ministerial statement, Parliamentary Debates, May 24, 1977.

24 Australia's application to return to ICEM as an observer was approved by ICEM's council at meetings on November 15–16, 1977.

25 UNHCR, "UNHCR Activities in Relation to Indo-Chinese Refugees and Displaced Persons since 1975," (Geneval: UNHCR, April 1979); and Australia, Department of Immigration and Ethnic Affairs, *Review '79* (Canberra: Australian Government Publishing Service, 1979).

26 Two transit centres known as Refugee Processing Centres (RPCs), were created: the largest one with accommodation for 17,200 refugees at Bataan in the Philippines, which was opened in the early months of 1980, and a second, smaller one on Galang Island in Indonesia a year later. About 2,700 refugees arrived at and departed from Bataan each month and more than 100,000 passed through Galang RPC since it opened. Both centres are very well organized, accessible to government officials and voluntary agencies, and offer language, orientation, and skill training courses for refugees. *See* UNHCR's monthly journal *Refugees*, No. 6, June 1984, pp. 13–16.

27 UNHCR, Opening Statement of the High Commissioner to the Thirtieth Session of the Executive Committee of the High Commissioner's Programme, Geneva, October 8, 1979; and Australia, Department of Immigration and Ethnic Affairs, *Review '80* (Canberra: Australian Government Publishing Service, 1980).

28 US Committee for Refugees, *World Refugee Survey 1983*, New York, pp. 62–72; and Australia, Department of Immigration and Ethnic Affairs, news release, "Refugees – A Gain for Australia," June 1984. Both Canada and Australia tend to claim from time to time that they have admitted more refugees than anyone else. However, the *World Refugee Survey 1983* shows that as of June 1982, Australia could boast the highest ratio of refugees to population, with Canada second, and the United States in third place.

29 The Canadian Foundation for Refugees was given a large initial grant but no further funding, except for the provision of accommodation, services, supplies, and salaries for a staff of five by the Canada Employment and Immigration Commission. The foundation saw itself as a service organization and resource centre for community agencies and groups working with refugees across Canada, as well as a useful source of public education in the problems and needs of refugees. It did not enjoy any special consultative relationship with government on Canadian refugee policies and programs, however, and was later disbanded.

30 Canada Employment and Immigration Commission, *Indochinese Refugees: The Canadian Response, 1979* and *1980* (Ottawa: Supply and Services Canada, 1982).

31 Canada, House of Commons Debates, vol. 124, no. 8, April 23, 1980, p. 338.

32 *See* the following articles on Australia's contemporary refugee policies and programs: Charles Price, "Immigration Policies and Refugees in Australia," *International Migration Review*, Special Issue on Refugees Today, vol. 15, Spring–Summer 1981, New York Centre for Migration; David Cox, "Refugee Settlement in Australia: Review of an Era," *International Migration*, Quarterly Review of the Intergovernmental Committee for Migration, Geneva, vol. 21, no. 3, 1983; and Trevor Griffiths, "The Australian Resettlement Approach," *Migration News*, Quarterly Journal of the International Catholic Migration Commission, Geneva, January–March 1983.

33 Australia, Department of Immigration and Ethnic Affairs, *Review '83*, Migrant Centres, pp. 72–76 (Canberra: Australian Government Publishing Service, 1983).

34 Charles Price, "Immigration Policies and Refugees in Australia," p. 104.

35 Australia, Department of Immigration and Ethnic Affairs, *Reviews '80, 81 and '83*, ((Canberra: Australian Government Publishing Service); and DIEA news release, "Refugees – A Gain for Australia," June 1984.

36 Trevor Griffiths, "The Australian Resettlement Approach."

37 Australia, Senate Standing Committee on Foreign Affairs and Defence, Report, *Indochinese Refugee Resettlement – Australia's Involvement* (Canberra: Australian Government Publishing Service, 1982).

38 Ibid., pp. xiii–xiv.

39 UNHCR, Executive Committee, *Note on Procedures for the Determination of Refugee Status*, Geneva, October 3, 1983; Ed Ratushny, Special Advisor to the Minister of Employment and Immigration, Report, *A New Refugee Status Determination Process for Canada* (Ottawa: Supply and Services Canada, 1984); Jean-François Durieux, "Refugee Status Determination Procedure in Germany, France, the U.S.A. and Australia," and Raphael Girard, "The Refugee Claims System," in *Refugee*, Special Issue on Refugee Status Determination, vol. 3, no. 4 (Toronto: York University, June 1984).

40 Ratushny, Ibid., p. x.

41 David Matas, "The Refugee-Claims Procedure – An Overview," *Refugee*, vol. 3, no. 4 (Toronto: York University, June 1984). Mr. Matas was a member of the Task Force on Immigration Practices and Procedures which produced a report for the Minister on the refugee status determination process in September 1980.

42 Canada, Office of the Minister of Employment and Immigration, W.G. Robinson, Special Advisor, *Illegal Migrants in Canada* (Ottawa: Supply and Services Canada, June 1983).

43 Canada, Office of the Minister of Employment and Immigration, Report of the Task Force on Immigration Practices and Procedures, *The Refugee Status Determination Process* (Ottawa: Supply and Services Canada, September 1981).

44 Ratushny, A New Refugee Status Determination Process for Canada, p. 61.

45 For more information about this proposal, see Barbara Jackman, "Models of Change in Canada's Refugee Status Determination Process," *Refugee*, vol. 3, no. 4 (Toronto: York University, June 1984).

46 UN General Assembly, Resolution No. 3449 (30), December 9, 1975.

47 G. Bertinetto, "International Regulations on Illegal Migration," ICM Seminar, Geneva, April 11–15, 1983 (see below).

48 Dr. James L. Carlin, Director, Opening Statement, Intergovernmental Committee for Migration, Sixth Seminar on the Adaptation and Integration of Immigrants on the theme of "Undocumented Migrants in an Irregular Situation," Geneva, April 11–15, 1983, *International Migration*, vol. 21, no. 2, 1983, pp. 97–100.

49 Ibid., pp. 103–16.

50 Ibid., Marta Peletier, "Rights and Obligations of Unauthorized Immigrants in the Receiving Countries, Protection of the Fundamental Rights of Unauthorized Immigrants," p. 175.

51 Ibid., W.A. Dumon, "Effects of Undocumented Migration for the Individuals Concerned," p. 227.

52 International Labour Office, Migration for Employment Project, Working Paper, David S. North, *The Canadian Experience with Amnesty for Aliens: What the United States Can Learn*, Geneva, 1979, p. 2.

53 Department of Immigration and Ethnic Affairs, *Review '76* (Canberra: Australian Government Publishing Service) pp. 16–17.

54 An earlier amnesty, described as "a special dispensation for people who are living in Australia illegally and who may be suffering from exploitation as a result," was proclaimed by the then Minister for Immigration, Al Grassby, on Australia Day 1974. No particular promotion or publicity effort was made, however, and only 400 undocumented migrants came forward.

55 Department of Immigration and Ethnic Affairs, *Review '77* (Canberra: Australian Government Publishing Service) p. 18.

56 Minister for Immigration and Ethnic Affairs, news release, "Amnesty for Illegal Immigrants," Canberra, January 5, 1976.

57 Department of Immigration and Ethnic Affairs, *Review '78*, p. 33.

58 Debate on Migrant Amendment Bill (No. 2) 1980, Parliamentary Debates, House of Representatives, November 27, pp. 151–54.

59 Debate on the Immigration (Unauthorized Arrivals) Bill 1980, Second Reading, speech by the Hon. Ian Macphee, Minister for Immigration and Ethnic Affairs, Parliamentary Debates, House of Representatives.

60 The Hon. Ian Macphee, MP, Minister for Immigration and Ethnic Affairs, news release, Canberra, June 19, 1980.

61 Department of Immigration and Ethnic Affairs, *Review '81* (Canberra: Australian Government Publishing Service) p. 57.

62 Ibid., p. 56.

63 International Labour Office, International Migration for Employment, Working Paper, Desmond Storer, "Out of the Shadows, A Review of the 1980 Regularisation of Status Programme in Australia," Geneva, 1982.

64 See Chapter 2, pp. 45–50.

65 The Canadians spent approximately C$2,000,000 on their Adjustment of Status program while the Australians spent A$100,000 on ROSP.

66 Canada Employment and Immigration Council, *Illegal Immigrants, Report to the Minister of Employment and Immigration* (Ottawa: Canada Employment and Immigration Commission, 1982.) *See* the discussion in the final chapter on the performance of the Liberal government in relation to advisory councils.

67 The Task Force produced two other reports: *Domestic Workers on Employment Authorizations* and *The Exploitation of Potential Immigrants by Unscrupulous Consultants*, both submitted in April 1981 (see Bibliography).

68 W.G. Robinson, Special Advisor to the Minister of Employment and Immigration, *Illegal Immigrants Issues Paper*, Discussion Paper, Canada Employment and Immigration Commission, Ottawa, February 15, 1983.

69 W.G. Robinson, Special Advisor to the Minister of Employment and Immigration, Report, *Illegal Migrants in Canada* (Ottawa: Supply and Services Canada, 1983).

70 *Illegal Immigrants Issues Paper*, p. 24.

71 The Hon. Lloyd Axworthy, PC, MP, Statement on Illegal Immigration to the House of Commons Committee on Labour, Manpower and Immigration (Ottawa: Canada Employment and Immigration Commission, June 29, 1983).

72 *Illegal Migrants in Canada*. The Robinson report contains both general discussion and specific recommendations. For reasons of space and sometimes clarity, several important statements from the general discussion have been included in the recommendations. Several recommendations on the same topic have also been amalgamated.

73 Axworthy statement on illegal immigration, p. 9

74 The Hon. John Roberts, PC, MP, Minister of Employment and Immigration, press release, November 17, 1983.

75 Australia News Bulletin, Australian High Commission, Ottawa, September 9, 1982.

76 Department of Immigration and Ethnic Affairs, *Review '83* (Canberra: Australian Government Publishing Service, p. 40).

CHAPTER FIVE

1 Some of the ideas in this chapter have also been included in a report for the Hon. James Fleming, PC, MP, formerly Minister of State for Multiculturalism, entitled *Multiculturalism in Australia: A Short Report and Evaluation* (Ottawa: Department of the Secretary of State, December 1980); in briefs to the former Australian Population and Immigration Council and the Australian Ethnic Affairs Council, Department of Immigration and Ethnic Affairs, Canberra, June 1978 and August 1980; and in an article in the *Journal of Canadian Studies* entitled "Multiculturalism in Two Countries: The Canadian and Australian Experience vol. 17, no. 1, Spring 1982.

2 Reservations of this kind were frequently expressed during the author's interviews with politicians and senior officials in Canada and Australia.

3 *See*, for example, a very interesting article on multiculturalism by W.W. Isajiw of the University of Toronto entitled "Multiculturalism and the Integration of the Canadian Community," *Canadian Ethnic Studies*, vol. 15, no. 2, 1983.

4 *See* the author's earlier study, *Canada and Immigration: Public Policy and Public Concern*, parts 2 and 3.

5 Report of the Royal Commission on Bilingualism and Biculturalism, Book 4, *The Cultural Contribution of the Other Ethnic Groups* (Ottawa: Supply and Services Canada October 23, 1969).

6 In October 1970, a Quebec cabinet minister, Pierre Laporte, was murdered and the British Trade Commissioner, James Cross, was abducted by a group of separatists. The crisis had evoked what was felt by many to be a considerable over-reaction by the federal government. Donald Smiley, a leading authority on Canadian federalism, said, for example, that multiculturalism introduced "a new irritant" into French-English relations in Canada from that point on.

7 Canada, House of Commons Debates, October 8, 1971, pp. 8545–46.

8 *Le Devoir*, November 17, 1981. *See* also Howard Palmer, ed., *Immigration and the Rise of Multiculturalism* (Toronto: Copp Clark, Issues in Canadian History, 1975) p. 151.

9 Report of the Second Canadian Conference on Multiculturalism, Guy Rocher, "Multiculturalism: The Doubts of a Francophone," (Ottawa:

Department of the Secretary of State, February 13–15, 1976), p. 47.

10 Ibid., p. 15.

11 *The Globe and Mail*, Toronto, December 1, 1975.

12 The Progressive Conservative government under Joe Clark held office from June 4, 1979 to March 2, 1980.

13 News release, Multiculturalism Canada, Department of the Secretary of State, November 14, 1983.

14 Canada, House of Commons, *Equality Now!*, Report of the Special Committee of the House of Commons on Participation of Visible Minorities in Canadian Society (Ottawa: Supply and Services Canada, March 1984).

15 The Hon. James Fleming, PC, MP, Minister of State for Multiculturalism, Open Letter, Multiculturalism Canada, Department of the Secretary of State, Ottawa, February 1.

16 Interview, Toronto, December 29, 1983.

17 *See* James Struthers, "Multiculturalism: Retrospect and Prospect" (editorial), Alan B. Anderson, "Canadian Ethnic Studies: Traditional Preoccupations and New Directions," Norman Buchignani "Canadian Ethnic Research and Multiculturalism," and other articles in *Multiculturalism: The First Decade*, a special issue of the *Journal of Canadian Studies* (funded by Multiculturalism Canada), vol. 17, no. 1, Spring 1982.

18 LNCP, Policy Statement, August 1975.

19 Australian Ethnic Affairs Council, *Australia as a Multicultural Society* (Canberra: Australian Government Publishing Service, 1978); Australian Population and Immigration Council and Australian Ethnic Affairs Council, *Multiculturalism and its Implications for Immigration Policy* (Canberra: Australian Government Publishing Service, 1979); Australian Council on Population and Ethnic Affairs, *Multiculturalism for all Australians: Our Developing Nationhood* (Canberra: Australian Government Publishing Service, 1982).

20 Ibid., *Australia as a Multicultural Society*, p. 4, *Multiculturalism and its Implications for Immigration Policy*, p. 9, *Multiculturalism for all Australians: Our Developing Nationhood*, p. 1.

21 Ibid., *Multiculturalism for all Australians: Our Developing Nationhood*, p. x.

22 Ibid., *Multiculturalism and its Implications for Immigration Policy*, p. 6.

23 The Hon. Stewart J. West, M.P., Minister for Immigration and Ethnic Affairs, news release, July 24, 1983.

24 Committee of Review of the Australian Institute of Multicultural Affairs, *Report to the Minister for Immigration and Ethnic Affairs*, vols. 1 and 2 (Canberra: Australian Government Publishing Service, November 1983), vol. 1, Chapter 7, Conclusions.

25 Ibid., Chapter 1, Summary of Main Recommendations.

26 Australian Institute of Multicultural Affairs, *Response to the Report to*

the Minister for Immigration and Ethnic Affairs of the Committee of Review of the Australian Institute of Multicultural Affairs, AIMA, December 17, 1983, p. 1.

27 Ibid., Section 1, Response to the Report.

28 The Council of the Australian Institute of Multicultural Affairs (AIMA), *Looking Forward: A Report on Consultations concerning the Recommendations of the Committee of Review of the Australian Institute of Multicultural Affairs* (Melbourne: AIMA, April 1984).

29 Parliamentary debates, House of Representatives, October 11, 1984, pp. 2174–77.

30 *The Globe and Mail*, June 4, 1984.

CHAPTER SIX

1 Australia, Department of Immigration and Ethnic Affairs, *Reviews '79 and '84* (Canberra: Australian Government Publishing Service).

2 Ibid., *Review '84*, p. 1.

3 Nancy Tienhaara, *Canadian Views on Immigration and Population*, Supplementary Study to the Green Paper on Immigration Policy (Ottawa: Department of Manpower and Immigration, 1975).

4 Howard Adelman, *Canada and the Indochinese Refugees* (Regina: Weigl Educational Associates, 1982), p. 2.

5 Liberal Party of Australia/National Party of Australia, *Policy on Immigration*, Canberra, October 1984.

6 The Hon. Stewart West, MP, Minister for Immigration and Ethnic Affairs, news release, Canberra, November 9, 1984.

7 The Immigration Planning Council, *Australia's Immigration Program for the Period 1968 to 1973*, A Report to the Minister of State for Immigration, the Hon. B.M. Snedden, QC, MP, tabled in the House of Representatives, September 10, 1968.

8 Canada Employment and Immigration Commission, *Background Paper on Future Immigration Levels* (Ottawa: CEIC, November 1984), p. 21.

9 The Hon. Stewart West, MP, Minister for Immigration and Ethnic Affairs and the Hon. Ralph Willis, MP, Minister for Employment and Industrial Relations, joint news release, Canberra, February 22, 1984.

10 Canada Employment and Immigration Commission, *Background Paper on Future Immigration Levels*, pp. 4–6.

11 Department of Immigration and Ethnic Affairs, *Review '84*, The Immigration Program (Canberra: Australian Government Publishing Service) pp. 23–32.

12 For the purpose of Canadian census classification, an immigrant is a resident of Canada who is not a Canadian citizen by birth. Thus, persons born outside Canada, except those whose parents are Canadian, are con-

sidered to be immigrants. As well, a few persons born in Canada who were not considered as Canadians at birth but later obtained Canadian resident status are included among the immigrant population. Thus "Immigrants" are people alive today who came to settle in Canada either as children or adults (Statistics Canada).

13 The information in this section comes from the following Statistics Canada publication with a few minor changes and omissions: *Canada's Immigrants*, 1981 Census of Canada (Ottawa: Supply and Services Canada, 1984).

14 Charles A. Price, *Australian Immigration: A Bibliography and Digest*, no. 4, 1979 and supplement, 1981 (Canberra: Department of Demography, Australian National University).

15 *The Australian Encyclopedia*, 4th Edition, Population.

16 *See* F.K. Hare, Provost, Trinity College, University of Toronto and Chairman of Canada's Climate Planning Board, *Future Climate and the Canadian Economy* (Ottawa: Environment Canada, 1981). Professor Hare writes: "scientific opinion is nevertheless tending to the view that true climatic change is just around the corner, and indeed in slow progress already. This change is expected to come from the rapid increase of carbon dioxide in the atmosphere, together with a parallel increase in other radioactively active gases.... These effects are the result of human interference – of fossil fuel burning, of forest decrease, of the wastage of soil humus, of increased fertilizer use, and of the release of industrial pollutants. They will work towards a substantial warming at the earth's surface, in the view of many authorities." *See* also A.B. Pittock, Commonwealth Scientific and Industrial Research Organization (CSIRO), Australia, and M.J. Salinger, University of East Anglia, "Towards Regional Scenarios for a CO_2 – Warmed Earth," *Climatic Change 4*, 1982; and A.B. Pittock, CSIRO, "Recent Climatic Change in Australia, Implications for a CO_2 – Warmed Earth," *Climatic Change 5*, 1983.

17 Leon F. Bouvier, "*Planet Earth 1984–2034: A Demographic Vision*," in *Population Bulletin*, a publication of the Population Reference Bureau, vol. 39, no. 1, Washington, D.C., February 1984.

18 Paul Ehrlich, *The Population Bomb* (New York: Ballantine, 1968).

19 Department of Immigration and Ethnic Affairs, *Review of Australia's Demographic Trends 1983* (Canberra: Australian Government Publishing Service, 1983); and David K. Foot, *Canada's Population Outlook: Demographic Futures and Economic Challenges*, The Canadian Institute for Economic Policy Series (Toronto: James Lorimer 1982).

20 Canada Employment and Immigration Commission, *Background Paper on Immigration Levels, 1984*, pp. 29–37.

21 The Hon. Chris Hurford, MP, Minister for Immigration and Ethnic Affairs, *Statement to Parliament on the 1986/87 Migration Program*.

22 Lorna Lippmann, "Asian Immigration and Public Opinion," *Migrant Action*, The 1984 Immigration Debate, vol. 7, no. 2 (1984), p. 12.
23 Kathy Laster, "Geoffrey Blainey and the Asianisation of Australia: A Debate Half Won," Ibid., p. 4.
24 Australia, Parliamentary Debates, House of Representatives, May 10, 1984, pp. 2231-35.
25 Ibid., pp. 2225-31.
26 Frances Milne and Peter Shergold, eds., *The Great Immigration Debate* (Sydney: The Federation of Ethnic Communities' Councils of Australia, 1984), pp. 61-65. *See* also other articles in this publication as well as in the special issue of *Migrant Action*, The 1984 Immigration Debate.
27 *See* Walter Pitman, *Now is Not Too Late*, Report of Task Force on Human Relations (Toronto: Council of Metropolitan Toronto, 1977), and *Equality Now!*, Report of the Special Committee on Visible Minorities in Canadian Society, House of Commons, Ottawa, 1984.
28 *See* Stuart L. Smith, "The Pacific Challenge," *International Perspectives*, September/October 1984.

Bibliography

Canada and Australia. Immigration: The Post-War Period

CANADA

Government Documents

Department of Citizenship and Immigration, 1950–1965
Annual Reports, 1950–1965.
Immigration Statistics, 1950–1965.
Sedgewick, J. *Report on Immigration*. Part I, April 1965. Part II, January 1966.

Department of Manpower and Immigration, 1966–1977
Annual Reports, 1966–1977.
Immigration Statistics, 1966–1977.
White Paper, Canadian Immigration Policy. 1966.
Green Paper on Immigration Policy. 4 vols. 1975.

SUPPLEMENTARY STUDIES TO THE GREEN PAPER

Breton, Raymond, Jill Armstrong, Les Kennedy. *The Social Impact of Changes in Population Size and Composition: Reaction to Patterns of Immigration.*
Epstein, Larry. *Immigration and Inflation.*
Hawkins, Freda, *Immigration Policy and Management in Selected Countries.*
Henripin, Jacques, *Immigration and Language Imbalance.*
Kalbach, Warren E. *The Effect of Immigration on Population.*
Parai, Louis. *The Economic Impact of Immigration.*
Richmond, Anthony H. *Aspects of the Absorption and Adaptation of Immigrants.*
Tienhaara, Nancy. *Canadian Views on Immigration and Population: An Analysis of Postwar Gallup Polls.*

Canada Employment and Immigration Commission
Annual Reports. 1978–
Immigration Statistics. 1978–
Annual Reports to Parliament on Immigration Levels. 1979–
Background Papers on Immigration Levels. 1983–
Task Force on Immigration Practices and Procedures
  REPORTS
  1) *The Exploitation of Potential Immigrants by Unscrupulous Consultants.*
     April 1981.
  2) *Domestic Workers on Employment Authorization.* April 1981.
  3) *The Refugee Status Determination Process.* November 1981.
Robinson, W.G. *Illegal Migrants in Canada.* June 1983.
Canada Employment and Immigration Advisory Council
  Annual Reports. 1979–
  Illegal Immigrants. November 1982.
  The Immigrant Settlement and Adaptation Program (ISAP). February 1984.

Department of the Secretary of State, Department of
Multiculturalism and Citizenship
The Canadian Family Tree. Co-published with Corpus Publications, Toronto,
1979.
Histories of Canadian Ethnocultural Groups. The Generation Series. Co-
published with McClelland and Stewart, Toronto.
  Abu-Leban, Baha. *An Olive Branch on the Family Tree: The Arabs in
    Canada.* 1980.
  Adachi, Ken. *The Enemy that Never Was.* 1976.
  Anderson, Grace M. and David Higgs. *The Portuguese Communities of
    Canada.* 1976.
  Chimbos, Peter D. *The Canadian Odyssey: The Greek Experience in
    Canada.* 1980.
  Con, Harry, Ronald J. Con, Graham Johnson, Edgar Wickberg, and
    William E. Willmott. *From China to Canada: A History of Chinese
    Communities in Canada.* 1983.
  Dreisziger, N.F., M.L. Kovacs, Paul Body, and Bennett Kovrig. *Struggle
    and Hope: The Hungarian-Canadian Experience.* 1982.
  Loken, Gulbrand. *From Fjord to Frontier: A History of the Norwegians in
    Canada.* 1980.
  Lupul, Manoly R. *A Heritage in Transition: Essays in the History of
    Ukrainians in Canada.* 1983.
  Radecki, Henry. *A Member of a Distinguished Family: The Polish Group in
    Canada.* 1976.
  Rasporich, Anthony W. *For a Better Life: A History of the Croatians in
    Canada.* 1982.

Reid, W. Stanford. *The Scottish Tradition in Canada*. 1976.
Cultures Canada. Regular bulletin of the Department of Multiculturalism
and Citizenship

Parliament
Special Joint Committee of the Senate and the House of Commons on
Immigration Policy. *Report to Parliament*. Ottawa, 1975.
House of Commons. *Equality Now!* Report of the Special Committee on
Visible Minorities in Canadian Society. Ottawa, 1984.
House of Commons. *Multiculturalism: Building the Canadian Mosaic.*.
Report of the Standing Committee on Multiculturalism. Ottawa, 1987.

Royal Commission on Bilingualism and Biculturalism
Report, Book 4. *The Cultural Contribution of the Other Ethnic Groups*.
Ottawa, 1969.

Books and Articles

Abella, Irving, and Harold Troper. *None is Too Many: Canada and the Jews of
Europe 1938-1948*. Toronto: Lester and Orpen Dennys, 1982.
Adelman, Howard. *Canada and the Indochinese Refugees*. Regina: Weigl
Educational Associates, 1982.
Anderson, Grace M. *Networks of Contact: The Portuguese in Toronto*.
Waterloo: Wilfrid Laurier University, 1974.
Berger, Carl. "The True North Strong and Free." In *Nationalism in Canada*,
Peter Russell, ed. Toronto: McGraw-Hill, 1966.
Berry, John W., Rudolph Kalin, and Donald M. Taylor. *Multiculturalism and
Ethnic Attitudes in Canada*. Ottawa: Department of Supply and Services, 1977.
Breton, Raymond, Jeffrey G. Reitz, and Victor Valentine. *Cultural Boundaries
and the Cohesion of Canada*. Montreal: Institute for Research on Public
Policy, 1980.
Burnet, Jean. "Ethnic Relations and Ethnic Policies in Canadian Society." In
Ethnicity in the Americas, F. Henry, ed. The Hague: Mouton, 1976.
– "The Policy of Multiculturalism within a Bilingual Framework: A Stock-
Taking." *Canadian Ethnic Studies*, 10:2, 1978.
– "Myths and Multiculturalism." *Canadian Journal of Education*, 4:4, 1979.
– "Separate or Equal: A Dilemma of Multiculturalism." In *The Social
Sciences and Public Policy in Canada*, A.W. Rasporich, ed., vol. 1. Calgary:
University of Calgary, 1979.
Corbett, David. *Canada's Immigration Policy, A Critique*. Toronto: University
of Toronto Press, 1957.
Dirks, Gerald E. *Canada's Refugee Policy: Indifference or Opportunism?*
Montreal: McGill-Queen's University Press, 1977.
Driedger, Leo, ed. *The Canadian Ethnic Mosaic, A Quest for Identity*.

Toronto: McClelland and Stewart, 1978.

Foot, David K. *Canada's Population Outlook, Demographic Futures and Economic Challenges*. The Canadian Institute for Economic Policy Series. Toronto, James Lorimer, 1982.

Green, Alan G. *Immigration and the Postwar Canadian Economy*. Toronto: Macmillan, 1976.

Hawkins, Freda. *Canada and Immigration: Public Policy and Public Concern*. Second Edition. Montreal: McGill-Queen's University Press, 1988.

– "Uganda Asians in Canada." *New Community*, Journal of the British Community Relations Commission, vol. 2, no. 3, Summer 1973.

– "Canadian Immigration Policy and Management." *International Migration Review*, vol. 8, no. 2, Summer 1974.

– "Destination Unknown: Difficult Decisions in Immigration Policy." *Queen's Quarterly*, vol. 82, no. 4, Winter 1975.

– "Immigration and Population: The Canadian Approach." *Canadian Public Policy*, Summer 1975.

– "Canada's Green Paper on Immigration Policy. *International Migration Review*, vol. 9, no. 2, Summer 1975.

– "Dilemmas in Immigration Policy-Making: The Problems of Choice, Political Will and Administrative Capacity." *Paper for the Seventh National Seminar of the Institute of Public Administration of Canada*. Seminar Proceedings, IPAC, 1976.

– "Canadian Immigration: A New Law and a New Aproach to Management." *International Migration Review*, Vol. II, No. 1, Spring 1977.

– "Canada: The Unintended Amnesty." *Migration Today*, vol. 5, no. 3, June 1977. New York: Centre for Migration Studies.

– "Immigration Law and Management in the Major Receiving Countries Outside the Arab Region." Paper for a *Conference on International Migration in the Arab World*. United Nations Economic Commission for Western Asia (ECWA), Nicosia, May 1981.

– "Multiculturalism in Two Countries: The Canadian and Australian Experience." *Journal of Canadian Studies*, vol. 17, no. 1, Spring 1982.

– "Towards a Population Policy for Canada." Canadian Population Society meetings, Learned Societies Conference, Montreal, May–June 1985.

– "Lessons to be Learned from the Immigration Experience of the United States, Canada and Australia," Paper for a *Conference on the Future of Migration*, Organization for Economic Co-operation and Development (OECD). Paris, May 1986.

Henripin, Jacques. "Quebec and the Demographic Dilemma of French Canadian Society." In *Quebec Society and Politics: Views from the Inside*, Dale C. Thomson, ed. Toronto: McClelland and Stewart, 1973.

– (with associates) *Les Enfants qu'on n'a plus au Québec*. Montréal: Presses de l'Université de Montréal, 1981.

Henripin, Jacques, and Jacques Légaré. *Évolution démographique du Québec et de ses régions, 1966-1986*. Québec: Presses de l'Université Laval, 1987.

Hill, Daniel G. *Human Rights in Canada: A Focus on Racism*. Canadian Labour Congress, 1977.

Hughes, David R. and Evelyn Kallen. *The Anatomy of Racism: Canadian Dimensions*. Montreal: Harvest House, 1974.

Isajiw, W., ed. *Identities: The Impact of Ethnicity on Canadian Society*. Toronto: Peter Martin Associates 1977.

– "Ethnic Identity Retention." Research Paper No. 125. Toronto: Centre for Urban and Community Studies, 1981.

– "Multiculturalism and the Integration of the Canadian Community." *Canadian Ethnic Studies*, vol. 15, no. 2, 1983.

Kalbach, Warren E. "Demographic Concerns and the Control of Immigration." *Canadian Public Policy*, vol. 1, no. 3, Summer 1975.

– "Growth and Distribution of Canada's Ethnic Population 1891-1971." In *The Canadian Ethnic Mosaic: A Quest for Identity*, Leo Driedger, ed. Toronto: McClelland and Stewart, 1978.

– and Wayne W. McVey. *The Demographic Bases of Canadian Society*. 2nd Edition. Toronto: McGraw-Hill, 1979.

Lachapelle, Réjean and Jacques Henripin. *The Demolinguistic Situation in Canada: Past Trends and Future Prospects*. Montreal: The Institute for Research on Public Policy, 1982.

Lupul, Manoly R. *Ukrainian Canadians, Multiculturalism and Separatism: An Assessment*, Edmonton: University of Alberta Press, 1978.

O'Bryan, K.G., J.G. Reitz, and O.M. Kuplowska. *Non-Official Languages: A Study in Canadian Multiculturalism*. Ottawa: Department of Supply and Services, 1976.

Palmer, Howard. *Immigration and the Rise of Multiculturalism*. Toronto: Copp Clark, 1974.

– *Land of the Second Chance: A History of Ethnic Groups in Southern Alberta*. Lethbridge: The Lethbridge Herald, 1972.

Pitman, Walter. *Now is Not Too Late*. Report of a Task Force on Human Relations. Toronto: Council of Metropolitan Toronto, 1977.

Porter, John. *The Vertical Mosaic: An Analysis of Social Class and Power in Canada*. Toronto: University of Toronto Press, 1965.

– "Dilemmas and Contradictions of a Multi-Ethnic Society." Paper delivered at a meeting of the Royal Society of Canada, Series 4, vol. 10, 1972.

Ramcharan, Subhas. *Racism: Non-Whites in Canada*. Toronto: Butterworths, 1982.

Reitz, Jeffrey G. *The Survival of Ethnic Groups*. Toronto: McGraw-Hill Ryerson, 1980.

– "Language and Ethnic Community Survival." *Canadian Review of Sociology and Anthropology*, special issue, Aspects of Canadian Society, 1974.

Richmond, Anthony H. *Postwar Immigrants in Canada*. Toronto: University
of Toronto Press, 1967.
- "Canadian Immigration: Recent Developments and Future Prospects."
International Migration, vol. 13, no. 4, 1975.
- "Immigrant Adaptation in a Post-Industrial Society." In *Global Trends in
Migration: Theory and Research*, M.M. Kritz and Associates, eds. New
York: Centre for Migration Studies, 1981.
- "Canadian Unemployment and the Threat to Multiculturalism." *Journal of
Canadian Studies*, vol. 17, no. 1, 1982.
- "Sociocultural Adaptation and Conflict in Immigrant Receiving Societies."
International Social Science Journal, Fall 1984.
Richmond, Anthony H., G. Lakshmana Rao, and Jerzy Zubrzycki.
Immigrants in Canada and Australia. Ethnic Research Program, vol. 1,
Demographic Aspects and Education. Toronto: York University, 1984.
Richmond, Anthony H., and Jerzy Zubrzycki. *Immigrants in Canada and
Australia*. Ethnic Research Program, vol. 2, Economic Adaptation. Toronto:
York University, 1984.
Rocher, Guy. "Multiculturalism, The Doubts of a Francophone." Paper for the
Second Canadian Conference on Multiculturalism. Ottawa: Department of
Multiculturalism and Citizenship, February 1976.
Romaniuc, Anatole. *Current Demographic Analysis, Fertility in Canada:
From Baby-boom to Baby-bust*. Ottawa: Statistics Canada, Department of
Supply and Services, 1984.
Stone, Leroy O. and Claude Marceau. *Canadian Population Trends and Public
Policy Through the 1980s*. Montreal: Institute for Research on Public Policy
and McGill-Queen's University Press, 1977.
Tepper, Elliot L., ed. *Southeast Asian Exodus: From Tradition to
Resettlement*. Ottawa: Canadian Asian Studies Association, 1980.
Timlin, Mabel F. *Does Canada Need More People?* Toronto: Oxford
University Press, 1951.
Wai, Lokky, Suzanne Shiel, and T.R. Balakrishnan. *Annotated Bibliography
of Canadian Demography 1966–1982*. London, Ontario: Centre for
Canadian Population Studies, University of Western Ontario, 1984.
Winks, Robin W. *The Blacks in Canada: A History*. Montreal: McGill-
Queen's University Press, and New Haven and London: Yale University
Press, 1971.

AUSTRALIA

Government Documents

Department of Immigration 1945–1973
Annual Reports.

Consolidated Immigration Statistics.

Department of Immigration and Ethnic Affairs 1975–
Department of Immigration, Local Government and Ethnic Affairs 1977
Annual Review of Activities 1976–
Consolidated Immigration Statistics.

STUDIES AND REPORTS

Immigration Planning Council. *Australia's Immigration Programme for the Period 1968 to 1973*. Report to the Minister of State for Immigration, 1968.

Immigration Advisory Council. *Inquiry into the Departure of Settlers from Australia*. Final Report, 1973.

National Population Inquiry, W.D. Borrie, Chairman, *Population and Australia: A Demographic Analysis and Projection*. 2 vols., 1975. Supplementary Report, *Population and Australia, Recent Demographic Trends and Their Implications*. 1978.

Australian Population and Immigration Council, *A Decade of Migrant Settlement*. Report on the 1973 Immigration Survey. 1976.

Australian Population and Immigration Council. Green Paper, *Immigration Policies and Australia's Population*. 1977.

Australian Ethnic Affairs Council. *Australia as a Multicultural Society*. 1978.

Australian Population and Immigration Council and the Australian Ethnic Affairs Council. Joint Statement, *Multiculturalism and its Implications for Immigration Policy*. 1979.

Australian Council on Population and Ethnic Affairs. *Multiculturalism for all Australians: Our Developing Nationhood*. 1982.

F.E. Galbally, Chairman. *Report of the Review of Post-Arrival Programs and Services to Migrants*. 2 vols. 1978.

W.D. Scott and Company. *Survey into the Information Needs of Migrants in Australia*. Report to the Department of Immigration and Ethnic Affairs. 1980.

Australian Institute of Multicultural Affairs. *Evaluation of Post-Arrival Programs and Services*. An Evaluation of the Galbally Report. 1982.

Committee of Review of the Australian Institute of Multicultural Affairs. *Report to the Minister for Immigration and Ethnic Affairs*. 1983.

Australian Population and Immigration Council. *Population Reports 1–7*.

Committee to Advise on Australia's Immigration Policies (CAAIP), Report, *A Commitment to Australia*, 1988.

Books and Articles

Appleyard, R.T. *British Immigration to Australia*. Toronto: University of Toronto Press and Canberra: The Australian National University, 1964.

- "Immigration Policy and Progress." Paper for the Australian Institute of Political Science 37th Summer School, *How Many Australians?* Sydney: Angus and Robertson, 1971.

Birrell, Robert. "The Social Dilemmas of Continued Immigration." Meredith Memorial Lectures. Bundoora (Vic): La Trobe University Press, 1978.

Birrell, Robert, and Colin Hay, eds. *The Immigration Issue in Australia.* Bundoora (Vic): La Trobe University Press, 1978.

Birrell, Robert, and Associates. *Refugees, Resources, Reunion: Australia's Immigration Dilemmas.* Victoria: VCTA Publishing 1979.

Blainey, Geoffrey. *The Tyranny of Distance.* Melbourne: Sun Books, 1966.

- *All for Australia*, North Ryde: Methuen Haynes, 1984.

Borrie, W.D. *Immigration: Australia's Problems and Prospects.* Sydney: Angus and Robertson, 1949.

- *Italians and Germans in Australia, A Study of Assimilation.* Melbourne: Cheshire, 1954.

- *Report of the National Population Inquiry.* 2 vols. and Supplementary Report. Canberra: Australian Government Publishing Service 1975 and 1978.

Buchanan, M. E. *Attitudes Towards Immigrants in Australia.* National Population Inquiry, Research Report No. 3. Canberra: Australian Government Publishing Service 1976.

Calwell, Arthur A. *Be Just and Fear Not, An Autobiography.* Hawthorn, Victoria: Lloyd O'Neill, 1972.

Cox, David. "The Role of Ethnic Groups in Migrant Welfare." Research Report for the *Commission of Inquiry into Poverty.* Canberra: Australian Government Publishing Service, 1975.

- "Community Attitudes to Refugees in Australia." Paper presented at the *Austcare Conference on Refugee Resettlement in Australia.* July 1976.

- "Pluralism in Australia." *Australian and New Zealand Journal of Sociology,* vol. 12, no. 2, 1976.

De Lacey, P., and M. Poole, eds. *Mosaic or Melting Pot.* New York: Harcourt, Brace, Jovanovich, 1979.

Ecumenical Migration Centre. "Family Reunion and Australia's Immigration Policy." *Multicultural Australia Paper No. 5.* Richmond, Victoria, 1979.

Ethnic Affairs Commission of New South Wales. *Participation: Report to the Premier.* Sydney, June 1978.

Francis, Ronald D. *Migrant Crime in Australia.* St. Lucia, Queensland: University of Queensland Press, 1981.

Grassby, The Hon. A.J., *Australia's Decade of Decision: A Report on Migration, Citizenship, Settlement and Population.* Immigration reference paper tabled in the House of Representatives, October 11, 1973.

- "Racial Discrimination Act: The First Two Years." *Ethnic Studies,* vol. 1, no. 3, 1977.

– "Australia's Cultural Revolution." In *Towards a Multicultural Tasmania*, W.W. Bostock, ed. Report of a Conference. Hobart: University of Tasmania, 1977.

– *The Morning After*. Canberra: Judicator Publications, 1979.

Howe, K.R. *Race Relations, Australia and New Zealand: A Comparative Survey, 1770s–1970s*. Wellington, Methuen, 1977.

Jupp, James. *Arrivals and Departures*. Melbourne: Lansdowne Press, 1966.

Kiernan, Colm. *Calwell: A Personal and Political Biography*. Melbourne: Nelson (Australia), 1978.

Kovacs, M.L., and A.J. Cropley. *Immigrants and Society: Affiliation and Assimilation*. Sydney: McGraw-Hill, 1975.

Kunz, Egan F. "European Migrant Absorption in Australia." *International Migration*, vol. 9, no. 1, 1971.

– "Some Aspects of Australia's Post-war Immigration." *Report of the National Seminar on World Population*. Australian Council for Overseas Aid, 1973.

– *The Intruders: Refugee Doctors in Australia*. Canberra: Australian National University Press, 1975.

– "Exile and Resettlement: Refugee Theory." *International Migration Review*, Special Issue: Refugees Today. Centre for Migration Studies, vol. 15, Spring–Summer 1981.

Martin, Jean I. "Migrants: Equality and Ideology." Meredith Memorial Lectures, Bundoora (Vic): La Trobe University Press, 1972.

– "The Economic Condition of Migrants." Research report for the *Commission of Inquiry into Poverty*. Canberra: Australian Government Publishing Service, 1975.

– "Ethnic Pluralism and Identity." In *Melbourne Studies in Education*, S. Murray-Smith, ed. Melbourne: Melbourne Unviersity Press, 1976.

– *The Migrant Presence, Australian Responses 1947–1977*. Studies in Society 2. Research report for the National Population Inquiry. Sydney: George Allen and Unwin, 1981.

– *The Ethnic Dimension: Papers on Ethnicity and Pluralism*. Studies in Society 9. Sydney: George Allen and Unwin, 1978.

MacKellar, The Hon. M.J.R., MP. *Implications to Business of Population Decline*. Address to the Corporate Planning Group for the Australian Institute of Management, Sydney, August 1976.

– *Options for a Population Policy*. Address to the Residential Workshop, "Australia's Population AD 2000." University of New England, Armidale, July 1977.

– *Australia's Immigration Policy and Immigration Principles*. Statement to the House of Representatives, June 7, 1978. Canberra: Australian Government Publishing Service, 1978.

Milne, Francis, and Peter Shergold, eds. *The Great Immigration Debate*.

Sydney: Federation of Ethnic Communities' Councils of Australia, 1984.

Price, Charles A. *Southern Europeans in Australia*. Melbourne: Oxford University Press, 1963.

– *Jewish Settlers in Australia: 1788–1961*. Social Science Monograph No. 23. Canberra, 1964.

– "Migrants in Australian Society." *Anatomy of Australia*, The Duke of Edinburgh's Commonwealth Study Conference. Melbourne: Sun Books, 1968.

– "Immigration 1836–1970." In *Australia in World Affairs: 1966–1970*. G. Greenwood and N. Harper, eds. Melbourne: Cheshire, 1974.

– *The Great White Walls are Built: Restrictive Immigration to North America and Australasia 1836–1888*. Canberra: Australian National University Press, 1974.

– "Beyond White Australia: The Whitlam Government's Immigration Record." *Round Table*, vol. 260, p. 369–77, October, 1975.

– "Australian Immigration: 1947–73." *International Migration Review*, vol. 9, Fall 1975. New York: Centre for Migration Studies.

– "Australia." In *The Politics of Migration Policies*, Daniel Kubat, ed. New York: Centre for Migration Studies, 1979.

– "Immigration and Ethnic Affairs." In *From Whitlam to Fraser: Reform and Reaction in Australian Politics*, Allan Patience and Brian Head, eds. Melbourne: Oxford University Press, 1979.

– "Immigration Policies and Refugees in Australia." *International Migration Review*, Refugees Today. vol. 15, Spring–Summer 1981. New York: Centre for Migration Studies.

Australian Immigration: A Bibliography and Digest. No. 1, 1966; no. 2, 1970; no. 3, Parts 1 and 2, 1975 and no. 4 and Supplement, 1979. These valuable publications have been edited by Charles Price and produced in the Department of Demography of the Australian National University in Canberra. They contain detailed bibliographies on various aspects of immigration, statistical material, an index of periodicals and organizations, and articles by Price and others on contemporary issues in this field. Following is a selection of articles from no. 3 (edited by Charles Price and Jean Martin) and no. 4.

Price, Charles A. "Australian Immigration: The Whitlam Government 1972–75." *Australian Immigration: A Bibliography and Digest*, no. 3, 1975, Part 1.

Pyne, Patricia, and Charles A. Price. "Selected Tables on Australian Immigration 1947–74, with Commentary." *Australian Immigration: A Bibliography and Digest*, no. 3, 1975, Part 1.

Price, Charles A. "Immigration and Population Policy: The Fraser Government." *Australian Immigration: A Bibliography and Digest*, no. 4, 1979.

Pyne, Patricia, and Charles A. Price. "Selected Tables on Australian Immigration 1947–78, with Commentary." *Australian Immigration: A Bibliography and Digest*, no. 4, 1979.

Pyne, Patricia, and Charles A. Price. "Australian Migration Tables." *Australian Immigration: A Bibliography and Digest*, no. 4, Supplement, 1981.

Derrick, Bernadette, Patricia Pyne and Charles A. Price. "Immigrants in the 1976 Census." *Australian Immigration: A Bibliography and Digest*, no. 4, Supplement, 1981.

Price, Charles A., Patricia Pyne and Elizabeth Baker. "Immigrants in the Vital Statistics." *Australian Immigration: A Bibliography and Digest*, no. 4, Supplement, 1981.

Price, Charles A. "Ethnic Origins." *Australian Immigration: A Bibliography and Digest*, no. 4, Supplement, 1981.

Richardson, Alan. *British Immigrants and Australia*. Canberra: Australian National University Press, 1974.

Rivett, Kenneth, ed. *Immigration Control or Colour Bar? The Background to White Australia and a Proposal for Change*. Immigration Reform Group. Melbourne: Melbourne University Press, 1962.

– (ed.) *Australia and the Non-White Migrant*, Immigration Reform Group. Melbourne: Melbourne University Press, 1975.

– "Race, Immigration and The Borrie Report. *Australian Quarterly*, vol. 48, no. 3, September 1976.

– "Immigration and the Green Paper." *Australian Quarterly*, vol. 50, no. 1, April 1978.

– "Towards a Policy on Refugees." *Australian Outlook*, vol. 33, no. 2, August 1979.

– "A Reassessment such as Blainey Asks For." *Migration Action*, Special Issue: The 1984 Immigration Debate, vol. 7, no. 2 (1984).

Roberts, Hew, ed. *Australia's Immigration Policy*. Nedlands: University of Western Australia Press, 1972.

Sherington, Geoffrey. *Australia's Immigrants 1788–1978*. The Australian Experience, No. 1. Sydney: George Allen and Unwin, 1980.

Smolicz, J.J. "Ethnic Cultures in Australian Society: A Question of Cultural Interaction." *Melbourne Studies in Education 1976*. Melbourne: Melbourne University Press, 1976.

– "Cultural Differences and Social Relations," and "Cultural Interaction in a Plural Society." In *Australia's Population AD 2000*, S.J. Booth, ed. Armidale: University of New England, 1977.

Smolicz, J.J., and M.J. Secombe. "Cultural Interaction in a Pluralist Society." *Ethnic Studies*, vol. 1, no. 1, 1977.

Storer, Des. "Migrants and Unionism." *Ekstatis*, vol. 3, no. 8, February 1974.

– "Ethnic Groups and Political Participation." *Ethnic Rights, Power and*

Participation. Ecumenical Migration Centre. Richmond, Victoria: Clearing House on Migration Issues, 1975.

– *But I Wouldn't Want My Wife to Work Here*. Fitzroy, Victoria: Centre for Urban Action and Research. 1976.

Taft, Ronald. *From Stranger to Citizen: A Survey of Studies of Immigrant Assimilation in Western Australia*. Nedlands, Western Australia: University of Western Australia Press, 1965.

– "Ethnic Groups." In *Socialization in Australia*, F.J. Hunt, ed. Sydney: Angus and Robertson, 1972.

– "Problems of Adjustment and Assimilation of Immigrants." In *Psychology and Race*, P. Watson, ed. London: Penguin Books, 1973.

West, M.P. The Hon. Stewart, *Australian Immigration Policy*. Statement to Parliament, November 1, 1983. Richmond, Victoria: Clearing House on Migration Issues. 1984.

Zubrzycki, Jerzy, *Settlers of the La Trobe Valley*. Canberra: Australian National University Press, 1964.

– (with M. Gibson) *The Foreign Language Press in Australia, 1848-1964*. Canberra: Australian National University Press, 1967.

– "A Note on Australia's Immigration Policy." *International Migration Review*, vol. 8, no. 2, Summer 1974.

– "Immigration and the Family in Multicultural Australia." Meredith Memorial Lectures. Melbourne: La Trobe University Press, 1978.

– "International Migration in Australasia and the South Pacific." In *Global Trends in Migration: Theory and Research on International Population Movements*, Mary M. Kritz, Charles B. Keely, Sylvano M. Tomasi, eds. New York: Centre for Migration Studies, 1981.

– (with Anthony H. Richmond and G. Lakshmana Rao) *Immigrants in Canada and Australia*. Ethnic Research Program, vol. 1, Demographic Aspects and Education. Toronto: York University, 1984.

– (with Anthony H. Richmond) *Immigrants in Canada and Australia*. Ethnic Research Program, vol. 2, Economic Adaptation. Toronto: York University, 1984.

Index

AUSTRALIA

CANADA

Immigration Act 1952: ministerial discretion and consequences, 38; need for new Act, 43; and White Canada Policy, 17, 38

Immigration Act 1976, 70–75; admission, 72; control and enforcement, 73–75; Immigration Appeal Board, 75; implementation, 79; inadmissible classes, 73; Minister's permits, 75, 76; nature of, xvii, 42, 70; planning and management, 71–72; principles, 71; refugees, 72–73; security, 75. *See also* Green Paper on Immigration Policy 1975; Special Joint Committee of the Senate and the House of Commons on Immigration Policy 1975

Immigration Appeal Board, 40, 47, 76

Immigration Appeal Board Act 1967, 40, 45; incorporated in Immigration Act 1976, 75

Immigration legislation before World War II, 16–22; continuous journey rule, 17, 18; Immigration Acts (1869, 1906, 1910, 1919), 16, 17; laws to discourage or exclude Chinese (1885, 1900, 1903, 1923), 16; orders-in-council, 17, 20, 21

Immigration management: Canadian points system, 39, 77, 78; dedication of immigration officers, xvii; foreign branch, 83, 84; fragmentation of immigration management, xvii, 36, 81–85; immigration service, early problems, 36; immigration within CEIC, 80; immigration within manpower, 44, 312n1; problems of, 244, 245; public access to immigration manuals, 146, 324n87. *See also* Canada Employment and Immigration Commission; Department of Citizenship and Immigration; Department of Manpower and Immigration; Immigration Acts 1952 and 1976; *Australia*: Immigration management

Immigration planning: Annual Reports on Immigration Levels, 88–92; consultative procedures, 89, 91; triennial programming, 88, 90

Immigration policies: consultation with provinces and public, 89, 91, 246; Green Paper on Immigration Policy 1975, 50–57; inter-war years, 25–30; King, Mackenzie, 1947 statement, 37, 38; liberalization and modernization in, 40, 41; non-discrimination and universality, 39; population and immigration, new policies, 256, 272; recession cutback, 255–58; Special Joint Committee of the Senate and the House of Commons on Immigration Policy 1975, 57–63; statement of principles, 71; White Canada and reasons for, 8–11, 16–21, 22–25. *See also* Immigration Acts 1952 and 1976; *Australia*: Immigration policies and law

Immigration policy-making: advisory councils in Canada and Australia, 253–55; annual consultation on immigration levels, 253; government leadership, xvi, 245, 247, 248; public attitudes, 247, 248; role of interest groups, 252, 253; role of Parliament, 248, 249; role of political parties, 249. *See also Australia*: Immigration policy-making

Immigration Regulations 1962: death of White Canada Policy, 39; reasons for, 39; remaining restrictive clause, 39

Immigration Regulations 1967: Canadian Points System, 39; Section 34, change of status, 45–48. *See also* Adjustment of Status Program; *International*: Commerce of migration